The State Department Boys

ADST-DACOR DIPLOMATS AND DIPLOMACY SERIES

Series Editor: MARGERY BOICHEL THOMPSON

Since 1776, extraordinary men and women have represented the United States abroad under widely varying circumstances. What they did and how and why they did it remain little known to their compatriots. In 1995, the Association for Diplomatic Studies and Training (ADST) and DACOR – an organization of foreign affairs professionals – created the Diplomats and Diplomacy book series to increase public knowledge and appreciation of the professionalism of American diplomats and their involvement in world history. Marciano de Borja's *State Department Boys* recounts how the U.S. Foreign Service helped train the first Philippine Foreign Service officer corps following independence in 1946 and how the Philippines went on to hold its own in the international arena.

OTHER TITLES IN THE SERIES

Gordon Brown, *Toussaint's Clause: The Founding Fathers and the Haitian Revolution*
Charles T. Cross, *Born a Foreigner: A Memoir of the American Presence in Asia*
Brandon Grove, *Behind Embassy Walls: The Life and Times of an American Diplomat*
Parker T. Hart, *Saudi Arabia and the United States: Birth of a Security Partnership*
Dennis Kux, *The United States and Pakistan, 1947–2000: Disenchanted Allies*
Jane C. Loeffler, *The Architecture of Diplomacy: Building America's Embassies*
William B. Milam, *Bangladesh and Pakistan: Flirting with Failure in South Asia*
Robert H. Miller, *Vietnam and Beyond: A Diplomat's Cold War Education*
William Michael Morgan, *Pacific Gibraltar: U.S.-Japanese Rivalry over the Annexation of Hawaii, 1885–1898*
David D. Newsom, *Witness to a Changing World*
Richard B. Parker, *Uncle Sam in Barbary: A Diplomatic History*
Nicholas Platt, China Boys: *How U.S. Relations with the PRC Began and Grew*
Howard B. Schaffer, *The Limits of Influence: America's Role in Kashmir*
Raymond F. Smith, *The Craft of Political Analysis for Diplomats*
Ulrich Straus, *The Anguish of Surrender: Japanese POWs of World War II*

*For a complete list of series titles, visit www.adst.org/publications

The State Department Boys

Philippine Diplomacy and Its American Heritage

Marciano R. de Borja

An ADST-DACOR Diplomats and Diplomacy Book

Washington, DC

Copyright © 2014 by Marciano R. de Borja

New Academia Publishing 2014

The views and opinions in this book are solely those of the author and not necessarily those of the Association for Diplomatic Studies and Training, DACOR, the Government of the Philippines, or the Government of the United States.

All rights reserved. No part of this book may be reproduced or transmitted in any form or by any means, electronic or mechanical, including photocopying, recording, or by any information storage and retrieval system.

Printed in the United States of America

Library of Congress Control Number: 2014940348
ISBN 978-0-9915047-8-7 paperback (alk. paper)
ISBN 978-0-9915047-9-4 hardcover (alk. paper)

 An imprint of New Academia Publishing

 New Academia Publishing
PO Box 27420, Washington, DC 20038-7420
info@newacademia.com - www.newacademia.com

Contents

Preface	vii
Acknowledgments	xiii
List of the State Department Boys	xvi
1. The Pioneers	1
2. Diplomatic and Consular Training	23
3. A Foreign Office for a New Nation	55
Photo Gallery I	97
4. Dealing with America	107
5. On the International Stage	135
6. Reaching Out to a Larger World	165
7. Surviving the Foreign Service	201
Photo Gallery II	243
8. "Father of the Philippine Foreign Service"	253
9. Leaving a Legacy	293
Appendix	319
Bibliography	323
Notes	329
Index	361
The Author	369

Preface

Before and after Philippine independence on 4 July 1946, the U.S. Department of State conducted technical courses known as the Philippine Foreign Affairs Training Program (PFATP) to train the first officers of the incipient Philippine Foreign Service. Forty Filipinos, divided into five groups, were selected to undergo training in diplomatic and consular work in the State Department and later on in selected U.S. Foreign Service posts. The trainees eventually formed the initial officer corps of the Philippine Foreign Service and were considered the pioneering Filipino career diplomats. They became the stewards of the future Philippine Foreign Service and were fondly and collectively labeled the "State Department Boys."

The State Department Boys were among those Filipinos originally called *pensionados*, meaning Philippine government scholars who were sent to the United States to study or train in the best institutions of that country during the American colonial regime. As time moved on, the term *pensionados* fell out of use. Besides, the term itself is generic and failed to distinguish the State Department trainees from other Filipino scholars in America. After their training in Washington, D.C., they called themselves "Mill's Boys" in honor of Edward W. Mill, their training director at the State Department. When Mill later left the U.S. Foreign Service, they became known as the "PFATP Boys." But the acronym "PFATP" is not just a mouthful and a tongue twister, it is also incomprehensible even to many Foreign Service personnel. Thus, a new name, "State Department Boys," with a stress on "State Department," was coined. The moniker is fancier and more modern and appealing to the younger generation. Perhaps the State Department Boys themselves popularized it. "Boys" in this context has a ring of youth, energy, and dynamism to it. It also denotes a select group of Filipino Foreign Service officers bristling with newly acquired knowledge from the United States. A sense of mystique also developed. Thus, being a State Department Boy eventually became a sort of status symbol and a badge of prestige.

Some officials in the Philippine Foreign Service, however, were critical of the term "boys," as they perceived it as subservient or amateurish. Indeed, they were grown "men" and not "boys." Most were in their thirties and early forties and were experienced bureaucrats and lawyers when they were sent to America. Strictly speaking, however, they were trainees rather than professional diplomats or experts on foreign relations. It is possible that the State Department Boys wanted to be called that way so that they would not be remembered by the new generation of Filipino diplomats as the "old timers," or they simply wanted to remain forever young in our minds. Yes, they were the "originals" or the "trailblazers," as some want to call them, but State Department Boys was the name that stuck. Some female diplomats in the Philippine Foreign Service were unhappy that all were men, with not a single woman included. Well, it was like that during those days – diplomacy, like so many other professions, was male-dominated.

The State Department Boys not only enjoyed the distinction of being the pioneers of the Philippine Foreign Service; they were also well respected and looked up to by the next generation of Filipino diplomats and admired by their peers in the Philippine government and abroad. Serving as mentors and role models, they left an indelible impression on those who knew them, especially those who saw and worked with them at close range. A retired ambassador I interviewed nostalgically recalled how as a vice consul he had the good fortune of working with a State Department Boy who taught him the nuts and bolts of consular work, effective interpersonal skills, office management, and social graces. Another retired ambassador fondly remembered how his chief of mission, a State Department Boy, cared for him and treated him like a son upon his arrival at post as a new third secretary. His boss made sure his adjustment to his new post was smooth, making all the necessary arrangements so that his family could settle quickly. Yet another retired ambassador remembered how the head of the Philippine delegation to a UN Conference, again a State Department Boy, brilliantly extricated the Philippines from taking sides in a crucial issue, to the amazement and amusement of other delegations.

Other insights and stories abound and are documented and narrated in this book. These anecdotal evidences and personal testimonies show the humanity of the State Department Boys through their respect for and positive outlook toward their work and their younger colleagues in the Foreign Service. Their lives, both public and private, inspired those who have followed their footsteps in the challenging world of diplomacy. Indeed, they were not only one of the most successful groups in the annals of the Philippine Foreign Service; but, more important, they left a legacy worthy of recognition and emulation. The career paths of the State Department Boys, however, were an interesting mix. Some became successful and rose to prominence, becoming distinguished ambassadors to major countries and permanent representatives to the UN, while others led less brilliant careers. A few left the Foreign Service shortly after joining.

This research project aims to reconstruct the stories of these pioneers of the Philippine Foreign Service and to discuss the evolution of Philippine diplomacy after independence and Philippine foreign relations during the Cold War. It also highlights Philippine-American relations, in particular the efforts of the United States to smoothly transition the Philippines from a colony to an independent state able to conduct its foreign relations with a core of professional diplomats. The present study aims to understand the beginning and evolution of the Philippine Foreign Service and examines other outstanding Filipino diplomats who led the development of the Philippine Foreign Service, including Elpidio Quirino, Carlos P. Romulo, Joaquin M. Elizalde, Narciso Ramos, Diosdado Macapagal, Bernabe Africa, Roberto Regala, and Melquiades Gamboa.

It is often assumed that simply because of the Philippines' former status as a U.S. colony, the country has patterned its institutions on the American model. Such a sweeping generalization, however, falls short and needs to be both qualified and quantified. To what extent did the Americanization of the Philippine Foreign Service take hold? Who were the American personalities or institutions that played a significant role in this process? How long did this influence or legacy last? These are some of the questions that we must answer to understand the extent of American influence on the Philippine Foreign Service.

The Philippines started well in the conduct of foreign relations. The American and Filipino leaders exerted tremendous efforts to ensure that the Philippines could hold its own in the international arena. The United States' nurturing of Philippine diplomacy was not confined to the training of the first generation of Filipino career diplomats under the PFATP. The State Department, on request of the Philippine government, also seconded an American foreign affairs adviser to the Philippine government to help set up the Department of Foreign Affairs. Furthermore, the two countries signed the Treaty of General Relations, the first bilateral agreement between the Philippines and the United States after Philippine independence, whereby the U.S. Foreign Service would represent Philippine interests in countries where the Philippines did not yet have a formal diplomatic presence. Thus, the State Department played a key role in the establishment of the Home Office and in shaping the early development of the Philippine Foreign Service. The Philippine government decided at that time to tap American expertise for assistance in professionalizing the Philippine Foreign Service both at home and abroad, because it needed sensitive guidance, especially in the early years of the Republic, to avoid committing so easily so many mistakes.

Did the Philippine Foreign Affairs Training Program and the secondment of an American foreign affairs adviser place the Philippines in the thrall of America? To a certain extent, yes. But the U.S. government did not foot the bill. The State Department agreed to conduct the training and send an adviser under the condition that the Philippines would shoulder all the expenses and compensation of the Filipino trainees and the American foreign affairs adviser. Despite the great financial constraints, the Philippine commonwealth government and later on the government of the new republic defrayed the cost of the PFATP conducted in Washington, D.C., and selected American Foreign Service establishments and the hiring of the American foreign affairs adviser. Under the terms of the Treaty of General Relations, the Philippine government deposited a lump sum in the State Department account to pay for the expenses of repatriation and other needs of distressed Filipino nationals overseas. There is a price to sovereignty. The Philippines early on learned that it had to bear the cost of independence and could not depend entirely on America to promote its national interests abroad. Notwithstanding its dependence on American tutelage in the conduct of its early foreign relations, the Philippines slowly and steadily crafted its own foreign policy based on its national interests and capabilities.

All of the above contribute to what I consider the "American heritage of Philippine diplomacy" about which there has been a dearth of research and serious study. This research project will, one hopes, fill the gaps in our knowledge and understanding of the beginnings of the Philippine Foreign Service and the American diplomatic and consular practice that permeated it. The fascinating story of the State Department Boys – the creation of the training program, the background and selection of qualified foreign affairs trainees, the nature of training in Washington and several American Foreign Service posts, and the establishment of the Department of Foreign Affairs – reflected a crucial time in Philippine history, the beginnings of Philippine navigation of international affairs and linkages with the world.

The training program in the State Department did not facilitate the career advancement nor ensure the professional success of the trainees. On the contrary, their careers were marked with frustration and disenchantment until a career Foreign Service was legally and firmly established. Rampant politicking by untrained aspirants and the absence of a career system were major obstacles that the trainees had to overcome, particularly those who did not have political connections. Furthermore, the growing nationalism and anti-American sentiment in Philippine society slowly diminished the prestige and distinction of having been American-trained. Those schooled in American diplomatic tradition and practice became vulnerable to criticism of being either too pro-American or being less attentive to the needs of the Philippines

In the State Department, Edward W. Mill, then the assistant chief of the Philippine Affairs Division, supervised the Filipino trainees. For his work as the architect and director of the Philippine Foreign Affairs Training Program from 1945 to 1947, he became known as the "Father of the Philippine Foreign Service." Mill had a hands-on approach to the training, conducting some sessions himself, and saw to it that the trainees were fully harnessed by the Philippine government after their training in America. He worked hard to ensure that his "boys" would be given appointments in the incipient Foreign Service and pushed for the creation of a career Foreign Service in the Philippines.

After his stint in the State Department, Mill was assigned to the U.S. embassy in Manila in 1948 and in Surabaya, Indonesia, in 1950. Two years thereafter, he left the Foreign Service to pursue a career in academe. While obtaining a PhD in political science from Princeton University, he returned to Manila as a visiting professor of political science at the University of the Philippines from 1953 to 1954. Throughout his life, Mill kept in touch with many of the State Department Boys, meeting them whenever he had a chance to visit countries where they were posted. His dedication transcended the training program he had managed, and he remained a lifelong friend to the State Department Boys and the Philippines.

The saga and legacy of the State Department Boys are largely unknown to the Filipino and American public alike, even to those who belong to the Foreign Service establishment. Sixty-seven years after the State Department conducted the first Philippine Foreign Affairs Training Program, the memory of the State Department Boys has inexorably faded. This book seeks to save their memory from total oblivion and to restore their worthy place in Philippine diplomatic history and Philippine-American relations.

Marciano R. de Borja
Department of Foreign Affairs
Manila, February 2014

Acknowledgments

I was fortunate to interview the late Ambassador Delfin R. Garcia, the youngest among the State Department Boys, in March 1997. I was awed by his reputation as an outstanding diplomat and one of the pioneer Filipino career diplomats. It never occurred to me at that time that I would eventually write and publish a book on them and their contribution to the Philippine Foreign Service. Although I interviewed him only out of curiosity, that interview provided me with the initial inspiration to work on this project.

In undertaking the research for this book, I relied heavily on the rich declassified documents and materials from the U.S. Department of State available at the U. S. National Archives and Records Administration (NARA) in College Park, Maryland, and the Edward W. Mill Collection of the Bentley Historical Library in the University of Michigan. I am particularly indebted to the Mark C. Stevens Travel and Research Grant that enabled me to conduct research at the Bentley Historical Library during the summer of 2008. I also consulted vital resources from the Carlos P. Romulo Library of the Philippine Foreign Service Institute, the Philippine National Library, the Filipiniana Section of the University of the Philippines Library, and the American Historical Collection at the Jose Rizal Library of Ateneo de Manila University.

I also benefited immensely from the relatives and friends of the State Department Boys who generously shared newspaper clippings, pictures, memorabilia, and mementos about them. Among these are Gina Bejasa, Nina, Joe, and Richard Alejandrino, Sonia Alejandrino Huang, Malloy Lardizabal, Ruth Baja Williams, Howie Severino, Marichu Sta. Romana Reverente, and Lito Fernando.

Acknowledgments

The book could have not been written and completed without the support and assistance of many people and institutions whose strong interest in the subject provided me with the impetus to continue my research. In the Philippine Foreign Service, I wish to thank retired ambassadors Rodolfo Arizala, Juan Ona, and the late Pablo Araque, who put their confidence in me from the very beginning of this project and who shared the interesting experiences they had with some of the State Department Boys; former Undersecretary of Foreign Affairs and ASEAN Secretary General Rodolfo Severino, Jr., Ambassador Delia Meñez Rosal, Ambassador Evan Garcia, now Undersecretary of Foreign Affairs for Policy; Leslie Baja, Philippine ambassador to Switzerland, Ambassador Leslie Gatan, Philippine ambassador to Canada; and Benito B. Valeriano, Philippine ambassador to India. My heartfelt appreciation goes to my direct superiors at the Department of Foreign Affairs, namely Undersecretary for Administration Rafael E. Seguis and Senior Special Assistant Rowena M. Sanchez, for their strong encouragement and support to this book project.

In the United States, I wish to acknowledge the assistance of the following: the late Paul Claussen, the chief of policy studies, and Christopher Morrison, both of the Office of Historian of the U. S. Department of State; Sara Schoo, the reference librarian at the Ralph J. Bunche Library of the Department of State; Michael Hussey, the archivist at the US National Archives and Records Administration in College Park, Maryland; William Wallach, the deputy director of the Bentley Historical Library, as well as Karen Jania, general reference division head, and Malgosia Mync, assistant reference archivist, at the Bentley Historical Library; Fe Susan Go, head librarian at the Southeast Asia Division, University of Michigan Libraries; Mereani Vakasisikakala and Natalyn Bornales, librarians, at the Dag Hammarskjold Library at UN headquarters in New York; and Zeny Avila and Dennis O'Leary of the Philippine Center in New York. Special thanks to Dr. Paul Kramer of Vanderbilt University; Dr. Dean Kotlowski of the University of Salisbury in Maryland and Ben Villanti, formerly adviser with the Mission of Japan. Special thanks to Alma Ambrosio Chand and Luz May, who kindly guided me during my stay in Ann Arbor. I also thank the Association for Diplomatic Studies and Training (ADST), particularly its president, Ambassador Kenneth Brown, and its publishing director, Margery B. Thompson, for accepting my work to be part of ADST's book series, for their editorial suggestions, and for placing this work with a U.S. publisher.

In Argentina, I wish to thank Rachel Davies Butrick, widow of Richard P. Butrick, the American Foreign Affairs adviser to the Philippines from 1946 to1947, for providing me with pictures and relevant information on her husband.

In the Philippines, I wish to thank Dr. Lou Apolinario Antolinao of Ateneo de Manila University for providing tips on how to conduct effective research in the U.S. National Archives and Records Administration and the Bentley Historical Library at the University of Michigan; Waldette Cueto and Dhea Santos, librarians at the American Historical Collection. Special thanks to Ruel Pagunsan, instructor at the Department of History of the University of the Philippines, who is my able researcher for this project. To Dr. Francis M. Navarro, historian and archivist, who is currently based in Madrid, Dr. Bernardita R. Churchill, historian, who divides her time between Manila and Washington, and Dr. Ricardo T. Jose, professor of history at the University of the Philippines, who all read the initial drafts of the manuscript and provided useful suggestions.

Notwithstanding the assistance I received from the people and institutions enumerated above, all the shortcomings and deficiencies of the book are purely mine. I also wish to emphasize that the opinions, views, and arguments expressed in this book do not reflect the official position of the Philippine Department of Foreign Affairs or the U.S. Department of State.

Lastly, I wish to thank my wife, Espie, for her understanding and sacrifice when I undertook this project. I hope that my time and attention, of which I deprived her and our children, Aristotle, Angela, and Agatha, while doing this project, were not used in vain.

THE STATE DEPARTMENT BOYS*

Group I
1. Manuel A. Adeva
2. Tiburcio C. Baja
3. Candido T. Elbo
4. Jose F. Imperial
5. Vicente I. Singian

Group II
1. Tomas G. de Castro
2. Delfin R. Garcia
3. Pelayo F. Llamas
4. Leopoldo T. Ruiz
5. Doroteo V. Vite

Group III
1. Anastacio B. Bartolome
2. Emilio D. Bejasa
3. Francisco P. Claravall
4. Juanito C. Dionisio
5. Pablo A. Peña
6. Aurelio M. Ramos
7. Eutiquio O. Sta. Romana
8. Alejandro D. Yango

Group IV
1. Jose M. Alejandrino
2. Marcelino V. Bernardo
3. Romeo S. Busuego
4. Carlos A. Faustino
5. Generoso P. Provido
6. Rodolfo H. Severino
7. Roman V. Ubaldo

Group V
1. Yusup R. Abubakar
2. Hortencio J. Brillantes
3. Irineo R. Cabatit
4. Irineo D. Cornista
5. Engracio D. Guerzon
6. Guillermo C. Fonacier
7. Marciano A. Joven
8. Reynaldo Lardizabal, Jr.
9. Luis Moreno Salcedo
10. Simeon R. Roxas
11. Eduardo L. Rosal
12. Tagakotta Sotto
13. Benjamin T. Tirona
14. Emilio Torres
15. Renato A. Urquiola

* The forty Filipino participants in the Philippine Foreign Affairs Training Program at the U.S. Department of State in Washington, D.C., from December 1945 to September 1947

1

The Pioneers

In mid-summer of 1945, the mood at the United States Department of State was upbeat. The unconditional surrender of Japan had just ended the Pacific War, and the Far Eastern Affairs Bureau was frantically sketching plans for America's relations with the newly liberated countries in Asia. One outstanding issue was the future of the Philippines, America's largest colony in the Pacific. Established in 1935, the Philippine Commonwealth government had been preparing for independence when the Pacific War broke out in December 1941. The Japanese occupation of the Philippines and the exile of the Commonwealth government in Washington, D.C. thwarted the Filipinos' quest for self-rule. But in February 1945, the United States liberated the Philippines, and the Department of State was working to ensure that independence would come about smoothly.

Although the Philippines enjoyed a high degree of autonomy as a Commonwealth government, the United States controlled its foreign relations. Toward the waning years of the Commonwealth and the onset of the new republic, the Philippine government realized that it lacked the capacity to rigorously train Foreign Service personnel for their future mission. Thus, the training of Filipinos for diplomatic and consular work by the U.S. State Department was one of the priority areas of cooperation between the Philippine and U.S. government.

As early as 1936, the Philippine House of Representatives approved H.B. No. 2263 to authorize, with the approval of the Department of State, qualified young people to train as Filipino attachés in American embassies in Paris, Berlin, Rome, London, Nanking, and Tokyo. Much later, members of the House of Representatives resurrected the idea by presenting bills with the same objective.[1] They introduced H.B. No. 1579 in March 1938 and proposed a Philippine Foreign Trade Service. Neither bill became law.

On 18 May1939, the Philippine Congress passed Commonwealth Act No. 429, authorizing the president of the Philippines to conduct negotiations with the president of the United States to secure assignments in American embassies and consulates abroad.[2]

During the academic year 1934–1935, the University of the Philippines (UP), the leading state university, adopted a four-year Bachelor of Science in Foreign Service in its College of Liberal Arts[3]. The program resembled other courses of study until its second half, when students began specialized courses in history, economics, geography, foreign languages (French and German), and international law.[4]

Likewise, the University of Santo Tomas in Manila, the country's oldest university, offered a Foreign Service degree program that was ahead of its times. Enrollment in both programs was tiny, partly because the specialized course did not guarantee a job offer after graduation. The Division of Foreign Relations in the Office of the President of the Commonwealth, established in 1937, was the only government agency where Foreign Service graduates could pursue a career that perfectly fit their academic background. But, the Division of Foreign Relations was too small to accommodate all Foreign Service graduates.[5]

Congressman Marcial Rañola of Albay, Bicol province introduced a bill in the Philippine Congress providing for the establishment of a Foreign Service School in the University of the Philippines. He explained the necessity of "a thoroughly trained corps of men" to handle our foreign relations, and stated that,

> Only those who possess an understanding of other peoples; who can develop an intimate acquaintance with their interests, their problems, conflict of parties, or course of action;

who have cultivated the ability to sift, to seize upon what is significant in the mass of news, rumors, assertions or debates; and who are able to know the character and particular aims of men who control the course of foreign governmental action, should be recruited for the service.[6]

Rañola added:

On or before 04 July 1946, U.S. sovereignty over the Philippines may be finally and completely withdrawn. Upon such withdrawal the country will begin to enjoy the rights and privileges, as well as to assume the responsibilities and obligations of an independent state. More active, close and direct intercourse with other countries will be inevitable. National affairs that may have a bearing on other nations will become more complicated, so that a special training will be needed to deal with them."

Rañola's bill provided that the dean and the professors of the Foreign Service school be chosen by the UP Board of Regents. The Regents would fix salaries and allowances from an appropriated sum of 5,000 pesos.[7]

Philippine Foreign Affairs Training Program

On 24 March 1944, Secretary of State James F. Byrne sent a letter to the Philippine Resident Commissioner to the United States Joaquin M. Elizalde expressing that the State Department would train selected Filipinos in diplomatic and consular work. However, Elizalde did not respond immediately. Frank Lockhart, a veteran Foreign Service officer who earlier served as consul in China, from inside the office that State Department personnel called PI (Philippine Islands), wrote a letter to Jaime Fernandez, the Secretary of Finance of the Commonwealth Government in Washington, D.C. Lockhart's fourteen-page memorandum was entitled "Preparations for the Handling of the Future Foreign Affairs of the Philippine Republic."[8] It set forth considerations for the Commonwealth government before the creation of a Department of Foreign Affairs and a Foreign Service. The document follows a similar document submitted to the Commonwealth government several years before on the same subject. The original document contemplated a preparatory period of about five years, but Lockhart omitted the lengthy preparatory period, assuming it would be reduced to a matter of months. In submitting the memorandum to Fernandez, Lockhart "made plain that it in no way reflected the official views of the United States Government but represented the personal views of several officers of the State Department."[9]

In July 1945, Lockhart convened an urgent meeting with his colleagues from the Foreign Training Division, Commercial Division, and relevant offices to draft a solution. They established the Philippine Foreign Affairs Training Program (PFATP) under the supervision of the Division of Philippine Affairs and in coordination with the Foreign Service Officers Training School. Lockhart appointed Edward W. Mill, his new assistant division chief, as director. Mill described the program's objectives as follows:

> The Philippine Foreign Affairs Training Program was designed to assist the Filipinos in preparing for the conduct of their foreign relations. This program was the outgrowth of preliminary studies made for several years by the Department of State. World War II and the subsequent occupation of the Philippines by the Japanese interrupted plans of the State Department for developing an active training program, but with the end of the war in the Pacific definite steps were taken to devise plans to assist in developing a Philippine Foreign Service after independence and to aid in the work incident to establishing a Department of Foreign Affairs for the new republic.[10]

On 25 July 1945, Carlos P. Romulo, who replaced Elizalde, sent a memorandum to Lockhart about the "Foreign Service Training Program for the Philippines." Romulo asked eight questions regarding the requirements of the training, assistance from the American consulate general in Manila in appraising applicants, and assistance from the State Department in selecting an experienced American adviser on foreign affairs for the Philippines.[11]

The State Department was racing against the clock to offer its assistance to the Philippine government. Lockhart consulted other State Department officials before proceeding to answer Romulo's memorandum. He emphasized that "no effort has been made to answer specifically all of Romulo's inquiries. An effort has been made to make the letter as general in its terms as possible and leave details to be worked out later."[12]

On 13 September 1945, the State Department informed Romulo that the Department was in a position to answer only some, but not all, of the questions Romulo posed and that additional information would be supplied as the project developed. Regarding the query about the number of trainees and the length of training, Lockhart replied that the State Department could extend its facilities initially to approximately fifteen Filipino trainees and that the duration of the training would run for approximately three or four months, including training in the Department and in the field.

On the specifics of the training in the State Department, Lockhart explained:

> It has been suggested that the activities of the Filipino trainees might be centered in the Division of Philippine Affairs of the State Department. The officers of this Division would be responsible for day-to-day direction of the work of the trainees. Various specialists of the Department, namely, commercial, legal and others would be called in from time to time to lecture and instruct the trainees and to answer their questions. Certain number of the trainees might also be assigned to divisions or sections of the Department for specified periods. At times the trainees would attend sessions of the Foreign Service Officer's Training School. The proposed program of studies and work is yet to be prepared but, generally speaking, it would include preparation in such fields as passport and immigration work, registration of births and marriages, certification of invoices of goods, preparation of economic and political reports, organization of protective services, drafting and negotiation of treaties, international organizations, and other subjects. It is expected that the training given to the Philippine personnel will

parallel that given to our own Foreign Service officers in preparation for their first assignment to the field.

As to the cost of the training, Lockhart stated: "*It would be expected that the Commonwealth government or the new independent government, would defray all expenses for salaries of the trainees, and all their travel and per diem expenses and allowances* (emphasis added)."

With reference to the American foreign affairs adviser, Lockhart explained: "In order to assist in the planning for the creation of the Philippine Department of Foreign Affairs and Foreign Service, the [State] Department is prepared, on the request of the Commonwealth government, to recommend a list of qualified Americans from which an adviser or advisers might be selected."[13]

The State Department also informed the American embassy in Manila that in connection to its report on the "Proposal to Establish a Foreign Service School in the University of the Philippines," they had created a committee on the Philippine Foreign Service under the chairmanship of Lockhart, with Julian Harrington as deputy director of the Office of Foreign Service, Woodbury Willoughby as associate chief of the Division of Commercial Policy, and Mill as secretary. The committee held its first session on 05 September 1945. At that point it was looking forward to developing a program of cooperation between the Commonwealth government and the State Department. Shortly after the first session, President Sergio Omen telegraphed Romulo to approve the program.[14] The committee vested the Division of Philippine Affairs with central supervision of the training program and worked closely with the U.S. Foreign Service Officer's Training School.[15] The Division of Philippine Affairs immediately drew up plans for the PFATP.

Back in Manila, Philippine independence added to President Osmeña and other government officials' urgency to create a Foreign Service. The American consulate general reported that Osmeña took up the matter at considerable length in his message to the last session of the Philippine Congress. Consequently, they passed Commonwealth Act. No. 683 and Osmeña approved it on 25 September 1945. The act organizes the Office of Foreign Relations, an initial step towards the organization of a Department of Foreign Affairs (DFA). The Commonwealth government also approved the appointment of a number of individuals to serve with the Department of State for training purposes. Application to the program was also opened to qualified individuals who might be appointed in the immediate future."[16]

Within the State Department, the Division of Philippine Affairs and the Division of Training Services discussed the finer points of allowing Filipino Foreign Service trainees to participate in the Service Officers Training School. The officers of the two divisions, Mill from Philippine Affairs and Mr. Carol H. Foster and Perry N. Jester, chief and assistant chief of Training Services respectively, agreed that the Filipino trainees should participate in as many of the lectures as possible, and special training would probably be necessary for visas, passports, shipping, and accounting; individual divisions would handle the logistics.[17]

Lockhart informed Romulo on 20 November 1945 that the new session of the Foreign Service Officers Training School would start on 03 December and requested that the Commonwealth government nominate at least five, but not more than ten candidates to participate in the initial program. He emphasized that the State Department reserved the right to admit only men of outstanding ability and character whose records were entirely clear of any direct or indirect collaboration with "the enemy." He further requested that arrangements be made between the Office of the United States High Commissioner, the U.S. Consulate General in Manila, and the Commonwealth authorities to select suitable candidates in the Philippines for the training program."[18]

The Secretary of State likewise sent the same message to the American consul general in Manila on the same date. He informed them that the Commonwealth government would have to defray the expenses of the trainees.[19] The trainees would spend six weeks at the Foreign Service Officers Training School and at least four weeks in certain work outlined by the Division of Philippine Affairs, after which they would gain practical experience at selected field posts.[20]

Initial Candidates

The Commonwealth government proposed several candidates for the first training: Manuel A. Adeva, Jose F. Imperial, Tiburcio C.

Baja, Vicente I. Singian, and Emilio Torres, who were already in Washington, and Eduardo Quintero, Tomas Benitez, Enrique Fernando, Antonio Sison, and Vicente Abad Santos who were in Manila. Adeva and Imperial were immediately accepted by the State Department. Torres's acceptance, however, was withheld because he reportedly served in the Department of Justice under the Japanese puppet regime, although he claimed clearance from the U.S. Counter Intelligence Corps (CIC). The State Department requested that the American consul in Manila provide more information from the CIC and other appropriate sources on Manila-based candidates. Similar reports were requested for Baja and Singian.

Subsequent U.S Army Intelligence reports cleared Adeva, Baja, and Imperial of any concerns of Japanese collaboration. Collaboration with the Japanese was a critical issue for the State Department. Proven loyalty to the U.S. and Commonwealth governments was essential for would-be trainees. On 28 November 1945, the secretary of state emphasized in his instructions to the American consular officer-in-charge in Manila that "this restriction would appear to be essential in order to avoid any possibility of misunderstanding on the subject of admissibility to the training program. The Commonwealth government in Washington has been informed of this attitude of the [State] Department regarding candidates and has been requested to select candidates in accordance with these high standards."[21]

Thus, the American consul general in Manila excluded anyone who had held a position in the Japanese-controlled Philippine republic even though that person may not have exercised any great power or influence or been guilty of overt collaboration with the enemy.[22] Antonio Sison and Vicente Abad Santos were among those denied acceptance. Sison was reportedly employed by the puppet government as investigator of price control at the Bureau of Commerce from September to December 1943 and as bank examiner at the auditing office of the Agriculture and Industrial Bank. Santos reportedly worked as a code committee law clerk from January 1942 to August 1944.[23]

From the outset the State Department and the Office of the Resident Commissioner in Washington agreed that "applicants should be completely free of all charges of collaboration with the enemy."[24]

Proven loyalty to the U.S. and Commonwealth governments was essential for trainees. The secretary of state's 28 November 1945 instruction to the American consular officer-in-charge in Manila emphasized that "this restriction would appear to be essential in order to avoid any possibility of misunderstanding on the subject of admissibility to the training program. The Commonwealth government in Washington has been informed of this attitude of the [State] Department regarding candidates and has been requested to select candidates in accordance with these high standards."[25] The American consulate in Manila faithfully enforced the State Department's trenchant instructions. The CIC carefully investigated all potential trainees. The American consul general excluded anyone who had held a position in the puppet government even if the person had little power or influence and did not overtly collaborate with the enemy.[26]

Aside from CIC clearance, the candidates faced other problems on their trip to Washington. U.S. consul Paul Steintorf reported that the issuance of passports and visas to Philippine-based trainees would be delayed because no fingerprint and registration forms were available. Furthermore, extreme congestion of air facilities made it impossible to obtain air transport for the trainees within a short time. Steintorf suggested the opening of the training school be deferred until January 1946.[27] The State Department, however, maintained the scheduled opening date and decided that Adeva, Baja, Imperial, and Singian could begin, as Group I, before the Manila-based candidates, who would join later.[28] The Filipino trainees would be detailed to the State Department and American diplomatic and consular posts abroad and would thereby be subject to the rules and regulations of the U.S. Foreign Service.

First Group

The delay and administrative constraints of sending trainees from the Philippines favored the Filipino candidates based in the United States. On 03 December 1945, the first group of Washington-based Filipino trainees entered the State Department, in particular the Foreign Service Officers Training School, and began their specialized training a week later.

Candido T. Elbo was a last-minute inclusion to Group I.[29] The first group was "mature and well qualified" by virtue of education and experience for this assignment.[30] The group's average age was forty—Adeva was the oldest at forty-four and Singian the youngest at thirty-one. All possessed three degrees and had graduated from leading American universities.

At the time of their selection, Adeva, Elbo, and Imperial were already working in the Philippine Commonwealth government-in-exile in Washington, D.C. Adeva, a native of Negros Occidental, studied law in Manila and New York. Prior to his training at the State Department, he served as chief of Nationals Division at the Office of the Resident Commissioner of the Philippines to the United States in Washington.[31] Elbo, a native of Santa Cruz, Laguna, served as secretary to the resident commissioner and, during the war, to the vice president of the Philippines.[32] In 1945, he became assistant secretary to the president of the Commonwealth.

Originally from Camarines Sur, Imperial obtained master's and PhD degrees in Foreign Service from Georgetown University and was a member of the Technical Committee of the Commonwealth President.[33] On 16 October 1944, Imperial received the newly created position of Foreign Service assistant and the responsibility of studying Foreign Office and Foreign Service organizations and procedures for the Philippines after independence. After seven months, Imperial submitted a 114-page report to the Philippine Commonwealth government-in-exile in Washington entitled, *Report on the Proposed Organization of the Foreign Service of the Philippines*.[34] Imperial's pioneering report became one of the foundations for the future DFA. Imperial and Adeva also served as technical advisers to the Philippine delegations at the United Nations Conference on International Organization in San Francisco from April to June 1945.

The other two trainees, Baja and Singian, were selected because of their connection with the Philippine government and their service during the war. Baja, a native of Batangas, received a master's degree in Foreign Service from the University of Southern California. During the war, he was language editor and radio writer for the Office of War Information in San Francisco.[35] He prepared and transmitted broadcast messages in Tagalog from the Pacific to the

Philippines. He exhorted his fellow Filipinos to hold fast and stand firm against the Japanese invasion, for the United States was building an unbeatable military force and arsenal and would soon come to their aid.[36]

On the other hand, Singian, a native of Pampanga, was studying at Princeton University in 1945 when he was selected to join the training program. Previously, Singian had served for two years as assistant to the Philippine resident commissioner to the United States and, before that, obtained a master's and PhD in Foreign Service from Georgetown University.

Pensionado Examinations

The selection of candidates for the PFATP at the State Department and the urgent recruitment of personnel in the Office of Foreign Relations in Manila prompted the Philippine Bureau of Civil Service to conduct competitive examinations, then called *Pensionado* examinations, to choose suitable candidates. Within seven months in 1946, the bureau gave three examinations, two under the Osmeña Administration and one under the Roxas Administration.

On 10 January 1946, the bureau announced that the examinations were,

> For filling of positions in the Office of Foreign Relations and/or selection of trainees in Foreign Service. The qualifications of applicants must satisfy the following: ages of 21 to 40, possession of a college degree with an average of at least 80% in their college record, and two years of relevant and responsible experience.

It was divided into three differently weighted parts: Theoretical Examination (70 percent); Experience and Training (15 percent); and Personal Fitness [Interview] (15 percent). The theoretical examination, the written portion, covered international law or international trade, history of diplomacy or modern history, Philippine economic conditions, Philippine history and government, and Spanish or French composition.[37]

On 09 February 1946, the bureau released a list of those that passed: Anastacio B. Bartolome, Emilio D. Bejasa, Hortencio J.

Brillantes, Francisco Claravall, Carlos A. Faustino, Gregorio M. Feliciano, Engracio D. Guerzon, Marciano Joven, Antonio L. Llanes, Manuel Y. Macias, Manuel Madarang, Cresencio S. Magbag, Luis Moreno Salcedo, Pablo A. Peña, Aurelio Ramos, Eduardo Rosal, Eutiquio O. Sta. Romana, Claro P. Sison, Renato A. Urquiola, and Alejandro D. Yango.

A second examination was held on 23 March1946.The purpose was "to fill positions in the Office of Foreign Relations or in the future foreign service of the Philippines"; and "those who qualify in this examination will also be considered in the selection of trainees to be sent to the Department of State in Washington, D.C. or to diplomatic and consular offices of the United States in foreign countries." As a word of caution, it said: "However, not all those who pass the examination will be sent abroad for training, as other factors are to be considered: namely, their activities during the enemy occupation, the availability of government funds to defray the expenses involved, etc."[38]

The examination was weighted differently than the first one. The percentage consisted of the following: Theoretical Examination (60 percent); Education, Training, and Experience (10 percent); and "Practical Examination" (30 percent).

The practical examination had the same oral interview, but included "actual tests of fitness in the Office of Foreign Relations for the purpose of securing further evidence of the candidate's qualifications." Perhaps, too much emphasis had been placed on the theoretical examination instead of practice and ability. The results were released on 04 May1946. Among the successful candidates were Pio G. de Castro, Octavio L. Maloles, Florencio D.R. Ponce, Rodolfo H. Severino, and Antonio A. Torres.

On 20 July 1946, the third examination was held in Manila. This examination's stated purposed and its weighted parts were the same as those of the March examination. The subjects of the theoretical examination were the same with two additions - Political and Economic Geography and English composition. Applicants only needed a college degree to take the examinations; the announcement said nothing about college average grade or work experience. On 26 October 1946, the bureau announced that only Jose M. Alejandrino, Romeo S. Busuego, and Carlos A. Faustino had passed.[39]

Second Group

The State Department expected the second group of Filipino trainees to report for training no later than 15 March 1946.[40] The second group was composed of Tomas G. de Castro, Delfin R. Garcia, Pelayo F. Llamas, Leopoldo T. Ruiz, and Doroteo V. Vite. Except for Garcia, all were already based in America; Garcia joined them in early 1946. The Philippine government had originally nominated five candidates from the Philippines, but the State Department rejected all except Garcia on the grounds of collaboration.[41]

De Castro, who hailed from Sorsogon, was a former law professor at UP and the Philippine Military Academy and a technical assistant at the Office of the Resident Commissioner in Washington, D.C. After the Pacific War, he joined the United States Armed Forces in the Far East and became a captain. Llamas, a native of Laguna, studied law at UP and worked as private secretary to the second deputy commissioner of Immigration and was detailed at the Office of Foreign Relations prior to his training in the State Department.

Originally from Aklan, Ruiz studied sociology and anthropology at the University of California, Columbia University, and the University of Southern California where he received a PhD. He was a senior analyst in the U.S. Foreign Economic Administration for three years and served on the Technical Committee of the Commonwealth President. Ruiz, however, was almost disqualified by the State Department because of his age and professional experience. At fifty-four, he was the oldest among the Filipino trainees and already had a great deal of professional experience.[42]

Vite, a native of Ilocos Sur, grew up in Hawaii and California. He graduated from George Washington University and studied Foreign Service at Columbia. During the Pacific War, he joined the U.S. army, serving in Papua New Guinea, Australia, and the Philippines. He worked as intelligence personnel in General McArthur's headquarters and attended the U.S. Army Signal Intelligence and Commando School for one year. He was discharged from the U.S. army in February 1946.[43]

The youngest member of Group II was twenty-four year old Delfin Garcia. He graduated from the University of the Philippines with a bachelor's degree in Foreign Service, one of the first two graduates of the program. Initially, he worked as an assistant at the Division of Foreign Affairs in the Office of the Commonwealth President shortly before the Pacific War. After, he worked at the Office of Foreign Relations and was nominated for PFATP.[44]

Group II began training on 21 March 21, and completed on 01 July 1946. They trained alongside American Foreign Service trainees at the Foreign Service Training School. After Group II, Acting Secretary Acheson informed the American consul in Manila that the State Department "considers trainees who have completed their work to be of high merit and qualified for responsible assignments. Adeva, Baja, Imperial, Castro, and Garcia were considered particularly able by officer in charge of the training program."[45]

Although PFATP was a pre-independence program, Commonwealth president Sergio Osmeña requested that the State Department continue it. The U.S. government agreed.[46] In his letter to the secretary of state on 01 June 1946, Osmeña's successor President Manuel Roxas requested that the PFATP continue indefinitely after the establishment of the Republic on 04 July 1946.[47] President Roxas expressed great satisfaction with the training of the first two groups of trainees, adding that "the Commonwealth government, however, feels that only a start has been made in obtaining the requisite number of trained Philippine Foreign Service officers. It therefore greatly desires that the present Philippine Foreign Affairs Training Program be continued for an indefinite period and is prepared to continue the training program on the same conditions as presently prevails."[48]

Third Group

Preparation for Group III was more complicated because it was the first time that the majority of the trainees were coming from Manila. U.S. Consul Steintorf reported on 02 April 1946, obtaining transportation for the new group was very difficult. Two weeks later, he reported his frustration to the State Department due to the delay in the issuance of the travel documents of the trainees, which he attributed entirely to the dilatory tactics of the Commonwealth government.[49]

Group III had eight trainees: Anastacio B. Bartolome, Emilio D. Bejasa, Francisco P. Claravall, Juanito C. Dionisio, Pablo Peña,

Aurelio Ramos, Eutiquio O. Sta. Romana, and Alejandro D. Yango. All but Dionisio were selected in Manila through the *Pensionado* examinations. Dionisio was a senior assistant at the Office of the Resident Commissioner to the United States in San Francisco when instructed to join the State Department training course. The background of Group III reveals that six were lawyers—Bejasa, Claravall, Peña, Ramos, Sta. Romana, and Yango. Bartolome and Dionisio had business and journalism backgrounds respectively. Sta. Romana and Yango were not only batch mates at UP College of Law, but they were both from the province of Nueva Ecija. Bejasa and Sta. Romana were distinguished by their service in the guerrilla movement against the Japanese invaders during the war.

On 27 April1946, Group III took the *SS John MacLeon*, a troop ship bound for America, and was expected to arrive in San Francisco on 24 May.[50] Sailing from the Philippines to America turned out to be an ordeal. As one of the trainees recounted:

> On 27 April 1946, the Foreign Service students left for Washington on a foul-smelling troopship, the *S. S. John McLean*. The 30-day voyage, which the starry-eyed students had expected to be pleasant, turned out to be a nightmarish experience. The trainees slept in bunkers, one over the other. Since there were no pillows, the lifebelt came in handy. During the 30-day crossing of the Pacific, the passengers formed long lines to eat their daily meal composed of mashed potatoes, broiled meat with gravy and grapefruit juice. The trainees' illusion of luxury cabins, deluxe toilets and bath facilities quickly vanished. The bathroom was a big compartment where three or four bathed at the same time with cold seawater.
>
> On deck, there were no chairs or improvised benches. The trainees sat down on coiled ropes, on chains, or on elevated platforms of the hatch. Luckily, one Manila businessman brought his rattan sofa and it quickly became a temptation for the trainees to sit or recline on it. Every time the businessman would leave the sofa, three or four of the trainees would sit on it. After a week, the rattan network of the sofa was torn by the excessive weight of the intruders

and the businessman wisely transferred his priceless possession to the other side of the deck far removed from any unholy intrusion. The almost inhuman living conditions on the ship became a butt of jokes even among the American GIs and sailors. Instead of calling the "MacLean" troopship, they called it a cattle ship! On 28 May 1946, the ship finally reached the port of Oregon.[51]

Former Philippine ambassador Eduardo Montilla was twenty-one at the time and new to the Philippine army. He shared his encounter with the members of Group III. On his way to the United States he was pleasantly surprised at the number of Filipinos aboard the ship: another student, three businessmen, and *pensionados* of the Foreign Service: Peña, Claravall, Yango, Bartolome, Sta. Romana, and Bejasa. During the month-long voyage, Montilla discovered the *pensionados'* dreams for their diplomatic careers and the forthcoming republic. Inspired, he abandoned his original plan to continue his studies in arms and ammunitions engineering and followed the *pensionados* to Washington, D.C. to apply for any position in the soon to be established Philippine embassy. Because of a port strike in San Francisco, they landed in Portland instead. On the first day of their arrival, the group told him he could commence his lesson in diplomacy by joining them in a cultural tour. So he did and found himself joining them in a visit to a burlesque theatre.[52]

They hardly had time to shake off the sea lag when they received a telegram from the Office of the Resident Commissioner in San Francisco telling them to take the earliest plane trip to Washington, D.C. Fortunately the manager of Northwest Airlines was able to reserve seats for all seven of them. It was their first plane ride. The trip took seventeen hours as they stopped at Billings, Montana, Minneapolis, Minnesota, and finally Newark, New Jersey. A bus took the trainees to New York where they stayed at the Embassy Hotel. During the wee hours of the morning, some of them visited the Empire State building while others rode in the famous New York subway train.

Coming back to the hotel, the trainees received instruction to take the first flight to Washington, D.C., the following morning amidst stormy weather. The plane jerked up and down in rapid successions causing one of the trainees to vow never to fly again. The following morning they met with Resident Commissioner Romulo and then with Edward W. Mill at the State Department. A photograph taken in June 1946 shows this group in gray and white double-breasted and three-button suits, serious faces, and penetrating looks, their black pomaded hair neatly combed, and wearing polished butterfly shoes. Mill stands at the center wearing a dark suit, towering over all of them.

On 03 June1946, Group III began training. The lectures were held in the State Department conference room, the Lothrop House, and the Department of Commerce or Department of Agriculture. They finished the course on 15 August1946.

Fourth Group

After Group III's graduation, Richard Butrick, the American foreign affairs adviser to the Philippine government, predicted that the State Department training program for Filipinos would end. Butrick was wrong, because two more groups were prepared to leave for Washington. But, Mill heeded Butrick's second recommendation that "some distinction should be drawn between those who definitely expect to be made officers and those who will be willing to accept clerical positions in the Philippine Foreign Service." The difficulty of finding appointments for the trainees caused Mill to postpone future groups until all past and present groups were placed in definite positions of responsibility at the Department of Foreign Affairs in Manila or in the Philippine Foreign Service.

Narciso Ramos, minister counselor at the Philippine embassy in Washington, agreed with Mill's policy recommendation. He had been receiving dozens of applications from Filipinos, including those based in the States, who wanted to participate in the State Department training program; and various sources were putting pressure on him to accept certain candidates. This policy afforded him a means to pass responsibility for accepting candidates to the State Department.[53]

Group IV consisted of seven trainees: Jose M. Alejandrino, Marcelino V. Bernardo, Romeo S. Busuego, Carlos A. Faustino, Generoso P. Provido, Rodolfo H. Severino, and Roman V. Ubaldo. Their training started on 06 January and ended on 12 June 1947.

When Mill received the American embassy in Manila's report on Group IV, he was immediately impressed by their qualifications and stature. He noted:

> The biographical records of these men show clearly that this will be the best group ever to enter the Department. One man, Generoso Provido, has a PhD from Stanford, another, Marcelino Bernardo has a PhD from Illinois, and the others are all established members of the bar. Most of them already hold important positions in the Philippine Department of Foreign Affairs. Needless to say we have an unusually fine opportunity here to further increase the good will already existing between our Department of State and the Philippine Department of Foreign Affairs.[54]

Alejandrino, Busuego, Faustino, and Severino were lawyers and passed *pensionado* examinations while Bernardo and Provido were already employed at the Department of Foreign Affairs. Ubaldo was the only U.S. based candidate. He was a senior assistant in the Office of the Resident Commissioner to the United States (Pacific Coast branch) in San Francisco.

Fifth Group

On 12 March 1947, twelve of the fifteen members of Group V sailed from Manila to the United States aboard the ship *General Gordon*. They arrived in Washington, D.C. fifteen days later. They were Yusup R. Abubakar, Hortencio J. Brillantes, Ireneo D. Cornista, Engracio D. Guerzon, Marciano A. Joven, Reynaldo Lardizabal, Jr. Luis Moreno Salcedo, Simeon R. Roxas, Eduardo L. Rosal, Tagakotta Sotto, Benjamin T. Tirona, and Renato A. Urquiola.

To the detriment of candidates who passed the *pensionado* examinations, some members of Group V were politically connected and were last minute substitutes. A nephew of the Sultan of Sulu, Abubakar, later became the first Muslim career ambassador of the Philippines. Three others were already in America when selected. Irineo Cabatit and Guillermo Fonacier, the only Filipino trainees who did not possess a college degree, were serving as assistants at the Philippine consulate general in San Francisco. Emilio Torres was assigned to the Philippine embassy in Washington as third secretary and vice consul. A last minute inclusion in Group V, Torres, was initially disqualified because of a derogatory report about his position in the Department of Justice during the Japanese occupation.[55] Estela R. Sulit, the first and only woman to be considered for the State Department training with Group V, was given another assignment. Sulit was then the administrative officer in the Philippine consulate in San Francisco.[56]

On 31 March, Minister Counselor Narciso Ramos of the Philippine embassy in Washington accompanied the trainees to the State Department and introduced them to Mill. The newcomers favorably impressed Mill. "I gained a very good impression of this group," Mill wrote in his diary that day. "They seem for the most part to be a fairly young group. They show considerable eagerness and enthusiasm for their new assignment and seem to have come to this country with the right attitude. Mr. Sotto, the son of the Philippine senator, in particular seemed eager to get off on a good start. He came to me and wanted to know just what books and materials he should get in order to get a good start in the training program. His attitude seems to be typical of that of the group as a whole."

He also shared this impression with Robert A. Burman of the U.S.-Philippine Financial Commission in his letter dated 14 April 1947:

A new group recently arrived from Manila. Several of the members of this group are sons of prominent Philippine senators. Despite the obvious political connections of some of the members of the new group, I think they may prove to be the best group we have had thus far. As time goes on I am more and more convinced of the importance of this program in strengthening the foreign policy ties between the two countries.

The collaboration policy was relaxed to accommodate some of Group V; half of them had collaboration records. Butrick said: "the collaboration issue is practically as dead as a dodo out here [Manila]." As Mill explained to Butrick:

> Hortencio J. Brillantes, Engracio D. Guerzon, Marciano A. Joven, Eduardo Rosal, Luis Moreno Salcedo, and Renato Urquiola held minor, non-policy posts in the puppet regime but that they have been subsequently cleared of any charge of active collaboration with the enemy. I have sent a telegram to the U.S. Embassy seeking further information on these men and hope that we may be able to admit them if nothing too adverse is reported.[57]

> Emilio Torres was not included in the State Department's 04 April 1947 Press Release, but was included at the last minute due to the intervention of Ambassador Joaquin Elizalde. Minister Counselor Ramos also wrote Mill to endorse Torres' participation in the training program. The inclusion of Torres in Group V created resentment among the original members of the group. One of the most vocal was Hortencio J. Brillantes who protested the inclusion of Torres in their group.[58]

Mill felt obliged to explain his side to Brillantes over the inclusion of Torres.

> In your letter of 22 September from Honolulu you wrote of the regret of the boys that a certain trainee should have not been admitted to the training program. I share your apprehension in this matter and refused for at least a year to allow this man to enter the training program along with the others and complete the work of the training program on the same basis. The Ambassador [Elizalde], however, was personally interested in his case and made it a matter of personal privilege to have him in the training program. I must say that once we had reluctantly agreed to admit him, he worked very hard and took the training program and work at the Foreign Service Institute seriously. I quite appreciate your desire to maintain the high standards set by men such as you and members of your group. I can promise you that if by any chance further trainees are sent to the State Department, I will insist on the same high standard of quality.[59]

Group V started on 07 April and ended on 23 July 1947. They followed a similar format to the previous groups, except that their training emphasized "the home office-side of foreign relations."[60] Group V did not train in any American diplomatic missions abroad; a few did practicum in relevant divisions in the State Department while others trained in the Philippine consulate general in New York or in San Francisco.

After Group V, the Philippine and U.S. governments agreed to discontinue the State Department training. Forty diplomatic officers were enough to cover the needs of the Foreign Service at the time. The Department of Foreign Affairs in Manila and the Philippine Foreign Service could not absorb more personnel. Besides, the cost of training the Filipino diplomats in Washington, D.C. and at U.S. Foreign Service posts was too much for the cash-strapped Philippine government. At this point, it would be interesting to know the details of the Foreign Service training program and how the Filipino trainees fared in their training in the State Department and selected U.S. Foreign Service posts.

2

Diplomatic and Consular Training

The Philippine Foreign Affairs Training Program was a crash course on diplomatic and consular work. The State Department offered the training facilities free of charge. State Department officials, many of them senior and experienced diplomats and consular officers, taught almost all the subjects. The trainees were briefed on the governments of different countries of the world and were taught on how to organize and administer a foreign mission or embassy, including details on operating a consulate. In addition, the trainees were assigned to various divisions of the State Department for specialized training and a few were selected for instruction at various American embassies.[1]

Each Filipino trainee entered into a contract with the Philippine Commonwealth government regarding the terms and conditions for training in the State Department. The terms and conditions covered the basic and extra pay, including clothing allowance, transportation cost, the place and period of service and so forth. The trainee received $180 per month if he was not yet working in the Philippine government. If he was already in government service, he only received his salary. If the salary was smaller than the allowance, he would receive the difference in addition to his salary. The trainees also received a lump sum of $150 clothing allowance for the duration of the training period. Nevertheless during their training at American Foreign Service posts, the trainees were entitled to additional allowance to cover the cost of living. The Philippine government shouldered all transportation expenses related to the performance of official duties by the trainees. As part of the contract with the Philippine government, the trainees were required to render three years of service to the latter and, in case of removal or early termination, the trainee concerned was required to reimburse the Philippine government all the expenses incurred during his training.

Training in Washington, D.C.

In 1945, the Department of State was still housed at the Old Executive Building, located at Seventeenth Street and Pennsylvania Avenue, which it shared with the War and Navy Departments. The Office of the Foreign Service, Division of Training Services, which managed the Foreign Service Officers Training School, was situated in a separate Annex called the Lothrop House, at 2001 Connecticut Avenue NW in Washington. Its official address was at Kalorama Triangle north of DuPont Circle. It was in the Lothrop House that the Philippine Foreign Affairs Training Program was conducted.[2]

Acting Assistant Chief of the Division of Philippine Affairs and PFATP Director Mill was initially ambivalent about the outcome of the program. "As director of this training program I can well recall our first meeting. None of us was very sure how far the program would go and how successful it would be," Mill admitted.

> It was evident from the beginning, however, that the first Philippine Foreign Service training group was most conscious of its historical role and determined to make a success of its important assignment. They tackled their work with great vigor and soon were making excellent records in the State Department.[3]

Mill described the first training program as follows:

> During the first week in the Foreign Service School the trainees attended a series of general orientation lectures on the work of the State Department and the American

Foreign Service. Malcolm Morrow, Chief of the Division of Public Inquires, Government Information Services, Bureau of Budget, spoke on the "Organization of the Federal Government," and Walton C. Ferris, Foreign Service officer detailed as Inspector, discussed the "Organization of the Foreign Service." John F. Simmons, American ambassador to El Salvador, talked to the group on "How a Diplomatic Mission Operates."

In the second week of work, Nelson T. Johnson, American Envoy Extraordinary and Minister Plenipotentiary to Australia, spoke on the subject, "Conduct and Contacts Abroad," and a special conference was held for the Filipino trainees on the organization and functioning of the Office of the Foreign Service, by Selden Chapin, Director of the Office of the Foreign Service, and Julian F. Harrington, Deputy Director of the Office of the Foreign Service.

During the third week, Eugene C. Rowley, member of the Board of Review of the Passport Division, conducted special citizenship work for the Philippine Group. During the fourth week, the trainees heard a lecture on "Writing of Economic Reports" by William C. Trimble, Assistant Chief of the Division of Northern European Affairs, and a lecture on "Handling of Political and Economic Reports in the Department of State" by Roger L. Heacock, Foreign Service officer, Chief of the Commercial Liaison Section of the Division of Central Services. Perry N. Jester, Acting Chief of the Division of Training Services, also lectured on "Service Etiquette."

In the fifth week, the trainees participated in the work on shipping and on commercial treaties. Other important and instructive lectures were given during this intensive six weeks' session of the Foreign Service Officers Training School. In addition, the trainees have participated in other work and lectures arranged by the Division of Philippine Affairs. Specialists in the Passport, Visa, Commercial Policy, and Shipping Divisions conducted special classes for the trainees in their fields of work. A representative of the Bureau of the Budget, Walter C. Laves, discussed the overall subject of the conduct of foreign relations by a modern government. The trainees have submitted regular reports on various phases of the work and have taken a series of examinations. Each Friday a general review session on the work of the week was held in the Division of Philippine Affairs.[4]

The trainees' sessions with the officers of the Division of Philippine Affairs were of particular significance. Here the program tied together their general training with the special problems and interests of the future Philippine Department of Foreign Affairs and Philippine Foreign Service. The entire training program was designed to be of concrete and immediate value to the trainees and their government.[5]

During the next six weeks the Filipino group joined their American classmates in an intensive program of lectures and studies in the field of Foreign Service work. The Filipino trainees were very conscious of their performance *vis-à-vis* their American classmates. Filipino trainee Pablo Peña from Group III observed:

> Our classmates were American Foreign Service officers, mostly newcomers who passed the Foreign Service examinations. In the class roster, one will be surprised to see a majority of them to be members of Phi Beta Kappa. Many are alumni of famous American universities such as Harvard, Yale, Princeton, Georgetown, Cornell, Columbia, and Catholic University. These young officers hold the appointment as vice consuls of the United States of America, signed by President Truman and confirmed by the U.S. Senate. Alongside them were the poor *Pinoys* (slang for Filipinos) who were nothing more than "trainees," covering the same course and absorbing the same subject matter. We had to be very attentive. We did not put our feet on the chairs. Also unlike our American numbers, we had to be busy taking notes instead of drawing caricatures, for our own information and for inspection by Mr. Mill at the end of the course.[6]

To round out the training, Mill helped the Filipinos make interesting friends in Washington and organized parties and informal discussion groups. On weekends he took them to historical places of such as Hyde Park in New York, Mount Vernon, Monticello, and Arlington National Cemetery.[7]

How did the Filipino trainees find the Foreign Service training program at the State Department? Jose F. Imperial gave the following impressions: "The course was difficult. Not only did the trainees submit regular reports on various phases of the work, but took also a series of five examinations. This is quite a contrast to the one general examination given to American vice consuls after the completion of their training at the Foreign Service Officers Training School."[8]

The State Department was particularly interested at the time in the recently created Office of Foreign Relations of the Philippine Commonwealth Government headed by Vicente G. Sinco. The department instructed the American consul in Manila to obtain available information on what was actually being done by Mr. Sinco's office. Such information would assist the State Department in replying to inquiries from the Filipino trainees regarding the functions and responsibilities of the Office of Foreign Relations in Manila and how its plans would possibly affect the future work of the trainees.[9]

Resident Commissioner Carlos P. Romulo was seriously concerned about the Filipino trainees and kept himself abreast of the program. In early February 1946, he inquired with Frank Lockhart regarding the progress of the trainees. Lockhart informed Romulo that the Filipinos devoted themselves assiduously to their work and that they had derived great benefit from the course. The course endeavored to provide them with every facility for acquiring as much information as they could give them regarding the work of the Department of State and work in the U.S. Foreign Service in general. Romulo said that the trainees were loud in their praise of the conduct of the school and the training that they had received. Romulo expressed great appreciation of the State Department's efforts to help them in this program. He added that on 15 February, he thought another group of ten or fifteen students would be selected and sent to Washington for this purpose since competitive examinations had been held in Manila recently to select additional trainees.[10]

Back in Washington, the first group completed the first phase of the training on 15 February1946. The occasion was observed with a ceremony that featured a discussion of the plans for the Philippine government's new Department of Foreign Affairs and its Foreign Service. The ceremony was attended by Romulo, Lockhart, Julian F. Harrington, deputy director of the Office of the Foreign Service, and Richard R. Ely of the Office of the High Commissioner for the Philippines.[11] The trainees made presentations in the latter half of the ceremony: Jose F. Imperial spoke on the proposed Department of Foreign Affairs; Manuel A. Adeva on the Office of Political Affairs; Tiburcio C. Baja on the Office of Economic Affairs; Vicente I. Singian on the Office of Administrative Affairs; and Candido Elbo on the Office of the Legal Adviser. The Filipino community in Washington celebrated the graduation of the first group with great fanfare. As a tribute to the graduates, the Filipino Executive Council sponsored a dance on Saturday, 30 March 1946 at the Burgundy Room of the Wardman Park Hotel.

With the completion of their work in the State Department and graduation, the trainees were detailed to American embassies, where they would receive training in the field. Estimates regarding the length of time required for the field training vary, but a period of three months abroad was considered adequate.

Training in U.S. Foreign Service Posts

At the State Department, there were active discussions between the Division of Philippine Affairs and the Office of Foreign Service on the detail of the Filipino Foreign Affairs trainees to American Foreign Service posts as they approached the completion of their training in the State Department on the second week of February 1946. On the other hand, the Philippine Commonwealth government was also anxious that the trainees be detailed abroad as soon as possible since it was paying the expenses of the trainees on a weekly basis. In the end, the Division of Philippine Affairs proposed the deployment of the trainees to the following posts:

Jose Imperial – Shanghai
Tiburcio Baja –Mexico City
Manuel Adeva – Sydney

Candido Elbo – Hong Kong
Vicente Singian – Santiago, Chile.[12]

The Division of Foreign Service Personnel, however, responded to the Division of Philippine Affairs, "None of our establishments in the Far East are yet sufficiently organized and staffed to afford training without adversely affecting the performance of essential functions for our own Government." Thus, Imperial and Elbo were instead assigned to Montreal and Havana, respectively.[13]

The State Department made it clear that per the detail of the trainees to American Foreign Service establishments, all expenses of travel, salaries, subsistence, and housing will have to be borne by the Philippine Commonwealth government. No State Department funds were available for this purpose and none would be made available in the future.[14] The State Department provided the American Foreign Service posts that would host the trainees with background information regarding the training program in Washington and instruction on how to accommodate the trainees. The posts were expected to afford them opportunity as observers to gain as wide a range of practical experience as possible consistent with the interests and available facilities of the posts. The extent to which confidential material was made to the trainee was left to the discretion of the posts.[15]

On 12 March 1946, Assistant Secretary of State Donald Russell wrote to Resident Commissioner Romulo regarding the deployment of the first batch of trainees to selected American posts abroad. Russell suggested that since the American Foreign Service granted its officers certain allowances while stationed abroad, the same practice should be followed with respect to the Philippine trainees. Accordingly, the State Department had prepared a series of figures covering allowances for each of the trainees at various posts. These allowances consisted of the usual heat, rent, and light allowances and cost of living allowances. The cost of living was fixed based on the rate of an unmarried American Foreign Service Officer Class V. In view of the temporary nature of the detail, the State Department suggested that each trainee be paid on a per diem basis: an estimated $7 a day for trainees in Montreal, Mexico City, Santiago, and Havana, and $6 a day for those in Sydney. Estimates on the transport expenses to and from Washington were also provided. He suggested that the Philippine government deposit a lump sum totaling six thousand dollars, tentatively, to pay for travel and per diem allowance to the trainees for an estimated period of three months. The amount, however, would not include disbursements for salaries for the trainees. He requested the Commonwealth government to fix trainees' salaries and that the sum required meeting these payments should be added to the six thousand dollars. Any remaining funds would be refunded to the Commonwealth government at the end of the training period. Lastly, Russell requested the approval of the Commonwealth government at an early date so that the trainees may be able to proceed to their respective assignments without delay.[16]

Performance in the Training at U.S. Foreign Service Posts

Tiburcio Baja was the first Filipino to be assigned to an American embassy under the training program.[17] He was assigned to the U.S. embassy in Mexico City. Manuel Adeva was assigned to the U.S. consulate general in Sydney, Australia; Candido Elbo to the U.S. embassy in Havana; Jose Imperial to the U.S. consulate general in Montreal; and Vicente Singian to the U.S. embassy in Santiago, Chile. Imperial, however, was unexpectedly appointed Public Relations officer of the Philippine Commonwealth government in Washington instead of his assigned post in Montreal. In his place, the State Department sent Singian.[18] Singian arrived in Montreal on 18 May 1946.[19]

At the posts, each trainee carried out special projects outside of the normal training. Adeva, for example, sought permission from the State Department to travel outside of Sydney to study the personnel and functional organization of the Ministry of External Affairs of Australia in Canberra. He requested a budget of thirty dollars for transportation and accommodations.[20] Arthur Richards of the British Commonwealth Division, in an internal memo to the Division of Philippine Affairs, approved Adeva's trip since "it might be helpful for him in his background study of diplomatic organizations and activities" and suggested that "a reply be sent to Adeva by cable without delay."[21]

The trainees were expected to return to Washington by 30 June.

Adeva requested special permission to return to Washington via Manila, so he could be present at the inauguration of the Philippine republic on 04 July 1946. In his letter, Adeva described the date as "a red letter day in the history of the Philippines and in the lives of the Filipino people." With nationalistic pride he concluded, "It will mean much to me and to my work as a Foreign Service officer to be a witness to the birth of our Republic."[22] Lockhart approved Adeva's request and instructed Consul General Steintorf to pay Adeva his salary for the last half of June; but he added that "no per diem payment should be made to Adeva during his stay in Manila."[23]

Tiburcio Baja arrived in Mexico City on 06 May. In his report to the State Department, Baja described the organization of the American embassy in Mexico City by divisions and sections. He studied the functions of each during his seven-week stay. He prepared, with the cooperation of the administrative officer, a schedule of the timetable he followed during his stay. In addition to studying the procedural aspects of the embassy, Baja delivered a radio broadcast on the program *La Verdad Es* (The Truth Is) and two addresses—one before the National Board of the YMCA and the other before the embassy staff. He also wrote an article in English that was later translated into Spanish for general circulation.[24]

Baja completed his training at the embassy on 22 June 1946 and departed for Washington the next day. He requested that a six piece silver tea set be allowed free entry into the United States, but Acting Secretary Acheson disapproved, citing that Baja's status did not entitle him for exemption.[25] Nevertheless, First Secretary and Consul General M. L. Stafford sent the State Department a glowing report on Baja saying: "Mr. Baja's good manner, pleasing personality, and constant diligence created a most favorable impression. He at all times conducted himself properly as a future agent of his country. It is suggested that the Philippine representative in Washington be informed in this sense."[26]

Candido Elbo benefited immensely from his training at the American embassy in Havana. Elbo submitted a comparative study on the work of the passport and visa in the State Department and the U.S. Embassy in Havana. In his letter dated 17 June 1946 to Morris N. Hughes, American consul general in Havana, Elbo summarized his observations of his training. He was profuse in appreciation for the "most generous attention and cordial courtesies that have been accorded to me by the diplomatic officers of the Embassy and the Consulate General's office." Having spent most of his training in the consulate general, Elbo said that the consular officers "have been more than generous and courteous to me. They have been fatherly in helping me understand and in explaining and calling my attention especially to the technicalities and intricacies of consular work."

Chargé d'Affaires Robert F. Woodward submitted a report to the State Department on Elbo's work in Havana, citing his strong interest in passport and visa work. He added that Elbo was uniformly considerate and agreeable and that he devoted much of his time observing the practical work of the officers in duty at the visa section.[27]

Vicente I. Singian arrived in Montreal at the end of May 1946. Vice Consul William Lakeland from the American consulate general met him at the train station. After staying at the Mount Royal Hotel, Singian found a nice apartment in front of the campus of McGill University. At the consulate, John D. Johnson, the executive officer, became Singian's mentor. He offered to share his office with Singian where they sat opposite one another. This enabled Singian to observe everything that was going on in the Consulate General.

Singian spent his first week studying overall organization, the functions of the consulate general's sections, and the Reporting Section. He studied by having conferences, observing, reviewing regulations, and evaluating the work of each section. His only complaint was related to his allowance: "I think you would be starting our Foreign Affairs organization on the right track if you could persuade *Malacanang* (Office of the Philippine President) to pay all trainees the same allowances. It hurts me a little to think that our colleagues can afford to live like gentlemen while Mr. Baja and I have to pinch and stretch pennies."[28]

For the first half of June 1946, Singian worked on Accounting, Shipping, and Invoices instead of Citizenship Protection, Notarial Work, and Extradition Procedure. After three weeks in Montreal, he heard news that he would be transferred to the embassy in Ottawa for a week from 17–22 June. Singian had requested the transfer from Mill to avail of the opportunity to pick up as much exposure to diplomatic work as possible while he was in Canada. Before leaving Montreal, Mrs. Winship hosted a luncheon for Singian at their home in fashionable Westmount.

When he arrived in Ottawa, Singian was impressed by the warm and hospitable reception he received at the American Embassy. He reported to Mill during his first week at the embassy that his American hosts treated him like a full-fledged member of the diplomatic corps. He was kept busy day and night. He was given plenty of work in the office during working hours. He was also required to attend many cocktails and dinners, causing him to feel like a "sponge."[29]

After Singian's training in Ottawa, Ambassador Atherton reported to the State Department that "Mr. Singian was acquainted with the methods and procedures of each section of the Embassy and was entertained by various members of the staff. He proved an eager and methodical student and made a very favorable impression."[30]

Upon completion of their training abroad, the State Department formally reported to the Philippine resident commissioner in Washington that each trainee had completed the program satisfactorily. In most cases, each man was graded and his record made available to the Philippine government.[31]

Group II

Group II followed a path similar to that of Group I, except that it was seven weeks longer. In a detailed outline prepared by Mill, one can appreciate the focus and rigidity of the program. The first three weeks centered on the history, organization, and functions of the State Department. The fourth and fifth week focused on the Foreign Service of the United States while the seventh to the ninth week dealt with the United Nations. Lastly, the tenth to the twelfth week were devoted to the organization and functions of the proposed Department of Foreign Affairs. Mill also prepared a list of recommended and required readings.

In their second phase of training, Group II was assigned to do special studies in the State Department. Doroteo V. Vite, for example, made a detailed study of management planning in the State Department. Due to lack of funds, Group II was not assigned to train at American Foreign Service posts. However, Mill did recommended Garcia, Group II's topnotcher, for training abroad. Garcia was unable to accept as he was recalled to Manila to serve as special assistant to Richard P. Butrick, the American adviser on Foreign Affairs to the Philippine government. From Group III to Group IV, the State Department only sent two or three top men abroad for field training. No member of Group V underwent training abroad as half of them did special training in the Department of State and other Federal agencies such as the Department of Commerce and the Department of Justice.

Group III

Group III's training placed more emphasis to individual development and specialization; this meant more reports and examinations. Group III needed more attention than the previous groups, Mill observed: "I received informal word from Manila that this group will desire less formal class instruction than the Foreign Service School provides, but more specialized instruction under my immediate supervision."[32] Pablo A. Peña, a member of Group III, in an article for the *Philippines Free Press*, described their training as follows:

> 03 June 1946 is the memorable date for Filipino students. On that day they started their training as the future diplomats in the State Department in Washington. They listened to world-famous lecturers on U.S.-Soviet relations and world affairs, American policies in Allied-occupied territories, passports and visas, shipping, immigration, management and personnel planning, protocol and public relations for Foreign Service, and other subjects related to the organization and functioning of the U.S. State Department. Subjects on international law were also taken up under competent professors. Training for a diplomatic post is no picnic. There are regular class recitations, taking research studies on sundry topics, weekly examinations, and reference work that require reading until late in the evening. The *pensionados* (trainees) seldom, if at all, got to bed before midnight. Some read lessons until one o'clock in the morning. But it is not all drudgery for the Foreign Service students. U.S. govern-

ment facilities are easily at their disposal. Newsreel pictures of them "in action" have been taken and shown throughout the United States. Dozens of complimentary articles have been written about them in various American papers and their photos have appeared in many periodicals. Then, too, there are the gay parties offered by friendly Americans from time to time.[33]

As with the first two groups, Mill provided a summary of the records of Group III to the Philippine embassy in Washington and the American foreign affairs adviser in Manila. In his letter to Butrick dated 23 August 1946, Mill said that he wanted a more detailed report on the performance of the trainees: "I propose to list the exact grades obtained by each man during the course of his training. A composite overall, final grade will also be given on a basis somewhat like this: Examinations (6 weekly and one final examination) – 60 percent; Class Discussion – 20 percent; General Attitude – 10 percent; Notebooks and Records – 10 percent."

For the first time in PFATP, Mill gave a comprehensive final examination. It lasted seven to eight hours. Those who were practicing lawyers described it as more difficult than the Philippine Bar examination. The grades on the final examinations were as follows:

Emilio D. Bejasa, 95 percent
Alejandro D. Yango, 91 percent
Pablo A. Peña, 90 percent
Anastacio B. Bartolome, 90 percent
Eutiquio O. Sta. Romana, 90 percent
Aurelio M. Ramos, 88 percent
Juanito C. Dionisio, 83 percent
Francisco P. Claravall, 82.5 percent

Mill was immensely satisfied with Group III's performance. In his letter to Butrick, he wrote: "I cannot stress how very sincere and diligent the members of this group have been. They worked harder and more faithfully than any group of students I have ever known. Their work has been of a high standard, and I believe that the members of the group should prove to be most valuable additions to the Philippine Foreign Service."³⁴

Mill informed his American friends of his admiration for the outstanding performance of the trainees. "After graduating three groups of Philippine Foreign Service Officers, *I am convinced that the educated Filipino is one of the most intelligent and most diligent of our world peoples*, (emphasis added)." Mill wrote Professor Kenneth Colegrove of Northwestern University.³⁵ To another friend in academe, Professor Harold W. Vinacke of the University of Cincinnati, he later boasted:

> My Philippine Foreign Affairs Training Program is still in full operation. I have trained 90% of the new Philippine Foreign Service. The records of these boys here have been outstanding. *I found the three training groups I have had to be as hardworking and as intelligent as any group of men I have ever known* (emphasis added). The fact that we have trained the nucleus of the Foreign Service should always be a great aid in fostering good relations between the two countries. Our impress will be reflected in these boys wherever they go in the world.³⁶

> Mill was excited to learn that a movie was made on the training program. He also requested his American friend in Manila to send him clippings of news on said film.³⁷

Mill, however, was preoccupied with Group III's return to the Philippines, with the exception of Peña and Bartolome, who would undertake training at the U.S. embassies in London and Paris respectively. The rest had no fixed schedule for their return to Manila. Thus, he wrote Butrick in Manila asking for assistance in following up with the Philippine authorities to expedite Group III's return. If the State Department graduates were inadvertently kept in Washington indefinitely, it would develop into a morale problem for both the Philippine embassy and the State Department.³⁸

Butrick briefed Mill about the not so favorable views of the Home Office regarding the predicament of Group III:

There is no evidence here that when Group III left Manila, they were informed that they would be away not more than 3 months. Neither was there any commitment that the trainees would be appointed Foreign Affairs Officers. I hope they are not misrepresenting things as I have on every occasion stressed the integrity of the trainees. Some of them will be ordered home; others will not. (Vice President and Secretary of Foreign Affairs) Quirino believes in a disciplined service in which personal motives are subordinated to the best interest of the Service. I read to Quirino and (Undersecretary) Africa the part of your letter stating that although the training program was completed on 15 September, the trainees have heard no word from their government. I trust that the trainees will not push this matter too far as it might backfire.[39]

Based on their performance, Mill was able to send the top two of Group III members to undergo training at the American embassy in London and Paris. Bejasa and Yango would have automatically qualified for the training by virtue of their ranking but his father's death forced Bejasa to return to Manila and the DFA requested that Yango return to Manila for duty. In their place, Pablo Peña and Anastacio Bartolome were chosen. They left for London and Paris respectively on 22 November 1946.

Pablo Peña in Montreal and London

Prior to London, Peña, however, had the good fortune of being sent to an international conference, the only Filipino State Department trainee to have done so. On the recommendation of Mill, Peña was selected to attend the International Labor Organization (ILO) conference in Montreal as an observer for the Philippine government. Peña spent a month and a half training in the Division of International Labor, Social, and Health Affairs at the State Department in preparation for his attendance at the ILO conference. Mill considered Peña one of the really outstanding trainees for his exceptional capacity for hard work.[40]

But before Peña proceeded to Montreal, he was summoned to the Philippine embassy in Washington. In his letter to Mill dated

22 September 1946, Peña provided a vivid account of his meeting with Ambassador Joaquin M. Elizalde in the Philippine Embassy in Washington before his trip. Peña wrote Mill that Elizalde must have summoned him to size up his appearance and his knowledge of international labor affairs. In the end, Peña made a good impression, and Elizalde wished him a pleasant trip and successful mission. A relieved Peña felt like a lump cleared down his throat."[41]

During the opening day of the ILO conference Peña was presented to the top officials of the ILO. They appreciated the Philippines' attendance at the conference and cordially welcomed them and their affiliation as a regular member. Peña did more listening than talking, as were his instructions. He managed to meet labor leaders from all over the world; South Africa, Costa Rica, Brazil, and Nigeria praised him for his command of the English language. But he deplored the Latin American delegates' command of English, which he found puzzling, given their geographical proximity to the United States.[42]

Peña reported to Mill the highlights of the conference. First was the speech of United Nations Secretary General Trygvie Lie, whom Peña described as having "a heavy muscular build with a personality that radiates vital force." The other highlight was the banquet given by the Indian delegation for the heads of the various delegations and important members. As the lone representative from the Philippines, Peña was invited. At the reception, he had a friendly conversation with Prince Sakol Varavern of Siam, who recounted a pleasant trip to Manila before the Pacific War. They talked about the organization of cooperatives in Siam as a solution to their varied economic problems.

Dinner was followed by speeches. In the speech by an Indian delegate Mr. Sal, the Philippines stole the thunder of the occasion when there was a tremendous ovation when Mr. Sal mentioned that their Indian hospitality was shared by the presence of a representative from the new Republic of the Philippines. In the course of the applause, U.S. Labor Undersecretary Morse winked at Peña as if it meant, hip hip hooray![43]

On 21 November 1946, Peña boarded the giant Flagship *Oslo* at La Guardia Airfield. The American Overseas Airlines flight flew via Gander, Newfoundland and Shannon, Ireland, Croydon and finally landed at Heathrow Airport in London two days later. It was a rainy day. Peña was given a lift by a Londoner passenger to the Park Lane Hotel, where the Visitor's Bureau of the American embassy had booked him a room. Life in postwar London was still tough.[44]

Peña later on transferred to the Strand Palace Hotel near Piccadilly and from there moved to Twenty Charles Street, Mayfair, in walking distance from the American Embassy at Grosvenor Square. He reported to Everett F. Drumright, first secretary of the American embassy and officer in charge of Peña's training. They previously met each other in the State Department prior to Drumright's assignment to London. Pena said, "Being a stickler for hard work, without much ado for preliminaries, Drumright charted my training program." After showing Peña his assigned office space, Drumright introduced him to Claude H. Hall, Jr., the administrative officer. Hall assured Peña that all available facilities were open to him for the accomplishment of his mission in the embassy. Peña was given access to the Embassy canteen, the commissary, and the Navy P.X. He was pleased with such privileges. In the embassy canteen, lunch and dinner cost about 70 cents, a price at which no adequate, well-balanced meal can be found elsewhere in London.

Peña recounted that his training at the American embassy in London, then America's largest Foreign Service post, started with his detail at the Consul General's office and ended with his assignment at the political, economic and labor sections. His American mentor also introduced him to some important officials of the British Foreign Office, which Peña thought should prove valuable contacts for the prospective Philippine Legation in London.[45]

Peña's successful training at the State Department, the ILO conference in Montreal, and field experience in London made him unique. He had the distinction of being the only State Department trainee who wrote and published accounts of his experience as a trainee in Washington, D.C. He impressed Mill with his essay "The Glamour and Grind of Foreign Service Training." Mill found it interesting and a comprehensive picture of State Department training.[46] He also published an article in the *Philippines Free Press*, "Filipino Foreign Service Students in Washington" on 14 September 1946. Finally, Peña and Bartolome published an account of their training and experience at the embassy in London and Paris respectively in *The American Foreign Service Journal* in June 1947 entitled "Philippine Trainees Gained Field Experience."

Anastacio Bartolome in Paris

Before leaving for Paris on 05 December 1946, Bartolome passed by the newly opened Philippine Consulate General in New York and visited Consul General Jose Melencio's residence. Melencio and the consulate staff brought him to Hotel Pennsylvania where the temporary office of the Philippine Delegation to United Nations in New York was located. He briefly met Carlos P. Romulo, the chief delegate of the Philippines to the United Nations.

In his voyage from New York aboard *America*, Bartolome met several foreign diplomats and consular officials. Among them were Henry B. Day, the first American consul in Manila who served there from 1934 to 1938 and Michael Verlinden, the Belgian consul in Manila from 1920 until the outbreak of the Pacific War. Verlinden reopened the Belgian Consulate in Manila in January 1946. Bartolome stayed in Hotel Vouillement during his training in the American embassy in Paris. During his first day of training, Bartolome arrived early in the Embassy and met with Second Secretary Walter Smith, who was in charge of his training. Smith introduced him to some of the personnel of the consular staff. Bartolome begun his training in the notarial and invoices sections and spent the rest of the week learning merchandise documentation. He also read the section on documentation in the *U.S. Foreign Service Regulations* manual.[47] Bartolome found consular work interesting despite its monotony. The friendly atmosphere at the Consular Section made his experience one of the memorable experiences of his life.[48]

Bartolome later received Smith's program of training. The first month of the training program was heavy on consular work—invoices and notarials, estates, welfare, passport and citizenship, and visas. The latter part of the training dealt with economic, accounting, and records. Bartolome wanted to familiarize himself with the whole embassy and learn the organization and functions of each section. He asked permission to spend time in the political and administrative sections. He anticipated Mill's advice that "you will likewise find it profitable to get instructions on how to prepare political dispatches and economic reports. Someday I hope to see you in charge of your post, and this knowledge will then prove useful."[49]

Bartolome was treated like a regular member of the embassy. The American ambassador invited him to spend Christmas day at his residence. Bartolome also socialized with other embassy officials—Hugh S. Fullerton, counselor and consul general, who invited him once to lunch with George Tait, counselor in London. The latter updated Bartolome about how his batch mate, Peña, was doing in London.

Mill wrote about the positive aspects of Peña and Bartolome's training in a letter to other former trainees. "Peña is doing a brilliant job in London. He is one of the most exacting men I have ever known. Bartolome has just arrived in Paris after a most interesting voyage on the America. These men will be of great value to their government after completion of their training abroad," he proudly wrote to Tiburcio Baja.[50] After his training, Bartolome went to London to meet with Peña, and together they sailed to New York aboard the *SS America* on 15 February 1947.

Meeting with Vice President Quirino

During the official visit of Vice President and Secretary of Foreign Affairs Elpidio Quirino to Washington and New York in May 1947, Mill organized a special meeting on 09 May between Quirino and Group IV and Group V to discuss the training program. Mill also emphasized the need to develop the career Foreign Service of the Philippines. The Filipino trainees had a chance to ask questions about the status of its expansion. Quirino informed the trainees that the Home Office and the Philippine consulates in the U.S. were undermanned and that some of the trainees may be sent to these offices for further practical training.

Quirino reminded the trainees about their obligation to the Philippines after their training in the State Department. He singled out and reproached Marcelino Bernardo upon learning that he was considering joining the World Bank. Quirino reminded the trainees that their training in Washington was to provide men for the Home Office and for the new Philippine Foreign Service posts.[51]

Mill brought Peña and Bartolome to Quirino's attention. The

State Department considered them two of the most outstanding trainees. He pointed out that these men had more extensive foreign affairs training than any other trainees. He indirectly conveyed to Quirino that the State Department was concerned about their future assignments in the Philippine Foreign Service, since they were the only graduates without definite appointments. Quirino assured Mill that something would be done to remedy the situation.

Group IV

Initially Mill believed that Group IV's performance fell short of the previous groups. "This group has not yet matched the high standards of its predecessors, but I have reason to believe that by the end of the training period it will have attained similar high rank."[52] Upon the completion of training, Mill selected the top three trainees from Group IV to undergo field experience. He selected Jose Alejandrino for the American embassy in Paris; Romeo Busuego for the American embassy in London; and Roman Ubaldo for the American embassy in Rio de Janeiro.

Jose Alejandrino was the top man of Group IV. He was highly regarded for his flair for organizing and planning. While in the Department of State, he had long assignments with the Divisions of Foreign Service Planning and Administrative Management before he was sent to France. Alejandrino arrived in Paris on 19 June 1947 where he stayed at the Vouillement Hotel, very close to the U.S. embassy. He was given his building entry pass and ration privileges for soap, candies, cigarettes, and other scarce commodities in Paris from the embassy commissary. Before starting formal training on 23 June, Alejandrino toured cafes, show places, nightspots, shops, and interesting places in the city in order to acquaint himself with the best and worst of Paris.[53]

Alejandrino began his training in the Passport Section where his American trainers gave him a desk, a typewriter, and files relating to Philippine interest. Consul Agnes Schneider, Mill's former student at the University of Michigan, was section head. Alejandrino only stayed in the section for three days because he was already familiar with much of the routine. He spent his last day reading passport laws and precedents published in one volume. While in Paris, he spent long weekends in Belgium, Holland, England, and Switzerland.

One of the highlights of Alejandrino's stay in Paris was meeting Vice President and Secretary of Foreign Affairs Elpidio Quirino during his first week there. After Paris, Alejandrino returned to Manila and was slated for assignment in the Philippine legation in Paris. The assignment never materialized but years later he would be appointed as Philippine ambassador to France.

Meanwhile, Romeo Busuego was given the permission to train at the U.S. embassy in London for three months. He left on 14 July 1947 and arrived in London the following day. He was eager to do a competent job at the embassy. In his letter dated 19 June1947 to Everett F. Drumright, first secretary of the American Embassy in London, Mill described Busuego as follows:

> Busuego is an extremely pleasant agreeable young fellow, and I can assure you that he will get along well with everyone there. His is most responsive to any and all suggestions for his work and will be very anxious to work with you very closely. He worked under Art Ringwald in the Division of Chinese Affairs for a while and got along with the people in Chinese Affairs very well. He ranked second among the members of Group IV training in the State Department.

While in London, Busuego took long weekends in France and Switzerland. After training, Alejandrino and Busuego met at Southampton in September 1947 and together returned to the United States.

Roman Ubaldo was initially slated to train in Bangkok, but it never materialized. Instead, Mill arranged to send him to the U.S. embassy in Rio de Janeiro. This was a fortunate change, Mill wrote, "Mr. Ubaldo in Rio is perhaps the most fortunate Philippine trainee abroad. He met and talked with President Harry Truman during the latter's stay at the American embassy in Rio. He also attended the sessions of the hemispheric conference and visited the famed *USS Missouri.*"[54] Ubaldo also benefitted from this training as it gave him the opportunity to see how the theories and principles he learned at the State Department were applied. He made the most comprehensive reports ever submitted by a Filipino trainee to the State Department. He made valuable contacts with the embassy personnel and the officials at Palacio Itamaraty (Brazilian Foreign Ministry).

Carlos Faustino was given a desk assignment at the Division of Foreign Reporting Services (FR) in the State Department where he learned the fundamentals of programming, distribution, and evaluation of economic reports. He requested practical training at the Office of Internal Coordination (OIC). During the course of his training at OIC, Faustino saw the need for an effective Philippine version of the OIC at home and abroad to promote Philippine culture and history as well as the country's social, political, and economic conditions.[55]

Marcelino Bernardo underwent training at the Division of Commercial Policy and Financial Policy under the Assistant Secretary of State for Economic Affairs at the State Department. During a radio interview in Manila after his training in Washington, Bernando recalled:

> I spent time acquainting myself with the operations of the Divisions of Commercial Policy and Financial Policy. These Divisions are important policy making branches of the Department of State and while there, I did not only collect for my personal use, various public materials and literature on the various commercial treaties, trade agreements, special studies, and reports on diverse topics, on commercial and financial policies, but also had the opportunity to contract, befriend and discuss intimately, various angles of the operations of these two specialized divisions… It was also during my stay in Washington that I had occasion to observe the organizations and operations of the International Monetary Fund and the World Bank.[56]

Group V

In a radio interview two years after graduating from the training program, Hortencio J. Brillantes summarized Group V's training as follows:

> We had two kinds of classroom sessions: one, together with American Foreign Service Officers or Foreign Service staff employees; and the other, exclusively among us Filipinos, with Mill as chairman. Our basic work included lectures on

visas, passports, documentation of merchandise, estates, notarials, and such other subjects. During our training we used such books as Stuart's American Diplomatic and Consular Practice; Schuman's International Relations; Kirk's Contemporary International Politics; the Organizational Manual of the Department of State; magazines, pamphlets, booklets and other publications carrying world events and important pronouncements of statesmen and diplomats. In addition, we were required to submit bibliographies of at least three countries, two book reviews and book reports. We studied the set-up, organization, and operation of all world and regional organizations dedicated to peace, particularly the defunct League of Nations, the United Nations Organizations and such other specialized or subsidiary agencies working under or attached to it. Mr. Mill also greatly emphasized the organizational and administrative practices attendant upon the organization of a Foreign Office and organization of diplomatic and consular missions.[57]

... Subject to the rules of security, we were given access to certain records and files of the Department of State. Experts in their own lines lectured to us in a masterly and scholarly fashion. During the lectures that covered the geographical areas of the world we were informed of the philosophical bases of the different governments as well as idiosyncrasies and mannerisms of the various peoples of the world. We had open forums and discussions on international issues and diplomatic problems. It was a pleasure to discuss these matters with our American colleagues. Periodic examinations were given by Mr. Mill. Ratings ranged from A to C; outstanding or excellent to satisfactory and one hundred percent downwards. In short, we took up everything related to diplomacy and consular practice, not only in theory but in practical operation as well. We were completely milled by Mr. Mill.[58]

Group V took their final examination on 18 July 1947, after which the State Department informed the Philippine government that the trainees were qualified to assume their duties in the Philippine

Foreign Service or the Department of Foreign Affairs. Yusup Abubakar, Hortencio Brillantes, Luis Moreno Salcedo, and Eduardo Rosal received an excellent rating. Brillantes was the top man in the group and Mill recommended that he be appointed as Foreign Affairs Officer Class III (top grade). In a very emotional letter to Mill after hearing the news, Brillantes said:

> I received a letter from my wife, and she is so eager to know the result of the training. You can imagine Mr. Mill, how I reacted to her inquiry. She told me that my kids are very desirous to know whether their poor father made good or not. This touched my heart so much as I have always looked upon my achievements as the only treasure which I could bequeath to them. Material wealth, I possess none. So I had to debate with myself whether to tell them what you told me in confidence. For two nights I lay restless on my bed. I was so deeply concerned lest my silence or failure to answer the inquiry from my family would be interpreted by them to mean my failure and their disappointment. I could not consult you then as you were away. So I decided to take the risk, and this is what I told her. I quoted your words to me, thus: "Mr. Brillantes, you are decidedly on the very top. Your closest competitors are Mr. Abubakar and Mr. Moreno." These, Sir, were your words to me in the morning. When I saw you in the afternoon you told me that there might be triple tie. I therefore presumed that in any event I was on the very top. Now Mr. Mill, if by writing this to my wife, I have done wrong to you, I must apologize very heartily. Be rest assured however, that I instructed her to keep it in the strictest confidence, and I know she will. On the morning when you told me that I was on the very top, and as soon as I turned back towards you, I felt teardrops on my cheeks, as I recalled my deceased parent—how proud and happy they would be to know that in spite of all hardships and poverty, their son is always trying to do his best. I know how a father feels—they are so proud of their children. You will therefore realize Mr. Mill that there are two voids in my life—orphanage and poverty. Orphanage—I make it up

with that I have a wife and children, ever willing to bear with my life's multifarious sacrifices; poverty—I make it up with my willingness to do anything for others, tempering my willingness with modesty and propriety.[59]

The competition to be the top man of Group V had been stiff, especially among Brillantes, Abubakar, Moreno Salcedo, and Rosal. Rosal's obsession with his ranking bordered on hysteria. Hearing rumors that Salcedo had overtaken him, he hastily dispatched a letter to Mill, saying:

> I was informed by Tencing (Hortencio Brillantes) and Simeon (Roxas) that Moreno got a higher grade than I did. I still do not believe them. I know that I had Moreno badly beaten. His 83% in Stuart (American Diplomatic and Consular Practice) was the one that pulled him down. I was just wondering whether you consented to disregard his grade of 83% and instead used all his two examinations in current events. That certainly could not be done. Stuart is one of the most important subjects in our training. Besides it will be unfair to us—particularly to me—that his two grades in one subject should be used. Please tell me all about this in your answer.[60]

Mediocre Performance

Not all the trainees, however, were concerned with their ranking. Some were content to coast along and simply graduate. The State Department had strict standards to assess performance for graduation and recommendation to the Philippine government. As it turned out, some performed poorly and almost did not make the grade. In his report on the performance of Group V, Mill expressed satisfaction over the group's overall performance except Guillermo C. Fonacier and Engracio D. Guerzon. Fonacier, in particular, had such a poor record in the training program that Mill almost failed him and denied him graduation. Since Fonacier was related to Narciso Ramos, minister counselor at the Philippine embassy in Washington, D.C., Mill confided to Ramos the problems with Fonacier. Ramos explained that Fonacier had to work in the most menial jobs to get ahead and that in doing so he had developed an inferiority complex. Ramos was afraid that Fonacier might give up and be useless forever if the State Department refused to graduate him. Upon hearing this, Mill said he would discuss with Richard Ely (who replaced Lockhart as chief of Philippine Affairs Division) as they were both anxious to see Fonacier graduate. Mill emphasized, however, that it was a favor to Ramos.[61] Fonacier was allowed to graduate. Fonacier and Guerzon only obtained a satisfactory rating, the lowest grade in Group V and were not recommended for appointment as Foreign Affairs officers.[62]

Special Training

Group V's training lasted from three to six months. After the regular courses at the Foreign Service Officers Training School, half of the trainees, namely Reynaldo Lardizabal, Hortencio Brillantes, Luis Moreno Salcedo, Benjamin Tirona, Eduardo Rosal, Irineo Cornista, and Simeon Roxas, were selected to undergo special training at the State Department, in the Passport, Visa, Administration, and Legal Division, and at other Federal agencies, such as Immigration and Naturalization Services. The rest of Group V attended a special session at the Foreign Service Officers Training School which was later renamed the Foreign Service Institute.

Lardizabal, assistant protocol officer in the Department of Foreign Affairs, was specifically selected by Undersecretary of Foreign Affairs Bernabe Africa to undergo training in the Protocol Division. In his letter to Raymond D. Muir, ceremonial officer of the Protocol Division, Africa expressed his desire to have Lardizabal specialize on protocol matters and if possible learn all details of procedures in protocol and etiquette, such as table arrangements and appointments in the White House and seating arrangements at state and other dinners of an official and semi-official character.[63] Lardizabal was admitted to the Protocol Division and he did some training at the Division of International Conferences. Lardizabal put his training at the Protocol Division to good use when he was appointed coordinator of the United Nations Economic Commission for Asia and the Far East (ECAFE) conference in Baguio City, the Philippines' summer capital, in the last quarter of 1947.

Brillantes undertook a two-week special training at the Passport Division on 21 July 1947. In his memorandum to Ms. Shipley, Passport Division Chief, Richard Ely introduced Brillantes in glowing terms, adding that Brillantes' training at the passport division was essential to his future work as assistant chief of the division of controls at the Department of Foreign Affairs in Manila.[64]

Afterwards, Brillantes moved on to the Division of Protective Services for a week. The purpose of his assignment was to learn how the State Department would represent Philippine interests abroad after independence.[65] Brillantes also undertook another two-week assignment at the Office of the Commissioner of Immigration and Naturalization Services of the Department of Justice in Philadelphia.[66]

Brillantes spent his last two days in Washington observing the Visa Division (VD). Part of his goal was to complete an information survey, but to gain perspective on how to revitalize the quota control section of the Philippine Foreign Service's Visa Division En route to Manila, Brillantes stopped in San Francisco. There he followed a two-week observation of the practical and fields operations of the Immigration and Naturalization Service at San Francisco, "thus rounding out one of the most comprehensive special training period ever given a Philippine trainee."[67]

Luis Moreno Salcedo's special training included a completed assignment at the Division of Aviation at the State Department and underwent further training at the Civil Aeronautics Administration and Civil Aeronautics Board of the Department of Commerce; Cornista trained in immigration and naturalization work in New York; Simeon Roxas trained in the Treaty Affairs Branch of the Office of the Legal Adviser at the State Department; and Guerzon trained in the Commercial Policy Division. Some of the trainees were deployed to the Philippine Consulate General in New York and San Francisco to gain practical experience. Tagakotta Sotto, however, was assigned to the Philippine Consulate General in New York while Irineo Cabatit and Guillermo Fonacier assumed their former positions at the consulate general in San Francisco. Irineo Cornista and Yusup Abubakar were the last trainees of Group V to complete their training on 01 October 1947.

Among the members of Group V, Abubakar impressed Mill the most. When Abubakar left Washington D.C., Mill wrote:

> I am mentioning Abu [referring to Yusup Abubakar] particularly since I have come to the conclusion that he is one of the most brilliant persons I have even known. I consider him nothing less than a genius. He has a phenomenal mind full of ideals and brilliant wit. It is a joy to be with him.[68]

Mill accentuated Group V's training with trips to places like Arlington Cemetery in Virginia, Hyde Park, Radio City, and Rockefeller Center in New York. The trainees also socialized with American friends. As Brilliantes recalled:

> We went every Tuesday evening to the house of some friends in Arlington, Virginia where we held informal discussions on American Government and International Relations. We used to call the house the Alabama embassy because the residents were mostly Southerners and one of the prettiest came from Alabama.[69]

Philippine Foreign Affairs Association

As early as 06 March 1947, Marcelino Bernardo and Jose Alejandrino of Group IV proposed to organize a Philippine Foreign Service Association composed of PFATP graduates. The idea was warmly received and supported by the Group III, Group IV, and Group V graduates. Thus, the Philippine Foreign Affairs Association was formed in Washington, D.C. Its main objective was to advance the interests of the career Foreign Service, particularly its officer corps, and protect the interests of individual members. Pablo Peña of Group III drafted its constitution and bylaws and these documents were adopted on 21 April 1947. On the same date, the association approved its first resolution expressing its "grateful recognition of the invaluable contribution of the Department of State of the United States to the healthy development of a Philippine career Foreign Service," and "its sincere appreciation of the great role played by Edward W. Mill in the direction and conduct of the Philippine Foreign Affairs Training Program."

Three months later, Ambassador Joaquin M. Elizalde swore in the officers of the new association. Bernardo became its first president while Roxas, Abubakar, and Tirona were head officers. The members pledged to work to realize the idea of a career Foreign Service of the Philippines.

Mill supported the association and believed that it would help develop the career Foreign Service. He invited the other graduates to participate in the organization. In Mill's report to his superiors at the State Department, he made an optimistic assessment of the association, considering it a very valuable means of further cementing good will between the United States and the Philippines since at least 90% of the Philippine Foreign Service during the next ten to fifteen years will be members of this organization.[70]

Membership to the Philippine Foreign Affairs Association consisted of active, associate, and honorary members. Active members are Foreign Affairs officers who are graduates or non-graduates of the U.S. Department of State; associate members are actual or former officers of the Department of Foreign Affairs as well as current or former attaches of other departments of the Philippine Government; and honorary members are the Secretary and Undersecretary of Foreign Affairs, the Chairman of the Committee on Foreign Relations in each House of the Congress of the Philippines, and diplomatic representatives of the Philippines with ambassadorial and ministerial rank. The active members, however, were the only ones who had the right to vote in the direction of the affairs of the Association. Active and associate members had to pay a fee of ten pesos annually. Article X of the bylaws of the Association also provides for the publication of a Philippine Foreign Service Journal.

Staff Support

In conducting the training program for Filipinos, Mill received full support from the staff of the Division of Philippine Affairs, especially his assistant, Edward Schefer, who instructed the Filipino trainees in economics, international trade, and trade promotion and substituted for Mill from time to time. A native of New York, Schefer obtained a degree in German Literature from Harvard College and took up graduate courses in economics and banking at the American Institute of Banking and New York University. He was fluent in German, Dutch, and French.

After working in the financial sector, Schefer joined the Foreign Commerce Service of the Department of Commerce as assistant trade commissioner in 1937, two years later the Foreign Commerce Service merged with the U.S. Foreign Service. From 1939 to 1942, he served in Washington, D.C. and was posted in Manila and Jakarta to handle public relations. In 1944 he became a Research Analyst and Foreign Affairs officer in the Philippine Affairs Division at the State Department. In addition, he participated in the exchange of Filipino and American students. He served as administrative and security officer of the Philippine and Southeast Asian Division.[71]

In Mill's recommendation letter on Schefer dated 01 March 1948, written before Mill left for Manila to assume his new post, he stressed Schefer's detailed knowledge of Philippine matters, particularly the country's economy, and his energetic and good personality.

Mill also depended on his secretary, Ms. Mordaunt, who helped him correct the examinations of the Filipino trainees while he was busy with the preparation for Philippine independence, state papers, and the training program. Mill also considered her as "a real star of the Foreign Service."[72]

End of the Training Program

The PFATP took two years to complete and the achievements of the Filipino trainees were in general outstanding. Ambassador Elizalde was particularly pleased with the performance of trainees assigned to the embassy in Washington after training. During a reception held in the residence of Minister Counselor Narciso Ramos, Elizalde informed the trainees that he was not going to accept any embassy officers who were not trained by the State Department. He said that the graduates were "50 times" as effective in performing their duties as those who had not received the training given by the State Department.[73] The knowledge and experience from the training provided the graduates with the expertise needed to represent the Philippines abroad and to direct the course of Philippine foreign relations.

In a letter to Mill dated 01 May 1947, the members of Group IV manifested their deep appreciation and heartfelt gratitude to Mill for the thorough and comprehensive training that they received under his enthusiastic guidance. For their part, Emilio Torres and Hortencio Brillantes of Group V sent letters to the Secretary of State praising the State Department for sponsoring the training program and the pivotal role played by Edward W. Mill in its organization and direction.[74]

Finally, the greatest compliment that Mill ever received from the Philippine government after the successful conclusion of the PFATP came from Vice President and Secretary of Foreign Affairs Elpidio Quirino in May 1947 who expressed the following:

> My Washington visit has enabled me to gain a fuller appreciation of the outstanding work you have been doing in connection with the training of our men for the Philippine Foreign Service. You have won the respect and affection of our trainees not only because of your high qualifications but also because of your devotion to their welfare and to the interest of the Filipino people. Your work in this regard has been and is of inestimable value to the Philippine Foreign Service and my government as well as I is grateful to you.[75]

Before we look into the individual careers of the State Department Boys, it is important to focus our attention to the beginnings of the Philippine Department of Foreign Affairs and Foreign Service.

3

A Foreign Office for a New Nation

Even prior to the formal establishment of the Department of Foreign Affairs (DFA) after the Philippines attained its independence from the United States in 1946, there were earlier attempts by Filipinos to set up a Foreign Office toward the end of the nineteenth century. As a colony fighting for its freedom, the Philippines needed to win independence from Spain and obtain recognition abroad as an independent state. Securing financial, economic, and military assistance as well as forging alliances to guarantee its security from external threats was also vital for the survival of a new nation. Hence, it was imperative to establish an agency to conduct foreign relations and open diplomatic missions abroad in accordance with the modern inter-state system.

Secretaría de Relaciones Exteriores

The first attempt to create a Philippine foreign affairs office took place on 01 November 1897 when General Emilio Aguinaldo, the leader of the Filipino resistance against Spain, and his troops set up the "Biak-na-Bato Republic" in Bulacan, a province just north of Manila, while fighting the Spanish forces. Aguinaldo, as head of the Supreme Council, designated Antonio Montenegro as secretary of foreign affairs the following day.[1] But Montenegro never had the chance to perform his functions as Filipino revolutionaries and the Spanish colonial officials entered into truce days later, which spelled the end of the young republic. Aguinaldo and twenty-six other top leaders agreed to a self-exile and sailed away to nearby Hong Kong after receiving indemnity from Spain in December 1897. There, they organized a junta together with other Filipino expatriates and plotted their continued struggle to attain Philippine independence.

When the Spanish-American War broke out in April 1898, Aguinaldo joined U.S. Admiral George Dewey in overthrowing Spanish control of the archipelago on the promise that the future independent Philippines would be recognized. The Americans, however, staunchly denied making a deal with the Filipino freedom fighters. Aguinaldo and his men returned to the Philippines in early May 1898. After initial success in fighting the Spaniards, Aguinaldo proudly proclaimed Philippine independence from Spain in Kawit, Cavite on12 June 1898.[2]

Aguinaldo established a revolutionary government on23 June 1898, with him as President. He issued an order creating four departments or secretaryships, consisting of Foreign Affairs; Police, Internal Peace and Order, Justice, Education and Hygiene; and Finance, Agriculture and Industry. Within the Department of Foreign Affairs, Navy and Commerce, the Division of Diplomacy was created to study and deal with all questions pertaining to the management of diplomatic negotiations with foreign powers and to take charge of the correspondence of the revolutionary government with them.[3]

Aguinaldo formed his first Cabinet on 15 July, without appointing a secretary of Foreign Affairs. On 28 September, he appointed Cayetano Arellano, a judge and the son of a Spaniard, as secretary of Foreign Affairs while Trinidad Pardo de Tavera was appointed as director of Diplomacy. Arellano, however, refused to accept the position.

On 10 August, Aguinaldo established "diplomatic committees" abroad and appointed "diplomatic agents" to represent the interests of the Philippines. The Hong Kong Junta was already doing, albeit in a low key, many of these functions. On 26 August 1898, Aguinaldo issued a "power of attorney" to Felipe Agoncillo, his legal adviser in Hong Kong, designating him as "minister plenipotentiary" of the Philippine Revolutionary government and instructed him to go to Washington, D.C. to negotiate with the American government regarding Philippine independence. Agoncillo was a brilliant Filipino lawyer who joined Aguinaldo and other exiles in Hong Kong in 1896.

At the U.S. capital, Agoncillo managed to get an audience with President William McKinley on 10 October, but not in his capacity as minister plenipotentiary but merely as a private citizen. He also unsuccessfully lobbied the United States Senate to block the ratification of Treaty of Paris between the U.S. and Spain. The Treaty was signed on 10 December 1898, whereby Spain ceded the Philippines to the U.S. for a payment of twenty million U.S. dollars. Despite the mission's failure, Agoncillo was honored in the annals of Philippine history as the first Filipino diplomat.

First Secretary of Foreign Affairs

Upon entering DFA headquarters along Roxas Boulevard, one is greeted by a statue of Apolinario Mabini at the lobby. Mabini is seated with a blanket draping over his legs; he was a paralytic and a towering figure in Philippine history. He was aptly called the "Brains" of the Revolution and the "Sublime Paralytic." He was carried around in a hammock. He is also recognized as the first secretary of Foreign Affairs, although others were appointed to the post ahead of him.[4]

Upon the establishment of a Revolutionary government in June 1898, Aguinaldo initially offered the secretaryship of foreign affairs, navy and commerce to Apolinario Mabini but Mabini declined due to his physical condition. On 02 January 1899, Mabini reluctantly accepted the position as secretary of Foreign Affairs in addition to his duties as head of the Aguinaldo Cabinet.[5]

In a dateless and unsigned letter to Aguinaldo, probably written when he was still the president's adviser and not as Secretary of Foreign Affairs, Mabini favored dealing not only with the U.S. but also with other Great Powers. As he observed:

> The state of our relations with other powers changes from day to day. At first I thought it was from America alone that we should seek advice; now it seems Germany wants to

meddle; and we cannot predict what is going to happen in the future. We will spend money of the country to let America know of our condition; and yet it may happen that we cannot be friends with America after all, because the wishes of other powers will prevail.[6]

Yet, Mabini admitted that there was nothing much he could do to dissuade the U.S. from taking over the Philippines: "All my efforts failed because the Treaty of Paris concluded on the 10th of December the previous year, had vested in the Congress of the United States the authority to determine the civil rights and political status of the Philippines..."[7]

In his final act as foreign minister, Mabini gave instructions to Colonel Manuel Arguelles of the Philippine army to negotiate an armistice with the Americans. He justified his decision given the superiority of the American forces in organization, discipline, war materials, and other resources.[8]

Mabini's tenure as foreign affairs chief lasted for only four months when he and other members of the Aguinaldo Cabinet resigned en masse on 04 May 1899, which Aguinaldo accepted three days later. Mabini turned over the government to the new Cabinet under Pedro A. Paterno on 09 May.

Despite the overwhelming firepower of the American forces and the increasing pro-American stance of the Filipino elite, Aguinaldo continued fighting until his capture in Palanan, Isabela, on 23 March 1901. It marked the end of the first Philippine republic. Further resistance was futile. General Miguel Malvar, the last remaining Filipino general of the revolutionary government, surrendered to the Americans a year later. Agoncillo and the other members of the Filipino Central Committee in Hong Kong, the nucleus of a future Philippine Foreign Service, disbanded on 31 July 1903.

Division of Foreign Relations

With the American occupation of the Philippines, the plan to establish a Foreign Office and Foreign Service had to wait until the attainment of complete independence from the U.S. Nevertheless, even before its formal establishment, the Philippines had limited foreign relations.

On 24 March 1934, the passage of the Tydings-McDuffie Act, otherwise known as the Philippine Independence Act, provided for the independence of the Philippines after a ten-year transition period. Thus, the Philippine Commonwealth was established and a new Philippine constitution was subsequently drawn up. Manuel L. Quezon and Sergio S. Osmeña were elected as president and vice president respectively of the first Commonwealth government and they assumed office on 15 November 1935. Although the Commonwealth government enjoyed substantial autonomy, the U.S. government saw to it that it would still be under strict surveillance by creating the position of High Commissioner.

Quezon knew the importance of preparing the Philippines to conduct its own foreign relations. Thus, he set up the Division of Foreign Relations at the Office of the Commonwealth President in early 1936. The U.S. high commissioner interposed no formal objection to its creation. The main purpose of the division was to lay groundwork for the future conduct of foreign relations by the republic and to assist Quezon in whatever dealings he might have with foreign countries through the U.S. high commissioner.[9] The Division also drafted plans for the organization of the future Department of Foreign Affairs and the Foreign Service and the recruitment and training of future diplomats. However, it did not have any substantive work since foreign relations were still under the control of the United States.

Quezon appointed Teodoro Evangelista as head of the Division and Eduardo Quintero as assistant division chief. Later on the Division expanded its personnel. It recruited three senior assistants— Jacinto Borja, Mauro Calingo, and Alberto Leynes. Quezon took personal interest and pride in the development of the Division and was anxious to strengthen it with funds and men. Since the Division was under the Office of the President, there was apparently considerable flexibility in the allocation of funds within the Division and in the use of position titles. Its budget for fiscal year 1941 was $21,120.[10]

Judge Roberto Regala later succeeded Teodoro Evangelista as head of the Division. In 1941, there were at least ten people working in the Division including Tomas Benitez, Silverio Almerañez, Alberto Yulo, Jose Evangelista, and Delfin Garcia. Some of them joined the Foreign Service after independence and reached the rank of ambassador. The work of the Division was, however, disrupted when Japan declared war on the U.S. on 07 December 1941.[11]

The Division of Foreign Relations tried to safeguard the national interests of the Philippines through "informal diplomacy." In 1936 and 1937, Quezon visited Europe, Asia, and America, which caused diplomatic and protocol difficulties since the Philippines was not yet an independent state.

Meanwhile, the State Department created the Office of Philippine Affairs within the Bureau of Far Eastern Affairs. The Office was set up to carry out the provisions of the Philippine Independence Act of 24 March 1934, in so far as they related to the State Department. The chief of the office was Joseph E. Jacobs, a Foreign Service officer of more than twenty years' experience in the Far East.[12] The Office of Philippine Affairs was later changed to Division of Philippine Affairs to conform to the other geographic divisions in the State Department (i.e. Division of Western European Affairs, Division of Mexican Affairs). The Division of Philippine Affairs would eventually organize and supervise the special training program for Filipino diplomats from 1945 to 1947.

In 1936 Henry B. Day was stationed in Manila as vice consul mainly to handle the question of Filipino emigration to the United States.[13] Under the Tydings McDuffie Act, Day need not secure an exequatur or authorization from the Philippine Commonwealth government to perform his functions and duties. In April 1937, Day was promoted to Consul and was relieved by Vice Consul Gregor C. Merril in October of the same year.[14]

In anticipation of Philippine independence and in the pursuit of their own national interests, various countries opened consular representation in Manila. By 30 June 1941, there were twenty-six foreign consulates accredited to the Philippines. Career consular officers represented China, France, Great Britain, Japan, the Netherlands, and Spain. The countries represented only by honorary consular officers were Argentina, Colombia, Costa Rica, Czechoslovakia, Cuba, Denmark, Dominican Republic, Ecuador, El Salvador, Guatemala, Mexico, Nicaraguan, Norway, Panama, Peru, Poland, Portugal, Sweden, Switzerland, Thailand, and Venezuela.[15]

The Office of the U.S. High Commissioner in its official report to the American president and Congress, said that "relations with foreign consular representatives stationed in the Philippines continued to be as a whole, amicable and cordial." There were some instances, however, when the high commissioner found it necessary to inform certain foreign consular officers, in one instance in writing, that "their activities extended beyond the limits of their duties either by engaging in activities more aptly handled through diplomatic channels or by approaching the Commonwealth authorities directly instead of the Department of State or the High Commissioner."[16]

As war raged in Europe, the U.S. government implemented anti-Axis policies in the Philippines. In several instances, the American high commissioner cooperated with the Philippine Commonwealth authorities to prevent the importation of undesirable German films and other forms of German propaganda. He also reproached various European consuls who complained about disagreeable statements appearing in the Philippine press, saying that the United States and its territories enjoyed freedom of the press. In June 1941, President Roosevelt ordered the closure of German and Italian consular offices in American territory. As a consequence, the Germans and Italian consulates in Manila closed down on 09 and 10 July respectively. The staff of both offices departed from the Philippines that month.[17]

Commonwealth Government-in-Exile in Washington, D.C.

On 07 December 1941, the Japanese sneak attack on Pearl Harbor triggered the war between the United States and Japan. General Douglas MacArthur, the Commanding General of the United States Armed Forces in the Far East (USAFFE) declared Manila an "open city" to spare it from devastation. On 02 January 1942, Japanese troops marched on the streets of the capital unopposed. The Japanese Imperial Army eventually defeated the combined American and Filipino forces in Bataan peninsula on 09 April. The Philippines endured three years of brutal Japanese occupation before the U.S. wrested back the archipelago in early 1945.

Fearful of the capture of top Filipino leaders by the Japanese forces, President Roosevelt invited Presidents Quezon and Osmeña to establish a "government-in-exile" in the U.S. Roosevelt made a solemn pledge to the Filipinos that "their freedom will be redeemed and their independence established and protected." This pledge was later enlarged to include the promise that the Philippines would be "assisted in the full repair of the ravages caused by the war." It was the quest to fulfill that promise that Quezon and his cabinet accepted the invitation to transfer the Commonwealth government to Washington, D.C.[18]

Several future State Department trainees were employed in the Philippine Commonwealth government-in-exile namely, Candido T. Elbo, assistant to the Commonwealth president; Jose F. Imperial, assistant in Foreign Service; Leopoldo T. Ruiz, senior analyst; and Emilio Torres, legal officer at the Office of the President.

America concentrated on Europe during the war, so it became Quezon's principal task to turn America's attention toward the Pacific War and the liberation of the Philippines. He held meetings with Roosevelt and embarked on an intense lobbying campaign in the U.S. Congress. In active support of Quezon, the members of his cabinet also made speeches throughout the United States, calling the attention of the American public to the Filipinos' loyal stand and urging prompt efforts for their early redemption.[19]

As a gesture of wartime cooperation and confidence in its ally, the United States increasingly permitted the Philippines to plan an independent role in foreign affairs. Roosevelt first signaled this when he invited Quezon to represent his country on the Pacific War Council. Congress, through Public Laws 380 and 381 (Joint Resolutions 93 and 94) of June 1944, also recognized the Philippines as a near-independent state.[20]

Ministry of Foreign Affairs

Japan's invasion of the Philippines was part of its long cherish dream of carving an empire in East Asia and turning it into the so-called "Greater East Asia Co-Prosperity Sphere." Since its victory against China in 1894 and against Russia in 1905, Japan had never tasted military defeat by any foreign power. It subsequently established itself as a colonial power taking possession of the Korean peninsula and the island of Formosa (Taiwan) in 1910. Japan also aspired for a greater role in global affairs. In 1931, Japan occupied Manchuria despite widespread international protest. In 1937, Japan triggered the Sino-Japanese War. Japan likewise signed the Axis Pact with Germany and Italy in September 1940 and subsequently occupied Indochina in the summer of 1941. This last act of Japanese expansionism set the alarm bells ringing in East Asia and the Pacific as it became evident that it was only a matter of time before Japan would clash with the U.S. and Great Britain to achieve hegemony in the region.

On 18 May 1942, following the fall of Bataan and Corregidor, Major-General Yoshihide Hayashi, Director of the Japanese Military Administration (JMA), announced that Premier Hideki Tojo had promised that "should the Filipinos henceforth comprehend the real intention of the Japanese Empire and cooperate with us as a member of the Greater East Asia Co-Prosperity Sphere, Japan would gladly grant them the honor of independence."[21] Tojo repeated this promise when he visited Manila on 05 May 1943. He gave orders for the swift organization of a Preparatory Commission for Philippine Independence that was set up on 20 June1943 with Jose P. Laurel, former Chief Justice of the Supreme Court and Secretary of Interior, as president. A new Philippine Constitution was also drafted and ratified in September 1943.

With the government framework in place, the Japanese decided it was time to grant independence to the Philippines. The country, however, would still remain under strict Japanese supervision. Meanwhile, the National Assembly, a Japanese-sponsored legislature, elected Laurel as president on 20 September 1943. The Republic of the Philippines under the auspices of Japan was inaugurated on 14 October. But even before its establishment, the Philippines, represented by Jose P. Laurel, Jorge B. Vargas, and Benigno Aquino, then National Assembly Speaker, attended the Greater East Asia Congress in Tokyo and signed a declaration calling for common prosperity, independence, fraternity, cultural exchange, and economic cooperation.

On 20 October 1943, the National Assembly passed Act. No. 1, creating the Ministry of Foreign Affairs. Senator Claro M. Recto was appointed foreign minister and Emilio Abello was designated as vice minister. The new ministry was appropriated five hundred thousand pesos for its constitution and operation. The proposed budget for 1944 called for an expenditure of 1,250,500 pesos or an increase of 750,000 pesos. The Office of the Minister was the largest with the total of fifty items or positions at the cost of 118,980 pesos.[22] On 11 February 1944, more foreign ministry officers were appointed: Teodoro Evangelista and Querube Makalintal as counselors; Salvador P. Lopez, press and publications officer; Francisco M. Africa, consultant on international cultural relations; and Mauro Calingo and Jesus P. Morfe, secretaries of the Ministry.[23]

The Philippine government also established an embassy in Tokyo, its lone Foreign Service post. On 23 October 1943, President Laurel announced the appointment of former Manila mayor Jorge Vargas as ambassador extraordinary and plenipotentiary to Japan. Vargas arrived in Tokyo four months later in February 1944 together with his two children and other embassy staff. Vargas carried a passport, numbered "1" and written in Tagalog, the first time a native language was used in a Philippine passport. The rest of the Vargas entourage also carried passports in Tagalog.[24]

The other members of the embassy were Francisco Lavides as counselor, Faustino Sychangco, and Leon Maria Guerrero as second secretaries; and Jose Carmona as third secretary and finance officer. A Japanese named Kazuma Nakayama, whom Vargas first met in September 1943, was chosen as the Ambassador's interpreter. Another third secretary, Amador Buenaseda, was added to the embassy staff in March 1944.[25]

On 29 February 1944 Vargas presented his credentials to Emperor Hirohito with the Japanese foreign minister as witness. He also paid a visit to Prime Minister Hideki Tojo on 22 March at the latter's home.[26] With the arrival of Vargas in Japan, the representation of the five nations forming the Greater East Asia Co-Prosperity Sphere was now complete. The ambassadors of China, Manchukuo, Thailand, and Burma had preceded Vargas.[27]

Using Philippine government money, Vargas purchased the embassy chancery in Fujimi-cho, which literally means "town where Mt. Fuji can be viewed" for one million yen. Vargas and his staff, however, did not stay in the Embassy until two months after their arrival. The transfer of building ownership to the Philippine government caused the delay and Laurel's cabinet approved the purchase of the land and building in November 1943. The embassy, a former millionaire's house situated atop Kudan Hill, carried this postal address: Yasuda Mansion No. 18-1 Fujimi-cho I Chome, Kojimachi-ku, Tokyo.[28]

The gate of the chancery sported a brass sign that read "Pasuguan ng Pilipinas" (Embassy of the Philippines). The chancery was the former residence of Iwajiro Yasuda, an artist who designed it in 1932 and completed its construction after two years. Its interior was of Romanesque design; its reception room, Gothic; its banquet room, Spanish; and its living room, a blend of Japanese and Occidental styles. Part of the garden was done in Romanesque style but the principal landscaping was Japanese with rock gardens and stone lanterns.[29]

Meanwhile Japan established an embassy and a consulate general in Manila and consular offices in Baguio, Davao, Cebu, Legazpi, Iloilo, and Bacolod. Aside from representing Japanese citizens and interests, the Japanese embassy was also tasked "to carry out policies of the Foreign Ministry, representing the Japanese government and ironing out irritants between the Philippines and Japan." The emperor appointed Syozo Murata, a former head civilian adviser to the Japanese Military Administration, as ambassador extraordinary and plenipotentiary to Manila on 05 October 1943. The Japanese ambassador, however, was under the newly created position of Greater East Asia Minister, instead of under the Foreign Minister who handled foreign relations with independent countries.[31]

Toward the end of 1943, the USAFFE launched an aggressive naval campaign in the Pacific to regain control of strategic islands. In September 1944, as the Americans started their military campaigns to retake possession of the Philippines, the Japanese government suggested to President Laurel that the Philippines declare war against the United States. However, Laurel pointed out that the Pact of Alliance with Japan was only defensive in nature and that there should be no conscription of Filipinos to join the Japanese Imperial Forces in fighting against the Americans.

On 10 October 1944, American forces landed on Leyte. By February 1945, the Japanese occupation had come to an end when the Americans liberated Manila and most of Luzon was cleared of Japanese military resistance. In March 1945, Japanese authorities evacuated Laurel and his family from Baguio City to Japan via Taiwan. In June 1945, the Laurels settled in Nara. Finally, on 17 August

1945, Laurel, while still in exile in Japan, issued a decree declaring that "in view of the reoccupation of the Philippines by the United States and the re-establishment of the Commonwealth of the Philippines, and the consequent termination of the war, the Republic of the Philippines has ceased to exist."[32]

Office of Foreign Relations

In October 1944 and after three years in Washington D.C., the Commonwealth government-in-exile returned to the Philippines with General MacArthur's forces. Sergio Osmeña succeeded Quezon as president on 01 August 1944 in New York, and other Commonwealth officials operated in Leyte Island while the American-Filipino forces moved north to the capital. When they liberated Manila in February 1945, the Commonwealth government had finally settled back in the nation's capital. War and liberation had ravaged the city since Manila was the site of one of the fiercest battles of World War II.

MacArthur turned the government over to Filipino civilian authorities headed by Osmeña. Little by little the Commonwealth government recovered its functions. The Philippine Congress reconvened and worked on relief and rehabilitation efforts. Preparation for independence was also resumed in full steam. To manage the country's foreign relations, Osmeña worked with the Philippine Congress to set up the Office of Foreign Relations.

Thus, Commonwealth Act No. 683 created the Office of Foreign Relations in the Office of the President on 25 September 1945. The Office of Foreign Relations was under the direct control and supervision of the president and permanently headed by a commissioner of Foreign Relations with the rank of an undersecretary of a department with presidentially appointed assistants. With the consent of the Commission on Appointments, the president could appoint delegates to the United Nations. The office was meant to be temporary inasmuch as it would cease to exist and its powers and functions would be automatically taken over by the future Department of Foreign Affairs (DFA) to be headed by a cabinet secretary. The Philippine Treasury appropriated 250,000 pesos in addition to funds already appropriated for salaries and other operational expenses in the office and for training Foreign Service personnel.[33]

Two months later on 11 November, Vicente G. Sinco, a political science professor at UP, was appointed as commissioner of Foreign Relations. As commissioner, Sinco summed up the *raison d'etre* of the Office of Foreign Relations: "Through its Office of Foreign Relations, the Commonwealth [government] will perform its duties to the international community, establish friendly relations in that sphere, cultivate the spirit of mutual assistance with its neighbors, and make its modest contribution to the peace and progress of the world."[34]

When Sinco became the dean of the UP College of Law, Bernabe Africa, another political science professor at the state university, succeeded him. Africa was a former *pensionado* who obtained a Ph.D. in Law from the University of Michigan. Seven months later, Africa became the first undersecretary of the new Department of Foreign Affairs. The former staff of the defunct Division of Foreign Relations, such as Delfin R. Garcia and Tomas C. Benitez, rejoined the new office. New recruits included Salvador P. Lopez and Octavio Maloles. The Office of Foreign Relations had five divisions: Political, Economic, Cultural, Legal, Controls, and Administration.

The office existed for barely seven months. Its structure and personnel, however, became the core of the future DFA. Nonetheless, one of its outstanding achievements was coordinating the Foreign Service training program in Washington and selecting candidates for the third, fourth, and fifth group of trainees.

After Roxas' election as president in April 1946, he hastily organized an official trip to the United States upon the personal invitation of President Harry Truman. In May 1946, Roxas and a small delegation spent only eight days in Washington, D.C. during which he held meetings with President Truman, acting Secretary of State Dean Acheson and representatives of practically every department of the U.S. government. Some issues relation to foreign affairs that were agreed upon during Roxas' trip was:

(1) Establishment of embassies in Manila and Washington;
(2) Philippine representation by United States diplomatic and consular establishments after 04 July, pending permanent establishment of Philippine diplomatic and consular missions;
(3) A formal request to the State Department for an adviser

on the organization of a Department of Foreign Affairs in the Philippine government.³⁵

In anticipation of the establishment of the Philippine Foreign Office upon the granting of independence on 04 July, Resident Commissioner to the United States Romulo wrote to Secretary of State James F. Byrnes on24 April 1946, requesting that the State Department provides the Philippine government with copies of its Foreign Service forms to be used as models by the new Philippine Foreign Service. On 31 May, Byrnes informed Romulo that a complete collection the forms had been transmitted to Romulo's office through Jose Imperial (who previously joined the first group of trainees in the State Department). The package included all forms used by the American Foreign Service.³⁶ The Philippine Foreign Service later on adopted these forms with little modification.

The Department of Foreign Affairs

The establishment of the Department of Foreign Affairs was a major priority for President Roxas. On 24 June 1946, he sent an urgent letter to the Philippine Congress transmitting a bill creating the DFA. The bill was couched in general terms and authorized the President to exercise complete discretion in the organization of the department.³⁷

When the United States granted the Philippines independence on 04 July 1946, the inauguration was a momentous and historic day. After centuries of foreign rule, the country was finally free to chart its own future and to conduct foreign relations according to its national interest. In the inauguration, the departments of Agriculture and Commerce, Finance, Interior, Justice, Labor and Public Works, and Communications were represented; the DFA was conspicuously absent because it still had to be organized. On the same day Roxas, appointed Vice President Elpidio Quirino, secretary of Finance, as concurrent secretary of Foreign Affairs.

Inauguration took place in a newly constructed grandstand adjacent to Luneta Park (now Rizal Park) along Manila Bay. A huge crowd of Filipinos witnessed the colorful ceremony. Representatives from twenty-five countries and distinguished American officials such as MacArthur and Maryland Senator Millard E. Tydings, co-author of the Philippine Independence Act attended the event.

The Office of the American High Commissioner, now converted into the new American embassy in Manila, assisted the Philippine government with administrative and protocol arrangements for the event.

There were conflicts between protocol-conscious diplomatic representatives, but they were solved behind the scenes. One American diplomat assigned to Manila wrote:

> The foreign delegates began arriving Monday and we were besieged by all sorts of requests and demands. The Turkish Ambassador thought the room assigned to him at the Manila Hotel was incompatible to his dignity. He was pacified. The French Consul General, having been designated a special assistant to the French Ambassador, thought his seat at table and on the grandstand was not prominent enough. And so on. But these things were ironed out in one way or another ...[38]

Other last minute snafus occurred: the messenger who delivered the invitations to the Manila municipal council stole the tickets to the grandstand and sold them. Thus, the city fathers were denied entry to the grandstand; on the evening of 03 July, the Office of the American High Commissioner received an urgent cable altering the text of President Truman's proclamation, so a new copy for the High Commissioner had to be prepared; the American flag, to be lowered during the ceremony, went missing and was replaced before the guests arrived. The American embassy was happy to assist the inexperienced and confused Foreign Office staff.[39]

The independence ceremony was impressive and emotional. Its climax came when Paul V. McNutt, the last American High Commissioner and first U.S. ambassador to the Philippines, lowered the Star-and-Stripes, and Roxas raised the Philippine tricolor to fly supreme. It symbolized the rebirth of the republic. As the two national anthems were played, howitzers boomed a twenty-one-gun salute and American, Australian, Portuguese, and Thai naval warships fired their guns. U.S. fighter planes saluted with a fly-by. The sight of the Philippine flag flying unfettered and unshadowed moved many to tears.[40]

In Washington, a simple flag-raising ceremony was also held in the Office of the Resident Commissioner at 1617 Massachusetts Avenue at 9:00 A.M on 04 July1946. Lockhart read Truman's Proclamation of Philippine Independence. Melquiades J. Gamboa, assistant secretary to the Philippine president, read Roxas' message. Leonides S. Virata, executive officer, read the message of the Resident Commissioner Romulo. They sang "Philippines, My Philippines" and "God Bless America." Father Joseph Kerr, S.J. said the invocation and Rev. Edward Hughes Pruden gave the benediction. The U.S. Army band played both national anthems.

One day before independence, the Philippine Congress passed Commonwealth Act No. 732 creating the DFA and giving the President of the Philippines blank check authority to organize the Home Office and the Foreign Service. Section 2 of the Act states that: "The Department of Foreign Affairs shall have the responsibility for the coordination and execution of the foreign policies of the Republic of the Philippines and the conduct of its foreign relations and shall perform such other functions as may be assigned to it by law or by the President relating to the conduct of foreign relations of the Republic of the Philippines."

The Act also appropriated three million pesos and provided for an embassy in Washington, D.C. and a permanent representation to the United Nations, the two main diplomatic activities of the new Republic.[41] However, the act only authorized the president to establish the Foreign Service. Roxas needed to issue an Executive Order to create the structure and organization of a professional Foreign Service. For this purpose, he sorely needed the expertise of an adviser on foreign affairs.

American Foreign Affairs Adviser

On 01 June 1946, Roxas sent a letter to Secretary of State Byrnes officially informing him of the need to establish a foreign affairs department. "The Philippine government lacked experience in this field," Roxas admitted, "and it is therefore urgent that we draw upon the experience of the United States in creating our own foreign affairs establishment." He added, "I am desirous of obtaining the services of a highly competent and experienced American who might be of assistance to me in helping to establish our new Department of Foreign Affairs." The American adviser would be detailed in Manila for a minimum of one year.

Roxas detailed the qualifications of the American foreign affairs adviser as follows:

> Such an officer should have administrative ability and would be expected to be of major assistance in developing the organizational outlines of our new Department of Foreign Affairs. He would also be expected to advise in regard to the drafting of the requisite legislation and rules and regulations governing our foreign affairs establishment. He would also be expected to be of assistance in formulating sound personnel standards and procedures and in helping us establish initial relations and correct working procedures with other governments. Considerable assistance would also be expected of the adviser with regard to the drafting of treaties. He would work directly with the head of the Department, under my personal supervision.[42]

Roxas followed up the status of his request with Paul Steintorf, the American consul general in Manila, who sent a telegram to the State Department on 07 June.[43]

Roxas's request for the secondment of a U.S. government official to the Philippine government was not unique. In 1938, when the Commonwealth government was drafting a new immigration bill, President Quezon sought U.S. assistance. Irving P. Wixon, deputy commissioner of Immigration and Naturalization in the U.S. Department of Labor, and George L. Brandt, a U.S. Foreign Service officer were sent to Manila to help draft the Philippine immigration bill. The bill became law in 1941.[44]

Lockhart telephoned Romulo on 11 June to discuss the appointment of an adviser on foreign affairs to the new republic. He told Romulo that the State Department was having considerable difficulty in finding a suitable person. He explained that the responsible administrative officers in the State Department had come to the conclusion that it would not be possible since there was a scarcity of Class I officers who might be suitable to detail; that the matter had been discussed with several qualified officers but various circumstances had prevented a detail up to this time; and that the prospect of an early designation of a foreign service officer was not promising.[45]

Lockhart asked Romulo whether the Philippine government was prepared to appoint some qualified persons, whom the State Department would recommend, and if so, what would be the salary and the nature of the allowances. Romulo told Lockhart that Roxas insisted upon the designation of a Foreign Service officer rather than an appointment by the Commonwealth. He added that Roxas, in a recent letter to the Philippine resident commissioner, expressed extreme disappointment that the State Department had not found a suitable adviser.

Lockhart repeated his early question to Romulo as to why the Commonwealth preferred the designation of a Foreign Service officer instead of an outright appointment. Romulo then clarified that the Commonwealth government wanted "someone detailed who could speak with the real authority of the Government of the United States." He stated that an officer serving under an appointment by the authorities of the new Republic would be disobeyed or circumvented by subordinates, but an American officer would not. Romulo added that it would establish goodwill between the Department of State and the DFA in Manila and that the designation of a Foreign Service officer or a high-ranking department officer would link them and work to the mutual advantage of both governments. Lockhart concluded that Romulo's main idea had someone in the Foreign Office who could implement a Foreign Office and a Foreign Service. Before the end of their conversation, Lockhart assured Romulo that the State Department would continue to search for an advisor and Romulo's views would be promptly brought to the attention of the appropriate authorities.[46]

A week after, Secretary Dean Acheson sent a telegram to the American consul in Manila with instructions to inform Roxas that the State Department still did not have an available Foreign Service officer or departmental officer for detail to the Philippine Republic to assist in the organization of the DFA and the Foreign Service. The State Department was also facing difficulty finding qualified and experienced officer who might be willing to accept the position because of inadequate remuneration and uncertainty of housing and transportation facilities to be provided by the Philippine government and the absence of other allowances which would justify acceptance.

Acheson wanted Roxas to review this situation and make concrete offer, which would necessarily have to be above the original offer of ten thousand dollars per annum plus living quarters, motorcar, and transportation expenses to and from Manila. Acheson said that retired officers and others who have been approached have expressed the feeling that the remuneration and allowances are inadequate in proportion to the importance of the work to be undertaken. He requested the comments of the American Consul Paul Steintorf and the American High Commissioner Paul McNutt after the matter has been discussed with Roxas. Nevertheless, Acheson ended his telegram on a positive note by saying that "the State Department is very anxious to be of assistance if at all possible."[47]

McNutt discussed the matter with Roxas and reported back to the State Department. In McNutt's telegram he emphasized that: "We can probably save ourselves and the Philippines much grief if this request (for a foreign affairs adviser) is acceded to promptly. Qualified adviser is desperately needed and urgently requested. Advantages of getting an American (adviser) are obvious. I hope you can give me early indication."[48] McNutt followed up his initial comments with a more detailed report:

> One. While admittedly the importance of a Foreign Office advisership justifies the highest remuneration, the Philippine government's ability to pay compensation for this position must be considered in relation to other advisers and Philippine government salaries. Roxas is resisting political pressure to raise government salaries despite empty Treasury. A high salary for a foreign adviser would weaken his hand. The salary of the President of the Republic is $15,000 plus generous entertainment, housing, servants, transportation, etc. Cabinet ministers receive $6,000. Precedents here for paying foreigners mean double that of local employees.(i.e., American same number of dollars as a Filipino is paid in pesos). Roxas offered $10,000 plus living quarters and a car in circumstances seem reasonable and

would set a pattern for financial and other needed advisers. Two. An experienced adviser to organize the Foreign Office and Foreign Service is important to our own as well as Philippine interests. Advantages of an American (Foreign Service adviser) are obvious and employment of other nationality is conversely undesirable. Interest of the work and patriotism should be added inducements.
Three. Names of suggested type of officer believed acceptable: Retired: (1) Ballantine (2) Salisbury (3) Dubois. Active: (1) Jacobs (2) Tenney (3) Harrington.
Four. Will (State) Department loan an active officer under Act of 25 May 1938? (The selected officer) should contemplate an assignment of about two years.[49]

After a frantic search, the State Department in the end totally disregarded the candidates proposed by Ambassador McNutt and finally decided to send Richard P. Butrick, a fifty-two year-old Foreign Service Officer Class I, who at the time was head of the Foreign Service Administration. Upon receiving his new assignment as Foreign Affairs adviser to the Philippine government, Butrick willingly accepted it. Years later, in explaining why he accepted the assignment, he said he never pushed himself at any time for any job he got.[50]

Richard Porter Butrick was born on 06 August 1894, in Lockport, Niagara County, New York. After studying Foreign Service at Georgetown and passing the Spanish language test of the State Department, Butrick joined the U.S. Consular Service.[51] He served as consular officer in Valparaiso, Chile, Guayaquil, Ecuador, and Hankow, China. While serving as head of the Foreign Service Administration at the State Department, Butrick was tapped to be the foreign affairs adviser to the Philippine Government. Since he was not in the short list of candidates for the position as proposed by the American ambassador in Manila, the State Department sent a detailed instruction to Ambassador McNutt on 15 July 1946, regarding the assignment of Butrick as adviser on foreign relations to the Philippine Government for a period of not less than one year. His detail was made on the basis of Public Law 63 (5 USC 118 E) of 03 May 1939, and that he would be given the personal rank of Minister during his detail.[52]

Before Butrick's departure for the Philippines, Mill convened a meeting on 26 June at the State Department to present Butrick to the members of Group I, II, and III of Philippine Foreign Service trainees in the State Department as well as to Eduardo Quintero of the Office of Foreign Relations who was then travelling to Washington, D.C. Other State Department officials such as Joseph Schaefer, Ralph Busick, and Ruth Hughes were also present. In his brief speech, Butrick expressed his appreciation for being given the opportunity to work with the Philippine government. He also stated that the most desirable qualities of a Foreign Service officer were, first and foremost, integrity and second only, ability.[53]

After another month of delay, Butrick finally arrived in Manila toward the end of July 1946, and immediately worked in the office of Vice President Quirino.[54] Delfin Garcia, a State Department graduate and a member of the second group of trainees, was hurriedly sent back to Manila right after the completion of his diplomatic training to serve as Butrick's special assistant.[55]

After a month in Manila, Butrick wrote his observation to Mill:

> The Secretary (Quirino) and his legal adviser, Judge Roberto Regala, are still so busy threshing out the (military) base agreement – of which I have been consulted only on a few fine points — that my plan of organization of the Department and the Foreign Service has not left their desks and I do not think the President is even aware that it exists. Meanwhile the budget hearings are going on and I may be faced with a *fait accompli* situation. I do not feel, however, that I should approach the President directly at the risk of alienating the Secretary, so you can see some of the difficulties facing me. Meanwhile the Department and the Foreign Service are operating on an ad hoc basis, which may be all right for the short term but cannot achieve the thoroughness of a well-organized department nor the long-term effectiveness.[56]

Butrick described his difficulties during his first months of duty in the DFA:

We are in the midst of drawing up travel, quarters, post, representation, and clothing allowance regulations. We seem to be in a spurt of activity at the moment. I think some of the highly placed persons are beginning to realize the necessity for proper organization, as matters pile up on their desks. Actually some of the men in the Department are too busy and others have very little to do. When the new organization is put into effect, this will be remedied. I have encountered great difficulty in putting it into effect because of the necessity for placing everyone now employed by the Department in a no less important position, absorbing all the employees—a number of whom have been employed recently on a political patronage basis—and ironing out budgetary difficulties, some of which are real and some of which are not so real.[57]

On 05 September 1946, Butrick reported to the State Department that Roxas would soon sign an Executive Order creating a career Foreign Service. He was also overseeing the preparation of the third group of Filipino diplomats who would train in the State Department. He inquired about the salary ratings of the third group and the State Department's suggestions on salaries of all trainees on appointment as Foreign Affairs officers.[58] The State Department answered Butrick's query and added that the State Department is keenly interested in the proposed Executive Order and requested to be informed of all developments.[59]

Since the completion of the Executive Order, Butrick had been engaged in the formidable task of actually bringing the order into effect. His influence had been used to formulate sound administrative principles and procedures and to bring the best possible men into the DFA. He also spent a great deal of time preparing the rules and regulations of the Foreign Service.[60]

In summing up the important role that Butrick played in shaping the organization of the Philippine foreign affairs establishment, the State Department justified the continuation of Butrick's services to the Philippine government in the following terms:

At the request of the President of the Philippines, Mr. Richard P. Butrick, was detailed to the Philippines as adviser on foreign relations to the Republic of the Philippines. In this capacity he has played an extremely important role in shaping the organization of the country's foreign affairs establishment. The United States has been keenly concerned with the type of foreign affairs establishment developed in the Philippines. The Department of Foreign Affairs and the Foreign Service of the Philippines can be powerful instrumentalities in preserving and fostering the close ties existing between the Philippines and the United States. The Foreign Service of the Philippines can be not only the voice of the Philippines abroad but can in a very real sense be the voice of American abroad. Philippine foreign policy linked with American foreign policy in the Far East can materially influence all Asia in the development of peaceful and progressive policies. In the United Nations the Philippines and the United States can work together for common goals. In acting as an architect of the new Philippine Department of Foreign Affairs and Foreign Service, Mr. Butrick is making an invaluable contribution to the implementation of these policy objectives.[61]

Butrick's mission in the Philippines proved successful and meaningful. He got along fine with Quirino but not with Roxas as he thought that the President "resented him a bit." Overall, Butrick's impression of the Filipinos was positive. He described the Filipinos as very good and very efficient. The Philippine social circles were wide open to him. Together with an American naval officer, they were the only foreigners who were invited to all the parties "where they really took their hair down and the women were present."[62]

While the relations between him and the Filipinos had been very good, there had been administrative difficulties in his assignment that had displeased him. When Quirino visited the United States in May 1947, Butrick joined him but decided not to come back to Manila. At the time he felt that his services would not be needed anyway since the Philippine Foreign Service had been thoroughly well organized as posts were opened in the United States and a few other places.

Butrick reported back to the State Department and was

subsequently assigned as Minister to the American Legation in Iceland in April 1948. He finished his tour there after just a little over a year. He returned to the State Department and was appointed director general of the Foreign Service, a position he held until April 1952. In recognition of his service to the Philippines, President Diosdado Macapagal belatedly awarded the Lakan of the Ancient Order of Sikatuna to Butrick on 16 October 1964.[63]

Executive Order No. 18

On 18 September 1946, Roxas signed Executive Order No. 18 "Establishing the Department of Foreign Affairs and the Foreign Service of the Republic of the Philippines and Fixing the Emoluments, Privileges and Allowances of the Officers and Employees Thereof." Upon reading E.O. 18, Mill wrote Butrick: "In general, Executive Order No. 18 appears to combine the best features of the Rogers Act, the Moses-Linthicum Act and the Foreign Service Act of 1946. It is an enlightened, comprehensive charter of organization for the new arm of diplomacy of the Philippine Republic."[64]

In his response to Mill on All Saints Day of 1946, Butrick could not hide his satisfaction over his achievement as he wrote:

> Naturally, it was a source of gratification to learn that you approved Executive Order No. 18. I put a terrific amount of work on it. The entire section on retirement was cut out and there are other evidences of compromises. On the whole, however, it is a good charter. When one thinks of the amount on man-hours put into the Rogers Act and the recent Foreign Service Act, you will have to admit that it is no small achievement for one poor little fellow like myself.[65]

Butrick, however, expressed his frustration on the lack of coverage on Executive Order No. 18 in the American press.[66] Mill agreed fully with Butrick's complaint on the lack of press coverage for E.O. 18. He also praised the political courage of Quirino and Roxas to come out so squarely for the merit principle in the Foreign Service. "Both of them must have been subjected to stiff political pressures to go easy on the merit principle in this field. I think that Roxas, Quirino, and you deserve the greatest credit for this Order."[67]

The American embassy in Manila duly reported the news on the issuance of E.O. No.18 to the State Department the following day:

> The Executive Order No. 18 was basically the work of Richard P. Butrick, although substantial modifications were made by the officers of the (Philippine) government before the Order was approved. The trend of these modifications was to transfer discretionary authority in the administrative matter from the Secretary of Foreign Affairs to the President. Another important amendment was the complete elimination of retirement provisions on the ground that a retirement system could not be legally established by Executive Order despite the broad authority conferred on the President by Commonwealth Act 732. [68]

On 20 September 1946, U.S. Ambassador Paul McNutt sent a detailed report to the State Department on E.O. No. 18. He praised Roxas as "he has taken great personal interest in the Foreign Service and has given it every encouragement." However, when Roxas made a press statement a day before the signing of E.O. No.18, he gave credit to the Philippine government for the accomplishment "without mentioning Butrick."[69]

Aside from providing a summary of the salient points of E.O. No. 18, the American embassy in Manila also made two important observations on the merits of the new Foreign Service: (1)"The Foreign Service has proved dynamic attraction to Filipino intellectuals. Many of the most brilliant and promising of Philippine writers, poets and critics are already enrolled in the Foreign Service, which has top prestige among all brackets of government service" and (2) New service borrows freely from the United States setup and best British and other foreign experience. Philippine government has created what it hopes will prove a model Foreign Service.[70]

Although Butrick was the main author of E.O. No. 18, the draft undoubtedly passed through the scrutiny of some of the brilliant minds in the Office of Foreign Relations such as Vicente G. Sinco, Bernabe Africa, Roberto Regala, and Mauro Calingo. Lastly, Vice President and Secretary of Foreign Affairs Quirino also examined the draft E.O. before it was submitted to the President for signature. It is also important to stress that two of the graduates of the first group, Jose F. Imperial and Manuel A. Adeva, were influential in blueprinting the original DFA setup as they helped materially to chart its early organizational framework and rules and regulations.[71]

Imperial, in particular, made the biggest contribution. While serving as Foreign Service assistant in the Commonwealth government-in-exile in Washington, D.C., Imperial submitted a proposal on how to organize the Philippine Foreign Service. His proposal envisions the creation of a DFA headed by a Secretary under whom there would be a permanent career undersecretary and three assistant secretaries—one for political affairs, one for economic affairs, and one for administrative affairs. The proposed Department would have a total of eight country divisions where all functional work such as political, economic, cultural, etc. sections would be done instead of having these functions performed in separate functional divisions. Imperial further recommended the appointment of an American career diplomat to advise the Philippines on its foreign affairs problems.[72] Together with Imperial and Adeva, we can also count Delfin R. Garcia who played an active role as special assistant to Butrick. Butrick, Garcia, and Imperial worked again together to write the *Foreign Service Regulations of the Philippines* in 1946.

Roxas' interest was strongly reflected in the statement that he issued on 17 September 1946, where he outlined the salient features of the organization and operation of the new DFA and of the Foreign Service of the Republic of the Philippines. After citing the legal basis for its establishment, Roxas remarked,

> The organization of the Department of Foreign Affairs has been set out at some length. Considerable study has been given to the organization. It is compact and close knit and should operate efficiently and effectively. The organization provides for the exercise of all necessary functions and the cooperation of other departments of the government. Complete coordination is provided for. A chain of command is established and authority and responsibility synchronized.[73]

It is also important to point out that from the beginning the Philippines had a single Foreign Service. The question of amalgamation of Departmental and Foreign Service people thrashed out by the Department of State in 1924 with the passage of the Rogers Act was settled by the Philippines at the outset in favor of an amalgamated service. Foreign Affairs Officers serve either the Department or the Foreign Service.[74]

Officers in the Foreign Service were prohibited from accepting, displaying or wearing any decoration, except those received as a member of the armed forces of the Philippines or of the United States prior to 04 July 1946. They were also prohibited from receiving any emolument from any foreign government and from engaging in business in the country to which they were accredited as well as from acting at attorneys, merchants, brokers, factors or other traders or agents.[75]

Secretary of Foreign Affairs

The automatic appointment of the vice president after election as concurrent secretary of Foreign Affairs was the practice during the early years of the republic. Elpidio Quirino was the first vice president to be appointed concurrent Secretary of Foreign Affairs. Butrick described Quirino as "a very exacting man and is cautious about appointments, a good characteristic."[76] On the other hand, Romulo praised Quirino for his role and stewardship of the DFA. "He was responsible for creating the Department of Foreign Affairs and the launching it on the international map."[77]

Quirino's placid face, chubby constitution, and patrician look in old age belie his humble origins. The son of a provincial warden, Quirino had grown up poor and struggled during his younger years to get a decent education. He, however, exhibited talent in painting, drawing and poetry. When he went to Manila to enroll in high school, he supported himself by selling drawings to magazines. While taking up law in the University of the Philippines at night, Quirino worked by day as a property clerk in the police department. He secured a job in the Philippine Senate as an assistant law clerk. It was then Senate President Manuel L. Quezon who first noticed his talents. Quezon hired him as a private secretary and took him to the United States during his trips.

Quirino's political career blossomed. He was elected to the House of Representatives, and later to the Senate where he became the majority floor leader. As a key ally, Quirino joined Quezon in Washington in 1933 to renegotiate the Hare Hawes Cutting Law earlier negotiated by Osmeña and Manuel Roxas. They succeeded in replacing it with the Tydings-McDuffie Law as the definitive Philippine Independence Act. Quezon exploited his success in securing the new Philippine Independence Act in his quest for the presidency of the Philippine Commonwealth. He persuaded Osmeña to be his running mate and they won handily over their rivals. President Quezon appointed Quirino to his cabinet, first as Secretary of Finance and later on Secretary of the Interior. At intervals while not serving in the government, Quirino practiced law and taught in various colleges and universities in Manila. He was dean of the Adamson College of Law before he was elected back to the Senate in 1941.

When the Japanese forces occupied Manila during the war, Quirino was imprisoned for two weeks and then released. Despite his sterling credentials, the Japanese never tapped Quirino to serve in the puppet regime. In 1945, during the battle for the liberation of Manila, the Quirino house was hit and caught fire. As the members of his family fled out of the house, rampaging Japanese soldiers gunned them down. Nine members of his family—his wife, three children, mother-in-law, brother, nephew and brother-in-law—were killed that day.

At the first session of the Senate after the liberation of the country from Japanese occupation, Manuel Roxas was unanimously elected as president and Quirino as president pro-tempore. Quirino worked on legislations regarding the Philippine Relief Administration, GI rights, and the rehabilitation of banks. Roxas picked Quirino as his running mate in the May 1946 presidential elections where they both won. As vice president and concurrent secretary of Foreign Affairs, Quirino laid the foundation for the Philippine Foreign Service and inaugurated the newly organized Department of Foreign Affairs. He went on a goodwill tour of the world, visiting the United States and Europe. In Washington, D.C., Quirino met with President Truman and Secretary of State Dean Acheson. In New York, he visited the United Nations office. In London,

King George VI and Foreign Secretary Ernest Bevin received him.[78] Quirino succeeded Roxas as president after the latter's sudden death. Quirino eventually won the presidential elections in 1949 and served as president until 1953.

Undersecretary of Foreign Affairs

Aside from the Secretary of Foreign Affairs, the DFA started with one undersecretary and three counselors. Bernabe Africa, the erstwhile Commissioner of Foreign Relations, became the first undersecretary. Aside from serving as the deputy secretary, Undersecretary Africa was also directly in charge of the Division of Coordination, Protocol and the Board of Foreign Service Personnel, Examination and Review.[79]

In practice, the undersecretary is the chief operating officer of the DFA. In the absence of the Secretary of Foreign Affairs, he runs the Department and also carries much of the load with the Philippine Congress. He is in close touch with the counselors and division chiefs. He is the chief instrumentality of departmental coordination and serves as the "eyes and ears" of the Secretary. Originally it was hoped by some that the undersecretary in the Philippine system would be a permanent, career officer. But the Philippines never formally adopted the idea of a permanent, career undersecretary and the position has continued to be political until the administration of President Diosdado Macapagal (1961-1965).[80]

Counselors

The counselors were responsible for the three main offices in the DFA. These offices with politico-geographic and administrative functions were the following: Political and Economic Affairs, Legal Affairs, International Organization and Conference and Administration, Budget and Control. Teodoro Evangelista was appointed counselor for Political and Economic Affairs; Roberto Regala as counselor for Office of Legal Affairs; and Felino Neri as counselor for General Affairs.

The Office of Political and Economic Affairs consisted of four divisions, namely American Affairs, European Affairs, Asian and Pacific Affairs and Commercial and Monetary Policy and Trade

Promotion. The Office of Legal Affairs, International Organizations and Conference had three divisions: United Nations Affairs and International Conferences; Legal Affairs, Treaties, Research and Publications; and Cultural Activities and Exchange. Finally, the Office of Administration, Budget and Control had the most number of divisions with seven. It was therefore necessary to divide it into two branches. The administrative branch consisted of the following: Management, Personnel, Welfare Supplies and Maintenance; Accounts, Foreign Service Administration; and Communications, Files and Records. The Controls and Citizenship Services branch was composed of three divisions: Passport and Citizenship, Visa and Immigration, National Shipping and Miscellaneous Services.

Quirino was on the lookout for talent as he combed other government agencies, law offices, companies, newspapers, and academe. He drafted gifted outsiders (and in some cases pirated them), which happened in the case of a young, brilliant lawyer named Diosdado Macapagal, a future president of the Philippines. Quirino appointed Macapagal as Counselor for Legal Affairs of the DFA replacing Roberto Regala who was assigned as Philippine Consul General to San Francisco. Macapagal was tasked to negotiate with Great Britain regarding the transfer of the Turtle Islands to the Philippines.[81] A frequent change in the hierarchy of the Department as shown by the Macapagal appointment was the order of the day. Likewise, Teodoro Evangelista left his position as Counselor for Political and Economic Affairs to assume the post of Executive Secretary of President Quirino. Serving as a right-hand man of the president was a big step in Evangelista's career. His leadership and services were sorely missed since he was considered a pillar of strength in the Foreign Office and was greatly respected by the foreign diplomatic corps in Manila.[82]

Finally, Felino Neri replaced Bernabe Africa as undersecretary when Africa was assigned as head of the Philippine Mission in Tokyo. Neri was a UP graduate and lawyer by profession. He started his government career as legal officer in the Philippine Sugar Administration. He became administrative assistant in the Office of the Commonwealth President, assistant Commissioner of Foreign Relations, counselor of Foreign Affairs and was undersecretary of Foreign Affairs at the age of forty-three. Although young by the standard of the time, future undersecretaries of Foreign Affairs, such as Raul Manglapus and Leon Ma. Guerrero, would be even younger than Neri when they got appointed to the position.

Career Personnel

President Roxas understood that the greatest asset of the new Foreign Office was the quality of its personnel. "No organization can be stronger than the caliber of its personnel. The Department must have persons of outstanding competence, balanced judgment and unquestioned loyalty. They must be adequately remunerated. The salaries provided are consonant with the duties performed." He admitted that the basic salaries of Foreign Affairs Officers are modest in comparison with those of other nations. But he believed that the combination of salaries and allowances would open the career to all competent Filipinos. And appealing to patriotism, he emphasized that, "as its name implies a Service, and it will not be found a highly remunerative profession, its members must look rather to the satisfaction of a life of patriotic endeavor and service to their country and fellowmen."

As there was a shortage of trained personnel, provision was made for the appointment of sixteen persons to the career foreign service without examination or having taken special courses abroad. This could be interpreted as a loophole to allow political appointees to be integrated in the newly established Foreign Service. As Butrick observed:

> Executive Order No. 18 provides that all Philippine diplomatic and consular officers, except chiefs of missions and consular agents, shall be Foreign Affairs Officers. To meet the need for personnel and to establish a nucleus of Foreign Affairs Officers in the Department of Foreign Affairs, provision is made in the Order for blanketing into the service 16 persons. Of these, eight will be "political" appointments, including Narciso Ramos, Melquiades Gamboa, Jose Melencio, and Roberto Regala and 4 others, among who will doubtless be the Consuls General at Honolulu, Shanghai, and Sidney. It may be necessary also to blanket in more of [Ambassador] Elizalde's appointees. The Secretary has wired for a complete list of his appointments.[83]

After the first year, Roxas assured that there would be no further appointments of this nature. This, however, would not be followed given the political nature of the jobs in the DFA and the Foreign Service.

Since the very beginning academic qualification was an important requirement in joining the DFA, particularly among the officers. Of the 117 officers listed in the *Directory of the Department of Foreign Affairs, December 1952*, only three did not have college degrees. The rest were all college graduates.[84] Even during the initial years of the DFA, Butrick observed the DFA officialdom's fetish for academic degrees.[85]

As to the Foreign Service, Philippine missions were classified into four classes and the salaries of the chiefs of mission were fixed. Extra allowances were granted to chiefs of mission to assist them in representing the nation and to uphold its prestige in diplomatic, official and business circles. To avoid multiplicity of Philippine agencies abroad, a single Foreign Service was established. Corollary to this, a career Foreign Service was made open on an absolutely non-political basis to any native-born citizen of the Philippines. The career service was known as the Foreign Affairs Service and its officers as Foreign Affairs Officers (FAO). They occupied all officer positions in the Foreign Service below the rank of *chargé d'affaires* and served as counselors of offices, chiefs of division and in other important positions in the DFA.

Home Office

The DFA was first housed in an elegant two-story mansion along Arlegui Street near Malacañang, the presidential office and residence. That area in the vicinity of Malacañang was once dotted with elegant mansions, some of which still survive. The Arlegui House was erected between 1933 and 1935 by the couple Josefina Escaler and Rafael Fernandez in a lot owned by the Escaler family. The exterior architecture of the house is a combination of baroque revival and neo-classical themes. Baroque revival is characterized by curvilinear designs and massive impressions; neo-classical portrays simplicity and balance. The towers in the left and right sides of the Arlegui house exemplify the symmetrical attribute in neo-classicism.

The house served as the office of the German Consulate before the war. During World War II, the Japanese-sponsored government took control of the property and the house was used as the office of Interior Commissioner Benigno Aquino, Sr.[86] Interestingly, the American consul general in Manila once occupied the mansion where the Foreign Office started its operations.[87]

The Arlegui mansion, however, was too small even for a fledgling Foreign Office. The personnel of the Department of Foreign Affairs increased from the skeleton force of 41 members on 04 July 1946, to 130 on 30 June 1947, and to 187 on 30 June 1948 in the Home Office and with personnel of 304 assigned to Foreign Service posts.[88] In no time, the space shortage at Arlegui was very evident as the employees were cramped side by side with the edges of their desks almost touching each other. Local and foreign visitors had to pass through the narrow space of tables as they made their way to a meeting a foreign affairs official.

A journalist covering the foreign affairs beat described the DFA building at Arlegui as follows:

> The hall in the ground floor is occupied by the administrative division, the "beavers" of the commercial, monetary policy, and trade promotion division, the secretary of the board of foreign affairs service personnel, examination and review, and the code experts. The acting undersecretary and two counselors occupied the left wing At the back of the left wing there is the crowded Record Section, full of cabinets, pamphlets, and other documents.
>
> There is an annex connected to the "big house" by a walk, where the "financiers" of the department work: the paymaster, the accountants, and allied employees work. In the same annex, there is the FACA (short for Foreign Affairs Cooperative Association) restaurant, where the officials and employees from the Secretary down to the messenger may spend a few minutes to sip a cold coke and nibble an upside-down cake. On the eastern part of the compound, there is another building where the auditors work and the caretaker lives.

The second floor of the big building is divided as follows: The hall, reached by a semispiral stairway is occupied by the controls division. "Controls office is foreign affairs parlance for the office where you arrange your passport, or a re-entry permit for a Chinese who wants to come back to the Philippines. The right wing is occupied by several assistants, some belonging to the United Nations Division, some to American Affairs, others to the European and African division. The left wing has rooms for the protocol division; for the Asian and Pacific Affairs, International Information and Cultural Activities, and the United Nations division. Barely sheltered by a small wall in the veranda on the right wing are stenographers; on the left wing, the "letterist" of passports and his helpers.

Go into any of these wings, literally a hive of activity, and you will find the assistant—the so-called "spade-workers' hoeing down the ground for important foreign policy decisions. One of them who works in a geographic division, you may find dictating an interpretative analysis of the latest development on the East-West wrangle over the Berlin question. This and other analyses of current happenings in other nations are forwarded to the President and the top brass of the ministry.

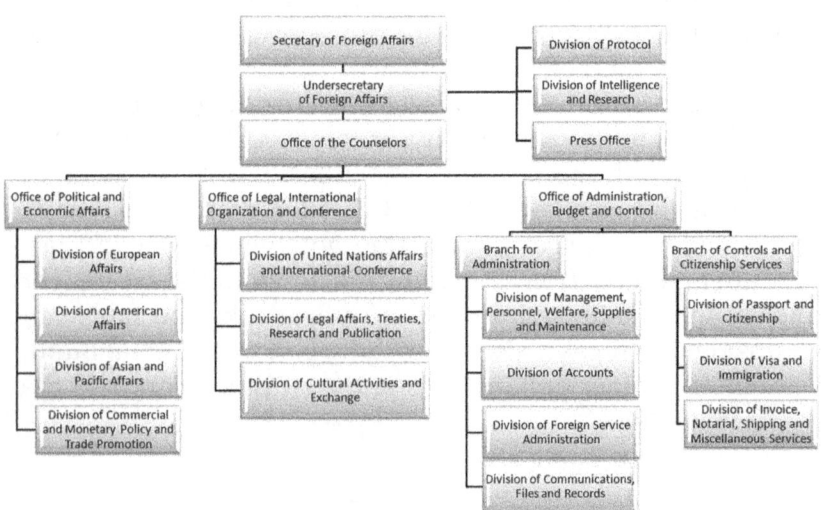

DFA ORGANIZATIONAL STRUCTURE 1946

Downstairs, the legal counselor may be briefing his assistants on the next phraseology of a treaty. Later you will find them huddled together with the representatives of the country with which the Philippine Republic wishes to establish friendly, commercial relations. Such conferences may be protracted, because of the care exercised in fashioning the clauses of the agreement or treaty before any signing can be done by the heads of the signing powers.[89]

The DFA's transfer to a bigger office was only a matter of time. In 1955 the DFA occupied the newly renovated and former UP library building along Padre Faura Street where it would remain until 1987. In the late 1970's, the DFA took over the two building across Padre Faura vacated by the Ateneo Law School that was occupied by the Office of Consular Affairs and the Foreign Service Institute. During the early 1980's, the Ministry of Foreign Affairs (as it was called after the shift to a parliamentary system) already made plans to construct a new edifice since the Padre Faura building was already too small for its expanding operations and increasing number of personnel. A scale model was built but the project was never implemented.

After Christmas of 1986, a mysterious fire damaged the MFA building, incinerating valuable diplomatic records. The Foreign Ministry moved to the Philippine International Convention Center (PICC) in 1987. The Consular Section meanwhile first occupied the Manila Film Center adjacent to the PICC and later transferred to old Jai Alai fronton at Taft Avenue. In 1991, when the Asian Development Bank (ADB) abandoned its old building along Roxas Boulevard and moved to its new headquarters in Ortigas Center, Mandaluyong, the property reverted back to the Philippine government. President Corazon Aquino signed an executive order assigning the old ADB building to the DFA.

Department Order No. 7

Secretary Quirino issued Department Order No. 7 on 20 January 1947 that reorganized and defined the functions of the various offices and divisions of the DFA to make it more efficient. The three offices under the direct supervision of the undersecretary were reduced to two divisions: Board of Foreign Service Personnel, Examination and Review and the Division of Protocol.

The Office of Political and Economic Affairs absorbed two divisions from the Office of Legal Affairs thereby increasing its four divisions to six. The new divisions were the Division of United Nations Affairs and International Conferences and the Division of International Information and Cultural Activities. The Office of Legal Affairs, International Organizations and Conference were renamed Office of Legal Affairs, Treaties, Intelligence and Research. On the other hand, the number of divisions in the Office of Administration, Budget and Control was reduced to five from the original seven.

From the outset of its organization there was a considerable awareness within the DFA of the need for internal coordination. Under Executive Order No. 18, a Division of Coordination and Review substantially patterned after the same division in the U.S. Department of State, was created under the Office of the Undersecretary. Department Order 7 of January 1947 changed this arrangement to provide for a drafting and research officer. These coordinating officers helped materially to foster department-wide coordination in correspondence and policy. Such an assignment demands men of particular ability, and it was fortunate that men of the ability of Emilio D. Bejasa and Delfin R. Garcia were assigned to this position at times.[90] Bejasa and Garcia both served as special assistants to the Secretary in 1952. "Nothing comes into or leaves the Department without passing through their hands."[91]

During the 1950s, the volume of Philippine bilateral and multilateral relations greatly increased. The country also established more embassies, legations and consulates abroad to represent Philippine interests. (This phenomenon will be discussed in more detail in Chapter VI.) As a consequence, these developments further stretched the resources of the DFA. Soon, personnel shortage was becoming evident. With the exception of the forty State Department Boys, the Foreign Service officials and staff dispatched overseas were in many cases ill-equipped or even received no formal training before their foreign assignments.

The expanding scope of diplomacy influenced the organizational setup of the DFA. It was necessary to modify and, in some cases, implement drastic changes in the structure of the department in order to make it more responsive and effective. Most of the initial organizational reforms followed the dictates of practicality and common sense. Thus, divisions were either merged or upgraded and even transferred to the direct supervision of the secretary or the undersecretary. In other words, it was a period of experimentation wherein the key problem was how to balance the substantive and administrative functions of the offices and divisions within the department.

In 1951, the Office of the Undersecretary was expanded. It was not only directly in charge of the Board of Foreign Affairs Service, Examination and Review (which was still inactive at the time) and Coordination but also of Intelligence and Legal matters. The three main offices in the DFA then were the Office of Political and Economic Affairs, the Office of Administration and Controls and the Office of International Social Cultural Affairs. The Office of Political and Economic Affairs consisted of two divisions: Division of Political Relations and Division of Economic and Trade Relations. The Office of Administration and Controls had four divisions: Foreign Service Matters, Passports and Visas, Administration and General Services and Communications and Records. Lastly, the Office of International Social Cultural Affairs was composed of two divisions: Information and Publication and United Nations and Cultural Affairs.[92]

Foreign Service Act of 1952

During its first six years of existence (1946–1952), the DFA was functioning mainly under Executive Order No. 18 and under several Department Orders. Thus, the DFA was then the only executive department of the Government whose organization and operation were based on an executive order and not on an act of Congress. While Executive Order No. 18 had proved adequate to meet the requirements of the Service in the first few years of the existence of the Department and the Foreign Service, it became increasingly evident that their orderly development would be handicapped unless the provisions for their reorganization and operation are embodied in the more stable form of a legislative enactment.[93]

Narciso Ramos, then Minister of the Philippine Legation in Buenos Aires, was one of the most vocal advocates of passing a law that would give the basic structure of the Philippine Foreign

Service a degree of permanence and solidity it needs in order to function with greater efficiency. Ramos deplored the fact that "one of the fundamental weaknesses of the Foreign Service is that its officers and employees do not have any assurance of a more or less permanent tenure of office. The threat of being laid off any time, regardless of their efficiency ratings and the need for their services, in an ever present preoccupation of the personnel and hang over their heads like the sword of Damocles. This sense of insecurity has been accentuated by the recent indiscriminate abolition of positions in the Service and the disproportionate reduction of salaries, particularly in the lower categories, by executive or legislative action."[94]

Congressman Diosdado Macapagal of Pampanga, a former counselor for Legal Affairs of the DFA and second secretary at the Philippine embassy in Washington, proposed two companion bills—one dealing with the DFA proper and the other with the Foreign Service as the overseas arm of the Department. The second bill, formally known as House Bill No. 47 entitled "An Act to Improve and Strengthen the Foreign Service of the Philippines" was co-sponsored by Congressman Tizon. The bill made some headway through the legislative mill that was approved in the House of Representatives in 1950. The bill, however, was pigeonholed in the Senate. No action whatever was taken with respect to the first bill dealing with the Home Office. In drafting the bill, Macapagal tapped the assistance of Jose Alejandrino, member of Group IV of the trainees. Alejandrino was a top-notched lawyer and was the top-ranked man in his group during their training at the State Department. He also hailed from Pampanga like Macapagal.

Despite the death of the Macapagal bill, the DFA continued its researches and studies along the same line. In early 1952, the DFA presented a composite bill dealing both with the Home Office and the Foreign Service, instead of two companion bills. The composite bill incorporated the salient provisions of the Macapagal bills and such features of the American Foreign Service Act of 1946 as could well be adopted to meet Philippine needs and purposes.

During the bill's deliberation in the Philippine Senate, Jose C. Zulueta, Chairman of the Senate Committee on Foreign Relations, praised the composite bill submitted by the DFA:

The main features of the bill are worthwhile noting. The first is the adoption of the career principle for the ranking personnel who man both the Home Office and the Foreign Service. This is in accord with the trend of the development in other countries, that is, towards a professional service made up of carefully selected, well-trained, and highly disciplined public servants who spend most of their lives and make their careers within the organization itself, just as it is with the army and the judiciary. It is a characteristic of this principle that the recruitment and promotion of personnel should be based primarily on merit and that a certain degree of permanence and security of tenure be assured. Only in this way can men of ability and integrity be attracted to the machinery of the government dealing with our foreign relations.

The second main feature is the integration of the Home Office and the Foreign Service by providing for the interchangeability of personnel. This has been found desirable in order that the personnel may have the opportunity for actual service in both the Home Office and the field. In this way they will acquire the balance experience and well-rounded background so necessary for the effective and efficient discharge of their delicate responsibilities.[95]

The bill sailed through the Senate without major problems as senators from the Nacionalista Party and the Liberal Party took a bipartisan stand. Librado Cayco of the Office of Legal Affairs, the main author of the composite bill, recalled his role in drafting the composite bill that was eventually enacted into law:

As the main author of the draft, I tried to convince Undersecretary Neri at that time that there was no sense in taking up the two branches of the organization in separate pieces of legislation when precisely our paramount objective, made implicit in the explanatory note to the bill, was the amalgamation and unification of the two services, as has been the tendency in the American Foreign Service and in similar organizations of other countries. Largely through the efforts of Senator Zulueta, at that time Chairman of the Senate Committee on Foreign Relations, the bill passed the Senate in May 1952 with few minor amendments.[96]

In June 1952, the Philippine Congress passed Republic Act No. 708, otherwise known as the Philippine Foreign Service Act of 1952, which reorganized the DFA. There was not much media hype about the passage of the Foreign Service Act of 1952. *Manila Bulletin*, the largest daily, only gave the law a short write-up while the *Philippines Free Press*, the largest magazine, which has a regular column entitled "The President's Week" had nothing about it. Indeed, there was nothing politically earth-shaking about the new law strengthening the Foreign Service by establishing a merit-based system for the employment and promotion of its personnel.

A close scrutiny of RA 708, however, will reveal that the law gives due recognition to participants in the State Department training program by exempting them from taking the future FAO examinations as required by law:

> No person shall be eligible for appointment as a Foreign Affairs Officer unless he has passed such competitive examinations as the Board of Foreign Service Examinations may prescribe to determine his fitness and aptitude for the work of the service and has demonstrated his loyalty to the Government of the Republic of the Philippines and his attachment to the principles of the Constitution: *Provided, however, that any person who has satisfactorily completed the Foreign Service Training Program in the United States Department of State* or who has rendered satisfactory service in a position of responsibility in the Department or in the Foreign Service or both for five years on the date of the approval on this Act *shall be exempted from both the written and oral examinations prescribed in this Act*...(emphasis added)[97]

Proposals for amendments to RA 708 were expedited, particularly with respect to the conversion of positions in the Home Office and the Foreign Service. One of them was made ostensibly to solve the problem of what rank to give personnel holding key positions in the Home Office when they are assigned abroad. The provision of RA 708 reads as follows:

> (Title III, Part B, Sec. 7) Conversion of positions—To permit rotation of career personnel between the Home Office and the Foreign Service as contemplated in this Act, the positions of counselor and, chiefs of divisions are hereby converted into positions of Foreign Affairs Officers Class I and II respectively occupying the rate of each class which the Secretary [of Foreign Affairs] deems appropriate.

In RA 895, this provision was amended to read as follows:

> To permit the rotation of career personnel between the Home Office and the Foreign Service as contemplated in this Act, the positions of counselors and the positions of chiefs of division and those equal rank and responsibility now occupied by *the graduates of the Foreign Affairs Training Program of the United States Department of State* (emphasis added) are hereby converted into positions of Foreign Affairs Officers Class I and Class II respectively, occupying the rate in each class which the Secretary (of Foreign Affairs) deems appropriate.

The amendment was made to favor the State Department Boys who could claim conversion of their positions to either FAO Class I or II, so long as they can point out that the positions they occupy are of "equal rank" to Counselors or chiefs of division. Instead of starting as FAO IVs, their minimum starting rank is FAO II. This amendment was thus made for the exclusive benefit of those who completed the State Department Training Program.[98]

Six years after Philippine independence, the DFA and the Philippine Foreign Service had reached a level of maturity and sophistication to manage the country's dynamic foreign relations. Initially patterned after the State Department, the inchoate Philippine DFA and Foreign Service started changing its organizational structure and operations little by little to suit the needs of the times. The Philippine Foreign Service Act of 1952, modeled along the lines of the

U.S. Foreign Service Act of 1946, gave it a solid legal foundation. More importantly, the Act recognizes the role of the State Department Boys by exempting them from taking the Foreign Service examinations required by the new law and the amendment to the Act gave them undue advantage in converting their positions in the Home Office and the Foreign Service. It would seem that the State Department Boys were a privileged group but this was not the case, as Chapter VII will show.

By the time the Treaty of General Relations between the Philippines and the United States was abrogated in 1961, the Philippines was more than ready to hold its own in the international community. The Philippines slowly expanded its foreign relations by setting up diplomatic and consular posts in countries that are crucial to its national interests. But despite the Philippines's bourgeoning relations with a growing number of countries, however, its most important bilateral partner remained to be America.

Photo Gallery I

The ceremony of Philippine independence on 4 July 1946. Representatives from twenty-five countries flocked to Manila to attend the historic event.
Source: Philippine Presidential Museum and Library, Manila, Philippines

The first Philippine Foreign Affairs Training Group entered the U.S. State Department for training on 10 December 1945. From left to right: Vicente I. Singian, Manuel A. Adeva, Jose F. Imperial, Frank P. Lockhart, Chief of the Division of Philippine Affairs; Tiburcio C. Baja, Candido T. Elbo; and Edward W. Mill, acting assistant chief of the Division of Philippine Affairs and director of the training program. *Source: Ruth Baja Williams*

The second group of the Filipino trainees at the U.S. State Department in 1946. From the top left: Tomas G. de Castro, Delfin R. Garcia, Pelayo F. Llamas. Below: Leopoldo T. Ruiz, Doroteo V. Vite. *Source: Edward W. Mill Collection, Bentley Historical Library, University of Michigan*

The third group of Filipino trainees at the U.S. State Department in 1946. From left – Emilio D. Bejasa, Francisco P. Claravall, Juanito C. Dionisio, Alejandro D. Yango, Edward W. Mill, acting chief of the Philippine Affairs Division at the U.S. State Department and director of the training program; Pablo A. Peña, Anastacio B. Bartolome, Aurelio Ramos, and Eutiquio O. Sta. Romana.
Source: Emilio D. Bejasa Family

The fourth group of Filipino trainees at the U.S. State Department in 1947. Clockwise: Rodolfo H. Severino, Roman V. Ubaldo, Marcelino V. Bernardo, Edward W. Mill (center), Jose M. Alejandrino, Carlos A. Faustino, Romeo S. Busuego, and Generoso P. Provido.
Source: Jose M. Alejandrino Family

The fifth and last group of Filipino trainees attending the Philippine Foreign Affairs Training Program, at the entrance of the U.S. State Department building in 1947. Front row, left to right: Yusup Abubakar, Tagakotta Sotto, Eduardo Rosal, Edward W. Mill (center), Marciano Joven, Renato A. Urquiola, Irineo Cornista, and Simeon Roxas; back row: Hortencio J. Brillantes, Reynaldo Lardizabal, Engracio D. Guerzon. Benjamin T. Tirona, Luis Moreno Salcedo, Irineo Cabatit, and Guillermo Fonacier. *Source: Edward W. Mill Collection, Bentley Historical Library, University of Michigan*

Edward William Mill (1916–1977) was the architect and director of the Philippine Foreign Affairs Training Program at the U.S. State Department from December 1945 to September 1947. He was known infomally as the "Father of the Philippine Foreign Service." *Source: Edward W. Mill Collection, Bentley Historical Library, University of Michigan*

The Old Executive Office Building, located at 17th Street and Pennsylvania Avenue, was still home to the U.S. Department of State when the Philippine Foreign Affairs Training Program was conducted in Washington, D.C., from December 1945 to September 1947. The State Department shared the building with the War and Navy Departments until the State Department moved to its new headquarters at C Street N.W. *Source: National Archives and Record Administration, College Park, Maryland*

Lothrop House, a separate "annex" building at 2101 Connecticut Avenue NW in Washington, D.C., at Kalorama Triangle, north of Dupont Circle, was the location of the Office of the Foreign Service Division of Training Services, which ran the Foreign Service Officers Training School, where the Philippine Foreign Affairs Training Program was conducted. The building is now known as Lothrop Mansion and serves as the Office of the Trade Representative of the Russian Federation. *Source: EHT Traceries, Inc. (1984).*

4

Dealing With America

The Philippine Embassy in Washington, D.C., was the first and most important diplomatic mission established after Philippine independence in 1946. In fact, the establishment of the embassy even preceded the formal organization of the Department of Foreign Affairs (DFA) in Manila and the Philippine Foreign Service. Philippine representation in the American capital, however, had begun even earlier through the Office of the Resident Commissioner of the Philippines to the United States. During its last years of existence, particularly during the war years 1942–1945, the Office of the Resident Commissioner was already functioning as a quasi-embassy dealing extensively with the U.S. Department of State, especially with regard to the organization of the training program for Filipino diplomats and the establishment of the DFA and the Foreign Service.

Office of the Resident Commissioner to the United States

The Philippine Bill of 1902 provided for the appointment of two Filipino resident commissioners to the United States to represent Philippines interests. It is important, however, to point out that in the beginning the resident commissioners were chosen by the Philippine Commission, the American-dominated civilian government that later evolved into a legislative body.

With the establishment of the Philippine Assembly in 1907, two Filipino resident commissioners, Benito Legarda, Sr. and Pablo Ocampo of the Progresista Party and the Nacionalista Party, respectively, were selected by the Philippine Commission to represent the Philippine Assembly in the U.S. Congress in Washington. The position of resident commissioner soon developed into a highly sought after post since its main task was to lobby the U.S. Congress as well as the American President to grant immediate independence to the Philippines. It did not only offer the opportunity of gaining national prominence but it also afforded the chance to be at the seat of power in Washington and to be exposed to the American way of life.

In 1909, with their newly-acquired political clout, the members of the Philippine Assembly insisted in selecting the two resident commissioners inasmuch as they were duly elected by the people while the Philippine Commission, majority of whose members were Americans, was only an appointed body. The dispute only ended when a Solomonic decision was taken. Since there were two Resident Commissioners, they agreed to nominate one candidate each. Thus, the National Assembly selected Manuel L. Quezon of the Nacionalista Party while the Philippine Commission decided to retain Benito Legarda in the post.[1]

Quezon, a representative of the district of Tayabas, and a former aide-de-camp of General Emilio Aguinaldo, the leader of the Philippine freedom fighters against Spain and the U.S., served as resident commissioner to the U.S. Congress from December 1909 to January 1917. Quezon was widely credited for the passage of the Jones Law of 1916 that allowed greater participation of Filipinos in running the affairs of the colonial government. He would later be elected senator, senate president and finally president of the first Commonwealth government in 1935.

The practice of sending resident commissioners to the U.S. continued by virtue of the Jones Law of 1916. Section 20 of the Jones Law defines their roles and, to emphasize the importance of the position, the Jones Law even mandates that the two resident commissioners be chosen by the Philippine legislature during its first meeting. Their term of office was fixed for three years and they were entitled to an official recognition as such by all U.S. government departments upon presentation to the President of the United States of a certificate of election by the American governor general of the Philippines. Furthermore, the Jones Law requires that a resident commissioner be a bona fide voter of the Philippines, be more than thirty years old and literate in the English language.

With the establishment of the Philippine Commonwealth in 1935, the number of resident commissioners was reduced to one. The power to appoint the Resident Commissioner was transferred from the Philippine legislature to the President of the Commonwealth. The American President also accredited the Resident Commissioner through the "presentation of credentials" much like the diplomatic procedure of accrediting foreign ambassadors. Like previous resident commissioners, the lone resident commissioner continued to have a seat in the U.S. House of Representatives with the right to participate in the debates but without the right to vote.

President Quezon appointed Joaquin Miguel Elizalde, former head of the National Development Company and a scion of the wealthy Elizalde clan, as the first resident commissioner of the Commonwealth government to the U.S. in 1936. Elizalde served as resident commissioner until the death of Quezon in August 1944. After Elizalde, President Sergio Osmeña designated Carlos P. Romulo, who served earlier as Quezon's personal secretary and later editor-publisher of the *Philippine Herald*, as resident commissioner on 10 August1945. The staff of the Resident Commissioner included Manuel A. Adeva, Roman V. Ubaldo and Juanito C. Dionisio. All three would later participate in the training program at the State Department. Adeva served as chief of Nationals Division, while Ubaldo was senior assistant. The Office of the Resident Commissioner also maintained a branch in San Francisco called the Western Division where Dionisio served as senior assistant.

With the Philippines officially proclaimed by the U.S. to be on its way to independence, the resident commissioner tended more and more to become a semi-diplomatic officer. Both Elizalde and Romulo carried on a very active representation of the Commonwealth government in Washington. During the war years, Romulo proved to be a particularly effective and eloquent speaker for the Philippine cause in the U.S. House of Representatives and aggressively championed the Commonwealth cause in Washington. The

Office of the Resident Commissioner was during this period an important advance for the Filipinos towards the conduct of their own foreign relations.[2]

His Excellency

The appointment of an envoy to the United States is the most important ambassadorial assignment in the Philippine Foreign Service today. Even more so in 1946 when the Philippines debuted as an independent state and would finally conduct bilateral relations as a sovereign nation with a former colonial master. The honor of being the first Philippine ambassador to the U.S. went to Joaquin Miguel Elizalde. He was seen as a shoo-in to the prestigious post given the fact that he already served as resident commissioner in Washington during the Commonwealth government and was among President Roxas' chief financial backers during the presidential elections of April 1946. What came as a surprise, however, was that Elizalde himself initially nominated another person, Jose Yulo, former Speaker of the House of Representative, to the much-coveted ambassadorship. Elizalde was reportedly more interested in getting an ambassadorship to London instead of Washington.

The State Department, however, was squeamish about the prospect of Yulo's appointment. Lockhart wrote a scathing memo to John Carter Vincent, Director of the Bureau of Far Eastern Affairs, on Yulo's record during the Japanese occupation. Lockhart quoted Joseph R. Hayden, former vice Governor General of the Philippines and a leading academic expert in Philippine affairs, as saying that "all those who were reported to have collaborated with the Japanese, he (Hayden) considered the offence of those who signed the Council of State papers as perhaps the most serious of the collaboration activities." Lockhart averred that, as a member of the Supreme Court, Yulo lent his name to what was theoretically one of the most important institutions functioning under the Japanese. Premier Hideki Tojo was reported to have warmly praised Yulo for his "unfailing efforts in the construction of the new Philippines."[3]

Lockhart's conclusion in his memo virtually vetoed the granting of an *agrément* to Yulo as he forcefully explained:

While Yulo has undoubtedly proven his administrative and technical competence, there is reason to believe that his conduct during the Japanese occupation was disloyal to the United States. Should he be selected for the position of ambassador to the United States, his appointment may well result in unfavorable repercussions in this country. In addition, those in the Philippines who remained staunchly loyal to the United States would feel badly let down to see appointed as ambassador to this country a man who had so openly and recently worked against the interests of this country in the Philippines.[4]

As a result, Yulo's purported assignment to Washington never materialized. President Roxas still had two excellent candidates in mind: Elizalde and Romulo, both of whom served as resident commissioners to the U.S. Romulo, however, was closely identified with former President Osmeña and did not campaign for Roxas. In his memoirs Romulo wrote about his conversation with Roxas:

"You see, Carlos," Roxas mused aloud, "I really wanted to make you the Philippine ambassador to Washington. But I cannot do it. Mike Elizalde is a good friend of mine. He contributed heavily to my campaign and I promised I'd make him our first ambassador to Washington. I'm committed to do that. But, "he said, "I have you in mind to be the permanent delegate to the United Nations and that is where I'm going to put you."[5]

Roxas' decision was perfect and proved to be the best under those circumstances. The choice of foreign assignments not only satisfied both Elizalde and Romulo but the new Philippine Republic thus benefited immensely from the talent and service of both men.

On 02 July 1946, Paul McNutt, the U.S. High Commissioner to the Philippines, telegrammed Secretary of State Dean Acheson inquiring on behalf of the Philippine government whether the appointment of Elizalde as Philippine ambassador to the United States would be agreeable to the American government. The following day, Acheson wrote a commendatory letter on Elizalde to

President Truman and concluded by saying that "I feel that the appointment of Mr. Elizalde as Ambassador of the Republic of the Philippines to the United States would be satisfactory, and if you concur in this opinion, I shall be pleased to inform the High Commissioner at Manila that your views may be communicated to the Philippine Government." Two days after, President Truman wrote "approved" and signed below Acheson's missive.

Back in Manila, the Philippines was granted full independence on 04 July 1946. In that same afternoon President Roxas received the credentials of former High Commissioner Paul McNutt as the first American ambassador to the new Republic of the Philippines. Roxas and McNutt then signed a provisional agreement of general relations, not subject to congressional concurrence for ratification. The agreement would be operative until the Treaty of General Relations become effective. Two of its four articles repeated U.S. recognition of Philippine independence and mutual diplomatic privileges and immunities. The U.S. was also to notify governments with which it had diplomatic relations of Philippine independence and to invite them to recognize the Republic. Further, the two parties were to enter into negotiations, as soon as feasible, on a treaty of friendship, commerce, and navigation; executive agreement relating to trade; a general relations treaty; a consular convention; and other treaties and agreements as might be deemed mutually agreed.[6]

Roxas appointed Elizalde on 12 July 1946 as the first Philippine ambassador to the U.S. His appointment was long anticipated and evoked little comment from the Philippine press. But it was not without critics. There were those who considered Elizalde as "not a true Filipino but merely a naturalized Spaniard." Indeed, Elizalde's Caucasian features easily stood out among predominantly Malay Filipinos. Like most Filipinos of Iberian descent, Elizalde was labeled as "Kastila" (Spanish).[7]

The *Evening Herald* in its editorial of 11 July 1946 hailed Elizalde's appointment. It asserted: "Mr. Elizalde is a Filipino citizen fully cognizant of his obligations to the Philippines as such citizen and of his rights and privileges, also as such citizen. He has demonstrated by deeds his loyalty to the Philippines with a greater zeal than many Filipinos have. In short, Mr. Elizalde has shown he is more Filipino than many of his countrymen. With his knowledge of the American high sense of justice and generosity and readiness to lend a hand to weak nations, Mr. Elizalde, wholly consecrated to the service of his country, is in a position to promote and keep ever warm and solid the friendship between the Philippines and the United States."[8]

Likewise, the editorial of *Morning Sun* on the same day echoed the *Evening Herald's* praise for and confidence on Elizalde.

> Ambassador Joaquin Elizalde goes back to the old scene of his service for the Philippines—Washington. He was our Resident Commissioner there under President Quezon. He did his job well then. He should do it well again now. The problems are many and complicated for the Philippines. The Philippine ambassador has no seat in the Congress. Things will have to be done now through different channels, through diplomatic contacts, through profitable connections. Much will depend upon the personality of our ambassador and Elizalde has that exactly as the best asset of the Philippines in the principal capital of the world.[9]

On 18 July 1946, at noon, Elizalde arrived at the Washington National Airport accompanied by Minister Counselor Narciso Ramos, First Secretary Urbano Zafra, and Lt. Senador Valeriano from the Philippine Army to finally set up the Philippine Embassy in Washington, D.C. Stanley Wood, the Chief of Protocol, informed the White House of Elizalde's assumption of duties and solicited the possible date of presentation of credentials. Elizalde need not wait too long. On 24 July, at noon, Elizalde presented his Letters of Credence to U.S. President Harry S. Truman. After the ceremony, the Protocol Division of the State Department certified that hence Elizalde would be addressed as "His Excellency Joaquin M. Elizalde, Ambassador of the Philippines."

> The Philippine ambassador's residence was and still is located in 2253 Sheridan Circle. The area is located in the famous "Embassy Row" in the U.S. capital where embassies and other diplomatic missions are concentrated. Washington's Embassy Row lies along Massachusetts Avenue, N.W., and

its cross streets between Thomas Circle and Ward Circle, although the vast majority of embassies are found between Scott Circle and Wisconsin Avenue. Considered as Washington's premier residential address in the late 19th and early 20th centuries, Massachusetts Avenue became known for its numerous mansions housing the city's social and political elites. The segment between Scott Circle and Sheridan Circle gained the nickname "Millionaires' Row".[10]

Mill, then assistant chief of the Philippine Affairs Division at the State Department was, however, not impressed by Elizalde's appointment as ambassador. Instead, Mill was betting on Romulo whom he worked with closely since his days in the Office of Strategic Services (OSS). As he wrote to his wife Wilma: "I met the new Philippine ambassador Joaquin Elizalde this week. The Philippines should have sent General Romulo back here as ambassador instead. Romulo did more good for the Filipinos than any twenty men they have sent here."[11] Notwithstanding this initial impression, Mill and Elizalde eventually developed a close working relationship.

Deputy Chief of Mission

Aside from Elizalde and Romulo, another major appointment that President Roxas made in the Foreign Service was that of Narciso Ramos as Minister Counselor in the Philippine Embassy in Washington, D.C. At the time of his appointment, Ramos was an incumbent congressman representing the fifth district of Pangasinan.

The Nacionalista Party, the main opposition group, and the Democratic Alliance, its junior partner, however, promptly attacked Ramos' diplomatic appointment on the ground of unconstitutionality. They cited Article VI, Section 16 of the Philippine Constitution, which provides that no congressman, "during the time for which he is elected," shall be "appointed to any civil office which may have been created ... while he was a member of Congress." In Ramos' favor it has been argued that his appointment to the embassy in Washington did not fall under the constitutional ban because the present Congress did not create the office. Article VII, Section 10 (7) of the Philippine Constitution empowers the President, with the consent of the Commission of Appointments, to appoint "ambassadors, other public ministers, and consul," This, it has been argued, implicitly creates subordinate diplomatic positions. Against this view the opposition's argument was made that the Act for the establishment of the Philippine Foreign Service authorized the President, by Executive Order, to "create" positions in the Service; therefore, the position of minister counselor in Washington was "created" by the President when he nominated Ramos.[12]

The Auditor General was reportedly impressed by the latter argument and ordered the suspension of Ramos' salary pending the opinion of Secretary of Justice Roman Ozaeta. The press had a field day covering the controversy, erroneously reporting that Ozaeta had ruled against Ramos and devoting ample space to speculation as to Ramos' future. Some papers claimed, not without basis, that Ramos would instead be appointed as Secretary of Public Instruction to replace the incumbent Manuel Gallego who would be assigned to London as Minister of the soon to be established Philippine Legation.

Due to the question on the legality of his appointment, Ramos' salary and emoluments were frozen for three months until a decision was reached by the Department of Justice in October 1946. In the end, Secretary of Justice Ozaeta rendered a favorable opinion for Ramos. As there was no precedent to the Ramos case in the fledgling Philippine Foreign Service, Ozaeta relied heavily upon American exemplars to support the ruling to justify the legality of the appointment. He conveniently used U.S. cases to drive the point that "diplomatic offices are created by international law and by the Constitution; not by act of Congress, nor by the President." He buttressed this argument by quoting Attorney General Caleb Cushing's answer to a similar query by the U.S. Secretary of State in 1855:

> It is the undeniable fact that "public ministers," as a class, are created by the constitution and law of nations, not by act of Congress. No act of Congress created the offices of minister to Great Britain, France, Spain, Portugal, the United Provinces, and other countries, to which ministers were sent by President Washington. They were not even mentioned in acts of appropriation. And thoughtful men have

held that wherever no "ambassador" or other "public minister" exists at the moment and the exigency for one springs up, there is a "vacancy" in the true spirit of the Constitution (7 Ops. Of Attys. Gen. [US] 212).[13]

With the Ozaeta opinion, the case against Ramos' appointment as minister counselor in Washington was finally laid to rest. Ramos himself heaved a sigh of relief after he received the good news that the Secretary of Justice and Legal Counsel of the Department of Foreign Affairs upheld the validity of his appointment, which was subsequently confirmed by the Commission on Appointments. In hindsight he confided to his friend Mill that: "I, myself, entertained doubts to the constitutionality of my appointment when I heard that this point was raised in Manila. When I was rushed into this Washington assignment, the constitutional aspect of the matter did not occur to me at all and if it had, I might have refused to come to Washington."[14]

Ramos acted as a reliable number two-man in the embassy and *chargé d'affaires* ad interim in the absence of Elizalde. This was most appreciated as Elizalde was often out of the U.S. capital due to his frequent travels. To show his confidence in Ramos, Elizalde gave him a free hand in firing or retaining people in the old Resident Commissioner's Office which was to be the nucleus of the Philippine Embassy, but not a single officer or employee was dropped in spite of the fact that practically everyone in the office was an Osmeña and not a Roxas sympathizer.[15]

The American embassy in Manila was particularly pleased by Ramos' assignment to Washington. As it reported to the State Department: "Ramos proved to be a capable and effective officer. His pleasant, easy-going manner won him many friends among both Filipinos and Americans. He is a well-balanced individual, not given to extremes of sort. From all indications, Ramos is very pro-American. He likes the friendship and association of Americans and goes out of his way to please them."[16]

After his assignment in Washington, Ramos would never return back to Philippine politics but would embarked on a successful diplomatic career as first Philippine Minister to Argentina, first Philippine Minister to India, first Philippine Ambassador to the Republic of China (Taiwan) and finally as Secretary of Foreign Affairs under President Ferdinand E. Marcos.

Embassy Officers

The Philippine embassy in Washington did not start from scratch as far as availability of qualified personnel was concerned. Elizalde wisely retained some of the personnel of the Office of the Resident Commissioner and Philippine Commonwealth government-in-exile to form the nucleus staff of the new embassy. He also brought in certain executives connected with Elizalde & Company and had them appointed as embassy officers. Nonetheless, Vice President and Secretary of Foreign Affairs Quirino (in some cases President Roxas himself) appointed highly selected and qualified men to staff the fledgling diplomatic mission. Aside from Elizalde and Ramos, the embassy started with three first secretaries, two second secretaries, one third secretary and a military attaché ad interim, all of them highly educated and qualified professionals. During the first two years of the embassy's existence, six former State Department trainees served there—Tomas C. de Castro, Leopoldo T. Ruiz, Emilio Torres, Doroteo V. Vite and Jose F. Imperial.

The three First Secretaries at the Philippine Embassy were Melquiades J. Gamboa, Urbano Zafra, and Juan Antonio Barretto. Gamboa was a brilliant lawyer and served as assistant secretary to the President of the Philippines. He was appointed as head of the political section of the Philippine Embassy.[17] Zafra, a former commercial adviser at the Office of the Resident Commissioner during the time of Elizalde, was made head of the economic section. Barretto, a former executive at Elizalde & Company, was assigned as administrative officer of the Philippine embassy.

The three second secretaries were Tomas G. de Castro, Leopoldo T. Ruiz and Godofredo Rivera. De Castro was a member of Group II of the Philippine Foreign Affairs Training Program in the State Department. He was among the first State Department trainees immediately assigned to the Philippine embassy right after his diplomatic training. He served as technical adviser to the Philippine delegation to the United Nations First General Assembly and as temporary member of the Philippine delegation to the Far Eastern Commission.[18]

Ruiz was another former State Department trainee and, like De Castro, was a member of Group II. Like Urbano Zafra, Ruiz served as adviser to the Philippine delegation at the fourth session of the United Nations Relief and Rehabilitation Administration held in Atlantic City, New Jersey in March 1946. Ruiz also authored several articles published by American scholarly magazines.[19] After his stint in Washington, he would be reassigned as the first Philippine consul in the Philippine Consulate in Chicago. Rivera like Barretto was another Elizalde recruit. He was an editorial writer in the Philippine Herald and before his assignment to Washington; he worked as a public relations officer for Elizalde and Company in Manila.[20]

The most junior officer in the embassy was Emilio Torres. Before his assignment in the embassy, Torres served as legal officer in the Office of the Resident Commissioner to the United States from 1945–1946. He was one of the officials retained by Elizalde to work with him the new embassy. He was appointed third secretary.[21]

To complete the roster of officers of the Philippine Embassy, a military attaché was also appointed. Lt. Manuel Q. Salientes, a graduate of West Point and the Massachusetts Institute of Technology, served as the embassy's first military attaché, although in an interim capacity.[22]

Not satisfied with the number of officers in the Philippine embassy in Washington, the Philippine Government further enlarged the embassy roster of officers. Before the end of 1946, two additional second secretaries were appointed—Octavio L. Maloles and Tomas C. Benitez. Maloles, a Harvard graduate, was assigned as second secretary in the Division of Political, Legal, and Cultural Affairs.[23] Unlike Maloles, the assignment of Benitez was more problematic. Prior to his appointment, Benitez was a protocol officer in the DFA.[24] When Benitez was appointed as second secretary in the Philippine Embassy in Washington, his record and activities during the war were again subjected to scrutiny by the State Department before a diplomatic visa was issued to him. Although he was an enthusiastic student of the Japanese language and was to some extent influential in promoting it, Benitez was believed to be friendly towards the U.S. In the end, Benitez was cleared, having occupied only a minor position and did not actively cooperated with the Japanese. He was finally issued a visa in November 1946.

Collaboration issues were no longer an impediment in appointing qualified personnel in the Philippine Foreign Service. As American consul general in Manila Paul Steintorf reported to the State Department: "the present policy of the Philippine Government in selecting Foreign Service officers is to pay little attention to their activities during the Japanese occupation period."[25] The Philippine Congress clamored for amnesty for collaborators for the sake of national unity. Pro-amnesty politicians pointed out that the people accused of political collaboration represented the cream of Filipino leadership whose talents the Republic needed during its young existence. The difficulty and slowness of prosecuting the culprits and the divisiveness of the collaboration issue forced Roxas to issue a General Amnesty on 28 January 1948.[26]

With the issue of collaboration finally settled, appointment of officials stained with collaboration in the Foreign Service became moot. Benitez' case was a litmus test for future appointments to the Philippine embassy in Washington as the U.S. government also relaxed its hard line position on the collaboration issue. The collaboration issue in the Philippines was not unique as similar situation also pervaded countries in Europe and Asia. Thus, the appointment of known collaborators such as Emilio Abello as minister in the Philippine embassy in Washington in September 1948, to replace Narciso Ramos never posed a problem to the U.S. government. Abello was executive secretary of President Quirino at the time.

By January 1947, additional personnel were assigned to embassy to reinforce its work. They were Abelardo L. Valencia, information and press attaché; Doroteo V. Vite, third secretary; and Lt. Senador D. Valeriano, assistant military attaché. Valencia was a veteran reporter for the *Philippine Herald* and was president of the Manila Press Club prior to his assignment to Washington.[27] Vite, a former State Department graduate, was appointed as third secretary and vice Consul. He also served as the embassy's liaison officer with the Filipino community in the U.S. capital. Valeriano served in the Philippine Army and the U.S. Armed Forces during the war. He was promoted to first Lieutenant in February 1946 and served as aide-de-camp to the Provost Marshall General.[28] He was handpicked by Elizalde to serve as assistant military attaché and also doubled as the ambassador's personal bodyguard.[29]

The State Department's Diplomatic List of 1947 shows the accredited officers of the Philippine Embassy in Washington, D.C., as follows:

Mr. Joaquin M. Elizalde, Ambassador
Mr. Narciso Ramos, Minister Counselor
Dr. Melquiades J. Gamboa, First Secretary
Dr. Urbano A. Zafra, First Secretary
Mr. Tomas G. de Castro, Second Secretary
Mr. Tomas C. Benitez, Second Secretary
Dr. Octavio Maloles, Second Secretary
Mr. Doroteo Vite, Third Secretary
Colonel Jaime C. Velasquez, Military Attaché
Captain Osmundo Mondonedo, Assistant Military Attaché
Lieutenant Senador D. Valeriano, Assistant Military Attaché
Mr. Jose Teodoro, Jr., Assistant Commercial Attaché
Mr. Abelardo L. Valencia, Press Attaché

As of 25 June 1947, fifty-four people were assigned to the embassy in Washington from the lowliest clerk up to the ambassador. Even then, additional personnel were assigned in 1948: four officers, three second secretaries—Bartolome A. Umayam, Vicente L. Pastrana, and Diosdado Macapagal—and State Department graduate Reynaldo Lardizabal as third secretary. The most notable appointment was that of Macapagal who became a member of the House of Representative and was later elected president of the Philippines. As a neophyte congressman, he sponsored the bill that eventually became the Philippine Foreign Service Act of 1952.

Embassy Chancery

The modest, chapel-like building located at 1617 Massachusetts Avenue NW, the erstwhile Office of the Resident Commissioner building, was converted into the Philippine embassy. Using Philippine government funds, Elizalde purchased the property during his stint as resident commissioner of the Philippines. During the war, it became the headquarters of the Commonwealth government-in-exile until it returned to the Philippines in October 1944. The Philippine Embassy remained in the aforementioned location for the next fifty years until the Philippine government finally inaugurated a new chancery across Massachusetts Avenue at the corner of Bataan Street in 1995. The transformation of the Office of the Resident Commissioner into the Philippine embassy was not merely symbolic but historic. For the first time the Philippines would now conduct relations with America as a sovereign state. Dissolving the colonial bonds, however, would still take decades to be achieved.

The immediate concern of the new Philippine Embassy was not substantive issues with the U.S. government but the mundane problems of administration. The embassy had to improvise an ad-hoc organizational set up and administrative rules on how to acquire furniture and office equipment while waiting for the approval of the Foreign Service Regulations of the Philippines. Elizalde tapped the services of Richard Butrick and Jose Imperial, who was later appointed as the first Filipino consul general in Washington, to draft the Philippine Foreign Service Regulations. It was approved during the last quarter of 1946.[30] The embassy received 428,680 pesos - 278,680 pesos for salaries, wages and post allowances and 150,000 for sundry and other expenses.[31]

Aside from the organization of the new embassy in Washington, D.C., Elizalde and the Filipino diplomats handled outstanding bilateral issues involving Philippine-American relations such as war damage claims, rehabilitation and development loans, war veterans' legislation, establishment of Philippine consulates in key American cities, and welfare of Filipino residents, among others.

To assist the Philippines to recover from the devastation of the war, the U.S. Congress passed the Philippine Rehabilitation Act. The Act provided for four-hundred million dollars compensation to war-damaged private property, one-hundred million dollars (fair value) transfer program of surplus war equipment, and $120 million to reconstruct damaged public works, as well as to defray costs of eight Filipino technical training programs. They considered the provisions generous, while the Philippine government believed them less than adequate in monetary terms since the total of $620 million was only about half of what the Filipinos (and Roosevelt) had believed just compensation. While Congress broke precedent to aid Philippine recovery, it attached as string the contingent clause that linked the rehabilitation and trade acts. And the formulation of the trade provisions proved even thornier than the debate over war damage costs.³²

In response to the passage of the GI Bill of Rights by the U.S. Congress to provide benefits to Americans who served in the regular U.S. army in the Pacific or in recognized guerrilla units during the war, President Roxas urged the Philippine Congress to speedily enact a GI bill of rights for Filipino veterans, granting essential benefits to widows and orphans, and educational privileges and employment preferences to veterans, pending the enactment of the US government of suitable provision for Filipino veterans. A GI bill of rights along the lines recommended by Roxas was enacted and a Philippine Veterans Board was set up to administer the benefits. The Philippine Congress authorized twenty million pesos when and if the money becomes available, for the administration of these benefits. Roxas allocated 2 million pesos for the first year operations of the Veterans Board.³³

The Philippine GI Bill barely satisfied the Filipino veterans inasmuch as they considered themselves entitled to many of the rights extended to American veterans under the U.S. GI Bill of Rights. Many American leaders, including President Truman and Ambassador McNutt, strongly endorsed their right to participate in a program of veterans' benefits provided by the U.S. A Philippine Veterans Bill was introduced in the U.S. Congress. It passed the Senate but failed in the House by a narrow margin.³⁴ This issue of Filipino veterans' benefits remains unresolved until today—the longest and thorniest issue in Philippine-U.S. bilateral relations.

One of the most difficult issues that Ambassador Elizalde ever handled in the U.S. capital did not concern bilateral issues but other international issues such as the partition of Palestine and the subsequent creation of the state of Israel. Although the issue was being heatedly discussed and resolved in the United Nations in 1947, the Philippine ambassador to the U.S. was under extreme pressure to toe the line of America. A veteran American reporter recounted the story of the Philippine vote:

> I remember one time Burt Wheeler, then out of the Senate and practicing law, had a fellow come to him, a Jewish gentleman, who said, "If you get the Philippines to vote for Israel we'll give you a fee of $30,000."

"Well", Wheeler said, "I don't know that I could do that. It's very difficult, I'm not making policy, and I'm not in the Senate," and he turned it down. But he ran into the Philippine ambassador Mike (Joaquin M.) Elizalde and he told Mike the story. And Mike said, "Well, it's good thing you turned him down." He said, "We can't recognize them. We got a lot of Moslems and Moros and we would be hurting with our own people, we would be in terrible shape."
About two days later he got a call from Elizalde, who had been called to the White House and told that if the Philippines didn't vote for Israel, we would withdraw financial aid by Mr. Truman. So Elizalde called up Wheeler and said, "Go back and get that client of yours and take his money, because we're going to have to vote."[35]

American pressure on the Philippines to follow the United States position in vital international issues, however, did not deter the Philippines from pursuing its national interests, even at the risk of clashing with the United States. For instance, the Philippines established full diplomatic relations with Spain against the will of America, opposed the United States with regards to Philippine reparation claims from Japan, and blocked Japanese participation in international conferences pending the conclusion of a peace treaty. These fundamental but honest differences in opinion would test Philippine-American relations in the early years of the Philippine Republic. The Philippines, after all, had to chart its own course and direction in the realm of international relations.

Philippine Consulates in America

In order to further strengthen Philippine relations with the United States and to provide consular services to approximately fifty thousand Filipinos in America, the Philippine government considered the opening of consulates in major cities in America as a priority. Before Butrick ended his tour of duty in Manila, he proposed the establishment of Philippine posts in New York and San Francisco.

On 25 September 1946, the Philippine Consulate General in New York City was established. It was and still is the hub for all Philippine consular matters in the eastern United States. Jose P.

Melencio was appointed as consul general. A graduate of UP and Georgetown Law School, Melencio served as undersecretary of Justice in the Commonwealth government before the war and was appointed later as associate justice in the Court of Appeals.

Three State Department Boys served as vice consuls under Melencio namely, Candido T. Elbo, Pablo A. Peña and Tagakotta Sotto.[36] Elbo was in charge of notarials, Peña with passports and visas, and Sotto with invoices.[37] *The New York Times* reported on 26 November 1946, on Melencio's initial activities:

> Jose P. Melencio, first Philippine Consul General in New York, was among Mayor O'Dwyer's visitors at the City Hall yesterday as he formally paid his respects on behalf of his government. The Philippine Consulate General will function from 40 Exchange Place next Monday and meanwhile will operate in Suite 607 of the Vanderbilt Hotel. He described his mission as the furtherance of trade and friendship between the two countries.

Next to be established was the Philippine Consulate General in San Francisco on 02 December 1946, with Roberto Regala. Prior to his assignment to San Francisco, Regala served as chief legal adviser at the DFA. Regala was considered as "one of the architects of the Philippine Foreign Service."[38]

Three former State Department trainees were appointed as consuls and vice consuls to assist Regala. The consuls were Jose Imperial and Tiburcio Baja while the vice consuls were Juanito C. Dionisio, Aurelio Ramos, and Benjamin T. Tirona.[39] Two other former trainees rejoined the Philippine Consulate General—Irineo Cabatit as administrative officer and Guillermo Fonancier as senior assistant.

On 09 January 1947, the Philippine consulate in Honolulu was established with Modesto Farolan as consul. Three consular officers were assigned to the consulate. One of them, Anastacio B. Bartolome, a former State Department trainee, served as vice consul.

On 18 February 1948, Philippine Consulates were established in Chicago, Los Angeles and Seattle. Leopoldo T. Ruiz, then Second Secretary in the Philippine Embassy in Washington, was appointed as consul in Chicago. Another State Department boy—Eduardo Rosal, assisted him as vice consul.[40] The Philippine Consulate in Chicago has jurisdiction over twelve Middle Western states with a total population of over fifty million people. It is situated in the heart of the richest commercial, agricultural, and industrial area in the U.S., and perhaps in the world. Approximately five-thousand Filipinos reside within this consular area. Ninety-five percent were already American citizens.[41]

In Los Angeles, a Vice Consulate was initially established with Marcelo T. Boncan as vice consul. Boncan was a former judge and member of the House of Representatives from Tayabas (now known as Quezon province). The post was subsequently raised to a consulate. The consulate had jurisdiction over southern California, Arizona and New Mexico. Assisting him were two State Department graduates – Pelayo F. Llamas and Yusup R. Abubakar who both served as vice consuls. When Boncan unexpectedly died on 10 July 1948, Sofronio Abrera, then serving as consul in the Philippine Consulate General in New York, was reassigned to Los Angeles to replace Boncan.[42]

Meanwhile the Philippine Consulate in Seattle was established with Pedro G. Ramirez as consul. Prior to his posting in Seattle, he served as assistant chief of the Division of Controls in the Department of Foreign Affairs in 1946 and was assigned to the Philippine Consulate in Honolulu in 1947.[43] Irineo Cornista, a State Department graduate, served under him as vice consul.

On 12 March1948, the Philippine Consulate in New Orleans was established with Jose Moreno as consul. Renato A. Urquiola, another former State Department trainee, was also assigned there as vice consul.

By 1950, the Philippines had three consulates general New York, San Francisco, and Honolulu; five consulates Los Angeles, Chicago, New Orleans, Portland, and Seattle; and one honorary consulate, Agana, in the U.S. The establishment and operations of the Philippine consulates in the U.S. received favorable comments from the rapidly growing Filipino community in America. As one Filipino journalist reported:

> The organization and operation of the Philippine Consulates

in the United States have been an outstanding success. They have been honest and efficient and have established a good name for themselves, their government and their country. The consular personnel are high in caliber and qualifications. They have been especially selected under the direction of the Vice President and Secretary of Foreign Affairs Elpidio Quirino.

Consuls General Jose Melencio in New York and Roberto Regala in San Francisco are responsible for the great success and high reputation of their respective consulates. Mr. (Tomas) de Castro, consul in Washington, and Judge Marcelo Boncan in Los Angeles are also deserving of commendation. Consul General Modesto Farolan in Honolulu is reported to be doing good work. A separate consulate was opened in Los Angeles a month ago and consulates are scheduled to open in Chicago and New Orleans.

During the first year of its existence, the New York Consulate collected in fees approximately $350,000 and that of San Francisco Consulate $250,000. As far as the Filipinos in the United States know, there is not even a whisper of irregularity in their collection or safekeeping. That is a record that the government may well set as its standard.[44]

Division of Philippine Affairs

The relationship between the Philippine embassy and the U.S. government was facilitated in great measure because of the existence of the Division of Philippine Affairs in the State Department. The Division, originally called the Office of Philippine Affairs, was set up to carry out the provisions of the Philippine Independence Act of 24 March 1934, in so far as they relate to the State Department. The first chief of the Office was Joseph E. Jacobs, a Foreign Service officer of more than twenty years' experience in the Far East.[45] The Office of Philippine Affairs was later changed to Division of Philippine Affairs to conform to the other geographic divisions in the State Department.

By 1944, the Division of Philippine Affairs became one of the most active divisions in the State Department as plans for the liberation of the Philippines from Japanese occupation were implemented. Besides having jurisdiction over the Philippines, the Division also exercised jurisdiction over all "American-controlled Islands of the Pacific" such as Guam, Wake, Midway, Samoa, Kure, Howland, Baker, Jarvis, and Canton & Enderbury (part British). In his memo to Mrs. Mathieu of DP, then division Chief Lockhart outlined his division's functions and activities: "The Division of Philippine Affairs concerns itself with the provisions, so far as they relate to the Department of State, of the Tydings-McDuffie Act of 24 March 1934, and the amendatory act of 07 August 1939, and other acts of Congress relating to the Philippines. It cooperates closely with the Office of the Resident Commissioner to the United States on matters of political and economic interest concerning the Philippines, and maintains a close liaison with the Commonwealth government in Washington."[46]

A committee on the Philippine Foreign Service, with Frank Lockhart as chairman, was set up within the State Department. More importantly for this study, Edward W. Mill would also organize and supervise the training program for the first Filipino career Foreign Service officers from 1945–1947. The other personnel at the division were E. Edward Schefer and Robert A. Burman, country specialists while Ilse Schott and Bertha M. Schweitzer served as stenographers.

In 1949, the Division of Philippine Affairs, however, was merged with other offices to form what came to be known as the Office of Philippine and Southeast Asian Affairs within the Bureau of Far Eastern Affairs.[47]

Philippine Club of Washington

To look after the interest of the Filipino community in the U.S. capital, the Philippine embassy spurred the establishment of the Philippine Club of Washington.[48] Candido R. Palting became its first president. The club was composed of Washington residents who were Philippine citizens, American citizens of Philippine parentage and a few American citizens friendly to the Philippines. The Philippine embassy encouraged the organization of the club with a view to assisting in the promotion of fellowship among the embassy personnel, the Filipino community, and American friends of the Philippines.

The State Department approved the establishment of the Philippine Club of Washington. In the letter of Stanley Woodward, the chief of protocol, to John Russell Young, president of the Board of Commissioners of the District of Columbia, Woodward stated that the State Department "perceives no objection to the formation of the club or to its being accorded the benefits of the Section of the District of Columbia Code.[49]

The clubhouse was located at 1708 New Hampshire Avenue, N.W. The five-story building was previously occupied by the International Students Club and the Food and Agriculture Organization. The first and second floors were used for Club purposes and the third, fourth and fifth floors were occupied by second secretary Doroteo V. Vite and his American wife Mickey, in whose name the entire premises had been leased from the lessor. Vite, in addition to his regular duties at the Philippine embassy, was also designated resident manager of the Clubhouse. Rooms in the fourth and fifth floors were rented to boarders most of whom were Philippine citizens, students or American citizens interested in the Philippines.

The Clubhouse had a social hall, music hall, recreation room, bar and dining facilities serving Philippine food. It served as a convenient meeting place, where the embassy staff met to lunch or to dine among themselves and with their friends; and Philippine societies and organizations held meetings and social activities in the Clubhouse. Products of Philippine handicraft and arts were exhibited in the Club and information about the Philippines was distributed to members and their guests.

Vite and his wife put tremendous effort in fostering closer relations between the Filipinos and Americans in Washington. Their project of launching a newsletter was also a way of breaking the monotony of Vite's work in the Philippine embassy in Washington. "There is nothing particularly exciting around this embassy. Work has settled down to a monotonous daily grind and whatever intellectual or spiritual stimulation one wished to have one will have to find it for himself elsewhere," Vite told his former mentor, Mill, in his letter updating the latter.[50]

Visit of Quirino to America

During Elizalde's assignment in Washington, Quirino visited America twice. The first was on goodwill in May 1947, as Vice President and Secretary of Foreign Affairs. Quirino's principal mission was to extend to President Truman the gratitude of the Filipino people for the grant of independence that made possible the establishment of the Philippine Republic. Quirino stayed in Blair House, the presidential guest house. President Truman received Quirino in the White House on 9 May 1947 where Truman hosted a small informal "stag luncheon." A historic photo of the visit to the White House shows Truman bantering with Quirino and flanking them were Philippine Ambassador Elizalde and US Ambassador McNutt.

Quirino's visit, however, turned sour when the *Washington Post* published an editorial denouncing the state of corruption in the Philippines, particularly the rampant irregularities involving the disposal and distribution of American relief and surplus goods. The opening salvo of the *Washington Post* blared:

> Smells of corruption emanating from Manila had preceded the visit here of Philippine Vice President Elpidio Quirino. It might seem ungracious on our part, to take note of them while the Vice President is enjoying our hospitality. There is no such intent. It is in the hope that our distinguished visitor will see the need of cleansing out the newly launched ship of state that will risk the imputation of discourtesy.

But the reproach continued:

> It is sad to see Filipinos making a bad start on the sea of independence which we and they celebrated less than a year ago. Remedial measures are called before the barque itself gets beyond repair. The scandals refer to charges of wholesale pilferage and the illegal sales of surplus war materials. Connivance of high Philippine government officials is alleged.

The editorial concluded with this indictment:

> Evidently they (Philippine government officials) can fatten on American aid and the Filipino budget without check ...

right now the officials in Manila seem trying to cover up their tracks by putting the blame on the American forces.[51]

Caught flat-footed by the *Washington Post* editorial, Quirino scrambled for answers to American reporters who hounded him for comment. His lame answer did not even satisfy himself:

> The matter is under thorough investigation by my government. I assure you there will be no stone at the top or the bottom left unturned. My country should not be judged by the acts of individuals but by its record. You cannot impugn the integrity of the Philippine government or the Islands' people. We have our internal political bickering but I assure you we present a unified front in our national duties.[52]

Elizalde tried to do some damage control but it was too little too late. In an official statement, he declared that the Philippine government "is proceeding to suspend, try, and convict those guilty of malfeasance in office." He declared, "President Manuel Roxas is now moving to provide that none would be spared from the heaviest penalties provided by law if proved to be guilty of such misuse of public trust." He explained further the possibility of the "existence of questionable practices by certain officials," but pointed out that press reports gave "greater emphasis to charges of scandal rather than to the efforts which are being made to root them out."

His first official visit to Washington was a big blow to Quirino's maiden foreign trip as Secretary of Foreign Affairs. It was a bitter pill to swallow, as it was the first time that it dawned on Quirino that the gravity of the bad news coming from Manila could easily wreck a foreign visit, particularly to America. By his own admission, he sadly acknowledged that his encounter with Washington press was a fiasco. "I consider this experience one of the most embarrassing moments of my public career."[53]

In April 1948, while delivering a speech in Clark Field, an American airbase in Pampanga, President Roxas collapsed. He was carried to a nearby American hospital but he could not be revived. Roxas' untimely death left a big void in the new Republic and the Filipino people were shocked at the news. Vice President Quirino took over the presidency without relinquishing the Foreign Affairs portfolio, although there were rumors that Jose C. Zulueta, the Secretary of Interior, would become the new Secretary of Foreign Affairs.

The rise of Quirino to the presidency did not augur well for Elizalde. Although the two men were civil to each other, there was a long-standing friction between them. Quirino resented Elizalde for consistently bypassing him when he was still the Vice President and Secretary of Foreign Affairs to take up matters directly with President Roxas. Quirino was suspicious of Elizalde and the latter's maneuver against him. Elizalde's power stemmed from his financial and economic clout in the Philippines and his reputation as a maker of Philippine presidents dating back from the time of President Quezon. He boasted, even to American officials, that he had contributed $300,000 to the election of Roxas.[54] With Roxas' death, Elizalde suddenly lost his patron and his influence ebbed. As a matter of expediency, President Quirino retained Elizalde as ambassador but his continued stay in Washington was now a source of speculation in the Philippine media.

As a show of force, President Quirino replaced Narciso Ramos against the wishes of Elizalde with his own man. He handpicked Emilio Abello, his executive secretary, to be minister counselor in Washington. As a consolation to Narciso Ramos, he was appointed minister extraordinary and plenipotentiary to Argentina, the first Philippine legation in Latin America. Elizalde lashed out at Abello's collaborationist records anticipating the he would have a hard time working in U.S. given his background. Abello served as vice minister of Foreign Affairs during the Japanese occupation. In truth, what unsettled Elizalde was the rumor that Abello would eventually replace him as ambassador to Washington. Abello would also report to Quirino everything that Elizalde was doing at post. Quirino also retaliated against Elizalde by keeping Elizalde in the dark regarding his forthcoming trip to the U.S. Elizalde was infuriated when he learned from the American embassy in Manila that Quirino reportedly told American officials to disregard Elizalde and directly communicate to him instead.[55]

In the end, Elizalde's great desire to prolong his stay in Washington was granted by Quirino. The two may have reached an understanding on the support of Elizalde for Quirino's presidential campaign in 1949. The truce was, however, short. After Quirino was elected as president, Elizalde's tenure as ambassador to the U.S. was again in peril. Elizalde had privately expressed to Quirino and close associates his personal objections to many administration policies involving the DFA. This difference of opinion was bluntly substantiated by Elizalde in his many unsuccessful attempts to resign his post and return to private business. He also froze the attempted deal between a presidential adviser and a member of the embassy to purchase at high prices airplane parts for the Philippine Air force way beyond the best open market rates and the actual requirements of the Philippine government. The purchase was not coursed through the Philippine Embassy in Washington but through a New York firm dealing with the War Assets Administration. Irked by the anomalous deal, Elizalde ordered it stopped and suggested to Malacañang (Office of the Philippine President) a thorough investigation of the transaction and similar others which may be current in Philippine Foreign Service posts abroad.[56]

In the long-term the beneficiary of the conflict between Quirino and Elizalde turned out to be Carlos P. Romulo as Quirino thought of Romulo as the ideal replacement for Elizalde. Besides, it was well known that Romulo and Elizalde were at loggerheads, with Romulo anxious to assume as ambassador to Washington.

After more than six years as Philippine ambassador to America, Elizalde bid farewell to President Truman on 10 January1952. But he was returning home to assume the position of Secretary of Foreign Affairs. President Quirino made it appear that Elizalde was being promoted rather than being demoted to a lesser position. Elizalde, however, left Washington with a heavy heart. A little over a month, Elizalde's successor, Romulo, presented his credentials to President Truman on 15 February.[57] The destiny of these two men appeared to be intertwined. The turnover was a déjà vu. In August 1944, Romulo replaced Elizalde as resident commissioner to the United States. Their job swapping continued. This time Romulo was replacing Elizalde as ambassador to the United States while holding on to his post as head of the Philippine mission to the United Nations in New York. Elizalde reluctantly took over Romulo's previous post as Secretary of Foreign Affairs in January 1952. "Elizalde dislikes

Romulo thoroughly, saying he talks too much and gets into all sorts of pickle for personal publicity," Mill noted after his long talk with Elizalde when the latter left Washington, D.C., for Manila.

Romulo, however, would be hardly remembered for serving as Philippine ambassador to the U.S. but more as "Mr. United Nations" for his exploits as Philippine chief delegate (now known as permanent representative) to the United Nations in New York and later as the first Asian to be elected president of the United Nations General Assembly in 1949. Romulo almost single-handedly put the Philippines in the world map of diplomacy. Romulo's extraordinary success in the nascent United Nations set the tone of Philippine multilateral diplomacy during its initial years as a new nation.

5

On the International Stage

Even when it was still an American colony, the Philippines was allowed by the United States government to enter into a number of multilateral agreements as an independent contracting party. On 28 August 1924, for instance, the Philippines signed the Universal Postal Convention and the country became a full member of the Universal Postal Union fifteen years later. As a major sugar producer, the Philippines likewise became a signatory to the Agreement and Protocol regarding the Production and Marketing of Sugar of 06 May1937.[1]

During World War II, U.S. President Franklin Roosevelt raised the international status of the Philippine Commonwealth to that of an independent state, if not *de jure*, at least *de facto*. Roosevelt extended an invitation to President Manuel L. Quezon to become a signatory to the Atlantic Charter, a joint declaration of the United States and the United Kingdom to resist the Axis Powers—Germany, Italy, and Japan. On 10 June 1942, the Philippines formally adhered to the Atlantic Charter, thereby giving its commitment to render material assistance and contribution to the Allies' struggle for victory against the Axis Powers. The Philippines was the second among the eighteen countries that later on adhered to the Atlantic Charter. Although sporadic, Philippine participation in international conferences before July 1946 served as a rehearsal for its active participation in the United Nations during its inception.

In June 1943, Secretary of State Cordell Hull transmitted to President Quezon for the consideration of the Commonwealth government a draft agreement for the establishment of the United Nations Relief and Rehabilitation Administration (UNRRA). In his letter Secretary Hull referred to the United States as "his Government" and from the context the Philippine Commonwealth was placed upon a position of equality with the United States and the other nations, which were to sign the agreement. The Philippines thus signed the agreement as an independent nation distinct from the United States.[2]

President Roosevelt defined the political status of the Philippines at that time in the following terms:

> The Philippine government is a signatory of the declaration by the United Nations, along with thirty-one other nations. President Quezon and Vice President Osmeña attended the meetings of the Pacific War Council, where the war in the Pacific is chartered and planned. Your government has participated fully and equally in the United Nations Conference on Food and Agriculture, and a Philippine representative is a member of the Interim Commission created by that Conference. And, of course, the Philippine Government will have its rightful place in the conference, which will follow the defeat of Japan.
>
> These are the attributes of complete and respected nationhood for the Philippines, not a promise but a fact.[3]

The U.S. Supreme Court confirmed this attitude of the U.S. president toward the Philippines in 1945 in the case of Hooven vs. Allison & Co. (324 US679). In said decision, the court described the status of the Commonwealth of the Philippines as an "independent government."

On 22 July 1944, the Philippines also signed the Articles of Agreement of the International Monetary Fund (IMF) as well as the Articles of Agreement on the International Bank for Reconstruction and Development (later renamed World Bank) at Bretton Woods in New Hampshire.[4] The Philippine Commonwealth government's adoption of the Bretton Woods Agreements was announced by the

United States to the other signatory states. The Philippines also participated in two conferences of the Food and Agriculture Organization (FAO) as well as in the International Aviation Conference.

Founding Member of the United Nations

In the summer of 1944, President Roosevelt ordered a group of officials from the State Department to draw up plans for what would be the structure of a world organization. In his first public announcement of the plan, however, Roosevelt called it the "World Security Union." As early as October 1943, Roosevelt had sent Secretary of State Cordell Hull to Moscow with a first proposal of what finally developed into the Dumbarton Oaks plan for a United Nations Organizations.[5]

The Moscow Declaration of 30 October 1943, signed by the foreign ministers of the Soviet Union (Vyacheslav Molotov), the United Kingdom (Anthony Eden), the United States (Cordell Hull) and the Ambassador of China to the Soviet Union (Foo Ping-Sheung), proclaimed that "they recognized the necessity of establishing at the earliest practicable date a general organization based upon the principle of sovereign equality of all peace-loving states, large or small, for the maintenance of international peace and security." Definite plans for the creation of a world organization, however, still took several stages—at Tehran in December 1943, at Dumbarton Oaks in the late summer of 1944, at Yalta in February 1945 and, finally at San Francisco in April 1945.

In the Dumbarton Oaks Conference, the Allied Powers envisioned the need for an Executive Organ of limited membership, which would be entrusted with primary responsibility of maintaining international peace and security. They also proposed the drafting of the United Nations Charter whereby aside from the four sponsoring states (United States, United Kingdom, Soviet Union, and China); other governments would be invited to the United Nations Conference on International Organizations in San Francisco for such purpose.

The Philippines' invitation to attend the San Francisco Conference was brought about by the Yalta Conference where the victorious Allied Powers tried to chart a new world order after the Second World War. In the original horse-trade at Yalta, the United States and the United Kingdom agreed to let Russia bring in Byelorussia and Ukraine as members of the first conference—in exchange for allowing the Philippines and India to participate.[6]

One night in 1945, Carlos P. Romulo, the Resident Commissioner to the United States, received a phone call from Philippine Commonwealth President Sergio Osmeña who was recuperating from surgery in Jackson, Florida, telling him that President Roosevelt would like to organize "a sort of world body". Osmeña added that if Roosevelt were to call a meeting of nations he would like Romulo to head the Philippine delegation.

Elated by his appointment, Romulo requested for an appointment with Secretary of State Edward Stettinius two days later. During their meeting Romulo complained to Stettinius that in previous international conferences the Philippine delegates were ignored because the Philippines was not yet an independent state. And if he (Romulo) were to be the chairman of the Philippine delegation to this new world body, he would like to be duly informed of what is happening. After their talks, Stettinius assigned an official from the State Department to serve as liaison officer between the Philippine delegation and the American delegation to keep the Philippine delegation informed of important developments. Romulo was obviously elated by Secretary Stettinius' decision.

Romulo headed a distinguished group of Filipino delegates to the San Francisco Conference which included Maximo Kalaw, dean of the College of Liberal Arts of the University of the Philippines; Carlos P. Garcia, senator and future president of the Philippines; Pedro Lopez, congressman from Cebu; Francisco A. Delgado, former senator and resident commissioner; Urbano A. Zafra, Colonel Alejandro Melchor and Vicente G. Sinco. Some members of the Philippine delegation played significant roles in the preparation and conduct of the San Francisco Conference. For instance, Pedro Lopez became a member of the Preparatory Commission while Vicente Sinco served as rapporteur of the First Commission.

Jose Imperial and Manuel Adeva, members of the first group of Filipino trainees at the State Department trainees and then working at the Commonwealth government-in-exile in Washington, served as technical advisers of the Philippine delegation. In a photo showing the Philippine delegation at the signing of the UN Charter, Imperial appears standing behind Romulo as the latter signs the UN Charter on behalf of the Philippine Commonwealth. Under Romulo's leadership, the Philippines actively participated in the drafting of the UN Charter from 25 April to 26 June1945. In the end, the Philippines, together with other fifty nations, became a signatory to and co-founder of the United Nations Organization on 20 October 1945, even before its formal independence.[7]

During the San Francisco Conference, the Philippine delegation contributed significantly to the framing of the UN Charter. Romulo "submitted 25 amendments" to the Dumbarton Oaks proposals on the structure of the United Nations: four were adopted in full in the new Charter and six were adopted in part or in principle. The four accepted amendments covered cultural matters which can be found in Section 3 of Article 1, Chapter 5 on purposes of the United Nations, Article 55, 57 and 62, and the provisions for international economic and social cooperation. The six others dealt with the equal rights provision in Section 2 of Article 1, Chapter I (the idea behind Article 21). The Philippines' main interest in cultural affairs was to foster global understanding through international cultural cooperation as a purpose of the United Nations, the discussion of cultural problems in the proposed Economic and Social Council (ECOSOC) and other specialized agencies, and the establishment of an educational and cultural commission.[8] The offshoot of these ideas was the creation of the specialized agency called the United Nations Educational, Scientific and Cultural Organization (UNESCO).

Aside from cultural affairs, security issues, and colonial peoples, the Philippine delegation batted for the sovereign equality of all law-abiding states, accepted compulsory jurisdiction of the International Court of Justice, and defined aggressors. To ensure equal geographic representation in the powerful Security Council, Romulo proposed the election of six non-permanent members from regions defined as North and Central America, South America, Europe, Africa, Western Asia, and the Western Pacific. He also insisted on the participation of non-members of the Security Council in enforcement action debates. The idea was for the Council to set as temporary voting members two states from the geographical region where the dispute arose, provided that the two were not Council members and not parties to the dispute. This became the idea behind Article 31, which states that: "Any member of the United Nations which is not a member of the Security Council may participate, without vote, in the discussion of any question brought before the Security Council whenever the latter considers the interests of that member are specially affected." The Philippines would wisely invoke this provision during the Council's deliberation over the Indonesian independence.[9]

Furthermore, Romulo, along with delegation heads of many small nations, challenged the veto power of the permanent members (United States, United Kingdom, France, Soviet Union, and China) of the Security Council. The veto power allows any permanent member to block any resolution contrary to its national interest. Romulo proposed that the Security Council's failure to arrive at a decision on substantive issues, by reason of the non-concurrence of one permanent member, should be remedied by submitting the issue to the General Assembly who will decide on said issues by an affirmative vote of three-fourths of all the members. This qualified majority reflects Romulo's strong belief that the democratic principle of majority rule should prevail. The provision for decision to be taken by three-fourths vote of Member States would enable legal action to be taken against one of the great powers that might become an aggressor. He repudiated the arguments that conflict among great powers would lead to anarchy, that unanimity was a necessary ingredient for world security, and that the democratic principle of rule by majority would weaken the Council's efficiency. He also argued that the veto power of the permanent members could be abused by any power.[10] The Philippine alternative proposal was in the end voted down as it was opposed by the great powers.

Another notable achievement of the Philippine delegation to the San Francisco Conference was on the issue of non-self-governing territories. This is truly significant since there were still many territories that were under colonial rule. The efforts of the Philippines would later contribute to the hastening of decolonization in many parts of Africa and Asia. The delegation was able to make such a valuable contribution to the United Nations by adding two important words " self-government or independence" in section b, Article 76, Chapter XII regarding International Trusteeship System, in the UN Charter. As it now reads, it provides that one of the basic objectives of the trusteeship system is: "to promote the political, economic, social and educational advancement of the inhabitants of the trust territories, and their progressive development towards self-government or independence." The colonial powers vigorously opposed the proposal of the Philippines to add the words "or independence." However, after prolonged debates both in the Committee meetings as well as in the plenary meeting of the General Assembly, the Philippine proposal was approved by majority vote. This Philippine amendment later on became the basis for the pursuit of independence of many Asian and African countries that were under colonial rule.[11]

During the debate on colonial issues, the Philippines' stand on freedom, human rights, international security, and the issue on war and peace, was clearly enunciated in the maiden speech of Romulo in the third day of the San Francisco Conference. He said we should make this floor the "last battlefield" and reminded his fellow delegates: "We are here to determine whether the human race is going to exist or whether it is to be wiped out in another world holocaust. Those of us, who come from the foxholes of battlefronts, have no illusions as to what another war will do to all men. This may be our last opportunity to achieve peace. We are here to fight for our lives…" The speech was a hit and Romulo received a standing ovation.[12] The following year, the Philippine delegation again headed by Romulo, made an extraordinary contribution to the United Nations Commission on Human Rights held in Geneva. In the working group on the declaration on Human Rights, the Philippine delegation either proposed or redrafted twenty-one out of the thirty-six articles.[13]

The Philippines continued its active participation in the United Nations as the country was bent on contributing to its construction and institutionalization. Maximo M. Kalaw, newly promoted Secretary of Public Instruction, participated in the London meetings in November 1945 that created the United Nations Educational, Scientific and Cultural Organization (UNESCO). Salvador P. Lopez, Romulo's deputy in the Philippine Mission to the United Nations, helped draft the UNESCO Charter, especially the section on United Nations Department of Public Information. The Philippines also became one of the first eleven members of the Far Eastern Commission, the highest policy-making body for occupied Japan, which was created in December 1945.[14]

Under the leadership of Vice President and Secretary of Foreign Affairs Elpidio Quirino, the Philippines became a member of many international organizations. "This is a great privilege for a young and small country such as ours," President Manuel Roxas observed. "The recognition was due to the fact that the Republic had already gained the respect and confidence of other nations. I'm happy to state that his achievement has been accomplished in large measure through the goodwill tour around the world of Vice President Quirino and to his brilliant leadership in our foreign affairs," Roxas said.[15]

Philippine participation in the United Nations also in a way veered the Philippine foreign policy away from its fixation on its bilateral relations with the United States. As one American scholar wrote: "The existence of the United Nations has also strongly affected Philippine foreign policy. Some Filipinos, indeed, say that their foreign policy is more closely tied to the United Nations than to the United States, which may be an effort to camouflage the degree of intimacy with America."[16]

UN Headquarters

The UN started with a working capital amounting to twenty-five million dollars. A provisional scale of contributions was devised to fix the contribution of member-states. The Philippine contribution was assessed at 0.256% of the entire UN budget amounting to $64,000. After the San Francisco Conference, the first UN General Assembly was held in London on 10 January 1946, at the Methodist Central Hall, Westminster. The first General Assembly was divided into two sessions. Thus, the Philippines sent two groups of delegates. The delegation to the first session was composed of Pedro Lopez, Tomas L. Cabili, and Manuel V. Gallego. The second, much bigger, delegation was headed by Romulo and composed of Mariano J. Cuenco, Pedro C. Hernaez, Raul T. Leuterio, and Lorenzo Sumulong. Alternate delegates included Leonides S. Virata, Salvador P. Lopez, Amado N. Bautista, and Jose D. Ingles.

The main problem of the new organization, however, was the

location of its permanent headquarters. San Francisco emerged as the main contender for the future site of the UN Headquarters. Having been the host to the UN Conference on International Organizations, which produced the UN Charter in June 1945, Romulo was one of the city's avid supporters. "The future drama of the world," Romulo claimed, "will take place in the Pacific." But many European delegations opposed San Francisco because of its great distance from European capitals. The Soviet Union objected to San Francisco's candidature from the very start and favored New York but was also open to Philadelphia as a compromise site. Even the US government later on said that the future UN Headquarters should not be too far from Europe. Several U.S. cities namely New York, San Francisco, Boston, and Philadelphia bid for the right to host the UN.

Soon, it became clear that New York was the front-runner for the UN headquarters. But even then there was still no consensus on where to locate it. Initially, New York City officials were anxious to host the UN permanently in Flushing Meadows, the site of the 1939 World Fair. In late 1946, the New York City committee offered to the UN a 350-acre site in Flushing Meadows Park. The City Building in the Flushing Meadows Park was converted into site for the General Assembly. The UN, however, turned down the proposal. The UN continued its search for a permanent home. Lake Success in Long Island also hosted several meetings of the incipient UN. But the growing number of personnel working at the secretariat had created problems for the organization. As the *New York World Telegram* reported:

> The permanent secretariat of the UN, which soon will number 2,000, plus families, already is beefing loudly at the isolation of the temporary site at Lake Success, Long Island, and the plaint is reassuringly human. "We are getting in one another's hair. We are too much together. We are too far from town. And it's going to be worse, when the wives and families come and everything is living in each other's pockets." These are but a few of the gripes registered by the residents of the makeshift headquarters.[17]

The search for a permanent site ended in December 1946 when John D. Rockefeller, Jr. and his family offered to donate $8.5 million to purchase a site between 42nd and 47th Streets along East River in Manhattan. To design and build the UN building, the U.S. government loaned the UN $65 million after the plan was approved by the General Assembly. Some were quick to hail the choice of New York City as the site of the UN headquarters. Senator Arthur H. Vandenberg of Michigan, a ranking Republican senator on the Foreign Relations Committee, turned out with a resounding recommendation in favor of the East River site arguing that the UN should not be in a large campus but should be in a large city close to all media of communications. There was also the danger that being in a more distant location would allow in the course of time to develop an independent existence and personality of its own. Besides, isolation of the Secretariat might well be prejudicial to the work of the Organization. No site should be selected which could not be reached by road or rail within an hour and half.

Philippine Mission

While waiting for the completion of the UN building in Manhattan, UN meetings were held in Flushing Meadows in Queens and Lake Success in Long Island. The foreign missions, including that of the Philippines, set up their offices in Manhattan. In 1946, the Philippine Mission to the United Nations rented Room 654 at Hotel Pennsylvania located at 401 Seventh Avenue, New York and converted it into a temporary office. Built in 1919, Hotel Pennsylvania was then the largest hotel building in New York. The Mission was relocated in the same year to a new address at Rm. 6231 of the Empire State Building, 350 Fifth Avenue, New York City, then the tallest building in the world.

In 1950, the officers of the Philippine Mission in New York included the following:

> Ambassador Carlos P. Romulo, Chief of Mission, Salvador P. Lopez and Jose D. Ingles, both Foreign Affairs Officers; Major Antonio P. Chanco, military attaché; Mauro Mendez, legal adviser; Narciso G. Reyes and Romeo T. Cristobal, public relations officers; and Captain Cesar B. Jimenez, assistant military attaché.[18]

In 1960, the Philippine government purchased a stately and opulent townhouse on 13-15 East 66th Street, New York City. In the same year the Philippine Mission to the United Nations and the Philippine Consulate General occupied the premises. Built in 1916, the "townhouse" currently houses the official residences of the Philippine Permanent Representative to the United Nations and the Philippine Consul General, New York. In November 1974, the Philippine Mission moved to its present site at the Philippine Center building located at 556 Fifth Avenue, New York, New York.

The Carrère & Hastings-designed building at 556 Fifth Avenue was built in 1912 to house the Knoedler Gallery, one of the leading art galleries in America at the time. When Knoedler's moved to a new home at 57th Street, the building at 556Fifth Avenue was leased to Schrafft's, a candy and chocolate company. In 1975 the Philippine Government altered the new building for the Philippine Center, which houses a tourist office, a trade board, the mission to the United Nations and the consulate. The Filipino architect Augusto Camacho gave the building a completely new façade of pebbled stucco, windowless above the ground floor. The lower façade is of soft, native Philippine rock, with a projecting wooden gable that evokes western Pacific architecture.[19]

Big Voice of Small Nations

In designing the official seal of the United Nations, U.S. Senator Warren Austin, the committee chair, circulated a proposed design to all heads of delegation in San Francisco. When Romulo saw the proposed design, he immediately went to see Senator Austin to complain. "The Philippines is not on the world map," he said. "But, General," Senator Austin explained, "your country is so small that if we tried to include the Philippines on a map of this scale, it would be nothing more than a dot." Romulo was not satisfied with the explanation but he had to give in. "All right," he said, "give us the dot!" So that is how the Philippines was included even as a mere dot in the official seal of the United Nations.[20]

With Romulo at the helm, the Philippines earned the reputation of being a "big voice of small nations." Romulo saw that Asia had no voice. Prior to the establishment of the UN, Asians had minimal or, if not, no participation at all. Romulo was looking for the role of the small nations in the UN since there was no coalition among small nations. As Romulo said, "Before, it was only Great Britain, Germany, France, United States, Soviet Russia who could speak to the world. Now small nations have their forum where they can air their grievances, speak for their ideals and aspirations, which was unknown before."[21] Thus, Romulo wisely concluded that the United Nations provided the Philippines with the opportunity to project itself and grow in international stature and fame. Romulo seized the role of spokesman for the rights of colonial peoples and small nations.

The Philippine delegation often clashed or engaged in heated debates with the great powers, particularly the Soviet Union. Records show that during the San Francisco Conference, Romulo had a verbal joust with Vyacheslav Molotov, leader of the Soviet delegation, when the latter demanded that there should be five rotating chairmen of the UN Conference instead of the internationally accepted norm that the host country is to be chairman of the Conference. This happened when Romulo supported the position of Mexican Foreign Minister Ezequiel Padilla in opposing the proposal of Molotov. Romulo's intervention infuriated Molotov who sarcastically asked "Mr. Chairman, why is the representative of the Philippines here? The Philippines is not an independent nation. He has no credentials to be in this meeting."

Molotov must have known well the *quid pro quo* in Yalta on the Philippine participation but would like to humiliate Romulo publicly for his temerity to oppose the Soviet position.

To such a statement, Romulo replied, "Mr. Chairman, may I ask him [Molotov] why is it that Ukraine and Byelorussia are here? They are not independent nations."

Molotov smirked, "It seems to me that the representative of the Philippines looks at all these international questions with color-tinted glasses from an American optometrist."

Unfazed, Romulo countered, "Mr. Chairman, for the information of Mr. Molotov, the Philippines is here by right, as a nation that fought the war with the other nations. We were an ally of the free nations, and we did our bit in the fight for freedom and democracy. I would like to know from Mr. Molotov by what right are the Byelorussians and Ukrainians here? They are not independent either;

they are part and parcel of Soviet Russia. . . . As to my glasses," said Romulo pulling out his glasses, "I wish to correct Mr. Molotov. These glasses I bought from a Russian optometrist whose name is Poldoski." Then putting on his glasses, Romulo joked, "That's why I seldom wear them because they distort my vision."[22]

As the world was divided by the Cold War, the Philippines gravitated on the side of the United States and its Western allies and Romulo earned the reputation as the nemesis of the Soviet delegation in the United Nations session hall. A famous incident took place in 1950 when Romulo was engaged in a heated argument with Soviet Deputy Foreign Minister Vishinsky, the Soviet representative at the United Nations, regarding Soviet proposal to abolish the Balkan Commission, a body established by the United Nations to report what was happening to Greece and mainly what activities the Russians were carrying out in Greece to subvert the Greek government. Romulo spoke against the Soviet resolution and it angered Vishinsky. The latter attacked Romulo by saying: "Mr. President, that small man with the big voice who represents an insignificant little country like the Philippines has dared attack Soviet Russia's motives. He reminds me of the Russian proverb "His ambition is worth a ruble; but his ammunition is only worth a cent." To such insulting remarks, Romulo answered in a humorous way: "Mr. President, we have been regaled by the use of personal vitriolic of the distinguished deputy foreign minister of Soviet Russia. I am not interested in his personal allusions to me because we are here not as persons but as representatives of governments. That he should refer to my insignificant little country must be understood as his usual way of dealing with small countries in this Council with arrogance. So I will not answer that either, but would like to remind Mr. Vishinsky that we the little Davids are here to fling pebbles of truth between the eyes of blustering Goliaths and make them behave." Romulo ended his rebuttal with a punch line: "As to my ambition being worth a ruble when my ammunition is only worth a cent, may I remind Mr. Vishinsky that at the present rate of exchange the cent is worth more than the ruble." Romulo's speech got an ovation from the audition and was widely written about by the international press. *Le Monde*, the French newspaper, published a cartoon showing Vishinsky as Goliath and Romulo as the little

David with a slingshot and a pebble hitting Vishinsky between the eyes.[23]

Romulo did not only possess oratorical prowess but had a bantering sense of humor. At one UN debate at the height of the Cold War the United States was uncustomarily being bested by the Soviet Union at the Security Council when a leading member of the "Free World" ran into Romulo at the men's room. "Romy," the diplomat said, "you shouldn't be here. You should be at the plenary rebutting [Soviet foreign minister] Gromyko!"

"Well, at least," Romulo answered with signatory equanimity, "here we can hold our own."[24]

In 1960, the Philippine delegation again engaged in a memorable debate with the Soviet delegation. This time, Lorenzo Sumulong, a senator and vice chairman of the Philippine delegation, tangled in a heated exchange with Nikita Khrushchev, Chairman of the Soviet Council of Ministers, during the debate on the item "Declaration on the Granting of Independence to Colonial Countries and Peoples."[25] In his speech, Sumulong said:

> It is our view that the declaration proposed by the Soviet Union should cover the inalienable right to independence not only of the peoples and territories which yet remain under the rule of Western Colonial Powers, but also of the peoples of Eastern Europe and elsewhere which have been deprived of the free exercise of their civil and political rights which have been swallowed up, so to speak, by the Soviet Union.

At this point, the Romanian delegate raised a point of order and the chairman of the Conference, Ambassador Fred Bohlen from Ireland, requested Sumulong to step aside from the rostrum while he deals with the point of order. The Romanian delegate told the chairman "this is not the proper forum for slander against a member of the United Nations." However, the Chair ruled that the Philippine delegate was not out of order and called him back to continue his speech. Again, the Romanian delegate raised a point of order reiterating his argument not to slander a member of the organization. The chairman ruled once more that the Philippine delegate did not say anything that has the element of personal insult.

Amidst this dispute, Soviet delegate Khrushchev rose to intervene:

> Why is it that the stooge of American imperialism here is speaking before you and is touching on questions which are obviously not procedural ones, and the President, who sympathizing with these colonialists and colonial domination, obviously is not stopping him? Is this justice?

Tension on the session floor had shot up. Francis O. Wilcox, a member of the American delegation, recalled:

> It was at that point that the chairman of the meeting, the ambassador from Ireland, Fred Bohlen began to pound his gavel for order, because when Khrushchev began to pound his shoe there was a lot of noise in the Assembly hall. The noise increased and he kept pounding, and pretty soon the gavel broke. All over the country this was shown on television so that after the elapse of a week or so. Fred Bohlen began to receive gavels from all over the country. I think he must have received twenty-five or thirty gavels to replace the one that was broken.[26]

Sumulong asked for the floor and stated that he and his delegation had no desire to wound the feelings and sensibilities of any member-nation or delegation but there is a need to make one's position clear as to the meaning of the word "independence" before the conference could act or vote on the issue. He ended his speech by saying that his delegation will support the proposal that the item should be discussed in the plenary of the General Assembly. This remark ended the Sumulong-Khrushchev debate.

Carlos P. Romulo

Despite his small stature, Carlos Peña Romulo was a giant figure in Philippine diplomacy. His distinctions include being the last Resident Commissioner of the Philippines to the United States, the first Chief Delegate of the Philippines to the United Nations, first Asian president of the United Nations General Assembly, appointed twice as Philippine ambassador to Washington, D.C., and served twice as Secretary of Foreign Affairs—his first stint lasted only for a year and half (May 1950 to November 1951) but his second term lasted for fourteen years (1968–1983). His early career, however, showed few clues that he would become the most successful Filipino diplomat in the 20th century and the most internationally renowned Filipino statesman during his time.

Romulo was born in Manila on 14 January 1899, to Gregorio Romulo and Maria Peña. He had two brothers and three sisters: Enrique, Lourdes, Soledad, Josefina, and Gilberto. He spent his childhood years in Camiling, in the province of Tarlac in the main island of Luzon. As a small child he enjoyed stories on Philippine history and legend as told by his grandmother Juana Besacruz Romulo. In school, the young Romulo was especially interested in language and literature. His first grammar teacher was an American, Leo J. Grove, from Ovid, Michigan. Romulo dreamt of becoming one of the best Filipino writers along such famous ones like Guerrero, Bernabe, Recto, Balmori, and Apostol.[27]

At an early age, Romulo also became interested in politics, especially when his father ran for and won as municipal councilor. His father was eventually elected mayor, and finally provincial governor of Tarlac. With the election of his father to the governorship, the family moved to the provincial capital. The young Romulo spent his first two years of high school in Tarlac but on his third year, his family transferred to Manila. In his high school in Manila, Romulo demonstrated his oratorical skills. His piece, "My Faith in America," won in an oratorical contest. While studying at the University of the Philippines as an English major, Romulo became the editor of the college paper. He also joined in the dramatic club play. He was a protégé of Rafael Palma, then UP president; he became the star of the debating team that held its own on a tour of American universities. Just before his graduation from the state university, he was chosen to study at Columbia University in New York. He left the Philippines in July 1918 and stayed at 106 Street near the Columbia University campus. He earned his Master of Arts degree in 1921.

After Columbia, Romulo went back to Manila and worked as a part-time civil service clerk and a cub reporter of *Manila Times*. He subsequently became the assistant editor of the *Citizen*. His meteoric rise in the media world caught the attention of Senate President Manuel Quezon who appointed Romulo as personal secretary. Thus, Romulo juggled several jobs as assistant professor of English at the UP and at the same time as private secretary of Quezon and assistant editor to Benitez of the pro-Quezon *Herald*. At age 25, he became associate professor and head of the UP English Department. Romulo left the *Herald* and joined the *Tribune* as editor upon the invitation of Alejandro Roces. In 1930, Roces named Romulo editor-in-chief of the TVT newspaper chain: *Tribune* (published in English), *La Vanguardia* (in Spanish), and *Taliba* (in Tagalog). Romulo was also a member of the UP Board of Regents from 1931–1941. In 1933, Romulo was sent to Washington to report on the progress of Hare-Hawes-Cutting Act. Quezon invited Romulo to return to *Herald* and Romulo accepted the offer. Because of the demanding work in *Herald*, Romulo resigned as professor and member of the UP Board of Regents. In 1939, he became managing director of radio stations KZRM and KZRF.

At the start of the Japanese occupation of the Philippines, General MacArthur appointed Romulo major in the Philippine Army and assigned him in charge of the press and radio in the Press Relations headquarters. He served as aide-de-camp of MacArthur in Bataan, Corregidor, and Australia. Romulo fed the press with news and communiqués from the battlefront. When the American forces retreated to Australia, Romulo joined General MacArthur's entourage. There, Romulo received the news that he won the 1941 Pulitzer Prize for his brilliant reporting on the war. On 16 June 1942, Lieutenant Colonel Romulo left for America. In the United States, President Quezon and US Secretary of State Stimson said that Romulo was to be the "Philippine Voice of Freedom" in America.

Romulo wrote books about his war accounts that endeared him to the American government and public. In 1942, Romulo published *I Saw the Fall of the Philippines*. He followed this with *My Brother Americans* in 1945. At the Philippine Commonwealth government-in-exile in Washington, President Quezon appointed Romulo as Secretary of Information and Public Relations from 1943 to 1944. When Quezon died in August 1944, President Sergio Osmeña named Romulo as Resident Commissioner to the United States and concurrent Secretary of Public Instruction. As Philippine resident commissioner in the U.S., the Romulo initiated the Filipino Naturalization Act, which was passed by voice vote in the U.S. Senate and Congress.

The U.S. military gave Romulo the rank of brigadier general in September 1944. "General" is a title he cherished and actively used. In fact, the US State Department officials would always address him as "General" during his stint as Resident Commissioner in Washington and even when he was the Secretary of Foreign Affairs under President Marcos, he preferred to be called "General Romulo" rather than "Mr. Secretary of Foreign Affairs." Some officials in the Philippine Foreign Service would furtively call him as "Secretary-General" not as a combination of Secretary of Foreign Affairs and General but to the position of Secretary General of the United Nations, which Romulo most coveted but failed to achieve. He could have become Secretary-General of the United Nations, succeeding the late Trygve Lie, were it not for the unwritten requirement that the Secretary-General should come from a politically non-aligned country.[28]

Romulo joined Osmeña and General MacArthur during the famous Leyte landing on 20 October 1944. Their picture wading in knee-deep water ashore was immortalized in WW II history books (although it was later discovered to be a mere re-enactment). Much later bronze figures were erected on the water's edge to commemorate the historic event. After the liberation of Manila, Romulo went back to Washington to resume his duties as Resident Commissioner. He was also appointed as chief delegate of the Philippine delegation to the United Nations Conference on International Organization in San Francisco in April to June 1945. One of Romulo's last achievements as Resident Commissioner was the successful coordination of the Philippine Foreign Affairs Training Program in the US State Department and the detailing of a senior American foreign affairs adviser to the Philippine Government to assist in the creation of the Philippine Foreign Service.

After the Philippines obtained its independence, President Manuel Roxas appointed Romulo as chief delegate to the United Nations with the rank of ambassador. The Philippine press hailed his appointment. The *Morning Sun's* editorial on 11 July1946, lauded Romulo's designation:

As for Romulo's appointment to the United Nations Organization no happier choice could have been made. His diplomatic background is rich and wide; his knowledge of affairs is the first-hand knowledge of someone who has lived through the most crucial years of the world's history, and right in Washington where great decisions were made and the greatest of minds held sway. The Philippines is lucky in having had its own men at historic moments in America—men whose services can be availed of to our advantage. One of these men is Romulo, worthy representative of our people wherever he may go.[29]

While serving as chief Philippine delegate to the United Nations, Romulo became the first Asian president of the General Assembly in 1949. Upon Romulo's election, a ticker-tape parade was held in New York in his honor. Seated between US President Harry S. Truman and New York Mayor William O'Dwyer, he rode through a hail of confetti, acknowledging the cheers of the crowd. Someone shouted: "Hey there's Romulo!" Romulo turned to his companions and remarked: "See, they see me in spite of my size." President Truman then looked at Mayor O'Dwyer and said: "Bill, you're the mayor of the greatest city in the world, and I'm the president of the greatest country in the world, but the general here —he's president of the entire world."[30]

Romulo presided over the fourth Regular Session of the General Assembly from 20 September 1949 to 12 December 1949 at Flushing Meadows, New York. For a young republic like the Philippines, this session offered great opportunities for leadership. Through the enviable performance of Romulo and the Philippine delegation, the Philippines earned tremendous international prestige and firmly established its right to play an active role in the conduct of world affairs.[31]

Although the 4th General Assembly was expected to be a "Peace Assembly," twelve weeks of intensive deliberations failed to materialize the "road to permanent peace." Three major events marred the first weeks of the session; namely, President Truman's announcement that an atomic explosion had been detected in Russia; Yugoslavia's election to the Security Council against Russia's bitter opposition; and Nationalist China's formal charges that Russia's aid to the Chinese Communists constituted a threat to peace in the Far East. The Assembly, however, overcame the adverse effects of these three shocks.[32]

The Philippine pride in the international body was widely known as "Mr. United Nations". Romulo's success in the United Nations remains unmatched by any Filipino diplomat up to the present. No other diplomat from any newly independent nation strode the world stage like Romulo. He was the last signatory of the UN Charter to die and was universally admired in the international community. During the Cold War years, Romulo received honorary doctorates from American colleges and universities, including Harvard, and boasted that he had more degrees than a thermometer.[33] During his distinguished career, Romulo received more than seventy honorary degrees from all over the world.

Narciso G. Reyes, former Philippine Permanent Representative to the UN in New York, summarized Romulo's fantastic career in the United Nations: "He had obtained in the United Nations all the honors and distinctions which was possible for a Filipino to attain—a participant in the formulation of the Charter; Chairman of the most important functional Commission of the Economic and Social Council; Chairman of the Special Political Committee of the General Assembly; President of the UN Conference on the Freedom of Information; President of the Security Council and President of the General Assembly itself."[34]

Notwithstanding universal adulation for him, Romulo also had his share of critics.[35] Even some of his former subordinates would lampoon Romulo. Ambassador Jose Zaide, former Philippine envoy to Paris, who at one time worked closely with Romulo, wrote:

> Carlos P. Romulo was both easy and hard to work for—easy because he was always news; tough because if he did not find his name in the front page, he might look for it in the obituary. I saw him close up—like many outstanding men, he was vain in his place in history. He would probably have coveted to die in office, preferably at a UN plenary session in New York for the world's adulation equal to his life's work."[36]

Not yet contented with his diplomatic glory, Romulo tirelessly worked to achieve more distinctions during his twilight years. As Ambassador Narciso G. Reyes observed in the late 1970s:

> The General [Romulo] continued attending the entire session of the UN General Assembly for three months, the only Foreign Minister to do so. As I observed in my letter to Secretary Melchor, the General Assembly was an occasion for the General's big performance every year, when he made his earth-shaking policy statement and reminded everybody that he was the last living founding father of the United Nations. What for? For the General, there were literally no more worlds to conquer in the United Nations. Why not the Nobel Peace Prize? I noticed that the General had been concentrating on amending the Charter, an earth-shaking achievement if it could be attained. And even if it could not, to be known as the champion of amending a key provision of the Charter, to go down fighting for a lost, glorious cause – who knows? In a lean year it might attract the attention of the Nobel Peace Prize Committee, and it would cap the General's fantastic career.[37]

Creation of the State of Israel

Romulo also had his share of disappointments. Despite his performance in the United Nations, at times the central government in Manila embarrassed him by contradicting his stance on critical issues. The passage of the UN resolution on the partition of Palestine and the creation of the State of Israel was one of the most difficult issues handled by Romulo during his stint in the United Nations.

The Question of Palestine as it was widely known was a thorny and complex issue that gripped the nascent United Nations. The Second World War and the Holocaust uprooted and displaced thousands of European Jews and provided the supporters of Zionism to push for the establishment of a Jewish Commonwealth in Palestine which was then under the British Mandate. As a first step, a powerful American Jewish lobby pressured members of the U.S. Congress and President Truman to urged Prime Minister Winston Churchill and later Prime Minister Attlee to open Palestine to Jewish immigration.

Initially, Truman endorsed the proposal to allow 100,000 Jews to settle in Palestine. The move displeased the British and enraged the Arabs. King Ibn-Saud of Saudi Arabia strenuously protested what he considered a violation of President Roosevelt's promise that the United States would not take any decision with respect to Palestine without full consultations between Arabs and Jews. Great Britain and the United States agreed to create a joint Anglo-American Committee to examine the whole question. Truman was pleased that the two sides unanimously endorsed his request for the admission of one hundred thousand European Jews. The U.S. government sent technical experts to London to study the financing and supervision of transporting one hundred thousand Jewish immigrants to Palestine.

On 24 July 1946, the American panel to the Anglo-American Committee devised a scheme, otherwise known as the Morrison-Grady Plan advocating the setting up of a system of autonomy eventually leading to a bi-national state or, alternatively, partition. Despite prolong efforts to find a compromise, the Arabs and the Jews continued their disagreements. Out of frustration, the British government submitted the Palestine problem, without recommendation, to the United Nations General Assembly in February 1947, to be taken up in September that year. The American delegation to the UN supported partition and immigration and started to lobby other delegations to accept the American position.

It was against this backdrop that the Philippines had to grapple with a decision. With a sizable Muslim population in Mindanao, around one million at the time, domestic consideration dictated that the Philippine delegation must oppose partition in order not to antagonize the Arab states and by consequence provoke outrage among its own Muslim community in southern Philippines. President Roxas surmised that the Arabs would never accept partition and if carried out would engulf the Middle East into armed conflict. After mulling over the problem, Roxas and Romulo agreed to vote against partition.

Days before the vote, Romulo made an impassioned speech in the UN against partition. It was followed by a big uproar. The speech satisfied the Arabs but caught the ire of the Jews. Romulo eloquently delivered the Philippine position on the Question of Palestine, which is worth quoting at length below:

My delegation takes part in this final stage in the consideration of the Palestinian problem with profound misgivings. We have carefully studied the report of the Special Committee on Palestine and as a result, the Philippine government has come to the conclusion that it cannot give its support to any proposal for the political disunion and the territorial dismemberment of Palestine.

We hold that the issue is primarily moral. The issue is whether the United Nations should accept responsibility for the enforcement of a policy which, not being mandatory under any specific provision of the Charter nor in accordance with its fundamental principle is clearly repugnant to the valid nationalist aspirations of the people of Palestine. The Philippine government believes that the United Nations ought not to accept any such responsibility...

In taking this position, my government is not unmindful of the sufferings of the great Jewish people, whom we hold in sincere admiration. We shall not speak here of our sympathy for them; the record shows what we have done to prove it. During the first dispersal of the Jews from Nazi Germany, the Philippines was among the very few countries that opened its doors to Jewish refugees and extended to them a cordial welcome. We gave them a haven in our country, and today they live and work with us in complete harmony and understanding.

The Philippines regrets its inability to approve of or to participate in a solution of the Palestine problem that would involve the encouragement of political disunion and the enforcement of measures that would amount to the territorial mutilation of the Holy Land.[38]

As he was leaving the UN building an unruly crowd surrounded and jeered him. Some threatened Romulo with bodily harm. At that point, Prince Faisal, the head of the Saudi delegation, sent his bodyguards to protect Romulo and escorted him safely to his car. Before leaving for his trip to attend a conference in London, he left instructions to his deputy, Jose D. Ingles, that the Philippine delegation would vote against the UN Resolution on Partition. The next morning, while aboard the *Queen Mary*, Romulo was called to the radio room to take a call. At the other end of the line was Sol Bloom, chairman of the US House Foreign Affairs Committee and a good friend of President Roxas. Bloom vigorously protested Romulo's position.

Two days later, while on his way to Geneva aboard the *Queen Mary*, Romulo received a cable from President Roxas stating that he was reversing the Philippine position, in the national interest, and he hoped that Romulo would understand. Romulo immediately cabled his resignation. After having made the speech that they both had agreed on, Romulo felt he had lost the confidence of the Philippine president. Roxas sent a cable asking Romulo to withdraw his resignation. American pressure on Ambassador Elizalde in Washington forced the Philippines to reverse its stance. Romulo recalled:

> Actually, as I pieced it all together later, it was not the President who had reversed himself. It was our ambassador in Washington Mike Elizalde who had taken it upon himself to force our delegation to vote for partition. He had called my surrogate, Judge Ingles, the day after I sailed and told him the Philippines must vote with the United States and implied that he had authority from Roxas, which was not precisely true. When Ingles had tried to contact me, a storm at sea prevented his call getting through, and he had then tried to clear directly with the President. What the President had actually advised was that the Philippines, considering the pressure from the U.S. Congress, which Elizalde described, should abstain. But Elizalde felt we must go further and took it upon himself to insist on the vote. Congress was threatening to cut off further aid to the Philippines. And only a vote in support of partition would appease them.[39]

Ingles, Romulo's deputy, who cast the Philippine vote, wrote years later:

> As early as 1947, when the plan of partition for Palestine came up for discussion in the UN General Assembly, the Philippines initially declared her opposition to the plan.

However, the Philippines changed her position when it was made known to the Philippine Ambassador in Washington, D.C., that American economic assistance to the Philippines depended on Philippine support to the partition resolution. Tacit support of the Israeli position against the return of the Palestinian people to their ancestral homeland thenceforth became the Philippine policy at the United Nations, which took the form of neutrality in the Arab-Israeli dispute.[40]

It was a roll call vote, breathlessly followed by Jews in Tel Aviv and other places, especially when the crucial ballot approached. The Philippine vote would give those in favor of partition the required majority. At one point the Philippine vote would have been the deciding vote, with the Arab bloc opposing, and the Americans and their allies in favor. But by the time the Philippine vote was actually cast, Haiti had reversed itself, and it was no longer a tie. Liberia also changed its stance at the last minute.

In the end the United States got the partition of Palestine. Earlier Great Britain served notice that it would terminate its Palestine Mandate on 15 May 1948. A day before the end of the British Mandate, the State of Israel was unilaterally proclaimed. The United States was the first country to accord recognition to the new Jewish state. There was an explosion of joy all over Israel, and frustration in the Arab countries. As expected, hostilities broke out. The combined armies of Egypt, Iraq, Lebanon, Syria, and Jordan invaded Israel the following day. But Israel repelled the Arab assault and even enlarged its territory years later.

The initial Philippine opposition to the partition of Palestine would, however, serve it in good stead in November 1973. During the Yom Kippur War, the Arabs threatened to cut off oil supplies to countries that they perceived as anti-Arab and anti-Muslim. The Philippines was among these countries. President Marcos immediately dispatched Romulo, who was then attending the UNGA Session in New York, to proceed to Riyadh. When Faisal (now King) heard of Romulo's presence in Riyadh, he at once invited Romulo to the royal palace and the two reminisced on their New York days, especially on Romulo's speech against the partition of Palestine. King Faisal assured Romulo that the Philippines would be kept out of the boycott list.[41]

Champion of Independence

In 1947, another crucial issue where the Philippines actively participated in was the discussion on Indonesian Independence at the Security Council as an interested third party. Philippine application to participate was promptly opposed by the colonial powers such as Belgium and Great Britain while the Soviet Union and Poland abstained seeing the Philippines as "under the thumb" of the United States. But Romulo advanced three reasons for the request of participation, namely concern for international peace, humanitarian desire to prevent further bloodshed and geographical propinquity.

On point # 3, Romulo invoked a "specially affected" area clause within the meaning of Article 31 of the Charter which states that: "any member of the United Nations which is not a member of the Security Council may participate, without a vote, in the discussion of any question brought before the Security Council whenever the latter considers the interests of that member are specially affected.

Australia, Belgium, Brazil, China, Colombia, France, Poland, Syria, the Soviet Union, United Kingdom, and the United States were all members of the council, and only Australia and Colombia supported Philippine participation. Columbia requested that the motion be put to a vote but the Philippines lost (6-0-5). France, Belgium, Britain, Poland, and the Soviet Union abstained.[42]

Romulo, however, was unfazed by the voting results and petitioned the Security Council to reconsider his country's participation in a memorandum dated 14 August1947, where he basically reiterated the same views. This time the indifferent Western powers could not provide any argument against the Philippines and the Philippines was allowed to participate at last.

The United States, on the other hand, remained absolutely quiet during the debates on Philippine participation, although she voted for Philippine participation but without much enthusiasm. The U.S. did not want to antagonize the Netherlands and other colonial powers that supported the Dutch return to Indonesia. The Americans were building a military alliance to counter the Soviet bloc and the European colonial powers were key allies in America's global ideological and military strategies. Romulo and other Philippine officials were of course frustrated by the U.S. attitude toward Indonesia. At any rate, the Indonesian issue afforded the Philippines with the opportunity to assert its independent foreign policy. The Philippines would therefore clash against the United States and its allies on independence issues, thereby throwing the Philippines and the Soviet Union into an informal partnership.[43]

The Philippines recognized Indonesia as a republic on 15 August 1947. Many countries recognized Indonesia's *de jure* sovereignty. After the The Hague Conference in December 1949, Indonesia and the Netherlands reached an agreement on the independence of Indonesia. The Philippines formally accorded *de jure* recognition to the new state on 27 December 1949.

Philippine Contribution to the United Nations

In general, the Philippine delegations to the UN and its affiliated agencies voted with the West and the United States on most major issues. This stance was not because of any sense of slavish obligation to the United States but purely on the basis of Philippine self-interest. Despite charges of excessive American leaning, the Philippines actually initiated and pursued a number of independent policies in the United Nations. The country not only voted independently, but sometimes against the United States on critical issues.

For example, the Philippines opposed various American policies on Japan, such as reparations, the revival of Japanese industry, the extension of Japanese fishing rights, the membership of Japan in international organizations; the Philippines refused to go along the recognition of the French-sponsored regime in Vietnam; the Philippines was out in front of the United States in its support of Indonesian independence struggle; and it has parted ways with the United States on various issues involving racial discrimination and segregation and the administration of trust and non-self-governing territories.[44]

At a time when the United States government was ready to disown China's Nationalist government, the Philippines publicly showed its support to that government and was actually prepared to bar Chinese Communist representation in the UN.

The Philippines also campaigned strongly to support Spain's membership in the UN, which had denied Spain's participation in the world body. Because of centuries old historical and cultural ties, the Philippines' support to the integration of Spain in the international community was obvious. At the Potsdam Conference in 1945, the Governments of the United Kingdom, the United States of America and the Soviet Union stated that they would not support a request for admission to the United Nations of the present Spanish Government "which having been founded with the support of the Axis Powers, in view of its origins, its nature, its record and its close association with the aggressor States, does not possess the necessary qualifications to justify its admission.[45]

Some of the specific contributions made by the Philippines in the UN may be summarized as follows: In the Trusteeship Council and the Special Committee on Non-Self Governing Territories, the Philippines consistently espoused the cause of dependent peoples everywhere. In the Commission on Human Rights, the Philippines contributed effectively to the drafting of the Universal Declaration of Human Rights and the implementing Covenant. As a member of the Economic Commission for Asia and the Far East, it helped to evolve a pattern of regional economic reconstruction and development designed to raise the living standards in the underdeveloped areas. In the Security Council, the Philippines undertook to support the Indonesian independence cause. In the General Assembly the Philippines spoke on many issues and in particular fought all vestiges of racial discrimination and violations of human rights. The Philippines sponsored in large part the United Nations program for the establishment of broad guarantees of freedom of information, including appropriate international conventions. For that purpose, General Romulo served as President of the UN Conference on Freedom of Information held in Geneva in 1948. The Philippines staunchly supported the independence of Korea and the defense of the territorial and political integrity of Greece. In addition to these activities, the Philippines participated in most of the specialized agencies of the United Nations, including UNESCO, the World Health Organization, the Food and Agricultural Organization, the World Bank, the International Monetary Fund, the International Civil Aviation Organization, the ILO, and the Universal Postal Union.[46]

Foremost among Philippine contribution to the United Nations was its support for Korean independence and its military participation, with other UN forces, in the defense of that state. The Philippines placed much confidence and reliance in the usefulness of the United Nations. The aforementioned record indicates that it supported the United Nations more than any other Asian nation.[47] Lastly, the Philippines was an active member in the Commission on Palestine and Commission on the Partition of Jerusalem. Simeon Roxas, a State Department graduate, served as technical staff to Senator Vicente Francisco, head of the Philippine delegation to the Palestine Commission.

Aside from its active participation in the United Nations, the Philippines took a pro-active role in fostering regional cooperation in the Asia-Pacific region. As one of the first countries in Asia to attain independence, the Philippines assumed the responsibility of promoting the principle of self-determination for Asian peoples and the right to self-government or independence but nevertheless recognized that such responsibility must be shared with other like-minded states to make it bearable. The first therefore to achieve this goal was to foster alliances and regional partnership that would build a firm and strong framework to promote peace and cooperation. Hence, the Philippines became a founding member of the Southeast Asia Treaty Organization (SEATO) in September 1954 and participated in the Asian-African Conference at Bandung, Indonesia on 18-25 April 1955. The Bandung Conference marked the beginning of the so-called Non-Aligned Movement (NAM), a group that disassociates itself from the rivalry between the West and East camp.

Despite its active multilateral engagements, the Philippines expanded its diplomatic missions to other continents and regions to help advance its bilateral ties and national interests. Only in establishing its presence in key capitals of the world could the Philippines accomplish this goal.

6

Reaching Out to a Larger World

In the wake of independence, the Philippine embassy in Washington, D.C. and the Philippine mission to the United Nations in New York became the epicenters of Philippine diplomacy. The Philippine Foreign Service, however, gradually expanded to selected countries and regions of the world based on national interests and the availability of human and material resources. The size and reach of the Foreign Service depended to a large extent on complex processes influenced by domestic factors, among them political considerations, budgetary constraints, and international political and economic developments.

After Manuel A. Roxas' victory in the presidential election of May 1946, Tiburcio C. Baja, then undergoing training at the American embassy in Mexico City, wrote the new Philippine president a letter congratulating him for his victory and offered him advice on the practice of Philippine foreign relations. President Roxas did not acknowledge the letter, but Baja's advice on the conduct of Philippine foreign relations accurately anticipated the future Philippine approach to expanding its international presence. Baja wrote:

> As you assume the leadership of our government, I wish to join the rest in calling attention to the vast problem of our international relations. I maintain the position that in the

decade or score immediately ahead our great hope lies with the United States of America. It is my considered conviction that we cannot over-emphasize this relationship and yet it can be underestimated. I join others in submitting that it be given the large attention that is its due.

With the rest of the world, I trust it would be a relationship of goodwill and friendship. Since coming here, I have realized potentialities in commercial and cultural ties with this country. In that respect, I see the whole Western Hemisphere a beacon to the Philippines. The twenty-one American republics are our sister republics, with language and culture much akin to ours. We will do well to cultivate their goodwill.

At the present time Europe lies in ruins, and Africa is still remote to us. Great Britain and France look to the Unites States for aid, while Russia remains the only threat to world security, if she chooses so to do. Japan and Germany will not be in our way, at least for some time. China appears ambitious for being considered one of the "big five", but much handicapped by internal strife. The European dependencies on the Asiatic mainland and the Southwest Pacific look to us for inspiration, and the United Nations Organization to which we are a signatory is in full swing.

Indeed, the Philippines, despite her full share of war damage, remains a beacon star because of her increased relations with the United States and her unusual position among the young and would-be independent nations."[1]

Baja's reference to the importance of bilateral relations with the United States was obvious to Philippine foreign policy makers since the Philippines wisely took advantage of American guardianship before opening up Foreign Service posts. Led by President Roxas, the Filipino leaders believed that the Philippines should proceed with caution in the establishment of diplomatic and consular presence abroad. Thus, they arranged for the U.S. State Department and its diplomatic and consular offices abroad to represent the Philippines before the Philippines established posts in those locations.

On 01 June 1946, President Roxas formally commissioned the

State Department, through the U.S. Foreign Service, to temporarily represent Philippine interests "in various areas in which we have particular Philippine interests." At any rate the United States smoothly integrated the Philippines into the family of nations.

Acting Secretary of State Dean Acheson expressed the United States' commitment and instructed the American high commissioner in Manila "to acquaint the Philippine authorities with services the U.S. government can perform and to obtain specific designation those countries in which U.S. representation Philippine interests desired." Acheson also instructed the high commissioner "to obtain directives from Philippine authorities regarding services to be performed for Philippine nationals within the scope of the State Department's handling, particularly regarding financial assistance and repatriation of Philippines." He clarified that "discussion should include provision for the Philippine to deposit a lump sum ($25,000 suggested fiscal year 1947) from which the Department may defray expenses for this representation. If the Filipinos are unable to make a deposit, the Department will explore the possibility advancing funds or arranging loan for this purpose, with the understanding that the expenses would be subject to reimbursement."[2]

Right after the Philippine independence ceremony, the Philippines and the United States signed a Treaty of General Relations, which outlines their bilateral relations. Upon Philippine request and at mutual convenience, the United States Foreign Service represented Philippine interests abroad where no Philippine representation existed. Two of its four articles reiterate United States recognition of Philippine independence and mutual diplomatic privileges and immunities. The United States was also to notify governments with which it had diplomatic relations of Philippine independence and invite them to recognize the republic. Further, the two parties were to enter into negotiations, as soon as feasible, on a treaty of friendship, commerce and navigation; an executive agreement relating to trade; a general relations treaty; consular convention; and other treaties and agreements deemed mutually necessary.[3]

On 18 July, acting Secretary Acheson instructed all American diplomatic representatives abroad to request from their host governments, recognition of the new Republic of the Philippines. On 14 October, the Philippine embassy in Washington informed the State

Department that it would deposit $25,000 into the State Department account so that American consular officers could extend welfare services to Filipino citizens abroad. Two weeks later, the Philippine embassy provided the State Department with clear and strident guidelines about the use of the funds. The guidelines required that the beneficiaries refund the Philippine government whatever amount is advanced to him; beneficiaries would be thoroughly investigated and repatriation considered a last resort; the Philippine government would await the recommendation of the American consular official concerned before taking action; and only necessary expenditures and third class accommodations were allowed.[4]

Under the above arrangements, U.S. consular officers were instructed to provide the following services: repatriation and financial assistance to destitute Filipinos abroad; extension of the usual notarial and consular services to Philippine vessels and seamen; administration of the estates of deceased Filipinos abroad; issuance of Philippine passports and visas to aliens proceeding to the Philippines; and certification of invoices and allied services.

Opening of Foreign Service Posts

Vice President and Secretary of Foreign Affairs Elpidio Quirino expanded the Philippine Foreign Service slowly and modestly because of budgetary constraints and the difficulty of finding available and trustworthy candidates for diplomatic posts. He believed the Roxas Administration should deem future officers essential to domestic politics.[5] But, the government's priority was to engage all talented individuals in the rehabilitation and reconstruction of the post war country.

The press, however, was abuzz with rumors about future foreign assignments of heads of posts. Names of cabinet secretaries, prominent politicians and occasionally big businessmen, surfaced as possible candidates. The general public was excited and interested as the Foreign Service slowly grew. Nevertheless, many potential candidates were wary of assignments outside of Washington and the United Nations and, in certain instances, even cabinet members and leading politicians politely refused.

Quirino initially envisaged legations in Washington, Nanking, London, Paris, The Hague, Bangkok, Canberra, Bern, and Madrid.

Bern caught a lot of people by surprise; at the Philippine independence ceremony the Swiss representative had expressed a polite hope for diplomatic relations, so the city was included. The Swiss consul later said that his government was in no hurry.[6] London and Nanking were priorities due to their governments' early request for accreditation of their ministers. The short-list of legations prepared in September 1947, reflected the priorities of Philippine foreign relations. This list included London, Nanking, Paris, Rome, Madrid, and Bangkok as well as consulates in Los Angeles, Seattle, Chicago, New Orleans, Portland, Sydney and Shanghai. From the outset, it was clear that only officers who had completed the U.S. State Department training course would fill the consulates. For the year ending on 30 June 1948, the amount of 732,320 pesos was allocated to fund operations in the above-mentioned posts.[7]

Many states recognized the Philippines diplomatically, except the Soviet Union and its satellites. In the summer of 1950 some thirty countries maintained diplomatic and/or consular officials in Manila including the United States, Great Britain, France, Nationalist China, Argentina, Australia, Belgium, Canada, Indonesia, India, Italy, the Netherlands, Thailand, and Spain. The Philippines had a mission to the United Nations and to SCAP (Supreme Command of the Allied Powers) in Japan, an embassy and several consulates in the United States, and legations or consulates in Formosa, Great Britain, Italy, Thailand, Argentina, Indonesia, Australia, Spain, India, Pakistan, and Hong Kong.[8]

The Philippines concluded treaties of friendship with Thailand, Turkey, and China and also a one-year air transport agreement with the latter. It signed similar treaties with France, Italy, Spain, and Greece and concluded an agreement with Great Britain allowing the Philippines to take over the administration of Turtle and Mangse islands beginning 06 September 1946.[9]

At this point, Philippine posts were categorized into embassy, legation, mission, consulate general and consulate. They differ based on the importance of the host State and the rank of the officers assigned to them; an embassy is headed by an ambassador, a legation by a minister, and a mission–as in the case of Japan–by an envoy. The distinction between a consulate general and a consulate is that the former is superior in rank. The legations and missions were all later elevated to embassies when the Philippines expanded relations with the host countries.[10] In January 1951, the legations in Madrid and Jakarta became embassies and in October 1954, the London legation followed; in 1956 the mission to Tokyo was elevated to embassy after the conclusion of the Philippines-Japan War Reparation Talks; in January 1953, the Philippine Consulate General in Calcutta was raised to legation and the following year, the Philippine Consulate in Karachi was also elevated. By the 1960's, "legation" and "mission" (except the missions to the United Nations) were no longer used; all existing legations were elevated to embassies.

Political and security developments in East Asia likewise transformed Manila into an essential diplomatic posting. The Philippines was the only stable country in the Orient and Manila developed into an important listening post; communists were expanding in China, Japan was occupied by Allied forces, Korea was unsteady, Indonesia was emerging as a new republic, and Indochina was at war. Correspondents and world travelers remarked that Manila had the glamour of Lisbon during the Second World War. Some even speak of "undercover agents" there trying to create psychological ground for the red advance. The situation in China caused the American embassy in Manila to enlarge its staff. By August 1949, there were twenty-six American diplomats stationed in Manila. Ambassador Myron Cowen, newly accredited U.S. envoy, was the dean of the diplomatic corps because he represented the oldest ambassadorship in the Philippines.[11]

As of July 1948, the Philippines maintained 18 posts, half of them in the United States—the embassy in Washington, D.C., consulates general in New York, San Francisco, and Honolulu, and consulates in Los Angeles, Seattle, Chicago, New Orleans and Portland. There were two posts in China—the legation in Nanking and the consulate general in Shanghai. In Europe, the Philippines had legations in Madrid, London and Rome. And, it had a mission to the United Nations in New York. Only five countries—United States, China, Spain, United Kingdom and Italy—had Philippine permanent diplomatic and consular representation.[12]

Even with financial limitations, the Philippines succeeded in establishing its own "listening posts" in various Asian and European capitals. With only 23 diplomatic and consular posts by 1949, it grew to 37 by 1953. This notable expansion was in keeping with the policy of "fortifying Philippine ties with its neighbors" in Asia as well as in Europe.[13]

Nationalist China

After the United States, the Philippines officially established relations with China, albeit on a consular level. Two weeks after independence, the Philippine government announced its interest in exchanging envoys with China before any other country. Believing China was very important, President Roxas and Vice President Quirino were understandably selective in making the appointment. They sought a reliable, common sense man of more than ordinary vision and patience for the Legation in Nanking. In fact, Roxas informally approached former President Osmeña with an offer to be the first Philippine minister to China.[14] Osmeña however, rebuffed the offer since he had already announced his retirement from government service after his failed bid for the presidency against Roxas.

The Manila newspapers, on the other hand, were floating the name of Undersecretary of Foreign Affairs Bernabe Africa as the most likely appointee as minister to Nanking, although he was also being considered for a ministership to Siam. The American embassy in Manila remarked,

> We know that Dr. Africa is not anxious to assume that post for financial reasons as well as for fear that the results of any mission to Nanking at the present time would not enhance the reputation of the minister as a skilled negotiator. Dr. Africa is an honest, well-meaning gentleman with high ideals, formerly professor at the University of the Philippines, and is slow-witted and methodical, very conscientious and hardworking, but he does not have a brilliant mind and apparently is aware of his shortcoming.[15]

After canvassing the field, Roxas and Quirino came to the conclusion that Senator Proceso Sebastian, a member of the Liberal Party and the Senate Foreign Relations Committee, was most qualified.

In early talks, Sebastian was not keen on going to Nanking; he had set his sights on Paris. Quirino, proposed another option; Siam had expressed interest in establishing formal diplomatic relations so Sebastian, could alternatively, establish a Legation in Bangkok.[16] Eventually, Sebastian accepted the Nanking assignment. On 19 April 1948, he presented his credentials to President Chiang Kai-shek. After the ceremony, he raced back to Manila to attend President Roxas' funeral. Roxas had died of a heart attack four days earlier. Neither Minister Sebastian's presentation speech nor the President Chiang reply was published in the press. After six months, Quirino considered elevating the Legation in Nanking to the status of embassy. But, with an annual budget of 4,000 pesos, he would still need congressional approval.[17]

Although selecting a minister to Nanking proved complicated and time-consuming, the government wasted no time establishing a consulate in Amoy to take care of vital interests since the majority of the Chinese immigrants in the Philippines hailed from Fujian province. The government had initially proposed Leopoldo T. Ruiz, a graduate of the State Department training program, as consul to Amoy. In November 1946, China granted an *exequatur* to Ruiz, but he would not leave Washington, D.C., where he was a second secretary in the Philippine embassy. Thus, Quirino hastily assigned Delfin R. Garcia, another State Department trainee and Ruiz's batch mate, as vice consul to Amoy in late 1946 to establish the first Philippine consulate in China. Garcia was then a special assistant to Richard P. Butrick, in Manila.[18]

Due to the number of visa applications from Amoy and neighboring Chinese provinces and the need to oversee immigrants from those regions, the government placed a representative in the mezzanine of the American consulate in the late 1930s, before establishing their own.[19] After more than a year in Amoy, Delfin Garcia was transferred to Shanghai. In March 1948, on the Bund, Garcia and an administrative officer set up a temporary Consulate at the Palace Hotel, one of the most famous and oldest buildings. The Consulate was officially set up on 05 April 1948. In 1949, Garcia would serve as liaison officer, second secretary and consul, to the Nationalist government at Canton. When the seat of the Nationalist government moved to Taiwan in 1950, Garcia became the chargé d'affaires *ad interim* at the Philippine legation in Taipei before Envoy Extraordinary and Minister Plenipotentiary Manuel Adeva arrived. Adeva, like Garcia, was a top State Department graduate. Adeva earlier served in the legation in Nanking as first secretary and consul general.

In Shanghai, Garcia served under Consul General Mariano Ezpeleta who was formerly legislative secretary to President Roxas. A brilliant lawyer, Ezpeleta had strong connections within the Roxas administration. The president was keen on the idea of sending Ezpeleta to Shanghai to protect him from political intrigues in an upcoming election.[20] He and the Philippine minister to Nanking Proceso Sebastian, who had recently returned to Manila for President Roxas' funeral, arrived in Shanghai in May 1948 aboard the steamer S/S *President Cleveland*. Hundreds of Filipino residents welcomed them at the wharf, waving "Mabuhay" (welcome and long live) placards and throwing garlands of flowers. Cheers were heard even before they reached the dock and four barges full of Filipinos circled the steamer in a surprising display of boisterous and festive reception.[21] Pelayo Llamas, another State Department graduate, joined the consulate in Shanghai. He was transferred to Nanking in 1949 where he served as chargé d'affaires.

Meanwhile in Amoy, Eutiquio O. Sta. Romana, another State Department graduate, succeeded Garcia in April 1948. Sta. Romana had the chance to visit the American Consulate in Amoy that the International Refugee Organization of the UNRRA managed. "Its walls, rooms, and environment remind me of my pleasant sojourn in Washington, D.C.," Sta. Romana recalled, "It refreshes my memories of yesteryears in 1946 when I used to grace the Department of State. This American Consulate is of the colonial type—truly American. I met here the American Consul in Shanghai, Mr. Sabin Chase, and a representative from the Foreign Buildings Operation Office of the State Department then on inspection of this Consulate building."[22] When the State Department vacated the property, the Philippine government signed a contract with the US government to rent the property for the Philippine consulate in Amoy. Sta. Romana moved to the new consulate in September 1948, which he rated as "the best among the Foreign Service establishment of the Philippines, excluding, of course, the Washington embassy."[23]

Fellow State Department graduate, Vicente I. Singian joined Sta. Romana. Toward the end of 1948, the Philippine government considered sending a military attaché to Nanking and, as the civil war worsened, they needed a competent military officer to assess the situation. They selected Major Nulogio Balao, head of the Philippine Ground Forces and a recent graduate from Fort Leavenworth in the United States. The government also considered the deployment of an officer and an enlisted man to the consulates in Amoy, Hong Kong, and Shanghai to dress as civilians and act ostensibly as visa experts. In reality, they would engage in counterintelligence work.[24]

As the war between Nationalists, led by Chiang Kai-shek, and Communists, headed by Mao Zedong, raged, the Philippine diplomatic mission followed the Nationalist government to Canton and in 1949 to Taiwan, then called Formosa. The Philippines continued to recognize Chiang Kai-shek's government as legitimate despite the recognition of India, Burma, and Indonesia of the communist government. For the Philippines, Formosa is of greatest strategic significance; about two hundred miles to the north of Luzon, the islands in the hands of an unfriendly power could constitute a direct threat to Philippine security. Philippine foreign policy makers stressed this. Chiang had made no secret of his intention engaging the Philippines in an active defense partnership. In June 1949, Generalissimo Chiang travelled to the Philippines to discuss a Pacific Pact with President Quirino.[25]

But, when the communists won, the consulate closed in October 1949.Since the Philippines did not recognize the Communist government in mainland China, all consular offices, except for the consulate general in the British territory of Hong Kong, were closed. This consulate was established in March 1947, by then Vice Consul Emilio D. Bejasa, a former State Department trainee. Originally Bejasa had planned to undergo practical training at the American Consulate for a couple of months, however, after his training Bejasa was not allowed to return to Manila. He was instead appointed acting consul tasked to open the Philippine Consulate. But holding office in the American consulate gave many people the impression that the Philippine Consulate operated out of the American Consulate in the Hong Kong and Shanghai building. Finally, on 01 August

1947, Bejasa inaugurated the Philippine office at the Filipino Club House in King's Park, Kowloon. Three months later the consulate transferred to the Marina House at Queen's Road. In 1958 it was elevated to a consulate general with Eduardo Rosal, another State Department graduate, as consul general.

Allied-occupied Japan

The establishment of diplomatic relations between the Philippines and Japan was a thorny issue due to the Japanese occupation of and atrocities in the Philippines during the Pacific War. After Japan's unconditional surrender on 07 August 1945, the Philippines became one of the first eleven members of the Far Eastern Commission (FEC), the highest policy-making for occupied Japan. The FEC was formed on 27 December 1945 during the Moscow conference of foreign ministers of Britain, China, Soviet Union and the United States. Its chief objective was to set policies for the administration of occupied Japan until achieving the terms of surrender. The United States directed and dominated the policies and actions on Japan. FEC's headquarters was located in Washington, D.C.

Philippine ambassador to the United Nations Carlos P. Romulo was the country's chief representative to FEC and Manuel Adeva, a State Department graduate, served as technical adviser. The Philippine delegation's goals were to obtain Japanese reparations and keep Japan militarily weak. The atrocities committed by the Japanese armed forces made the Philippines fear a resurgence of a strong militaristic Japan once again threatening its security. In April 1946, the reparations survey mission (created by President Truman and headed by presidential adviser Edwin W. Pauley), recommended the removal of Japan's industrial facilities for security reasons. As reparations, Pauley suggested distributing the industries to countries that Japan had occupied and destroyed. The commission, through the initiative of the United States, adopted Pauley's recommendations and arranged a program. Elated by this decision, Romulo submitted a list of twenty-two kinds of industrial plants and amenities that the Philippines wished to claim as reparations. However, the Soviet's veto kept the program from approval in the FEC's final deliberation.

The United States continued to initiate reparation programs

but the FEC disapproved them. In 1949, the American delegate announced that the United States would end its reparations initiatives, citing FEC's inability to arrive at a decision for their implementation.[26] This made the Philippines antagonistic toward U.S. policies on Japan, particularly about reparations.

Post-war bilateral trade between the Philippine and Japanese governments had been discontinued. On behalf of Japan, General MacArthur as Supreme Commander for the Allied Powers (SCAP) tried to resume post-war trade relations with the Philippines. America was concerned about Japan's economic recovery and the tide of communism in East Asia. Notwithstanding the lack of a commercial agreement, bilateral trade was rising in favor of the Philippines from 1947 to 1949. By the first quarter of 1949, the Philippines exported 43.5 million pesos worth of goods to Japan and imported 9.8 million pesos worth of goods leaving a balance of 36.6 million pesos in favor of the Philippines.[27] The Philippines also sent four economic missions to Japan, the first one headed by Undersecretary of Foreign Affairs Bernabe Africa.

Vice President Quirino and Africa decided that it was in the national interest to promote commercial relations with Japan until bilateral relations could be normalized. On 27 September 1948, Quirino appointed Africa as chief of mission to Japan with a rank of Minister Plenipotentiary and Envoy Extraordinary. Since Japan was still under SCAP, the Philippine embassy in Washington suggested Africa as a representative to SCAP. The State Department favorably endorsed Africa's nomination.[28]

On 10 October SCAP approved the establishment of the mission and accepted Chief of Mission Africa, with a rank of Minister, to SCAP. They also granted clearance to Africa's daughter Paz, Private Secretary Remedios Orlanes, Second Secretary Jose Espino, and Third Secretary Enrique Garcia.

On 22 October Africa, who was averse to flying, departed aboard the ship S/S *Kjibadak* for Hong Kong. He visited the Philippine consulates in Hong Kong and Amoy before proceeding to Kobe aboard *S/S Shirala*. Two days earlier, Enrique Garcia, acted as advance man, departed Manila via Northwest Airlines and arrived in Tokyo on 20 October. The mission was officially established in Tokyo on 07 November 1948. The embassy in Washington informed the State

Department that on 15 November1948, the mission in Tokyo would assume the representation of Philippine interests throughout Japan.[29]

Africa wanted the mission in Tokyo as both living and office quarters. His predecessor Ambassador Jorge Vargas purchased the property for the Philippine government during the Japanese occupation and the Philippines wanted it back. The building was then being used as a billet by fifteen Philippine Reparations and Restitution Delegation personnel, two dependents, and seven government personnel expected to arrive. At the behest of the U.S. political adviser for Japan, the State Department notified the Philippine government that allowing Africa to use the former embassy as a residence and office would require providing and reconditioning possible alternative facilities for government personnel. In the meantime, the American embassy recommended that Africa and his daughter stay at the Imperial Hotel and Orlanes, Espino, and Garcia stay in another U.S. army billet.[30] The embassy's title was eventually given to the Philippines. Africa and his family moved into the former embassy, while mission personnel were accommodated in a procured building, the Koremaga House.

The U.S. political adviser for Japan reported to the State Department that the Philippine Mission was established on 07 November 1948, the consular section, however, was opened to the public on15 November. American officials turned over all pertinent Philippine consular files to the mission. The Philippine Reparations and Restitution Delegation, located at the Hattori building in Tokyo, was integrated into the mission adding mission status to their previous status as a Reparation and Restitution Delegation.[31] By December 1948, the Philippine Mission in Japan consisted of the following:

Bernabe Africa, Minister and Chief of Mission
Bernardo P. Abrera, Chief, Reparations and Restitution Section
Jose Ma. Espino, Second Secretary and Consul
Enrique M. Garcia, Third Secretary and Vice Consul
Estanislao P. Angeles, Assistant, Reparations and Restitution Section
Isidro A. Soriente, Assistant, Reparations and Restitution Section

Major Constancio R. Velasco, Assistant, Reparations and Restitution Section
Remedios S. Orlanes, private secretary to the Chief of Mission

Marcelino V. Bernardo, a State Department graduate, was also assigned to the mission as commercial counselor. Bernardo, an economist by training, was the foremost Philippine expert on Japanese reparations and restitution. The American embassy in Manila reported to the State Department that Tiburcio C. Baja, then Philippine Consul in Hong Kong, might become first secretary in the Philippine mission to Japan. "Change would be probably best for American interest as Baja, who is a graduate of the State Department's Philippine Foreign Affairs Training Program, particularly pro-American," the American embassy said. In the end, Baja was instead posted to the consulate in Sydney.

Through Africa's work, economic relations between the Philippines and Japan were restored. Timber, iron, ore and other raw materials were exported to Japan while the Philippines imported mainly consumer goods and construction materials. In 1950, a barter trade agreement was reached, developing a new phase of relations for both countries. The peace treaty formally ending the Pacific War was signed in San Francisco in 1951, slowly restoring normal diplomatic relations. With the end of the occupation of Japan in 1952, the Philippines and Japan began establishing semi-diplomatic missions with the condition that no Japanese who had served in wartime military and civilian offices could become mission staff.[32]

In the last year of the Quirino administration, aide memoires passed between foreign offices, but attitudes stiffened. Yet slow progress was made along other lines. In February 1953, and after Jose Imperial, head of the mission in Tokyo, met with the Japanese Emperor and Empress, Quirino met with the Japanese chief of mission in Manila. The Japanese envoy arrived in Manila on 29 October 1952 to promote commercial and cultural relations. On 04 July 1953, Quirino pardoned 58 Japanese war prisoners and commuted to life imprisonment the death sentences of 56 others. Two days later, he turned over 114 Japanese war prisoners to Japanese custody.[33] Despite this friendly gesture, the Philippines harbored bitterness; Quirino had lost his wife and other close family members during the war; reparation remained unresolved. The reparation claims are contained in the *"Basic Post Surrender Policy for Japan,"* approved by FEC on19 June 1947. A United States interim directive to General MacArthur's Tokyo headquarters authorized SCAP to make available to China, the Netherlands, the Philippines, and the United Kingdom, thirty percent of the overall reparations pool in Japan using advance transfers. The Philippines was allotted a five percent share in this allocation or one-sixth of the pool. It received out of the advance reparations from army and navy arsenals 24 million pesos worth of machine tools, laboratory apparatus, and equipment such as motors and generators.[34]

Two years after, the United States government rescinded its ad interim directive of 04 April 1947, ending the advance transfers program. It also withdrew its proposals on the Japanese reparations shares. This unilateral action dismayed Romulo and his delegation. But even before the disagreement became public, Romulo's hard-line position on Japan was already well known in the State Department. In an internal memo at the Division of Philippines Affairs, between Division Chief Richard Ely and Assistant Chief Mill, noted Romulo's position. "Please note the attached AP dispatch from Spencer Davis in Manila dated17 February 1948," Ely advised Mill. Davis reported that:

> You will observe that Romulo takes a particularly vigorous stand against liberalizing our policy towards Japan. An example is his remark: "If anybody willing to trade tested friendship for uncertain friendship of traitorous nation, lest he forget, eighteen million Filipinos have behind them other Orientals whose wounds are still fresh from Japanese aggression. We stand shoulder-to-shoulder, back-to-back in our demands that Japan be kept militarily and economically impotent.[35]

Philippine opposition to the policy shift grew stronger. On 21 August 1951, Romulo, now secretary of Foreign Affairs, declared, "the payment of these reparations by the Japanese has become in some respects almost sacred (or fetish) of the Filipinos… it is perhaps true to say that no other objective of our foreign policy has been pursued with greater consistency and persistence than our claims for reparation from Japan."[36]

The reparation question surfaced at the Japanese Peace Treaty Conference in San Francisco in September 1951. Before the conference and to ensure their receipt of reparations, Philippine negotiators amended the first American draft, which threatened to waive the Allied Powers' reparations claim. As a result, Article 14 of the treaty made available Japanese services, production, salvaging, and other work. In the end, the Philippine delegation signed the treaty but, Romulo said, "with the greatest possible reluctance." Memoirs of Japanese terror during the war, a fear of a resurgent Japan, and an estimate of insufficient reparations were the cause for hesitation. But, at the same time, Soviet communism was growing in Asia and Japan, if rebuilt, could help hinder its spread.[37] On 15 July 1956, the Philippine Senate finally approved the reparations agreement and the treaty.

In 1953, Jose Imperial replaced Africa as chief of mission in Tokyo. Counselor Tomas G. de Castro joined the mission as Imperial's deputy. Both Imperial and de Castro were State Department graduates. The mission had four sections: the Political and Legal Section, the Military Affairs Section, the Consular Section, and the General Affairs Section. The budget was 136,980,000 pesos. In addition to the Foreign Service personnel, a unit in the military section focused on the administration of the Philippine contingent fighting in Korea.[38]

Considering the need to expand consular services in the Kansai region in southwest Japan, the mission also urged the opening of a consulate in Kobe, where sixty percent of the consular documents submitted for certification came from.[39] On 28 August 1958, the consulate in Kobe was inaugurated with Pelayo Llamas, a State Department graduate, as consul. Thus, the leadership of the Philippine diplomatic and consular missions in Japan was in the hands of State Department graduates.

Legation in London

Since the 18th century, Great Britain has had a strong interest, particularly a business interest, in the Philippines. It was no surprise that she immediately recognized Philippine independence and became the second nation, after China, to establish a legation in Manila on 30 October 1946. The gesture was warmly received and hastened the establishment of a London legation; a *chargé d'affaires* was assigned for the time being. Quirino initially favored Narciso Ramos, then minister-counselor of the embassy in Washington, for the position.

In January 1947, the DFA began scouting for a possible head of post. Quirino strongly backed Salvador Araneta as minister to London. A Harvard graduate, Araneta was a powerful financial figure having owned several big businesses (i.e. real estate and FEATI airline). Quirino was anxious to fold him into the Liberal Party. President Roxas, although initially sympathetic to the nomination, opposed Araneta's outspoken antagonism to the parity rights and the government's economic dependence on the United States. Quirino stated privately that Araneta agreed to, in the future, be silent about the parity issue.[40]

Roxas, however, preferred Supreme Court Chief Justice Manuel Moran for the position, but Moran refused to leave the court. Roxas allegedly wanted to transfer him and replace him with Secretary of Justice Roman Ozaeta. Failing to get Roxas' nod, Quirino suggested Joseph McMicking, an American-raised-and-educated businessman of British, Spanish, and Filipino descent. However, McMicking, after serving in the U.S. Army, had recently changed his citizenship from Filipino to American. Roxas optioned renouncing the American citizenship to be considered for the London post. Although his Filipino citizenship may have been in question, McMicking considered the possibility.[41]

The State Department closely monitored the London appointment. Upon reading the report by the American embassy in Manila, Director Ely wrote a memorandum to Mr. Vincent and Mr. Penfield of the Bureau of Far Eastern Affairs expressed misgivings about Araneta's appointment.

> I think that Araneta's appointment to the British post would not be to our advantage. He is a very able man and his family is very powerful and influential, but he is not

particularly friendly to us. Araneta is very opposed to any special relations between the Philippines and the United States and has opposed free trade with the United States for many years. His family is one of the few wealthy Filipino families that have attempted to enter commercial life in the Philippines and I have always thought that his opposition to special trade relations was that he wanted to be in a position to go into manufacturing in a small way and felt that if he had the protection of a Filipino tariff against American products, he would be able to operate more successfully. I suspect he wants this London post with the thought that he may be able to secure the cooperation of the British in breaking down free trade between the Philippines and the United States. I have often heard him say that it was the free entry of American products that prevented the industrial development in the Philippines. However, I do not suppose that there is anything we can do about it. McMicking's appointment seems out of the question. I do not see how Roxas could justify to his own people, the appointment of a Spaniard (Elizalde) and a British (McMicking) to his two most important posts.[42]

Selecting a Philippine minister to the Court of Saint James and opening of the legation would have to wait several months more. Earlier, Pablo Peña, a State Department trainee at the American Embassy in London, had made initial contact with the British Foreign Office to pave the way for the accreditation of the Philippine envoy. In January 1947, Peña accompanied Everett F. Drumright, first secretary of the American embassy, to meet with Vice Marshal of the Diplomatic Corps Marcus Cheke to discuss the protocol for presenting a Philippine minister to the Court of Saint James. Peña also called on the Head of the Japanese and Pacific Foreign Office D.F. MacDermont, an office that supervises Philippine affairs. MacDermont cordially received Peña and assured him that the British government desired Philippine representation at the Court of Saint James, posthaste. He added that the Foreign Office would gladly help procure a satisfactory chancery and living quarter.[43] Peña wrote a report to the State Department in anticipation of the mission in London. After reading the report, Drumright commented, "Peña has prepared a better report than the one prepared by this Mission."[44] Peña was motivated to write an excellent report by his aspiration to work in the imminent Legation. Instead, the post was assigned to State Department trainee Romeo S. Busuego of Group IV who had also trained in the American embassy in London.

Meanwhile at the U.S. State Department, Octavio Maloles, second secretary at the Philippine embassy in Washington, met with Mill to discuss whether officers of the proposed Philippine legation could use the American Embassy's commissary. Maloles stated,

> "We are sort of adopted children of yours, you know", and then went on to discuss the advantage to be derived by the Legation in sharing commissary privileges with our embassy. He intimated that the Philippine use of the commissary would be for only a temporary period and that sooner or later the Philippine Legation would set up its own commissary. However, no formal request for commissary privileges has been made by the Philippine government.[45]

On 02 June 1947, Vice President Quirino visited London with an entourage that included his daughter Vicky, his son Tomas, President Roxas' son Gerardo Roxas, Aide and Press Officer Major Carlos Quirino, Social Secretary Helen B. Pellicer, and stenographer Teofilo Rivera; U.S. Foreign Affairs adviser Richard P. Butrick begged off at the last minute. The Hospitality Department of the British government received Quirino and royally entertained him. Quirino set his heart on finalizing an Anglo-Philippine friendship and commerce treaty. Time constraints and the Philippine delegation's limited knowledge of British treaty procedure prevented signing the treaty. The American embassy in London closely monitored these developments. Drumright reported to the State Department how lack of preparation and knowledge of the British system put the Philippine delegation at a disadvantage in negotiating with the British Foreign Office.[46]

The Americans watched on the sidelines with concern, ready to assist upon Philippine request. Drumright said,

As for my part in all this, I am simply keeping a respectable distance from the whole business. I have seen neither draft nor counter draft and I have discussed the matter in a perfunctory fashion only with the Foreign Office. My feeling is that the Filipinos have got to stand on their own feet, and that for appearance's sake, we ought to let the two parties work out their own solution. Of course, if Mr. Quirino comes to us for assistance or advice, we shall do what we can in a discreet way to assist him.

By mid-1947, the plan for the London legation was implemented. President Roxas named Ramon J. Fernandez, a shipping magnate and former senator, as the first Philippine minister to the United Kingdom. The legation was inaugurated on 17 November 1947 and its chancery was located at Hans Place. It was also officially accredited to Norway, Sweden, and Denmark. Officers included First Secretary and Consul General Jose Imperial, Second Secretary Octavio Maloles, and Third Secretary and Vice Consul Romeo Busuego. Imperial and Busuego were graduates of the State Department training program.

Mother Spain

Because of historical and cultural ties, the Philippines prioritized Spain when considering the establishment of diplomatic relations with Europe. Spain had already set up a legation in Manila on 30 January 1947, with Teodomiro de Aguilar y Salas as Envoy Extraordinary and Minister Plenipotentiary, and was eager to gain a corresponding legation in Madrid. But, President Roxas deferred all embassy plans for locations outside the United States. As a Hispanophile, Vice President and Secretary of Foreign Affairs Quirino first tackled the finalization of an amity treaty with Spain. The Department of Foreign Affairs, however, delayed discussing the treaty with the Spanish legation in Manila lest the treaty offend the United States or the United Nations. President Roxas and Spanish Minister Aguilar finally signed the Treaty of Friendship on 27 September 1947. But Spain's poor international standing labored their relations. Spanish Prime Minister Francisco Franco's attitude during World War II caused the Allied Powers to exclude the country from the Marshall Plan and the United Nations. [47] Out rightly accrediting a Philippine minister plenipotentiary in Madrid would antagonize the world body.

Quirino decided to establish a small mission instead under a chargé d'affaires. For this post, he chose Colonel Manuel Nieto, then managing director of Manila Hotel and chairman of the Board of the National Tobacco Corporation. Nieto served as military aide to the late President Quezon and joined the Philippine Commonwealth-in-exile in Washington, D.C., during the occupation of the Philippines. Nieto was predominantly of Spanish blood and the Franco government thought him acceptable. He had close ties with the Compañia General de Tabacos de Filipinas, commonly called Tabacalera, the last of the large Spanish commercial or industrial enterprises in the Philippines.[48]

Nieto's appointment as chargé d'affaires in the Madrid legation alarmed the State Department. In a confidential memorandum to Mr. Penfield of the Bureau of Far Eastern Affairs, Richard Ely, chief of the Division of Philippine Affairs said:

> The appointment of Nieto as chargé d'affaires in Madrid would be very unfortunate. He is predominantly a Spaniard and is very closely allied with a group of Spaniards and people of Spanish-Filipino blood who have always been very active in support of Franco. He is not a particularly able man but is more of the "playboy" type, although no longer a boy. It is possible that this appointment springs from (President) Roxas' desire to find a suitable place for Nieto, for he would be under very strong pressure from Mrs. (Aurora) Quezon to take care of him; and Roxas probably wants to get him out of the management of the hotel for which he has no qualification.[49]

Also appointed as first secretary and consul general, Nieto arrived in Madrid on 03 July 1948, and promptly assumed his duties. The Spanish press referred to Nieto as the "Philippine minister." Francisco Claravall, a State Department graduate, joined Nieto at post as third secretary and vice consul.

When Nieto arrived in Madrid, the legation had been open for several months thanks to Second Secretary Manuel Escudero who was working closely with the American embassy in Madrid to assume responsibility for Philippine matters.[50] A descendant of a distinguished Philippine family and a well-known judge in the Philippines, Escudero was popular in the Filipino colony and was highly regarded by the U.S. embassy. He was outspokenly pro-American and seemed entirely sympathetic to its democratic viewpoint.[51] This stance would eventually cause Escudero and Nieto to clash.

Nieto fumed when he discovered that Escudero was sending diplomatic notes to the Spanish Foreign Ministry in English instead of Spanish. Nieto immediately required the use of Spanish for all future communications to the Spanish government. Escudero was pro-American, but Nieto was pro-Spanish, aligning himself with the anti–United States movement known as *Hispanidad*. The movement emphasized the racial, cultural, linguistic, and religious bonds between Spain, Latin America, and the Philippines. The American embassy in Madrid reported:

> This attitude of Mr. Nieto has not only cost him popularity amongst some of his own people but has caused a rift in the Philippine Legation between himself and Mr. Escudero. Typical of their differing attitudes is the fact that whereas Mr. Escudero came to the embassy very frequently to discuss many of his problems, to date Mr. Nieto has not even come to call on the American chargé d'affaires *ad interim*. Within a month after his assumption of duty as Charge, the visit of Victoria Quirino, daughter of President Quirino, afforded Nieto the opportunity to make the acquaintance of many leading Spanish officials as he travelled around Spain accompanying Ms. Quirino. It appears that Mr. Nieto endeared himself to Spanish officialdom during Ms. Quirino's visit by creating an impression that he was solidly on the side of the [Franco] Regime and that he was playing right along the government's Hispanidad propaganda.[52]

Eventually, Nieto had Escudero transferred to the newly opened Philippine legation in Buenos Aires. Nieto's pro-Spanish stance and closeness with the Franco government changed the relationship between the two countries. In 1950, the Philippines led efforts to restore full diplomatic relations with Spain. When the Philippines elevated the Madrid legation to an embassy in April 1949, it made Spain the second country after the United States with a Philippine embassy. This embassy was also accredited to the Vatican. The Philippines strongly lobbied to admit Spain to the technical organizations of the United Nations and to terminate the diplomatic boycott of Spanish government.[53]

France and Italy

Quirino visited Paris on 09 June 1947, to discuss the conclusion of a Treaty of Friendship and Commerce with the French government and to conclude the establishment of a legation in Paris. Jose Alejandrino, a State Department graduate, was positioned to become second secretary, but the Paris legation did not open on schedule. Alejandrino underwent training at the U.S. embassy in Paris in the summer of 1947. He met Quirino when the latter visited Quay d'Orsay to witness the signing of the Treaty of Friendship and Commerce. The Philippine legation in Paris was established on 13 March 1951, with Proceso Sebastian as minister.[54] This legation was also accredited to Belgium and The Netherlands.

On 09 July 1947, the Philippines and Italy signed a Treaty of Friendship. The following year, on 28 January 1948, a legation was established in Rome with former Senator Domingo Imperial as minister. Five months after, the Department of Foreign Affairs informed the U.S. embassy in Manila that the Rome legation had assumed diplomatic and consular representation for Philippine interests in Italy. It expressed appreciation for the services rendered by the American Foreign Service officers in Italy on behalf of the Philippines.[55]

To reinforce the Rome legation, President and Acting Secretary of Foreign Affairs Elpidio Quirino made prestigious and well-publicized appointments. He appointed Felipe Buencamino III as second secretary. Buencamino left Manila aboard a Pan-American World Airways Clipper to San Francisco, Washington, and then to Rome. He was accompanied by Francisco Oira, finance and property officer. The Philippine press covered Buencamino's departure. Buencamino came from a prominent family and was married to Zenaida Quezon, daughter of the late President Manuel L. Quezon.[56]

Experienced officer Octavio L. Maloles, then second secretary at the Philippine Embassy in Washington, was transferred to Rome to serve as first secretary and consul and to support the neophyte Filipino diplomats. Like Buencamino, Maloles was a member of the Philippine elite.[57]

Aside from promoting friendly relations, commercial interests, and protecting citizens abroad, the legation also represented the country at the Rome headquarters of the Food and Agricultural Organization of the United Nations. But promoting trade relations with Italy was the legation's priority and echoed the priority of the Italian government.[58]

Australia

In Australia, the Philippine Consulate General was established in Sydney on 19 February 1947, with Manuel A. Alzate as consul general. Alejandro Yango and Emilio Bejasa, two State Department graduates, were posted to Sydney to assist Alzate. While waiting for Alzate's arrival, Yango scouted locations for the consulate general. In his letter to Mill, Yango said:

> I am temporarily holding offices at the above-named address (Hotel Grand Central, 151 Clarence St., Sydney) and I hope that I may soon get established in some permanent place in the city or at least in a suburb conveniently near the city. The American Consul General here, Mr. Nielson, has been most kind to me and has promised his assistance in the matter of housing and office accommodations for me and the rest of the consular staff. I have spent my first week here familiarizing myself with my new post of assignment and I expect to be great help to the Philippine Consul General, Mr. Manuel A. Alzate, when he arrives in Sydney sometime by the middle of next month. I am also happy to inform you that Mr. Emilio Bejasa, one of my classmates in the Third Training Group, will join us here as Consul. I am sure you will be proud of him for getting this satisfactory assignment.[59]

Tiburcio C. Baja was assigned to the embassy in Sydney from 1949 to 1952. He worked under Consul General Roberto Regala at the Philippine Consulate General in San Francisco. The consulate general was elevated to a legation in 1950 and Regala, formerly consul general in San Francisco, was appointed as minister. The legation was also accredited to New Zealand. Regala was regarded for his insight and effort to improve Philippine-Australian relations. In December 1955, the Philippines and Australia agreed to raise its legation in Sydney and the Australian Legation in Manila to embassies. Regala became the first Philippine ambassador to Australia.

Relations with the Rest of Asia

Elsewhere in Asia, more posts opened:

> 09 May 1949, Philippine Legation in Bangkok with Jose Alejandrino as Chargé d'Affaires, *ad interim*
> 08 September 1949, Philippine Consulate in Karachi, Pakistan, with Tagakotta Sotto as Consul
> 06 November 1949, Philippine Consulate in Djakarta, Indonesia, with Vicente Pastrana as Consul
> 16 November 1949, Philippine Consulate in Calcutta, India, with Meynardo Farol as Consul
> 18 December1952, Philippine Consulate in Singapore with Yusuf Abubakar as Consul
> 28 February 1955, Philippine Legation in Seoul with Tomas de Castro as Minister
> 04 February 1955, Philippine Consulate in Menado, Indonesia, with Leon T. Garcia as Consul
> 1955, Philippine Legation in Phnom Pehn, Cambodia[60]

Indonesia

The Consulate in Djakarta, previously named Batavia, was established before Indonesia became an independent state. Both the Netherlands and the Free Indonesia Governments accredited the first Filipino consular officials. Because the Philippines championed the cause of decolonization in the United Nations, the support of the Philippines was invaluable to Asian countries struggling for independence. Philippine support for Indonesian independence at

UN conferences illustrates this type of support and illustrates its good neighbor policy toward its Southeast Asian neighbors.

Indonesia and the Philippines share ethnicity, race, languages, colonial history, and other things. On27 December 1949, the day Indonesia declared its independence, the Philippines sent two representatives to witness the occasion. The consular office in Djakarta was elevated to a legation. On 28 February 1950, Manuel V. Gallego, former Secretary of Education, became Envoy Extraordinary and Minister Plenipotentiary to the United States of Indonesia. Two weeks later, Vicente L. Pastrana became first secretary while Marciano Joven, a State Department graduate, became third secretary. Jose F. Zaide was detailed as press assistant.[61] With the opening of the legation, Foreign Affairs Secretary Carlos P. Romulo visited Djakarta. In May 1951, the legation was elevated to an Embassy and an Indonesian Embassy in Manila was set up.[62] It was the third embassy in the Philippine Foreign Service and the first Philippine embassy in Asia.

Upon President Quirino's invitation, President Sukarno made a state visit in 1951. It was the "highest watermark" in the relations of the two countries. Since the country's independence five years earlier, Sukarno was the first foreign head of state to make a state visit to the Philippines. The Philippines and Indonesia also signed a Treaty of Friendship. The first article of said treaty states that "there shall be perpetual peace and everlasting amity between the Republic of the Philippines and the Republic of Indonesia." The agreement also provided for consular, cultural, commercial relations, air transportation, and communication. The foreign affairs departments of both countries offered scholarships to allow Indonesians to study in Manila and even sent an Indonesian cultural mission to the Philippines.[63]

Thailand

Thailand was one of the first countries to recognize the Philippine Republic. Before the war, the Philippines imported the bulk of its rice from Thailand and more than three hundred Thai students studied in the Philippines. Opening formal diplomatic relations, however, had to wait.

On 05 February 1949, the Department of Foreign Affairs announced that Vice Consul Carlos Faustino would travel to Bangkok to handle Philippine Affairs at the American embassy in Siam. He would remain at the American embassy until the organization of a Philippine Legation in Bangkok.[64]

On 23 April, Undersecretary of Foreign Affairs Felino Neri announced that the Philippines would open a legation in Bangkok, Thailand with Jose Alejandrino and Carlos Faustino, both serving at the home office, assigned to the post. Both Alejandrino and Faustino were graduates of the State Department and the Philippine Foreign Affairs Training Program. Alejandrino ranked as the top man in his group and Faustino also had a very good record.

A law graduate from the University of the Philippines, Alejandrino served as a labor attorney for labor unions prior to the war. He was a son-in-law of Secretary of Interior Sotero Baluyut. While training in the State Department, Alejandrino had long assignments at the Divisions of Foreign Service Planning and Administrative Management. In recognition of his outstanding work in the Department of State, Alejandrino was assigned to the American embassy in Paris for training. He made a detailed study of the administrative organization of the Philippine embassy while in Washington and is known to be very interested in the subject of embassy organization and structure. While in the Department of Foreign Affairs, he drafted organizational plans for the Department as well as a basic Foreign Service statute modeled along the lines of the United States Foreign Service Act of 1946. Alejandrino had reportedly performed "an A-1 job" while working as Undersecretary Neri's his right-hand man.[65]

As for Faustino, the American embassy in Manila described him as follows:

> Carlos Faustino was a comparatively young man. He is a law graduate from the University of the Philippines and practiced law before entering the training program for Philippine diplomats. He was a member of the fourth group where he had a very good record. Since completing the work in the Department of State, Faustino has been assigned in the Protocol Office of the Department of Foreign Affairs, serving

as an assistant to Luis Moreno, Chief of Protocol. Faustino has not advanced as rapidly as Alejandrino (and his other batch mates) and one of the reasons for this has been the apparent lack of political connection. He has been known to be anxious for a foreign assignment and particularly for one in the United States.[66]

The American embassy in Manila enthusiastically reported to the State Department about the two State Department graduates taking over the helm in Thailand.

Officers of the American embassy in Bangkok will find that Alejandrino and Faustino are both very friendly to the United States. They will be found to be cooperative in about all matters. Both of them consider themselves as career men and are grateful to the Department of State for their diplomatic training. Alejandrino is expected to act as *chargé d'affaires* pending the arrival of Minister Domingo Imperial. Imperial has until recently been serving as Philippine minister in Rome.[67]

PHILIPPINE FOREIGN SERVICE POSTS

POSTS	1946	1951	1955	1969	1981	1990	1996	2002	2013
Embassy	1	3	4	31	54	54	54	60	60
Mission	1	2	2	2	3	2	2	2	4
Legation	-	7	10	-	-	-	-	-	-
Consulate General	2	2	2	16	20	16	14	18	20
Consulate	-	8	12	-	-	2	3	1	-
Extension Office	-	-	-	-	-	-	1	1	-
Total	4	22	30	49	77	74	74	82	84

The American embassy in Bangkok reported the arrival of the head of the Filipino legation, Alejandrino on 29 May 1949. Accompanying him were third secretary and vice consul Faustino, administrative officer Ernesto Garrido, and staff assistant Faustino Reuroladar.

The U.S. embassy observed Alejandrino's initial activities with great interest and promptly reported developments to the State Department. Alejandrino presented his credentials to the Regent on 02 June, and subsequently made a statement to the press. He expressed his government's eagerness in finalizing a civil aviation agreement with the Thai government to grant reciprocal rights to their commercial airlines and improve trade relations. Alejandrino suggested that exploring barter trade would overcome currency problems. He added that the Philippines considered commercial relations with Thailand of great importance and would therefore appoint a commercial attaché in Bangkok. Moreover, he mentioned that Thailand was independent long before the Philippines and maintained independence "even during the heyday of Western imperialism." In reaction, the American embassy in Bangkok said, "This Embassy hopes reference to independence and imperialism was a matter of exigency of moment and not indication of the outlook of the Philippine legation."[68]

India

On 16 November 1949, the Philippines established a consulate in Calcutta with Meynardo Farol as consul. It was not until 04 January 1952, that the Philippines established a legation in New Delhi with Narciso Ramos as minister. Ramos, who had previously served at the legation in Buenos Aires, took ten months before transferring to New Delhi. On 30 October 1952, he presented his credentials. Jose Moreno, second secretary and former acting Philippine consul general in Calcutta, was *chargé d'affaires* ad interim until the arrival of Ramos.[69] The first minister of India to the Philippines, Mirza Rashid Ali Baig, in contrast, was accredited in Manila six months earlier.

To serve as chancery and his temporary official residence, Ramos rented a suite at the Maidens Hotel, Old Delhi. During the late 1960s the chancery was moved to a two-hectare property located at the diplomatic enclave of New Delhi.[70]

Developing relations with India was not an easy task. Philippine and Indian exports—sugar, copra, and coconut oil products—were similar and often competed in the world market. But, the Manila cigars had somehow penetrated the Indian market. The number of Filipinos in India was too small to merit attention; the climate and the job opportunities had deterred Filipino migrants, and from 1952 to 1953, there were only two recorded Filipino residents in India.[71]

In their early years of independence, both countries were cautious of each other. Some Indian leaders considered the Philippines an American puppet; the Philippines perceived India arrogant, seeing itself as the leader of Asia. Indifference spurred by lack of mutual need kept the countries apart. The prime function of the legation in New Delhi was political, to help the Indian government, press, and other groups understand Philippine policies.[72]

As a former journalist, Ramos occasionally confronted the Indian press about negative reporting. He asked them to refrain from using "Banana Republic" when writing about the Philippines. An article in the New Delhi Times had used the phrase and Ramos called this "false and defamatory" saying it was employed "with apparent intent to ridicule and hold in derision a friendly country."[73]

Ramos said "Banana Republic" was a derogatory epithet for certain Central American countries, where chaotic political and economic conditions resulted in frequent revolutions. "Our government is not perfect as the governments of other countries are not perfect," he said. "But we have a stable government which has given the Filipino people living standards and a literacy percentage higher than those found in most Asian countries. Last November the reigning political party was thrown out of power not by bullets but by the ballots in an orderly election in which, unlike India, only literate voters took part."[74]

South Korea

The Philippines staunchly supported Korean independence in the United Nations serving conspicuously on various UN Commissions on Korea. When the Korean War broke out in 1950, the Philippines and Thailand were the only Asian countries that participated in the UN defense of the Republic of Korea. However, the Philippines was slow to establish diplomatic relations with South Korea. The first Korean mission headed by Y. T. Pyun, special envoy of President Syngman Rhee, visited Manila in February 1949 to lay the groundwork for a formal relationship. After the Korean War, the Philippine and Korean governments took steps to exchange diplomatic representatives.

On 07 February 1953, the Department of Foreign Affairs announced that the Philippine Representative to the UN Commission on the Unification and Rehabilitation of Korea (UNCURK), Minister Maximo Bueno, would establish the first diplomatic office in Seoul. He was *chargé d'affaires* of the mission.[75] Seven months later on 17 September, Tomas G. de Castro, a State Department graduate, was appointed Envoy Extraordinary and Minister Plenipotentiary to Korea. He took his oath before Vice President Carlos P. Garcia and assumed his post a week later. As a reciprocal gesture, the first Korean minister to the Philippines, Kim Young Kee, arrived in Manila on 06 January 1954, to establish a Korean legation.[76]

Relations with Latin America

When Philippine ambassador to Washington Joaquin M. Elizalde attended the inauguration of President Carlos Prio in Havana on10 October 1948, he announced that the Philippines was planning to establish diplomatic relations with Mexico and Cuba. On 24 May 1949, Elizalde became Envoy Extraordinary and Minister Plenipotentiary to Cuba. Notwithstanding, the Philippine government requested that the State Department continue to represent Philippine interests in Cuba.[77]

Close historical and economic ties made Mexico and Cuba likely choices for Philippine legations. But surprisingly, the Philippines selected Argentina for their first diplomatic mission in Latin American. President Quirino was impressed with the importance of Philippine-Argentine relations during the visit of the Argentine cruiser *La Argentina* in July 1948. The Argentine minister to London helped establish a Philippine diplomatic mission in Buenos Aires by working with the Philippine minister to London.[78] They established formal diplomatic relations by exchanging notes between their embassies in September 1948.

Narciso Ramos, minister-counselor at the Philippine Embassy

in Washington, was designated as minister to Argentina. The American embassy reported to the State Department:

> Narciso Ramos has shown little enthusiasm for the assignment. Ramos reportedly referred to his assignment to Buenos Aires as an "exile" and stated frankly that he does not plan to stay there very long. He expressed puzzlement at the reason for the establishment of a Philippine Mission in Buenos Aires prior to Mexico City or Havana. He said that it was possible that after a short stay in Buenos Aires he would be shifted to Mexico City as chief of a Philippine Mission that may be established there in the near future. Ambassador Elizalde, who is also currently in Manila and under whom Ramos has worked for the past two and one half years, also questioned the Buenos Aires assignment and said that "Ramos will not be there very long."[79]

From New York, Ramos and his wife, Angela, and daughter, Gloria, boarded the *S.S. Uruguay* on 25 February 1949, and arrived in Buenos Aires on 15 March. Accompanying them were first secretary and consul general Manuel Escudero, administrative officer Augusto Ramirez, cryptographic and records clerk Constantino Alvarado, and consular clerk Felicisima Barza. Escudero initially served in the legation in Madrid but fell out with his boss, Manuel Nieto, who transferred him to Buenos Aires.

During their voyage to Argentina, the Ramos entourage received many acts of good will, courtesy, and cooperation from the State Department and the US Foreign Service posts in South America. In a note sent to the State Department dated 7 April 1949, the Philippines in Washington cited the assistance extended by Consul Kenneth J Yearns in Bahia; Ambassador Herschel V. Johnson and Second Secretary and Consul Randolph A. Kidder in Rio de Janeiro; Consul Arthur G. Parsloe in Santos; Ambassador Ellis O. Briggs and Second Secretary and Consul Sidney Kennedy Lafoon in Montevideo; Consul General Cecil M.P. Cross in Sao Paulo; *Chargé d'Affaires* Guy W. Ray and Messers. Maleady, Grady, Massibie, Krieger, Rice and other members of the American Embassy staff at Buenos Aires. Narciso Ramos finally assumed his new post in Buenos Aires on 04 April 1949.

Mexico

The Philippine legation in Mexico City was established on 23 April 1953, with Mariano Ezpeleta as minister. Ezpeleta previously served as Philippine consul general in Shanghai and as consul general in London. He flew to San Antonio, Texas, and took the train to Mexico City. Philippine consul Estela Sulit and the Mexican chief of protocol welcomed him at the Central Station.[80] To reinforce the legation, Luis Moreno Salcedo, a State Department graduate, was assigned to Mexico City as second secretary.

One of the first tasks of Ezpeleta and the legation was to relax visa requirements between the Philippines and Mexico. A reservoir of good will from the Manila-Acapulco galleon trade had linked them for more than two hundred years of Spanish colonial rule and helped them reach their diplomatic goals. Toward the end of the Pacific War, the Mexican government sent the Squadron 201, an air force squadron of three hundred men, to the Philippines to help fight the Japanese. With Philippine independence, Mexico believed it would be the site of the Philippines' first Latin American embassy. The Philippines opened their Mexico legation in 1953. Mexico rejoiced, establishing diplomatic ties "satisfied the ego of the Mexicans," Ezpeleta wrote in his memoires. "It brought about for us a separate category, that of a friendly Asian country, which became later that of a little sister country – *la hermana menor de Mejico*."[81] The legation was elevated to embassy status in 1960.

Growth of the Philippine Foreign Service

By the end of 1955, the Philippines had thirty posts:

> Four Embassies —Washington, Madrid, Jakarta, and London
> Two Missions — the UN and Tokyo
> Ten Legations — Paris, Rome, Bangkok, Sydney, Taipei, New Delhi, Seoul, Mexico City, and Karachi
> Two Consulates General —New York and San Francisco
> Twelve Consulates —Honolulu, Los Angeles, Seattle, Chicago, New Orleans, Hong Kong, Singapore, Agana, Hamburg, Manado, Cairo, and Vancouver[82]

By June 1957, the Philippines had an embassy in the Holy See and legations in the following capitals: Vienna, Jerusalem (under the embassy in Rome), Brussels, The Hague, Berne (under the embassy in Paris), Copenhagen, Helsinki, Oslo, Stockholm (under the embassy in London), and Vientiane (under the legation in Saigon). In the same year, the consulate in Kobe, Japan, was established with Pelayo Llamas, a State Department graduate, as consul general. A non-resident Consulate in Macao (under the Philippine consulate in Hong Kong) was set up.[83]

Vice President and Secretary of Foreign Affairs Emmanuel Pelaez announced on 23 August 1962, the opening of the Philippine mission to the European Office of the United Nations in Geneva. A career minister would head the mission, represent the Philippines at local conferences, handle relations with UN specialized agencies and international organizations with Geneva headquarters. Pelaez also disclosed that President Diosdado Macapagal had approved establishing an embassy in Brussels, to complement the Belgian embassy in Manila. Brussels was not only the seat of the European Common Market and the Philippines' substantial trade with Western Europe.[84]

On 12 May 1964, the Philippines established diplomatic ties with the European Community (EC), precursor to the European Union. Vicente I. Singian, a State Department graduate, headed the first Philippine mission to the EC in Brussels. On 16 May 1964, the EC recognized the mission.

On 03 January 1964, Secretary of Foreign Affairs Salvador P Lopez announced the opening of nine Foreign Service posts; embassies would open in Canada, Sweden, Portugal, and Brazil, and new consulates in Portland, Oregon, USA; Auckland, New Zealand; Rotterdam, The Netherlands; Copenhagen, Denmark; and Barcelona, Spain.[85] On 20 March 1965, President Macapagal issued Administrative Order No. 116, which classified diplomatic missions into three categories for chiefs of missions based on post significance and salary. The classifications were as follows:

Diplomatic Missions, Class I: the Philippine Embassy in Washington, the Philippine Embassy in Tokyo, Bangkok, Jakarta, London, Bonn, Paris, Madrid and the Philippine

Mission to the United Nations in New York;
Diplomatic Missions, Class II: the Philippine Embassy in The Hague, Rome, Holy See, Taipei, New Delhi, Canberra, Brussels, Saigon, Kuala Lumpur, Karachi, Berne and Mexico City; and the Philippine Mission in the European Office of the United Nations in Geneva,
Diplomatic Missions, Class III: the Philippine Embassy in Seoul, Rangoon, Buenos Aires, Cairo, Tel Aviv, Phnom Penh, Colombo, Lagos, Vientiane, Ottawa, Stockholm, Lisbon, Brasilia and Tananarive (Madagascar).

By 1965, the Philippine mission expanded from eleven in 1952 to thirty-six.[86] This expansion was brought about by the abrogation of the Philippines-United States Treaty of General Relations in 1963 that ended American tutelage in Philippine foreign relations, when the Philippine Foreign Service had already come of age. The State Department Boys dominated the leadership in the Philippine Foreign Service. Of the 25 active State Department graduates, 11 held ambassadorial posts while 14 occupied deputy chief of mission positions or similar important responsibilities at the Home Office. They no longer needed to consult their American counterparts on how to open and operate a diplomatic and consular mission.

At this point, we may get the impression that the Philippine Foreign Service has grown and developed naturally, though protractedly, without a glitch. The same, however, could not be said of the diplomatic careers of the State Department Boys who faced an uphill climb in order to firmly establish themselves in the complex world of diplomacy.

7

Surviving the Foreign Service

After the completion of their training at the U.S. State Department and Foreign Service posts, the Filipino trainees were given a diplomatic rank based on their performance in the training program, academic and professional qualifications, and by virtue of Program Director Edward W. Mill's recommendation. The DFA in Manila did not yet have a linear roster of officers. In the State Department's telegram to U.S. Foreign Affairs adviser Richard P. Butrick, Mill recommended the following ranks based on a regular series of examinations, oral and written reports, educational work, background, and close observation of the Filipino trainees:

> First Group: Class I—Manuel A. Adeva, Jose F. Imperial, Tiburcio C. Baja
> Class II—Vicente I. Singian, Candido Elbo
> Second Group: Class I—Tomas De Castro, Leopoldo T. Ruiz
> Class II—Delfin R. Garcia, Doroteo V. Vite
> Class III—Pelayo Llamas
> Third Group: Class II—Emilio D. Bejasa, Pablo Peña, Anastacio Bartolome, Alejandro Yango
> Class III—Eutiquio O. Sta. Romana, Aurelio Ramos, Juanito C. Dionisio, and Francisco Claravall[1]

Butrick balked at Mill's recommendations, which he thought were too lenient. He requested that Mill reclassify them so that some officers would start at Class IV. He thought it improbable that no more than two were appointed to Class I.[2] Mill took note and, instead, recommended the following trainees for Class IV: Llamas, Sta. Romana, Ramos, and Claravall. He reclassified Vite and Singian to Class III, but firmly retained Bejasa as Class II.[3] Notwithstanding Mill and Butrick's efforts, the Department of Foreign Affairs ignored most of their recommendations and started a majority of the State Department graduates at Class IV. As Butrick wrote to Mill: "There is a considerable pressure to keep the salaries of the trainees down at a low level and to make them vice consuls (it was even suggested that (Manuel) Adeva be made a vice consul)."[4] After a lot of haggling, Vice President and Secretary of Foreign Affairs Elpidio Quirino appointed Manuel A. Adeva, Jose F. Imperial, Tiburcio C. Baja, Leopoldo Ruiz, Tomas de Castro, and Vicente Singian at Class II.

Appointment to a particular class or rank not only determines position, but basic annual salaries. Class I received 9,000 pesos, Class II earned 7,500 pesos, Class III received 6,500 pesos, and Class IV received 4,500 pesos. In comparison, ambassadors earned 12,000 pesos annually. Some graduates who were not appointed as FAOs were designated as senior assistants in the Department of Foreign Affairs at 4,200 pesos per annum. The salary scale in the Home Office and the Foreign Service was such that there was no relationship between a consul general's job and that of a division chief. As Butrick noted:

> The only well-paid officers, from an American standpoint are: the undersecretary and the heads of the three offices (Political and Economic Affairs, Legal and International Conference Affairs and Administration and Controls), known as counselors. The top salary for counselors is 8,400 pesos. Because of the salary scales in the Department, I had great difficulty in setting the salary scales for Foreign Affairs Officers, but I think it has finally been worked out satisfactorily.[5]

While many State Department Boys accepted their appointments without a fuss, Jose M. Alejandrino was an exception. As the top ranked man in Group IV, Alejandrino refused to take his oath as Foreign Affairs Officer Class IV. In his letter to Mill dated 16 March 1948, he complained:

> I was appointed FAO IV at 4,500 pesos per annum a week ago. Being unhappy about the appointment, I did not take my oath of office. Instead, I requested for a reconsideration of my case with a view to raising my appointment to Class III at least. Ex-Secretary Sotero Baluyut (my wife's uncle who will soon be called back to the Cabinet as Secretary of Public Works and Communications), Senator Lorenzo Tañada, Congressman Roy (Chairman of the House Committee on Banks and Corporations), Congressman Lorenzo Sumulong (Chairman of the House Committee on Foreign Relations) and Congressman Hermenegildo Atienza (Chairman of the Committee on the Department of Foreign Affairs of the Commission on Appointments) strongly backed me up. With my qualifications, your report on my performance during the training course and their combined recommendations, the Vice President saw his way clear to reconsidering my case. For last Saturday a special messenger from the Department came to my residence to notify me that the Vice President wanted to see me. I happened to be out in the province then. However, upon my arrival in Manila yesterday, I went to see him in his house where he is convalescing. After the usual exchange of greetings he told me that he had reconsidered my original appointment by having me appointed to Class III with assignment to our Paris Legation which will be opened soon. I thanked him for the new arrangement.

Alejandrino was one of the few State Department Boys who possessed such tenacity and political clout. Although the graduates were being groomed to be officers, not all of the State Department trainees were recommended for the position. Mill saw to it that officer appointment was based on academic and professional qualifications as well as one's performance in the training program. On this basis, Mill did not recommend Guillermo C. Fonacier and Engracio D. Guerzon of Group V to be officers. Fonacier almost flunked the training program, eventually receiving a satisfactory rating. He returned to the Philippine Consulate in San Francisco in 1948 to work as an administrative assistant. It took him five years before was finally appointed FAO Class IV and became vice consul in 1954.

Mill also saw to it that his former wards were placed in positions that would utilize their training and talents. Emilio Torres, a State Department graduate, wrote, "Mr. Mill's valuable help does not terminate at the end of the training program. In his own very diplomatic and firm way he sees it that "his" trainees are given a suitable place in the scheme of the Philippine Foreign Service. This is indeed a big thing, worthy of any man's pride."[6]

First Assignments

Fresh from training, the State Department Boys had responsible positions in the Home Office and the Foreign Service. Delfin R. Garcia proudly noted, "There is a graduate of the (Philippine Foreign Affairs Training) Program in every Philippine Foreign Service establishment who provides the technical direction and assistance essential for the proper conduct of the office."[7] Group I received the following assignments: Adeva as consul in the Philippine consulate general in New York; Baja as consul in the Philippine consulate general in San Francisco; Elbo as vice consul in New York; and Imperial and Singian were detailed to the DFA in Manila.[8]

Mill was particularly pleased with Baja's appointment as consul of the Philippines in San Francisco.[9] He wrote about Baja in his letter to Richard Butrick: "So far as Baja is concerned, I want to emphasize that the Department considered him to be thoroughly outstanding. His record at the American embassy (in Mexico City) was excellent, and he has gotten along particularly well in this country."[10] Baja was eyeing the assistant to the American Foreign Affairs adviser position in Manila, but his posting to the Philippine consulate general in San Francisco dashed his plan.

Meanwhile, Vicente Singian's status at the Home Office discouraged him. He confided to Mill: "Among the trainees here now,

I am, unfortunately, the only one who holds a position of some importance. For some reason or another, the Department feels that it is only in matters of protocol where some specialized training is required. As a result, other key positions are given to outsiders regardless of the availability of trained men."[11]

The ease with which Group I received their appointments was unusual; some of the succeeding groups were less fortunate. Members of Group II more or less followed the examples of Group I. Almost all of them were deployed in the United States. Tomas de Castro, Pelayo Llamas, Leopoldo Ruiz, and Doroteo V. Vite were all assigned to the Philippine Embassy in Washington. De Castro and Ruiz were appointed as second secretary and consul while Vite was vice consul. Unfortunately, Delfin Garcia, the youngest member of the group found himself in a bind. After the training, he anxiously awaited in Washington for his formal designation. Despite his excellence as a trainee, Garcia was not immediately appointed. Alarmed, Mill wrote a letter to Butrick on 23 August 1946:

> Regarding Mr. (Delfin) Garcia, I wish to ask your cooperation in seeing that his case is personally brought to the attention of the Secretary of Foreign Affairs. Garcia was probably the top man ever to take the training program in the Department. He had an average of 98 or near perfect in all his tests. He is moreover blessed with an exceedingly fine personality. His one handicap may be his youth; he is only 24. For some reason, the Department of Foreign Affairs has been slow in giving him any appointment, and he has been waiting around Washington and the Embassy for some word from his government. There is no reason whatsoever why Garcia could not be of immediate and valuable service to his government.

As a solution, Butrick requested that Garcia become his special assistant in Manila. There, Garcia helped him and other DFA officials draft the Philippine Foreign Service Regulations. After serving under Butrick, Garcia was eventually appointed vice consul and opened the Philippine Consulate in Amoy in November 1946.

Notwithstanding appointment difficulties for the State

Department Boys, Mill was pleased. He wrote to Butrick, "Generally speaking, I would say that the Philippine government has done

> In appointing these career men the Philippine Government has shown an initial determination to develop a merit foreign service which is most commendable. I only hope that this will be kept up. You and Secretary Quirino, backed up by the President, of course, deserve great credit for this.[12]

But, permanent and relevant appointments were difficult. Mill pestered Butrick every time he received bad news about former wards with "floating" status. But, because of a legal loophole, Butrick couldn't do much about formal appointments. Butrick reminded Mill that before departing for the United States, the trainees had signed an agreement with the Office of Foreign Relations and subsequently the Department of Foreign Affairs stating that "the Philippine government was under no obligation to provide employment to the trainees upon the completion of their training." Butrick helped the graduates even though interceding as Foreign Affairs adviser was difficult. He confided to Mill in his letter of All Saints Day of 1946:

> While I have made repeated efforts to have the trainees appointed, the process has turned out to be a slow one indeed. There is a tendency to belittle them. Even the principal officers, themselves appointed FAOs, seem reluctant to have the trainees appointed FAOs until they themselves have passed on them.

Mill and Butrick worked in tandem to shield the State Department Boys from the complex and destructive politics at the Home Office. At one point, Imperial was recalled to Manila for "political orientation" so Butrick warned Mill in a handwritten note to Mill: "I have boosted Imperial. He will probably be ordered to Department for duty but principally to be "sized up." You might wish to tip him off – in person not over telephone – if you think it safe."[13] Mill confided to Everett F. Drumright, First Secretary of the American embassy in London, about the reason for the recall:

There is some jealousy and envy of Imperial among his compatriots in the Foreign Service, due in large part, I think, to his heavy academic background. Imperial holds a Doctor of Foreign Service degree from Georgetown University. He is an extremely suave and gracious sort of person. He is probably more keenly alert to diplomatic practice and usage than anyone I know in the Philippine Foreign Service. He is inclined to stand on protocol and to observe diplomatic niceties very carefully.[14]

Following his brief stay in the Home Office, Imperial was sent back to the United States as Consul in the Philippine Consulate General in San Francisco and subsequently as First Secretary and Consul General in the Philippine Legation in London.

By March 1947, members of the third group were holding the following positions: Anastacio Bartolome and Pablo Peña were assigned as technical assistants to the consulate general in New York; Emilio Bejasa was acting consul in Hong Kong; Francisco Claravall was vice consul in Honolulu; Juanito Dionisio and Aurelio Ramos were vice consuls in San Francisco; and Eutiquio Sta. Romana and Alejandro Yango were detailed in the Home Office.[15] Yango was acting chief of the Division of Passports, Visas, and Immigration.[16]

Anastacio Bartolome and Pablo's assignments displeased them. After training at the State Department and American embassies in Paris and London respectively, they were in high spirits and expectation. But unlike their peers, both were designated as technical assistants not vice consuls or consuls.

Generoso Provido, a member of Group IV, wrote Mill:

I understand that Mr. Peña, Mr. Bartolome and the rest of the members of my group have not yet been accommodated pending the arrival of the Vice President. I am sure that when the Vice President arrives there will be jockeying for position with no holds barred. I wish the trainees of the fourth group as well as Mr. Peña and Mr. Bartolome are accommodated. Perhaps this is possible if you postpone the graduation of the last group. There is no difficulty accommodating the last group since most of them have strong political backers.[17]

More than a year later in January 1948, Peña and Bartolome became Foreign Affairs Officer Class IV—a result of Mill's efforts. They were promoted to vice consuls in the Philippine consulate general in New York.

Top ranked Group III graduate Emilio Bejasa, Alejandro Yango, and Eutiquio O. Sta. Romana returned to Manila immediately after training. The sudden death of Bejasa's father caused him to rush home, while Yango and Sta. Romana had personal and business affairs to attend to in their hometown of Cabanatuan. Bejasa was originally slated to continue training in the American Consulate General in Shanghai but it lacked staff and training facilities to accommodate him. Rather than overburden the China post, the State Department's Office of Foreign Service sent Bejasa to the American Consulate General in Hong Kong. He trained there for four months before receiving instructions from the Home Office to establish the Philippine Consulate in Hong Kong and to become acting consul.[18]

Eutiquio O. Sta. Romana had a rather disappointing start in the Philippine Foreign Service. Vice President Quirino's ire placed his career in limbo. Right after State Department training, Quirino appointed Sta. Romana as vice consul to the Philippine Consulate General in New York. Instead of accepting, Sta. Romana returned to the Philippines to take care of some family business. He reportedly wanted a post in China or Thailand to "know and study our oriental neighbors." This insubordination caught the Quirino who froze his appointment to any position at the Home Office and the Foreign Service. At home in Cabanatuan City, Sta. Romana desperately waited for news of his status from the DFA. He bitterly complained to Mill:

> The way the present Department of Foreign Affairs is run is far from satisfactory – below the standard of any of your graduates. For it is run by people who know little, if at all, of foreign relations. I know Dr. Jose Imperial made the same impression. There is much to be desired here, but unfortunately trainees of the State Department are not given the square deal for the evil influences of the former Ministry of Foreign Affairs during the Japanese Regime are in the Department of Foreign Affairs. Such is the sad lot of the

young department of the Republic of the Philippines. The office routine is characterized by confusion, duplicity and inefficiency. There is no coordination of work. The Department of Foreign Affairs is in awful mess. Out of jealousy and sheer vanity, the officials of the Department are critical of the trainees – as if they know better. I sincerely hope in the years to come, these observations are remedied and fruitful reforms carried out – the initiative to come from the Philippine Foreign Affairs Training Program and its honored graduates.[19]

Mill commiserated with Sta. Romana and pleaded to Quirino to reconsider an appointment. In his letter to Sta. Romana, Mill wrote:

I can appreciate that your situation since your return to the Philippines has not been an easy one. I regret that you did not see fit to accept the position of vice consul in New York, but at the same time I understand the reasons which made you feel that you must return to the Philippine first. Your decision to return to the Philippines first was perhaps a mistake, but it should not be held against you indefinitely. You will be interested to know that I very strongly recommended you to various ranking officials and urged them to review your case and give you a new assignment if possible. For your strictly confidential information (and please do not quote the reference), I wrote to Mr. Butrick on 25 February and strongly urged favorable consideration for your case. This was done entirely on my initiative and without any request from you or anyone. I was very much impressed with your splendid attitude while in training in the State Department, and I felt that you could render your country most valuable service abroad in a Foreign Service capacity.[20]

When Quirino and Counselor Teodoro Evangelista visited the United States, Mill spoke highly of Sta. Romana, he lobbied with other ranking officials as well. On 12 January 1948, Quirino relented and granted Sta. Romana a Foreign Affairs Officer Class IV status. Three months later, Sta. Romana became vice consul at the

Philippine consulate in Amoy, China. Compared with New York, Amoy was a hardship post. And he accepted to redeem himself, perhaps remembering his former mentor's words:

> From my own standpoint I think it is highly desirable that our graduates be spread about the Far East rather than concentrated in the United States. You can do the cause of Philippine-American friendship more good by getting around the world and showing people what sort of graduates the State Department has produced.[21]

Indeed, Sta. Romana redeemed himself in Amoy. In August 1949, as the Communist forces approached the city, he safely led the evacuation of the consular staff and their families and household members from Amoy to Manila. The Philippine Consulate closed and its personnel were recalled to Manila. Sta. Romana's heroism made headlines in the *Manila Bulletin*.[22]

In 1953, Sta. Romana wrote Mill proudly that his "problem trainee" had redeemed himself. He admitted but considered his past mistake a blessing in disguise.

> "In accepting a position in the Foreign Service in 1948, my primary aim was to redeem myself for my error of judgment in 1946 for not accepting a position as vice consul in New York. But my decision in 1946 proved to be a blessing in disguise for since 1948 I have seen China, India, Italy, and Thailand not to include Switzerland (for the ILO conference, 1950). Among our group, I believe that I am the most moved.[23]

Group IV also experienced mixed fortunes. Those without political connection did not automatically receive their appointment and anxiously waited. Jose M. Alejandrino was among those who were swiftly appointed. He became special assistant to the Undersecretary of Foreign Affairs. Other appointments were Marcelino V. Bernardo, chief commercial and monetary policy and trade promotion division; Romeo Busuego, third secretary and vice consul in the London legation; and Generoso Provido, assistant chief, division of European affairs in the Department of Foreign Affairs.

On the other hand, Rodolfo H. Severino, Carlos A. Faustino, and Roman V. Ubaldo were not as fortunate. Severino and Faustino, in particular, returned home to lackluster reception and waited long for their appointment at the DFA. They wrote to Mill with resentment about the DFA. Severino wrote Mill about the cold treatment he received from Undersecretary Africa and the gloomy prospect of getting a permanent position:

> By the looks of things, there cannot be reasonable optimism about my getting into the Foreign Service, my training and preparation for it notwithstanding. Two high-ranking officials in the Department advised me that there must be one to pull strings for me and push my appointment if I don't want to be left behind. As I do not know how to play this game of push and pull and with nothing to back me up but my past record in the government service, my prospects of getting in look pretty slim. Even if I had one who could pull wires for me, I would not consent to employing the suggested method, than which nothing is more undesirable.[24]

Faustino echoed the same sentiment and frustration of Severino as he painfully realized that the DFA hierarchy would not give special treatment to State Department trainees. He wrote Mill confidentially:

> Dr. Africa said he welcomed us but he could not give Severino and me jobs in the Home Office because "there are no items available." He told us to wait for the opening of new legations and consulates in the near future, where we "might" be placed. I could see he took pains in stressing the word "might" so we do not get the feeling of assurance of landing even a foreign assignment. My impression is that in so far as Dr. Africa (who acts as Secretary of Foreign Affairs in the absence of Quirino) is concerned, returning trainees will find it hard to land positions in the Home Office or abroad, unless they pull political wires. I don't think Dr. Africa is to blame, as in this dear old country of mine, political pressure especially in pre-election times is a one great factor to reckon with.

Faustino reported the DFA's misgivings regarding the value of the State Department training, particularly its top officials:

> Dr. Africa also asked me as to what I learned at the State Department. Other officials in the department (jealous of the trainees) even expressed doubts as to the value of the training. I defended the training program in all these occasions and gave them an idea of what we went thru in the training of the State Department. I told them that all I know of diplomatic and consular practices were learned at the State Department. I have given a newspaperman friend of mine here in Manila the article on the training program which I prepared in Washington and which was passed over by you. I have requested that the same be published sometime in the middle of July 1947 when Secretary Quirino and other Philippine Foreign Service men will meet in Manila to reorganize the Philippine Foreign Service.[25]

Mill lamented Faustino and Severino's situation. He encouraged them to defend the State Department training and never lose hope:

> One thing I wish you would attempt to do while in Manila is to make clear to the officers of the Department of Foreign Affairs that the training received by the trainees in the Department of State is not simply theoretical training. The training received here is, in fact, the most practical training offered anywhere in the world. There seems to be a great misconception in the Department that the trainees discuss only matters of great world concern; but while some of this is, of course, done, most of the work is basic, bedrock consular and diplomatic work. Some of us here feel regretfully that there is a lack of appreciation in certain circles in Manila of the great contribution we have made in the training of the Foreign Affairs officers of the Republic. We have most willingly and gladly, out of our desire to assist the newly independent Republic, extended our utmost cooperation in assisting in the development of a Foreign Service for the Philippines. I think it would be most regrettable if this con-

tribution were to go unappreciated by certain officials in Manila. I appreciated your attempt to make clear to the concerned officers just what we have been doing and just what you have learned while stationed here.[26]

In the end, Severino and Faustino received their appointments. Severino was designated attorney in the Legal Office and later as assistant in the Division of Asian and Pacific Affairs; Faustino was appointed assistant protocol officer.

Roman V. Ubaldo also struggled with his appointment after training in the American embassy in Rio de Janeiro. He waited in Manila and thought it a mistake to have returned to the Philippines. With nothing to do, he complained to Mill:

> When I arrived (in Manila) I went to pay my respects to the Undersecretary (Africa). He told me that my status as a trainee detailed at the Home Office will continue together with my allowance of $180 a month. The Accountant raised a question to the effect that I should be terminated upon arriving Philippine shores, but Dr. Africa stuck to his point – I having been away from the islands too long and should be detailed here to familiarize myself with the methods of operation. The next week when I asked for an assignment, however, in order to get my remuneration, Dr. Africa changed his stand. He followed the Accountant's contention so now I'm here without anything – job, salary, and assignment.
> The Undersecretary's opinion is that I should go back to Washington, since there's no place for me here. And the worst part of it is that I'll have to pack, rather prepare to leave soon. To this point, I wish to acquaint you with the facts. Since the Undersecretary said there was no place for me here, I went to see Mr. Juan Barreto, Administrative Officer (of the Philippine Embassy in Washington, D.C.) and he offered me my former item of $300 a month, an item which is equal to a salary of some of the Embassy clerks. I bargained but "no soup." Anyway when I saw the list at the Department's personnel division, my item became $400.

The position is that one held by Dr. Ruiz, not as FAO, but a glorified clerk. It's very discouraging to aspire for FAO berths because these are persons who have the "pull" and those who know who, outsiders are given preferences over those who had been trained, or even those in the Department.[27]

News of Ubaldo travelled from the embassy in Washington to Tiburcio C. Baja at the consulate in San Francisco. On February 2, Baja wrote Mill: "There is no place for him and that the chances are that he will have nothing for a long time. I think the plan now is to bring him back to Washington. I hope he gets something either here or there soon." Fortunately, Ubaldo did not have to wait long. The help of a congressman in his province resulted in an appointment as senior assistant in the American Division of the DFA in Manila.

Group V fared better. The DFA and the Foreign Service were already two years old when they completed their training. In two years, the DFA and the Foreign Service quickly developed and expanded. New positions meant more available jobs. The State Department informed the Philippine government that Group V must have definite positions as soon as they returned to Manila. Home Office appointments of Group V were as follows: Luis Moreno Salcedo, acting Chief of Protocol; Hortencio J. Brillantes, assistant chief, division of controls; Engracio D. Guerzon, chief Division of Invoice, Shipping and Miscellaneous Services; Marciano A. Joven, senior assistant, commercial and monetary policy and trade promotion division; and Simeon R. Roxas, attorney, Office of Legal Affairs. Assignments abroad were: Yusup R. Abubakar, vice-consul, Los Angeles; Irineo R. Cabatit, staff member, consulate general in San Francisco; Irineo D. Cornista, vice-consul Seattle; Guillermo C. Fonacier, staff member, consulate general in San Francisco; Reynaldo Lardizabal, third secretary, Washington; Eduardo L. Rosal, vice consul, New York; Benjamin T. Tirona, vice consul, Chicago;[28] Renato A. Urquiola, vice consul, New Orleans; and Tagakotta O. Sotto, vice consul, New York. Emilio Torres, who posted as third secretary in Washington, D.C. before joining Group V, was promoted to second secretary. But, Torres was not satisfied. He confided to Mill that he wanted a Chicago or New Orleans assignment.

Although pleased with many of his protégés' appointments, Mill continued to assist other graduates. He asked Benjamin Tirona and Tagakotta Sotto, members of Group V and sons of two prominent senators, to help their batch mates and those from other groups. To Tirona, Mill wrote:

> One thing which is causing me such concern these days is the apparent indifference of Manila to the need for appointing career men to the Service. The home office has received a number of the graduates of the program rather coolly after their arrival in Manila. After having been treated as kings while here, it is bit ironical to go "home" and be treated like strangers. Ben, I wish you would use your personal influence to see that all your classmates, not only of Group V but of the other groups as well, are appointed to the Service ahead of political appointees. Surely your father must be interested in this ideal also. Your country will benefit ever so greatly if this objective can be realized.[29]

Sounding like a crusader, Mill sent a letter to Sotto a month later:

> A very significant telegram in behalf of you boys went out of the [State] Department today. This telegram, which I drafted, instructed our Ambassador in Manila to press for the appointment of graduates of the Philippine Foreign Affairs Training Program to the new diplomatic and consular posts to be opened. Names of individuals recommended were listed in the telegram. This telegram capped the many efforts I have made to get you men appointed to the Foreign Service. I have reason to believe now that my never-ceasing fight to put the trainees in key positions will end victoriously. I cannot say more just now, but unless something comes up at the last minute, the cause of the career service is about to get a very big boost.[30]

In addition, Mill took time from his busy schedule in Washington to visit many of them. Mill recounted:

> During my visit away I made a trip to the Philippine Consulate General in San Francisco and the Philippine Consulate in Los Angeles. I met with Judge Regala and Judge Boncan, but most of my time was devoted to my "boys," Mr. Imperial, Mr. Baja, Mr. Dionisio, Mr. Rosal, Mr. Ramos, Mr. Cabatit, and Mr. Llamas. I am proud of these men. They are the real heart of the Foreign Service and the hope of the future.[31]

Group I member Tiburcio C. Baja, was not satisfied with his posting as consul at the Philippine Consulate General in San Francisco. The amount of work, responsibility, and income at the consulate exceeded that of the consulate in New York and the embassy in Washington where the Foreign Affair Officers were ranked two. Yet, as Baja complained to Mill, consuls in the San Francisco consulate were paid less.

> It is this anomalous situation which I seek to correct in my letter to the Secretary of Foreign Affairs, maintaining that if allowed to remain uncorrected, the Philippine Foreign Service will be establishing a poor precedent. For one thing, the San Francisco Consulate General will not attract the best men from the point of view of class and salary. And it will be tragic for such an important post.[32]

Mill sent the letter to Butrick for assistance, but he returned it with marginal notes:

> Baja wrote me also. I did not reply. If this gets to the attention of the Vice President [Quirino], it will do Baja no, repeat no, good. The trainees are already in bad odor, owing to Sta. Romana's not going to New York and Singian's difficulties with (Narciso) Ramos, etc. There is resentment in the Department which Adeva and Imperial have done much to correct but still exists. Letters such as Baja's do not help in getting jobs for the trainees.

Baja's frustration with the politics of the Foreign Service was understandable. He wanted to contribute to the strengthening of the career system. Baja assured Mill:

> I have been thinking of the struggle ahead for the career character of our Foreign Service. In our Republic politics is keen and powerful. I do not like politics as I know it. In fact, this retarded my decision to return to the government service. But precisely because of what politics is at present, that I was induced to get into it believing that perhaps what I am and what I can do may be a wholesome influence in Philippine politics. This point is what seems to be holding me in my position, hard as my situation at times is.[33]

In August 1946, Delfin Garcia became special assistant to Richard Butrick, the American Foreign Affairs adviser, but reported to Mill that it was difficult to strengthen the career system. Mill replied with words of encouragement:

> From our experience in this country it is always an uphill battle to develop a real merit service. There is always considerable jealousy of the career men and a disposition to by-pass them. In the long run, however, a country comes to depend on its career men for the most effective service. While career men should work for common objectives, it is also important that career men do not segregate themselves too much from the rest of the working force. During the first years of the new Foreign Service, it will be important for all the career men to stick together, but it is to be hoped that as time passes the career men will come to embrace the entire service personnel instead of a small group within the overall force.[34]

Because officers were needed to open new posts, the initial assignments proved to be only temporary. After a brief stint in the San Francisco consulate, Jose F. Imperial and Manuel A. Adeva were reassigned as first secretaries and consuls general in London and Nanking respectively. Tiburcio Baja was also serving in San Francisco when he learned about a transfer to an emerging legation in

Bangkok. But the transfer became problematic. Like his batch mates Adeva and Imperial, Baja was initially appointed as first secretary and consul general. He had received the letter of appointment and took the oath of office. But Baja was devastated when he learned that he had been downgraded to first secretary and consul; he considered it a demotion. Fortunately, it took so long for the legation to be established that the transfer never materialized. He transferred instead to the consulate in Sydney as first secretary and consul.

Politics in the Foreign Service

Career advancement for the graduates varied because of the prevalence of politics in the early days of the Foreign Service. The promotions of many State Department graduates with weak or no political connection was delayed or bypassed to favor political protégés. In these cases, they all turned to Mill for help. In 1950, Anastacio B. Bartolome was serving as vice consul in the consulate in Honolulu when he asked Mill to intervene. When the deputy position at the consulate became available, Bartolome and another vice consul Andres Ferrer were vying for it. Ferrer, reportedly a protégé of the Speaker of the House of Representatives, had never taken the Foreign Service entrance examinations or training. He was transferred to Honolulu only after a brief stint in Amoy. Bartolome didn't want to lose face and be overlooked for the position. He believed that his training at the State Department and the American Embassy in Paris qualified him for the position. Bartolome appealed to Mill:

> It is for the above reasons, Chief, that once again I seek your help, knowing full well that you have and always will have the welfare and interest of "your boys" at heart. You have batted for me and Mr. Peña and other ex-trainees many times before, and I earnestly hope you will bat for me once again. Unlike Vice Consul Ferrer, I have no political "padrinos" (sponsors) in the Philippines to recommend me. I am relying entirely on my personal merits and qualifications, hoping that my superiors would take cognizance of same. With your valuable assistance, however, which I hope you will not deny me, I stand a pretty good chance of landing the No.2 position.[35]

Even the politically connected, like State Department graduate Yusup Abubakar, abhorred politics. As vice consul in Los Angeles, the state of politics in Manila disappointed Abubakar and caused him to contemplate leaving the Foreign Service. "I do not know of the present plan of the Foreign Office regarding my assignment. It seems that there is so much politics going on in Manila and promotions are given to persons who could pull strings regardless of their showing or accomplishments," Abubakar wrote to Mill.

> I am a little bit discouraged and am bidding my time to watch further developments. In the event that I shall be convinced that there is no future in the Foreign Service, I will go into politics where there is a great opportunity to be had. Senator Pecson who just returned from Washington informed me that the younger element in Sulu wants me to become the governor of the province. I told Senator Pecson that I would be willing to accept the position should the President offer it to me.[36]

Doroteo Vite also had to fight to be promoted to consul. "I finally got the promotion I have been fighting for so long, and not without a big struggle and pressure I made," he happily reported to Mill.

> I simply told them (people in the Home Office) that I deserved the promotion and also that it was not possible for me to live with the dignity of an official of the Philippine Republic if I did not receive a higher remuneration. I pulled some wire here and there and so finally my colleagues in the Department (of Foreign Affairs) probably got so pestered they dug up the recommendation which had been approved by President Quirino while he was still Secretary. It did not take long for him to sign it once he had it on his desk. The Manila papers are almost always skewy on many things. I have been vice consul for two years and I still remain a vice consul although my FAO rank is two steps up. I have been promoted to FAO III at 5,500 pesos per annum and should automatically become second secretary and consul but since there is no vacancy in the post here for a consul then I remain as a vice consul.[37]

During its initial years many lawyers and judges joined the Philippine Foreign Service and dominated its appointments, especially those in the United States. The Foreign Service overlooked many capable State Department graduates for promotion and cited its preference for lawyers as an excuse. As a non-lawyer, Baja criticized this practice. He wrote to Mill at the American embassy in Manila:

> I am glad that you are there to refute the claim that only lawyers make good Foreign Service officers. You need only to point the undersecretary and the first two ambassadors of the Philippine Republic are non-lawyers. In my talks with the Consul General here, reference is made to the policy of giving preference to lawyers in appointments to Foreign Service. But with due respect to the profession, I submit that it is my observation that while the knowledge of the law may be an advantage, a literal lawyer is a handicap. Moreover, what is there in the law book that I cannot learn if it has to be learned in the performance of my duties as a Foreign Service officer? It is again my observation that lawyer officers have to run to the shelf as I have when confronted with the need of a provision of law. I believe therefore that having taken law is no *summum bonum* (utmost good) in the Foreign Service. On the other hand, a broad cultural and social background is sure foundation of effective human dealings, which constitutes much of Foreign Service. This has been demonstrated again and again in my experience with other peoples everywhere. So let the howlers howl and the scowlers scowl and the growlers growl – I stand pat on the proposition that the Philippine Foreign Service needs men of law, yes, but of broad and liberal human love, nonetheless.[38]

Separation from the Service

In early 1951, an austerity program by the Philippine government separated several State Department graduates from the Foreign Service: Yusup Abubakar, Marcelino Bernardo, Candido Elbo, and Delfin Garcia. A disillusioned Garcia wrote to Mill:

Since I consider myself a career man, ready to devote an entire life, I was greatly surprised to be one of those laid off, more so when I believe my record has been very satisfactory compared to others. It seems that no definite criteria were used in determining which positions were to be abolished.[39]

But, Baja thought the salary and allowance cuts was justified. "Our salaries and allowances have been slashed and Congress is yet determined to make further cuts. The conduct of some of our officers abroad is causing unfavorable impressions among certain congressmen. In some instances, I believe, the adjustment being made is justified."[40]

Out of desperation, Garcia asked Mill for assistance with a job at the UN or the Economic Commission for Asia (ECA). Mill recommended Garcia to Vincent Check, head of ECA in the Philippines. Mill encouraged a downhearted Garcia:

"I am confident that nobody or no one can ever keep you down. You are sure to surge to the top sooner or later in almost anything that you do. I have explicit confidence in you. No, don't worry Delfin. I am sure everything is going to turn out all right in your case. You can know that your old mentor is pulling for you with all his might. One of these days, you'll be up there as an Ambassador or a Cabinet Minister. But regardless of what happens, I'm all for you.[41]

Fortunately, Garcia and Yusup Abubakar were reinstated; Garcia was appointed as second secretary at the Philippine mission to the United Nations in New York and Abubakar was assigned as consul to the consulate in Cairo. Candido Elbo left his post in the Philippine Consulate General in New York and settled in the United States while Marcelino Bernardo decided to go back to academe and became an economics professor at the University of the Philippines.

The development and expansion of the Foreign Service took its toll on the graduates. Several decided to quit or retire early because of dissatisfaction, career change, or dismissal from the service. By December 1952, Emilio Torres, Doroteo Vite, and Leopoldo T. Ruiz were no longer in the DFA directory of active officers. Torres resigned after his stint at the Embassy in Washington. The departure of Ambassador Elizalde, Torres' mentor, may have influenced this decision. Vite thought he had joined the carrier service but in 1950, he was separated from the Foreign Service. To bury his frustration and broken heart, he moved to Hawaii to join academe.[42] After his stint as consul in Chicago, Leopoldo T. Ruiz decided to leave the Foreign Service and went back to his first love – academe but this time to Dumaguete City in Negros Oriental where he became the fourth president of Silliman University. He was also the first Filipino to hold the Silliman University's presidency after the Board of Trustees unanimously elected him on its meeting on 26 August 1952.[43]

Revamp after the Election of President Magsaysay

After the victory of Ramon Magsaysay, the Nationalista Party standard bearer, over the incumbent President Elpidio Quirino of the Liberal Party, President Magsaysay appointed Vice President Carlos P. Garcia as concurrent Secretary of Foreign Affairs and Leon Ma. Guerrero as undersecretary of Foreign Affairs. Garcia made no bones about his disgust over the current state of affairs in the Foreign Office and lost no time revamping the organization of the Department of Foreign Affairs and the Foreign Service. He froze the transfer and designation of new officers to the various Foreign Service posts and immediately recalled the chiefs of mission who had resigned after President Magsaysay's victory to give the new administration a free hand in the appointment of new heads of posts.

Garcia never hid his political intentions behind the revamp. In an official statement upon assuming his post as Secretary of Foreign Affairs, Garcia said: "The Department of Foreign Affairs is the only department in the government that was created, staffed, and maintained throughout its life under a single party, the Liberal Party. As a result a new administration finds itself compelled to implement its foreign policy with the appointees of the former administration with whose policies the Nacionalista Party was in profound disagreement."[44]

He added that "it is only fair that the new administration should be given an opportunity to select officials who subscribe to its objectives and tactics in foreign policy." But he allayed the fears of many when he promised that he would not allow the Foreign Service to be a "dumping ground of political protégés.

He also proposed to amend Republic Act No. 708, otherwise known as the Philippine Foreign Service Act of 1952. He averred that "career officers of the Foreign Office have barricaded themselves behind the provisions of the Foreign Service Act. And as long as the act is not amended, they are confident of retaining their positions." According to Garcia, the amendment of the Foreign Service Act and the subsequent revamp in the Foreign Office "was solely to improve the quality of service, against which there has been much complaint among Filipinos who have gone abroad." He lashed at the defects of the Foreign Service Act which he claimed "failed to provide for a coordinated service embracing both the Home Office and the Foreign Service, this leading to unfair discrimination in matters of promotions and allowances."

Furthermore, Garcia criticized that although the Foreign Service Act contemplates the organization of a Foreign Service based on competitive examinations, nobody in the Foreign Service had really taken or passed any examination. This accusation, however, was wrong inasmuch as civil service examinations were conducted to select people to join the defunct Office of Foreign Relations and to participate in the State Department training program. However, since the passage of the Foreign Service Act of 1952, the DFA had not conducted a single FAO examination. Again, Garcia claimed that the Act was worded "to exempt all Liberal Party appointees from the examination required by it." This statement apparently alludes to the State Department graduates who were exempted from taking the examination.

Garcia pointed out the defects of the Foreign Service Act. First, only allowing persons between 23 and 30 years old to take the Foreign Service examination discriminates against mature and experienced professionals. Garcia proposed that the age limit be increased to 39 years old. Second, the Act fails to make provisions for Foreign Affairs officers specializing in the promotion of trade. "Since trade expansion will be one of the cardinal objectives of our foreign policy under my direction, an amendment will be necessary if this policy is to have any success." Third, the Act does not have provisions for the rotation of personnel between the Home Office and Foreign Service in order to give everyone well-rounded experiences. Lastly, the procedure for the removal of Foreign Affairs officers with unsatisfactory records is cumbersome and vague. There are many FAOs appointed by the past administration who have disgraced the nation with their scandalous acts and yet under the provision of laws, it is extremely difficult to dismiss them.[45]

The Manila press had a field day reporting on the impending overhaul of the Foreign Service. It was also divided as to the advantages and disadvantages of the revamp that Vice President Garcia wanted to carry out. *The Manila Times* editorial of 23 January 1954, labeled Garcia's proposal to reorganize the Foreign Service as "unwise." "The Secretary of Foreign Affairs tinkers with a dangerous proposal when he suggests the dismissal of a majority of our career officials as an essential feature of his sweeping reorganizational proposal," the *Manila Times* declared. As a clear defense of the State Department graduates, the editorial explained:

> Career officials are the hard core of the Foreign Service organization. They joined the Foreign Office at its inception, after passing rigid qualifications tests. They underwent special training here and in the US State Department in Washington, and were chosen not on the strength of their political connections but on the strengths solely of their merits. The performance of these career officials has been satisfactory and has enhanced the prestige of the country they represent.[46]

The *Evening News* condemned Garcia's proposal in its 23 January1954 editorial entitled "It's the Spoil System." "In the midst of talk that the Foreign Service should be staffed with men representative of the best of our Republic, it develops that Vice President Carlos Garcia wants them rather to be representative of political supporters." It concludes by stating "This is the spoils system, pure and simple, in a department of government that can least afford it, where qualifications and experience are vital, especially in the lower echelons."[47]

Benigno S. Aquino, Jr., a columnist at the *Manila Times* and a future senator, however, defended Garcia by pointing out the rampant politicking concomitant with a change of administration.

> We are sure the Vice President had only the sincerest motives when he proposed the DFA's reorganization. As he said: "it is solely to improve the quality of our Foreign Service. But we also know that there is always a flock of Nacionalista Party politicians cooling their heels at Arlegui (Foreign Office building) every morning seeking a Foreign Service position, or recommending some "protégés" for "any foreign assignment, as long as it would mean a free trip abroad." And to the many applicants, it would indeed be a "foreign" assignment."[48]
>
> As to the dismissal of erring Foreign Service officials, Aquino in the same column fully agreed with Garcia: "We concur with Vice President Garcia that there have been many FAOs appointed by the past administration who have disgraced the nation abroad with their scandalous acts. Yet under the present provision of laws it is extremely difficult to dismiss them. This brand of misfits should really be booted out of the service but fast."

To give full powers to the Secretary of Foreign Affairs to revamp not only the Department of Foreign Affairs but also the entire Foreign Service, Garcia asked his Nacionalista Party mates in Congress to file a bill that would permit the reorganization of the Foreign Office. The bill would have two salient points: 1) Creation of what will be known as the "Foreign Service Reserve Corps" where otherwise technically capable FAOs would be reverted from active status because they do not enjoy the confidence of the administration; and 2) Creation of two levels of foreign service officers, the first to be known as "highly confidential and technical" which would include all FAOs from vice consul to ambassador, and the other to be known as "confidential and highly technical which would include staff officers such as disbursing and administrative officers of overseas missions, and also stenographers, typists, and receptionists.

The proposed bill seeks to correct R.A. 708 or the Foreign Service

Act of 1952, which, according to Garcia, overemphasizes seniority and technical skill as primary considerations for assignments and promotions. When the proposed bill takes effect, the Secretary of Foreign Affairs will have the power to designate, subject to the confirmation of the Commission on Appointments, all FAOs from vice consul up, regardless of the rigid standards set by R.A. 708.[49]

Garcia, however, failed to get a single Nacionalista senator to back the proposed bill. Senators Gil J. Puyat, Lorenzo Sumulong, and Tomas Cabili, all Nationalists, cautioned Garcia to "go-slow" on the reform of the Foreign Service. Cabili went further and said the move "smacks of political persecution" and could "spell the ruin of the Foreign Service."[50] Unfazed, Garcia referred the proposed amendments to R.A. 708 to Secretary of Justice Pedro Tuason to render an opinion on the issue. This move was interpreted as a ploy to get Garcia "off the hook" as he desperately sought support for his proposal.

On 23 March 1954, Secretary of Justice Tuason issued an opinion to the effect that the proposed changes in the Foreign Service Law were clearly unconstitutional. He stated that the proposed amendments would "destroy the constitutional provision regarding permanent tenure of office except for cause and after due investigation." He took particular exception to the provision calling for the creation of a Foreign Service Reserve Corps to which career diplomats who did not have the confidence of the administration would be assigned. Confronted with the Tuason opinion, Garcia abandoned his drastic plans to reorganize the Foreign Service.[51]

Tuason Opinion on RA 708

Garcia's quest to overhaul the Foreign Service did not stop with his failure to get support for his proposed bill. On 16 March 1954, he again sought the opinion of Secretary Tuason specifically on the following questions: (1) "whether the provisions of Republic Act 708 limit the appointing power vested by the Constitution in the President" and (2) whether the phrase "public ministers" as used in the constitution includes Foreign Service officers other than consuls." The contention of Garcia and Guerrero, his deputy, was that President Magsaysay (and by extension the Secretary of Foreign Affairs and Undersecretary) was free to appoint anyone he wished regardless of the appointment provisions of R.A. 708.

Secretary Tuason, in his Opinion No. 82 of April 3, 1954, found the two questions to be closely related to each other and therefore discussed the two questions as one. Citing Article VII, section 10 (7) of the Constitution, which gives the President the power to appoint ambassadors, other public ministers and consuls, the Secretary ruled that an act of Congress cannot infringe this power and that therefore Republic Act 708 does not limit the power of the President to appoint ambassadors, other public ministers and consuls. He found Foreign Affairs Officers to be essentially within constitutional categories of diplomatic and consular officers. Secretary Tuason concluded, "It is my opinion that the President may also appoint Foreign Affairs Officers without complying with the eligibility requirements under Republic Act No. 708. The provisions of this law imposing certain limitations for appointment s Foreign Affairs Officers should be deemed to be merely directory and not mandatory upon the President."[52]

Much exception was taken to the Secretary's ruling, particularly with regard to the appointment of Foreign Affairs Officers. It was pointed out that Republic Act 708 was patterned after the US Foreign Service Act of 1946 and that in the United States, a country with a similar constitutional pattern, no such ruling had been sought to invalidate the restrictions on the appointing power of the President of the United States. It was also pointed out that the ruling would open the floodgates of the service to all sorts of political appointments in defiance of the merit system. But from a strictly legal standpoint there were not too many who challenge the President's authority under the Constitution to appoint "ambassadors, other public ministers, and consuls" as he saw fit. In large part, the problem seem to resolve itself into a question whether the President, in keeping with the civil service traditions of the Philippines was willing to abide by a career Foreign Service law and thus accept some limitation on his constitutional power of appointment of diplomatic and consular personnel.

Congressman Diosdado Macapagal, the author of R.A. 708 disputed the opinion rendered by Secretary Tuason. He branded the opinion as "erroneous" and "immoral." "The opinion of the Justice Secretary will destroy the merit system and weaken the Foreign Service, the country's first line of defense." Secretary Tuason's opinion," Macapagal said, was "immoral" because it sanctioned a disregard of an act of Congress and led to the "packing of the Foreign Service" with political protégés." Because of the Justice Secretary's opinion, "politicians are being dumped in the Service to the despair of the career men." Macapagal expressed the opinion that the administration should not involve a strict technicality in disregard of sound public policy.[53]

As the Tuason Opinion cleared the way for President Magsaysay to exercise his prerogative to appoint, Magsaysay immediately named two veteran political allies as consuls general –Raul Leuterio, former Majority Floor Leader of the House of Representatives as consul general in New York and Nicanor Roxas, former member of Congress as consul general in San Francisco. "These appointments seem to be not in accordance with the spirit of the new Foreign Service Act (Republic Act No. 708) because under this law nobody can be appointed as Foreign Affairs Officers without taking an examination," observed Roberto Regala, a former judge and then serving as Philippine Minister to Sydney, "Now, it is likely that these appointments were based upon the fact that the President has the appointing power to appoint consuls, ministers, and ambassadors and that this constitutional power of the President cannot be restricted. It may be correct from a strictly legal standpoint, but it is not in line with the spirit of the Foreign Service Act. Precisely the Foreign Service Act places the Foreign Service as a career and, therefore, nobody should be appointed to the said service without passing an examination and that the persons to be appointed as consuls general must be those ones certified by the Board from those who have been in the service."[54]

In Mill's letter to Regala dated 24 May 1954, he shared Regala's preoccupation about the political inroads on the career Foreign Service. "The powers of the American and Philippine presidents to conduct foreign relations under their respective Constitutions are basically the same. Yet I cannot imagine anyone seriously arguing that the American president could make any Foreign Service assignments he saw fit in disregard of the Rogers Act of 1924 and (Foreign Service Act of) 1946. The argument of the Philippine Secretary of Justice here seems untenable to me."[55]

Regala lamented the adoption of the Tuason Opinion and its

negative effect to the career foreign service. "As a result of this opinion, many people outside the Foreign Service were able to enter into it without previous examination. The opinion practically disregards seniority rule as shown by some promotions or appointments as published in the papers. This is really very discouraging and has reduced the morale of the people connected with the service."[56]

Appointment and Promotion Problems

In practice, Congress exerts a great deal of, if not the decisive, influence in the making of diplomatic and consular appointments. Congress, beset by equally strong patronage pressures, has aggressively maintained its role in the appointment process by constantly using the Commission of Appointments (CA) as a check on all executive appointments.[57] The CA's action or inaction, however, also could be damaging to the careers of the members of the Foreign Service. As tension rouse to higher levels with proposed reorganization of the Foreign Service, Garcia strictly scrutinized the promotion of erstwhile Quirino appointees even in grade and in salary within the same class by letting the CA decide on their fate or block their advancement. This was partly provoked by the memorandum submitted by Minister Roberto Regala to the Department of Foreign Affairs stating that promotions in salaries or grades of FAOs within the same class need not be submitted to the CA. Regala's memorandum could be interpreted as an oblique defense of Tiburcio Baja who served under him at the Philippine Consulate General in San Francisco.

In late May 1954, the CA bypassed the promotion of eleven FAOs whose promotions (mainly in grade) were submitted to the CA for confirmation. Although these officers were appointed to Class II, there was no increase in their salaries, but merely involving a consolidation of basic and excess salaries. Six FAOs were re-appointed by President Magsaysay but left out the remaining five, which include two State Department Boys—Tiburcio Baja and Tagakotta Sotto. Baja was then first secretary and consul in the Philippine Embassy in Jakarta while Sotto was consul in Karachi and at the same time *chargé d'affaires* of the Philippine legation there. Without CA confirmation, it appeared that the five officers might have their services terminated and be out of the service.

Regala's letter to the DFA regarding the issue of promotions in salaries and in grades of FAOs within the same class provides an authoritative elucidation on the why there is no need for CA consent for such promotions. As Regala asserted: "With due deference to the action of submitting these promotions to the Commission on Appointments, I feel that after a careful examination of the language of the Foreign Service Act, the promotion in salary of a Foreign Affairs Officer within the same class does not need nomination by the President and consent by the Commission on Appointments."[58]

Not satisfied with Regala's argument, Undersecretary Leon Ma. Guerrero again consulted Justice Secretary Tuason to render an opinion on the case of the FAOs bypassed by the Commission on Appointments. Secretary Tuason found, as was previously explained by Minister Regala, that since the so-called promotions of these men actually involved only consolidation of already existing salaries and/or in-grade promotions, that it was not necessary for the Commission on Appointments to pass on them and that they might continue in service regardless of the inaction of the Commission on Appointments. This ruling on the part of the Secretary of Justice helped to bolster morale in the Foreign Service, particularly among the men affected.[59]

Still the Philippine Foreign Service underwent major changes in the first semester of 1954. The rash of political appointments to the top posts in the Foreign Service signaled the fact that the raid on foreign assignments was on. The *Manila Bulletin* editorial banners:

> Quietly the Commission on Appointments, while applying the by-pass to qualified Foreign Service officers, demothballed a politician from retirement and approved his nomination as minister plenipotentiary with the personal rank of ambassador. He is being groomed for a key post in Asia. His training for the job? He is a Nacionalista old guard .... The hardest hit is the Philippine delegation to the United Nations in New York City ... What of the work and prestige so patiently built up by the men of the Foreign Service at the United Nations? The acting chief delegate to the United Nations is being shifted to Washington. The able legal assistant is to be recalled to Manila. A competent researcher

finds that his item in the budget has been given to the son of a Congressman... The new appointments show that this merit system can easily be bypassed. The special training, competence, experience, and resourcefulness demanded of men on foreign assignment are being brushed aside. And the yardstick? Political pull.[60]

For the career men in the Foreign Service, it was a period of demoralization. Sensing the discontent and insecurity in the service, Undersecretary Guerrero tried to mend fences reassuring the career men that appointment and promotion in the Foreign Service would be based on, despite the initial resistance of Vice President Garcia, the Foreign Service Act. The Nacionalista administration, however, exercised the power to appoint its men to replace out-going chiefs of mission who tendered their courtesy resignations. By the end of August 1954, there were only four chiefs of mission whose resignations were not accepted by President Magsaysay. Among them were Roberto Regala in Sydney, Narciso Ramos in New Delhi, Manuel Alzate in Rome, and Manuel Adeva in Taipei. Adeva was the highest ranking among the State Department graduates at the time. Their future in the Foreign Service, however, remained bleak.

Narciso Ramos submitted his formal courtesy resignation – unqualified, forthright, and unequivocal—to President Ramon Magsaysay in time for him to receive it upon his assumption of office on 30 December 1953. Angela Valdez Ramos, wife of Ramos, wrote Mill from New Delhi to ask for the latter's intercession on behalf of her husband. Her letter dated 04 January 1954, partly reads:

> By this time the President and the Foreign Secretary must be considering the persons to be retained and those persons to be changed in the Foreign Service. As Narciso must have told you, he is prepared to be replaced, for although he has his efficient record to stand on and is at the same time considered a career man, being one of the very first sent out after 4 July 1946, still our political activities in the last elections could be used by the present administration against him. He has rendered twenty years of continuous service to the government and has only ten years more to go. It would

be a pity if he would be separated now and therefore would lose all future advantages of retirement.

While he seems optimistic about some business plans that he has, I know that Narciso is not cut for business. While we have the two girls still in the States, a stable job would be more desirable.

Aside from the financial consideration, I believe that Narciso can still contribute towards a better and stronger Foreign Service for the Philippines. I am sure that he is better qualified (modesty aside) than most of those whom the new administration may choose from the Nacionalista Party or Democracy Party, having more than seven years of experience to his credit.

Because of your close association with our Foreign Service and your keen interest in Philippine affairs, your advice may be sought, or you may volunteer to give your opinion about the men who you think are qualified to carry on our diplomatic work abroad. Please do not hesitate to say a word or two in favor of Narciso.[61]

By April 1954, Ramos was still in New Delhi. He wrote to Mill:

I have been waiting for the axe to fall, but my neck is still intact. Apparently, the new administration in Manila does not have enough honest and competent men for the diplomatic jobs which we "obnoxious" Liberal party appointees have been holding. I know the new Foreign Secretary, Mr. Garcia, subscribes to the political concept that to the victors belong the spoils, and he wants to eliminate us, but if I am still in the service, I am inclined to believe that it is due to the good sense and moral courage of President Magsaysay, who up to now, has refused to be stampeded into ousting indiscriminately all appointees of the past regime.[62]

In the end, Ramos remained in New Delhi and was subsequently appointed as ambassador to the Philippine embassy in Taipei. He would be appointed as Secretary of Foreign Affairs in 1966 during the first term of President Ferdinand E. Marcos. Meanwhile, Roberto Regala was retained in Australian and promoted to ambassador in December 1956. Manuel Adeva was transferred to Bangkok and was promoted to ambassador to Thailand, the first State Department graduate to earn the rank of ambassador extraordinary and plenipotentiary.

Amidst the gloom, there was also light. President Magsaysay promoted two State Department graduates in 1954. Simeon Roxas was promoted from Class IV to Class II. Although some members of the Commission of Appointments objected to the promotion, the majority succeeded and confirmed Roxas. In all fairness, Roxas had served, without promotion, as chief of the Treaties Division at the Home Office and subsequently as third secretary in the Philippine Legation in Rome for three years. When he returned, he discovered that his peers had used political connections to bypass him while he remained Class IV. When the Magsaysay administration took over, Roxas employed his seniority to obtain an appropriate promotion.

President Magsaysay also announced that Tomas de Castro, counselor at the Mission in Tokyo, would be appointed to career minister. Unlike Roxas, De Castro's promotion was considered "good and well-deserved."[63] Some State Department graduates were not as fortunate. Delfin Garcia was stuck as consul for 8 years with no prospect of a promotion.[64] A significant number of the State Department graduates, however, received their promotion in 1957, notably Jose Alejandrino, *chargé d'affaires* of the Philippine Embassy in Madrid, was promoted from FAO Class I to rank of career minister; Juanito C. Dionisio and Emilio Bejasa from FAO Class II to FAO Class I; Pelayo F. Llamas from FAO Class II (medium grade) to FAO Class II (maximum grade); Aurelio Ramos, Anastacio B. Bartolome, Rodolfo Severino from FAO Class II (minimum) to FAO Class II (medium); Carlos A. Faustino from FAO Class III (minimum) to FAO Class III (maximum).[65]

Dismissal in the Foreign Service

True to his promise, Vice President and Secretary of Foreign Affairs Garcia cleansed the Foreign Service of "FAOs appointed by the Quirino administration that had disgraced the nation abroad with their scandalous acts." Unfortunately, two State Department graduates got entangled in widely publicized corruption cases early in their diplomatic career. One was exonerated while the other ruined and lost his Foreign Service career for good.

One of the first celebrated cases of dismissal in the Philippine Foreign Service was that of Hortencio J. Brillantes. While serving as Philippine consul to Seattle in 1954, Brillantes was accused of misappropriating funds and misconduct in office. Due to these alleged offenses, President Ramon Magsaysay ordered the dismissal of Brillantes.[66] His colleagues in the Foreign Service, especially Luis Moreno Salcedo, his batch mate at the State Department, were deeply worried about Brillantes's career. In his letter to Edward W. Mill, Moreno Salcedo expressed disbelief over the news: "I don't know if it's true but last week's issue of the *Free Press* says that the President has dismissed Tencing Brillantes because of the charges against him. Poor Tencing! I do not know whether or not he is guilty but it certainly is terrible to be separated from the Service one has learned to love, in disgrace, with eight children and when one is no longer young. If he has erred, he's surely paying dearly for it."[67]

In the end, it turned out that Brilliantes was a mere victim of a smear campaign and was eventually cleared of any wrongdoing. At any rate, his reputation was badly damaged by this episode. He was also psychologically devastated when he was bypassed for promotion. But Brillantes was resilient and determined to prove his detractors wrong about him. In December 1957, as an Alternate Representative of the Philippine Mission to the United Nations in New York, Brillantes wrote a poignant letter to Mill:

> I have long intended to correspond with you, but since my assignment here, I have been working so hard, harder than at any time in my life. I wanted to disprove to the whole world the clouds of smear that had been overcast on me; I wanted to show to my boss whom I did never know before and who never did know me in return, that I can deliver the goods. He in fact tried me, but with my avidity for work and the fundamentals sipped from the State Department fountain of wisdom plus the experience I have had, I understood all assignments, - and in fact, after a week's time, I became his closest adviser in the Mission. So, important assignments came unto me one after another.[68]

The controversial case that eventually destroyed the career of a former State Department graduate fell on Tagakotta O. Sotto. On 8 September 1949, the Philippine Consulate in Karachi, Pakistan was established with Tagakotta Sotto as consul. Bilateral relations between the Philippines and Pakistan started well and developed fast. Philippine importation of rice from Pakistan was one of the cornerstones of bilateral trade. When the Consulate was raised to a Legation, Sotto was designated as *chargé d'affaires*.[69] As head of post, Sotto was instrumental in facilitating rice transaction between the Philippines and Pakistan. In fact he overplayed his role and was embroiled in a controversy that he could not extricate himself from.

On 11 February 1956, President Magsaysay signed Administrative Order No. 179 removing Consul Tagakotta O. Sotto from office. (Removal of Consul Tagakotta Sotto, 11 February 1956; Official Gazette, Vol. 52, No. 2. P. 595-596) Sotto was charged of misconduct, disloyalty to the Philippine Government and malfeasance in office. The administrative order against him consisted of the following:

1. That as *chargé d'affaires* of the Philippine legation at Karachi, he [Sotto] signed an agreement without the authority of his Government for the purchase and sale of rice in the amount of 30,000 long tons between the Government of Pakistan through its Secretary of Food and Agriculture and the Republic of the Philippines;
2. That without authority from the Government of the Republic of the Philippine, he designated the Ivlom Corporation of Karachi as the executive agent of the said government to handle all transactions in connection with the aforesaid agreement;
3. That he is guilty of insubordination in that he refused to follow the instructions of the Department for him to come to the Philippines as contained in its radiogram No. 246;
4. That he left his post without the permission of the Department and without submitting the necessary clearances in violation of existing regulations;
5. That he filed a suit before a Pakistan Court making the Republic of the Philippines party plaintiff against Ivlom Corporation and other dependents without obtaining previous authority from his government, thereby placing the Republic of the Philippines under the jurisdiction of a foreign court;

6. That he withdrew the aforesaid suit during its pendency without the consent of the Philippine Government, to the prejudice of the Filipino rice dealers in whose interest the case was filed; and
7. That he continued and still continues to remain absent from his post without an authorized leave and keeping the Department ignorant of his whereabouts.

Sotto admitted charges numbers 1, 2, 3, and 5 and denied the rest. His case was referred to the Board of Foreign Service of the Department of Foreign Affairs for formal investigation. The DFA instructed Sotto to return to Manila to refute the charges against him and to confront the witnesses against him. Sotto still refused to report to the Home Office. In a radiogram, he manifested conformity to his dismissal provided he would not be required to return to the Philippines. During the hearing of the case, Sotto's counsel was given the chance to refute the evidence against his client. Nonetheless, the evidence presented against Sotto was overwhelming and he was found guilty of the irregularities adduced against him. Thus, Secretary Garcia, upon the recommendation of the Board of Foreign Service, recommended the dismissal of Sotto to President Magsaysay. As can be gleaned from the last part of the Administrative Order, President Magsaysay avoided the precipitous decision he made against Hortencio Brillantes and treated the Tagakotta Sotto case with more caution and deliberation. After all, Sotto was not just an ordinary career diplomat but was also the son of a former Philippine senator. Thus, the president's carefully worded verdict reads as follows:

> After carefully going over the records of the case, I agree with the Board's findings which are concurred in by the Secretary of Foreign Affairs. In view of the seriousness of the irregularities committed by the respondent, I am constrained to take drastic action against him (Sotto) as recommended by the Secretary of Foreign Affairs and the investigating body. Wherefore, Consul Tagakotta O. Sotto is hereby removed from office effective as of the date of his preventive suspension.

On 06 May 1956, President Ramon Magsaysay approved the recommendation of Vice President Garcia for the suspension of Sotto for "abandonment of office" and not on the administrative charges leveled against him.[70] Sotto faded and disappeared like a bubble. Nothing was heard of about him in the Foreign Service since then. Many years later, he was reportedly sighted in Canada where he was living all along after his dismissal from the Philippine Foreign Service.[71]

A Decade after the State Department Training

Ten years after the Philippine Foreign Affairs Training Program was launched, Mill proudly claimed that the State Department-sponsored program had by then paid rich dividends. As Mill wrote: "The program was important not only as a means for helping the Philippines to build a career foreign affairs establishment but that it was also important as a means for strengthening Philippine- American relations. Most of these key foreign affairs officers will always be particular good friends of the United States."[72]

The State Department graduates as a group made a historic contribution to the advancement of their country. As Mill wrote: "It must be recalled that this past decade has been a period of building for the Republic of the Philippines and its Department of Foreign Affairs and Foreign Service. The principle of a career Foreign Service has had to be enunciated and fortified, an organizational framework abroad and at home created, standards of performance set, and the foreign policy goals and objectives of the Republic clarified. In other words, it has been a pioneering time for career foreign affairs officers. It would be fallacious to credit the graduates of this program with having accomplished all these things. Many non-graduates of the program must share credit with the graduates for building accomplished during this period. But there can be little doubt that the PFATP graduates have been the active spearhead of the movement to build a career foreign affairs establishment for the Philippines."[73]

Since the organization of the Department of Foreign Affairs, the State Department Boys filled all the top positions of the Department, except those of Secretary and Undersecretary. A majority of the Division Chiefs in the Foreign Office had been State Department trainees. But it was in the Foreign Service where they had been particularly conspicuous. In 1956, five of the graduates of the program achieved the rank of Minister (already considered head of post at the time, although still a category lower than ambassador). They were: Manuel A. Adeva, Minister to Nationalist China; Jose F. Imperial, Minister to Japan; Tomas G. de Castro, Minister to Korea; Jose Alejandrino, Minister to Thailand; and Yusuf Abubakar, Minister to Egypt.[74]

Adeva became the first graduate of the State Department training program to become a career ambassador in 1956 as Philippine ambassador to Thailand. Those State Department Boys working in the Home Office were serving as either division chiefs or counselors. They inspired other qualified people to join the Foreign Service and mentored future generation of career diplomats. However, out of the original 40 trainees, only 32 were still in active service in 1955.

The death of President Ramon Magsaysay in an air crash in 1957 was a tragic event for the Philippines. The Philippine presidency seemed to have been a cursed position. Already three Filipino presidents had died while in office – Manuel L. Quezon, Manuel A. Roxas, and Ramon Magsaysay. Vice President Carlos P. Garcia assumed the reins of government. He appointed Felixberto Serrano as Secretary of Foreign Affairs. The appointment of Felixberto Serrano as Secretary of Foreign Affairs was heaven-sent for the State Department Boys. As a former ambassador to the Philippine Mission to the United Nations, Serrano was familiar with the work and good performance of the State Department graduates, some of whom served under him. Unlike his predecessor, Serrano was not too concerned about the politics in the Foreign Service. There was no witch hunting and political loyalty check that characterized the first years of the Secretaryship of Carlos Garcia. In effect, the career service had been given a boost.

Months later after the assumption of Secretary Serrano, Anastacio Bartolome, member of Group III, broke the good news to Mill about the State Department graduates: "02 November 1959 is a memorable day for many officials in the Department. On that day they received promotions either as Foreign Affairs Officers in the various classes or as career ministers. I am happy to inform you that a number of ex-trainees of the State Department Philippine Foreign Affairs Training Program are among the recipients of these promotions. They include Simeon Roxas who is now a career minister; Rodolfo H. Severino, Irineo D. Cornista, and I as Foreign Affairs Officers, Class I; and Marciano A. Joven as Foreign Affairs Officer, Class III," an excited Anastacio Bartolome wrote to Mill. "The oath of office was administered separately to each group of officers belonging to the same class by Secretary of Foreign Affairs Felixberto M. Serrano." Bartolome also added that Generoso Provido, Vicente Singian, and Tiburcio Baja were also promoted to Foreign Affairs Officer, Class I.[75]

Mill also celebrated the good news conveyed by Bartolome. In his response Bartolome, he said: "You say that 02 November 1959 is a memorable day for many officials in the Department. Let me say that it is also a memorable day for me, for as you can imagine, I always take keen pride in the accomplishments of the graduates of the program. I think that Secretary Serrano, whom I have never had the pleasure of meeting, deserves much credit for approving these promotions."[76]

In general, the State Department graduates continued to reap success in their Foreign Service careers. By July 1963, 27 of them were already holding the ranks or positions of ambassadors, career ministers, or consuls general in the Foreign Service. It was also in the 1960s that the degree of success of the State Department graduates became evident. Many of them were deeply conscious of their ranks and positions in the Foreign Service. Not all of them, though, would reach the coveted ambassadorial position or even if they reach a chief of mission rank, some still retired without getting an ambassadorship to a particular country. Some simply lagged behind and became bitter as they see that time was no longer on their side. One of them was Tiburcio Baja who, while serving as Philippine minister to London, wrote to Mill in August 1965 to express his disappointment. "I am disappointed and impatient. Many of my very juniors are now ambassadors – Abubakar, Tirona, Rosal, Roxas, and Garcia to name some. Will I ever make it at the top by the time I retire at 65? I have sometime a notion of quitting at 63 and take it easy. After all they do not seem to care. I am ever doing my best but my best is not their best and is not good enough. Somehow there is always a hindrance to promotion. Why stick around?"[77] Baja retired as minister in the Philippine Embassy in London. He was recommended to be the Philippine ambassador to Nigeria but it did not materialize.

Other State Department graduates chose to retire as number two in the Foreign Service post due to personal or family reasons. This was the case of Jose F. Imperial who after serving as head of posts in Japan and Thailand, spent the last years of his career as deputy chief of mission in the Philippine Embassy in Washington, D.C. He was also the victim of much criticism from the Manila press for his alleged pro-American ways. As one Filipino columnist sneered: "Ambassador Jose F. Imperial, who is married to an American lady twice his size, is said to show more interest in the businesses of the State Department than those of Padre Faura (former headquarters of the DFA); that he believes more in Secretary Dean Rusk than in Secretary (Narciso) Ramos and that his style of living is more of an American than that of a Filipino. To the members of the Washington embassy personnel, it has also been observed that Imperial has always appealed for strict compliance with American laws. If Ambassador Imperial who is said to be 67 would not be able to extend again his term, he would acquire American citizenship and live in retirement in American territory."[78]

Since its beginning in 1946, the Foreign Service was not immune to the influence of politics. Politics still remained one of the factors for advancement in the Foreign Service. Any change of administration would certainly affect the career advancement or stagnation of the State Department graduates. Toward the end of the term of President Diosdado Macapagal in 1965, several ambassadorial appointments were made, including the appointment of Eduardo Rosal as ambassador to Portugal. However, upon the assumption to the presidency of Ferdinand E. Marcos, all the Macapagal appointees were unceremoniously recalled. As one Filipino career diplomat recalled: "Ambassador Eduardo Rosal is a career ambassador but a President Macapagal's midnight appointee as ambassador to Portugal, left for Lisbon, where Charge d' Affaires Amante Manzano with Portuguese foreign ministry officials and the press were waiting for him at the airport. He committed the mistake of contacting our embassy in Madrid, who relayed to him the order to return to Manila immediately. He ended up in the DFA freezer formerly occupied by his arch-enemy Manuel Collantes who became undersecretary upon the assumption of office of President Ferdinand E. Marcos. Since he had taken his oath as ambassador to Portugal, he was automatically dismissed in January when the special meeting of Congress adjourned. Much later President Marcos relented and allowed him to return to DFA to head the North Borneo Office."[79] The North Borneo (Sabah) Office was then considered the "freezer" section at the DFA.

As of 15 January 1967, only twenty-five of the original 40 of the State Department graduates were still in active service.[80] They were holding the following positions in the Philippine Foreign Service and the Department of Foreign Affairs:

1. Abubakar, Yusup: Ambassador to Ceylon
2. Alejandrino, Jose: Ambassador to France
3. Baja, Tiburcio: Minister and Chargé d'Affaires, London (with the rank of ambassador)
4. Bejasa, Emilio: Ambassador to the Federal Republic of Germany
5. Bartolome, Anastacio: Minister to Saigon
6. Busuego, Romeo: Ambassador to Malaysia
7. Brillantes, Hortencio: Ambassador to the United Nations (Geneva)
8. Cornista, Irineo: Minister to New Delhi
9. De Castro, Tomas: Ambassador to Argentina
10. Dionisio, Juanito: Ambassador to Pakistan
11. Faustino, Carlos: Consul General, Hong Kong, with rank of Minister
12. Garcia, Delfin: Ambassador to The Netherlands
13. Imperial, Jose: Chargé d'Affaires, Washington, D.C (with the rank of ambassador)
14. Joven, Marciano: Consul General to Phnom Pehn, Cambodia
15. Llamas, Pelayo: Consul General to New Orleans (with rank of Minister)
16. Moreno, Luis Salcedo: Ambassador to the Republic of Vietnam
17. Peña, Pablo: Assistant Secretary for Political Affairs (Manila)
18. Provido, Generoso: Consul General to Chicago, Chief of Mission II

19. Ramos, Aurelio: Minister to Madrid
20. Rosal, Eduardo: Head, North Borneo Office (Manila)
21. Severino, Rodolfo: Minister, Chief of Coordination and Policy (Manila)
22. Singian, Vicente: Ambassador to Belgium
23. Tirona, Benjamin: Ambassador to Burma
24. Urquiola, Renato: Consul General to San Francisco
25. Yango, Alejandro: Minister, Philippine Mission to the United-Nations, New York

Those who recently left the Foreign Service were Guillermo Fonacier and Manuel A. Adeva who retired in 1965 and 1966, respectively. Those who already passed away were Candido Elbo, Irineo Cabatit, Engracio Guerzon, Eutiquio O. Sta. Romana, and Roman V. Ubaldo. Earlier five State Department graduates had left the Foreign Service to join either the private sector or academe. They were Doroteo Vite, Emilio Torres, Reynaldo Lardizabal Jr, Marcelino Bernardo, and Leopoldo T. Ruiz. One, Tagakotta Sotto, was dismissed from the Service.

The State Department graduates listed in the Biographical Register in 1970 were down to twenty-five – eighteen of them were ambassadors or chiefs of mission and four were career ministers. By 1983 there were only five of them in the active service — Emilio Bejasa, Hortencio Brillantes, Delfin Garcia, Luis Moreno Salcedo, and Alejandro Yango — and four of them were already retiring. Bejasa had actually retired in 1979 but was plucked out of retirement to serve as deputy to Ambassador Benjamin Romualdez in Jeddah, Saudi Arabia. He was eventually transferred to New Delhi and was appointed as Philippine ambassador to India.

In 1986, Delfin Garcia was the only State Department graduate in the active list of Foreign Service Officers. He was Philippine ambassador to the German Democratic Republic. He was then the most senior career diplomat in the Philippine Foreign Service. A year later, Garcia finally retired. His retirement marked the end of an era. The State Department Boys had disappeared from the roster of the Philippine Foreign Service.

Photo Gallery II

The U.S. Foreign Service Institute. The fourth and fifth group of Filipino trainees attended the newly established U.S. Foreign Service Institute in 1947, then located at 2115 C Street NW in Washington, D.C. *Source: National Archives and Record Administration, College Park, Maryland*

Richard Porter Butrick (1894–1997), the American Foreign Affairs Adviser detailed to the new Philippine Republic from August 1946 to May 1947 to help establish the Philippine Department of Foreign Affairs and the Foreign Service. *Source: Rachel Davies Butrick*

Arlegui House, the first building of the Philippine Department of Foreign Affairs at Arlegui Street in Manila, circa 1946. *Source: American Historical Collection, Rizal Library, Ateneo de Manila University*

The Department of Foreign Affairs moved to the newly rehabilitated University of the Philippines Library Building at Padre Faura Street in 1955. The Padre Faura Building served as DFA headquarters until 1988. *Source: Lopez Museum and Library, Pasig City, Philippines*

One of the reunions of Edward W. Mill and the State Department Boys in Manila in 1948. Included in the picture is Undersecretary of Foreign Affairs Felino Neri (third from left). Front row, left to right – Jose Alejandrino, Marcelino V. Bernardo, Felino Neri, Edward W. Mill, Luis Moreno Salcedo, and Rodolfo H. Severino; back row, Generoso P. Provido, Engracio D. Guerzon, Carlos A. Faustino, Emilio D. Bejasa, and Roman V. Ubaldo. *Source: Edward W. Mill Collection, Bentley Historical Library, University of Michigan*

Ambassador Joaquin M. Elizalde (sixth from left) with the officers of the Philippine Embassy in Washington, D.C., circa 1947. *Source: Benito B. Valeriano*

U.S. President Harry Truman received Vice President and Secretary of Foreign Affairs Elpidio Quirino in the White House in May 1947. With them were Philippine Ambassador Joaquin M. Elizalde, at right, and U.S. Ambassador Paul McNutt, at left. *Source: American Historical Collection, Rizal Library, Ateneo de Manila University*

The Philippines was a founding member of the United Nations. Carlos P. Romulo, chief delegate of the Philippine Commonwealth to the United Nations Conference on International Organization held in San Francisco in June 1945, signs the United Nations Charter. He is flanked by other members of the Philippine delegation and foreign delegates. Jose F. Imperial (third from the left) served as technical adviser to the Philippine delegation. Imperial would later join the first group of Filipino trainees in the U.S. State Department in December 1945. *Source: American Historical Collection, Rizal Library, Ateneo de Manila University*

The Philippine Delegation to the United Nations General Assembly in 1962, headed by Secretary of Foreign Affairs Salvador P. Lopez (front row, extreme right). The members include Luis Moreno Salcedo (back row, extreme right), Hortencio J. Brillantes (back row, third from left), and Emilio D. Bejasa (front row, extreme left), all top graduates of the Philippine Foreign Affairs Training Program at the U.S. State Department. Moreno Salcedo and Brillantes later in their careers became Permanent Representatives to the United Nations in New York and Geneva respectively, while Bejasa served as Deputy Permanent Representative at the Philippine Mission to the United Nations in New York. *Source: Emilio D. Bejasa Family*

8

"Father of the Philippine Foreign Service"

On 13 July1977, Edward W. Mill, then Chairman of Diplomacy and World Affairs Department at Occidental College, died in his home in Eagle Rock, California. His death was sudden and unexpected. The day before his death, Mill received a clean bill of health at his annual physical examination. In fact, Mill was looking after his wife Virginia who the hospital had recently discharged after a major surgery. "On the 12th of July, when he returned from his physical exam we discussed his health," Virginia recalled. "He felt so good over such a fine report. I said to him, "Honey, you will live to be 105." His answer was, "One never knows." The shock upon seeing him on the morning of 13 July has almost been too much. He looked as though he were peacefully asleep. The autopsy revealed that it was an aneurysm."[1]

Five days later, Secretary of Foreign Affairs Carlos P. Romulo wrote to Virginia: "We learned with sorrow the death of your husband Dr. Edward W. Mill. He was the author of the Philippine Foreign Service Training, U.S. State Department shortly after Philippine Independence and we are indebted to him for the initial training of many of our Foreign Service Staff now occupying important diplomatic posts in many parts of the world. We mourn his death and we will always remember his memory with profound gratitude."[2] More condolence letters poured in. In one, Philippine Consul General to Los Angeles, Armando C. Fernandez, wrote:

> The entire staff of the Philippine Consulate General joins our colleagues in Manila in expressing our most profound sense of loss and grief on the untimely demise of your late husband, Dr. Edward W. Mill. As former Director of the Philippine Foreign Affairs Training Program of the US Department of State, the name of Dr. Mill will always be remembered in high esteem by the career corps of our foreign service.[3]

A year later, Virginia received a letter from Juan M. Arreglado, secretary general of the Philippine Ambassadors Association, transmitting a laminated resolution passed by the Philippine Ambassadors Association in its meeting of 16 March 1978, in Makati that reads:

> In this resolution, it was resolved to pay tribute to the memory of Dr. Edward W. Mill as an inspiring and outstanding professor, diplomat, scholar, a great and sincere friend of the Philippines, and to make of record this humble token of the Association's highest regard and appreciation of all that Dr. Mill had done for the Republic of the Philippines in the development of the Foreign Service.[4]

The outpouring of condolences and homage from Philippine Foreign Service officials exemplified Mill's relationship with the Philippines and its foreign affairs officialdom. He was not only a mentor but a lifetime friend of the State Department trainees. Long before his untimely death in 1977, Mill was already regarded as the "Father of the Philippine Foreign Service."

Family Roots and Education

Edward William Mill was born on 14 June 1916 in Mason City, Illinois. He descended from immigrants from North Devon, England, and Malmö, Sweden.[5] As a young boy, Mill played the trumpet; tennis was his favorite sport, and he loved the outdoors. Since his family owned a cottage on the lake, Mill grew up amidst the rivers and lakes of Wisconsin. His father, Edward J. Mill, was a hardworking farmer who later in life became a wealthy landowner. Mill's parents moved to Belvidere, Illinois when young Edward went to college.

Mill attended public schools in Rockford, Illinois, and Madison, Wisconsin. At an early age, he knew he wanted to be a politician or a civil servant. Mill studied Political Science at the University of Wisconsin and majored in International Relations. He also took up courses in international law, comparative government, and international organization. Grayson L. Kirk, Walter R. Sharp, John T. Salter, William Ebenstein, and Fred Harrington were his professors and became his long-time friends. Mill's diligence and brilliance caught his professors' attention, particularly Prof. Salter who was also chairman of the Political Science Department. Nearing the conclusion of Salter's class on municipal administration, Salter told Mill: "I just wanted to tell you that I consider you the outstanding man in class; I have no doubt as that, only as to who is the second."[6]

Months later, Prof. Salter encouraged Mill to join the teaching staff since he saw Mill's potential in academe. In fact, Mill helped him write *The Pattern of Politics*, a book about the approach to studying politics. After Mill took part in a heated discussion in a political science class, one of his classmates, Frank D. Sprutel of Milwaukee, approached Mill and said: "Mr. Mill, you have the best speaking voice I've ever heard. I could listen to you all day." This boosted Mill's confidence. Coupled with his mastery of the art of public speaking, his speaking voice became one of his greatest assets in the coming years.

Mill graduated with honors in Political Science in June 1940. Thinking about what lay ahead, he wrote in his diary: "Politics and doing something for the people represent my great passions."[7] Before graduating, the University of Michigan offered Mill a scholarship. He worried about supporting himself the following year, but he decided to go to Ann Arbor.

At the University of Michigan

After only one semester of straight As at the University of Michigan, the school appointed him an instructor of an American state government course. Since every member of the Political Science Department had a doctorate degree, the appointment was a great honor. Prof. James K. Pollok, the department chairman, who had nominated Mill, was the last to earn the distinction himself sixteen years earlier. Pollock had authored numerous books on Michigan civil service amendments and nationally famous speakers. The department faculty included Prof. Joseph Ralston Hayden, former vice governor of the Philippines; Prof. Jesse R. Reeves, Ford Professor of Constitutional Law and former judge on the 10th Federal Court of Appeals; Prof. Arthur W. Bromage, generally considered the most outstanding man in state and municipal administration in America; and Prof. Lawrence Preuss, an international lawyer. Mill was thrilled to be in the company of these brilliant men. Mill focused his graduate work on Pacific affairs—Japan, China, and the Philippines. He took a special interest in the development of the Japanese Navy. He subsequently earned an M.A. in Political Science in June 1941.

Mill greatly enjoyed teaching and working with students. He had 36 freshmen and sophomore students in his American government class and he co-taught a course on political parties for juniors and seniors. Aside from his regular courses, Mill occasionally delivered lectures in other courses and seminars when the head professor was absent. He approached the task with gusto and considered it a privilege. As he wrote:

> At 2 o'clock I took Prof. Pollock's place and lectured to his seminar group on Prof. Salter's "The Pattern of Politics" (which I helped to write) as an approach to the study of politics. In this group were two Negro students (both very sharp), two Philippine students (We have more "rah-rah" in our politics.) and a rather unusual Michigan State senator. It was a privilege to talk to this group.[8]

To augment his salary, Mill earned ten dollars a day correcting papers and proctoring exams. Mill found teaching was his greatest strength, even boasting that he had a natural talent for it. He successfully delivered a lecture on "The Conduct of American Foreign Relations" to three hundred students to cap his first year of teaching. He was also sent to the University of Indiana as a University of Michigan representative for the Mid-West International Relations Conference. Mill excitedly wrote home: "I was given a car marked

State-Owned, University of Michigan and supplied with all gas and oil. Could one imagine this in these days of rubber shortages and the likes? I took along four university seniors majoring in political science and acted as faculty adviser to them. I can tell you that my talk there on Chinese Communal Life and the Development of the Civil Service Concept was a great triumph."[9]

Mill worked hard to prepare his lectures and it paid off handsomely. His reputation as an outstanding lecturer spread among his students and reached the ears of senior faculty members. One Tuesday during a Political Science faculty lunch at the Michigan Union, Professor Bromage described one of Mill's student's reactions:

> Say Ed, one of my boys came rushing in to see me after your lecture and said: "Boy that fellow (Mill) must know his stuff. I'll bet he put three to four hours of work in preparation." Mill was very satisfied with this compliment although deep inside he had this to say: "They don't know that it takes hours of preparation to deliver those lectures even if you are an expert in the particular field, but of course, 3 or 4 hours to him meant a great deal, and he thought he was really expressing himself when he said this.[10]

Mill was preoccupied with the war raging in Europe. He followed it with a keen eye, fearing its impact on the United States. He was among the thousands of Scandinavians who opposed Hitler; he looked forward to the draft rather than shirked it.

During a debate with his English friend Jeff Seed, Mill pointed out how "indifferent and apathetic the run-of-the-mine American was to the great cause of the war." He detested the lack of patriotism of college men in Michigan, which was typical of "the deplorable sentiment existing among all too many of our American college men today," Mill wrote in his diary.

> They can't see the necessity of being drafted and regard it as a great imposition upon them. How selfish, how despicable! Intellectualism has its values but when it produces minds narrow, cynical and purely self-seeking its value may well be questioned. It was people of this stamp who laid

the foundation for the degradation of France. I regard being drafted and serving my country as a privilege to be gladly accepted.[11]

The outbreak of war in the Pacific on 07 December 1941 drastically changed the lineup of the Political Science Department. By September 1942, the University lost many top professors to the U.S. government and the war effort. Hayden was sent to China on a diplomatic mission; Preuss was seconded to the State Department to work on a special project relating to postwar reconstruction; and Henem was commissioned as a captain in the army intelligence unit.

Mill had long felt that he could be of some assistance to the U.S. Navy because of his detailed study of the Japanese navy. He had applied four times to the navy and army but was rejected on physical grounds for being underweight and near-sighted. Although he claimed that he was "organically sound," standing at six foot one, Mill was lanky, slightly stooped, and looked frail. Mill applied, as a first choice, to be an instructor in the naval pre-flight schools. He possessed the required teaching experience, but had 3/20 vision, with 12/20 the minimum for consideration and 18/20 desired. Mill was disappointed that these physical standards weren't waived for teachers. Besides, his corrected vision was 20/20. He assumed he would end up as a private in the Army, but failed the physical test again. He consoled himself by reflecting on his career in academe. "I expect to make some decided progress on my doctorate this year—at least so long as the army refuses to take me."[12]

Love Life and Political Plans

Mill's academic interests never thwarted his love life. Gail was his steady girlfriend in Wisconsin; they separated when he moved to Ann Arbor. While teaching at the University of Michigan, he met Wilma Stevenson during the first semester of his political science class in 1941. Their relationship began professionally and a semester later blossomed into a love affair. Mill visited Wilma regularly at her home in Concord, Michigan. By April 1942, after a whirlwind romance, they got engaged. On 15 August 1942, they got married at the Concord Presbyterian Church. As Mill noted in his memoirs: "Wilma is an unusually fine girl whose tastes run side by side with my own. She has a world of common sense and about everything else that I have always desired in my wife."[13]

Mill's interest in politics also never waned. He may have run for public office, but the Pacific War altered his plans. He believed the U.S. faced a crisis of domestic politics:

> As a people it seems to me that greed for personal power has become all too dominant in our way of life; the public interest comes but second in the minds of our contemporary politicians. I believe that young men detached of loyalty to the special interests and capable of the highest actions must make sacrifices and enter the political arena before democracy has hung itself. I do not know that I fit into this particular category of person, but I do know that I am consumed with a passion to do something for democracy and the common man. Perhaps I may get a chance someday.[14]

At the Foreign Broadcast Intelligence Service

Despite his success in Michigan, Mill started looking for career opportunities beyond academe. His initial attempts failed. Through Dr. Joseph R. Hayden, he got an offer to help write President Manuel L. Quezon's biography. Quezon was at the head of the government-in-exile Washington, D.C. But the job did not materialize because, according to Dr. Hayden, "the kind of book which he (Quezon) now proposes to write will not require documentary research."[15] In July 1942, Mill applied to the Department of the Interior in the Division of Territories and Island Possessions. They told him that there was no vacancy for which he was qualified.[16]

His opportunity to government work came in early 1943 when he received a letter, dated 25 February 1943 from Goodwin Watson, Chief of Analysis Division at the Foreign Broadcast Intelligence Service (FBIS). Watson informed him that he was recommended for a position in a government agency and would involve analyzing current broadcast news from the Far East. Mill was pleased and surprised but thought that: "The analyses of foreign propaganda efforts appear to be a highly important phase of our general intelligence work and I should be very happy to have a role in this work."[17] He had never applied and knew little about FBIS.

He consulted his mentor Dr. Hayden who knew nothing about it either. Mill discovered that FBIS heard about Mill's articles on Japanese and Pacific affairs published, for free, in *Current History*. His knowledge of Pacific affairs fit the requirement for the "analysis of Pacific broadcast."

On 05 March 1943, Mill received a curt telegram from Watson: "Would you accept a position as previously described? Salary $3,100 plus overtime. Could you commence work on 15 March?" Mill rushed an excited letter to his folks about the job. "This is the second great offer I have had in the past few months. The first one from President Quezon from Washington fell through because of my uncertainty with regard to the draft. I am afraid this will happen again. And the tough part is that I may well be rejected again and left holding the bag."[18]

Leaving the University of Michigan was difficult, but despite his hesitation, the offer was too good to refuse. Not only was it an opportunity to work in the federal government, but also both of his mentors, Hayden and Pollock, supported the offer since Mill would be using his specialization in Pacific affairs. Still hoping to join the army, Mill packed his things and headed to Washington, D.C.

Mill accepted the temporary FBIS job with a leap of faith. On 27 April, Mill was appointed Assistant Broadcast Analyst, salaried at $2,600 per annum—much lower than what had been promised. Mill's official title was "Military Analyst, Far Eastern Division, FBIS." He had written his Aunt Ida that: "This work is intimately related to the war effort; most of our work being with the army and navy intelligence, the FBI, the Board of Economic Warfare, and the Office of Strategic Services. We have some of the greatest minds in political science working here with us."[19]

Mill's job was unique and highly confidential.

> I have been delegated, however, to be the expert on all phases of Japanese life; in other words I must be able to write as exhaustively and as accurately of Japanese economic life – the price of commodity structure, materials mobilization, banking policies and procedures, insurance systems, savings methods as well as the ordinary professor of Japanese life; I must know the Japanese political structure, the position

of the Emperor, of the Diet, Privy Council, Imperial Household Ministry; I must know the Japanese military and naval policies, methods, and personnel to the letter (and would you be surprised if you know what we were doing in that regard); in short I must know Japanese life as well as I know American life. Where did I learn all this? Did I ever have a course on this? The answer is I had no formal training whatsoever; my knowledge was acquired by my own reading and thought. And in all sincerity, I can tell you right now that I have just about the top responsibility in the federal government for the analysis of this material. I am the only one in Washington doing this. On very short notice I typed up on Saturday and Sunday, working eleven hours each day, a 35 page summary which will be published on Wednesday of this week for use only by leading government officials and officers working on Far Eastern matters.[20]

In fact, Prof. J. T. Salter, Mill's professor in Wisconsin, wrote him to inquire if there was any available job for him in FBIS. When Mill consulted with the head of agency on Salter's behalf, but was told: "A man must be known as a foreign expert before we take him" and that he would try to get Salter a job more suited to his field of specialization.[21] Although saddened by the response, it boosted Mill's confidence about his abilities and reputation.

At the Office of Strategic Services (OSS)

Mill's intelligence work at the FBIS helped him advance toward a higher paid job at the Office of Strategic Services, America's wartime intelligence agency and precursor to the Central Intelligence Agency (CIA). As early as January 1943, Mill had heard about available positions at the OSS but remained discouraged by his rejection by the navy and army. On 30 June 1943, just two months after joining FBIS, L. Gurier Durant, acting director of personnel of OSS, sent Mill a letter and various forms for employment application. Mill submitted them with low expectation. On 15 July 1943, Mill received a letter from Hayden about a possible transfer to the OSS. Mill, however, was still not confident with his prospects.

Nevertheless, Hayden's excellent recommendation enabled

Mill to get a job at the OSS. Mill formally joined the OSS as a Pacific area specialist in October 1943. His letter to his parents reflects the confidentiality of his work:

> The work is surrounded with the most intensive and drastic secrecy; every new employee has to run a withering gauntlet of FBI, Army Intelligence, and Naval Intelligence scrutiny before being accepted for duty. We are technically warned against discussion of any possible military movements with anyone, even the best friends and closest relatives; no one is to be trusted. So as far as discussion of the war goes, therefore, you will have little of anything from me from now on. But you know that I am right in the middle of things.[22]

Mill's work involved a lot of traveling around Washington. He spent a great deal of time at the State Department and at the U.S. Congress. In April 1944, Mill and Hayden worked together again on Southwest Pacific affairs. At the time Hayden was already General Douglas MacArthur's adviser and right-hand man. Through Hayden, Mill met General William "Wild Bill" Donovan, the chief of OSS, and other top officials (colonels) of the War Department. During this time, Mill began serious work on the Philippines and their preparation for liberation from Japanese occupation. Much of his work was research and writing; he wrote six PhD-size theses on various topics, including one of the basic handbooks used in the invasion of the Philippines.

As the Allied Powers advanced in the European theater, it was just a matter of time before the Philippines would be center stage. On 12 June 1944, Mill met, for the first time, Col. Carlos P. Romulo, MacArthur's aide and secretary of information of the Philippine Commonwealth government at the Statler Hotel. Awed by Romulo's reputation as "the last man of Bataan," they discussed the Pacific War; Mill noted that Romulo was "sharing encouraging and most interesting inside information."[23]

Mill's Washington experience allowed him to meet at least seventy-five percent of the ranking Far Eastern personnel in the country and opened up the sources of research material – Library of Congress, National Archives, Departmental Archives, Institute of

Pacific Relations, Library of the Carnegie Endowment for International Peace, etc. He grew his interest in the Philippines and made extensive contact with Philippine officials. When President Quezon died of tuberculosis on 01 August 1944, Mill attended his funeral at Arlington Cemetery. After Quezon's death, Mill quickly established close relations with Vice President Sergio Osmeña whose succession to the presidency "was hailed as certain to bring about closer Filipino-American collaboration. Philippine-American affairs have teen tangled in uncertain channels for a number of months, and a more clear-cut course of action was now expected."[24]

Mill entertained the idea of working for President Osmeña especially when the latter took him under his confidence. Osmeña even invited Mill to have lunch with him in his residence. This brought Mill much added prestige with his superiors at the OSS, particularly after he became one of the few Americans to attend a formal meeting of the Philippine Cabinet. As Mill wrote his folks: "I can honestly tell you that I have played a real role in the historic decisions now being reached in the Southwest Pacific. Someday, when time permit, I shall show you some amazing things."[25]

Staff agencies concerned with the reoccupation of the Islands wanted Mill's excellent performance and growing expertise on the Philippines. At one point, the OSS and the SWPA, General MacArhur's Headquarters, were fighting for him. Hayden wanted Mill to join General MacArthur's staff as adviser on Philippine Affairs. Hayden wrote General W.J. Donovan to release Mill. "This suggestion calls for a lot of "nerve,"' Hayden wrote Donovan, "but perhaps you will feel that the end in view, i.e. the speedy winning of the war here and the maintenance of good relations between the United States and the Philippines, justifies it."[26] Hayden received a cordial note from Donovan saying that if requested by General MacArthur he would release Mill.[27]

Toward the end of September, MacArthur requested Donovan to release Mill to work directly with him as an adviser of civil affairs. The request caused quite a furor in OSS circles. Mill quickly wrote back to his folks that he was offered a position as "adviser to General Douglas A. MacArthur on Civil Affair." He cautioned them, "because of the important character of this position, I wish you would keep the news confined to the family for the present.

Naturally it has caused the greatest excitement here. I hope to be able to write you more soon."[28]

But, Donovan and the OSS were determined to keep Mill; he had become too important. Donovan approached Mill and they spoke in length about releasing him to MacArthur. Mill's outstanding record and his closeness with President Osmeña and cabinet officials were indispensable to the OSS. By then, Mill had just written a seventy-page study on the Philippine government entitled "The New Government of the Philippines," which Hayden and the State Department enthusiastically endorsed. The study became standard reading in MacArthur's headquarters.[29] Mill was working on a study of police organization in the Philippines. To entice him, the OSS promoted Mill to Deputy and Acting Chief of the Pacific Islands Section. The fifteen-person section covered the affairs of the Japanese mandated islands, Hawaii, Australia, New Zealand, New Guinea, the Philippines, and the Netherlands East Indies.[30]

On 20 October 1944, General MacArthur, President Osmeña and other top American and Filipino officials landed on the island of Leyte; it was the first step toward Philippine liberation and MacArthur had fulfilled his promise to return to the Philippines. Mill felt he had contributed to the liberation of the Philippines and celebrated from his OSS office. He recalled that in July 1944, he launched the initial negotiations leading to President Osmeña's return to the Philippines with MacArthur's forces. He had worked closely with Osmeña and got a good inside picture of Philippine affairs. He would have wanted to be part of that historic event. As he wrote to a friend: "I was supposed to be in on the invasion of the Philippines personally, but got tangled up in a jurisdictional squabble and failed to obtain my release here (OSS).[31]

At the U.S. Department of State

Despite his expertise, Mill did not intend to focus solely on the Philippines. His interests extended to the overall problems of the Pacific region. He was still hoping to launch a political career. Nevertheless, other career opportunities beckoned. In November 1944, after thirteen months in OSS, Mill approached Frank P. Lockhart, then Chief of the Office of Philippine Affairs at the U.S. State Department, about his interest in working in the State Department. Mill expected to go to the Philippines to work in MacArthur's headquarters. On18 March 1945, Mill broke the news of his transfer to the State Department to his parents:

> The U.S. State Department has completed all steps in my appointment to the Department as a Far East Deputy Division Chief and the Bureau of the Budget has approved my appointment. Because I will have administrative duties, Gen Holmes, the Assistant Secretary of State, has personally approved my appointment. The salary is to be $5,200 a year. A few more jumps and I'll be in the category of having to be approved by the Senate. The big question now is getting my release from OSS, but the situation in that respect looks much better that it did when Gen. MacArthur asked for me as an adviser... As I look back on my past few years of teaching in one of the best colleges in the country, service with the Federal Communications Commission, a honorable discharge from the army, service with the Office of Strategic Services, a request from Gen. MacArthur, and now what looks to be the best of them all, a fine job with the State Department. It makes me feel much older than I am.[32]

Unlike his previous jobs, which were tied to the war effort, a position in the State Department would be a permanent, lifetime employment. Mill was excited but assumed the job would last no longer than six months to one year. He believed that his experience at the FCC, the OSS, and now at the State Department would help him get a teaching job or prepare him for a political career. Joining the State Department would mean towing the official line. "I am aware that my liberal views may not find general expression in State Department policy, and I suppose that it can lead to discouraging results. I will be freer to express myself in the teaching field or in politics or in editing or reporting on a paper."[33]

Mill received his formal appointment as a P-5 Country Specialist from Secretary of State Edward M. Stettinius. It was a major career advancement, especially when one takes into account what Mill had to go through before he secured the position. As he wrote his folks:

> Much red tape was involved in my case as I had never been in the Philippines (hardly west of the Mississippi for that matter), had never served in the Foreign Service, had no PhD, and was only 28 years old. I did, however, receive some of the highest endorsements that one could desire, and my reports and studies on Pacific questions, and my contacts with high-ranking Government officials and members of Congress turned the tables in my favor.[34]

The timing was perfect. Mill's expertise was at peak value. He confided to a friend: "As you realize Washington is a beehive of Philippine activity among other things these days. Affairs in the Philippine Islands field are really at a peak."[35] As a world peace advocate, Mill thought the timing was historic because of the on-going United Nations Conference on International Organizations in San Francisco.

State Department officers and staff gave Mill a cordial reception. He was excited to join the Office of Far Eastern Affairs — the office in charge of American policy toward China, Japan, the Philippines, and the entire Pacific—and work under the famed Ambassador Joseph C. Grew, the last American ambassador to Japan before the Pacific War. Mill's immediate boss was Frank Lockhart, a veteran Foreign Service officer who had served as American consul general in Shanghai.

The State Department was located at the Old Executive Building on Seventeenth Street and Pennsylvania Avenue in Washington, D.C. It was next to the White House and across from Blair House, the official guesthouse; President Truman was currently residing in the Blaire House while the White House underwent repair. In the morning, Mill could see people line the streets to watch President Truman leave the Blair House on his way to the White House. Three months into the job, Mill was promoted to acting assistant chief of the Philippine Affairs Division. He replaced Paul Steintorf, a seasoned career diplomat, who was assigned to the Philippines as United States consul general after liberation from Japanese occupation.

The relationship Mill maintained with top Philippine officials while at the OSS was an asset as assistant chief of the Philippine

Affairs Division at the State Department. Mill had direct contact with President Osmeña and Philippine Resident Commissioner to the United States Romulo and they regularly received him in the Office of the President of the Philippine Commonwealth at 1716 Massachusetts Avenue. He conferred with the two officials on vital issues about U.S.-Philippines relations. In November 1945, two of the outstanding issues that Mill discussed with President Osmeña were Japanese collaboration and Philippine independence. Mill conveyed that the U.S. government wanted the Philippine Commonwealth government to proceed as effectively as possible against collaborators. Osmeña replied that his government would deal sternly with all former Japanese puppets, and Romulo stated that this was imperative.[36]

Regarding Philippine independence, some Filipino and American officials lobbied to postpone the date because of war damages. Osmeña maintained that the Philippine Commonwealth government would accept independence no later than 04 July 1946. Mill told Osmeña that independence should be granted by that date. But, Osmeña was skeptical and insisted on meeting with Secretary of State Byrnes to discuss independence. Mill wisely replied, "The Secretary would be glad to talk with him (Osmeña) on the point but that such a high policy statement of that character would presumably have to come from the President of the United States. Since President Osmeña has been conferring with President (Truman) frequently, I suggested that President Truman might soon issue such statement."[37]

Philippine Foreign Affairs Training Program

Mill's most important assignment in the State Department, and for which he earned the informal title "Father of the Philippine Foreign Service," was as director of the Philippine Foreign Affairs Training Program (PFTAP). He considered it the most interesting, significant, and best part of his life and career. The Philippine trainees fondly called Mill "Chief."

Mill's academic background had prepared him for the difficult task of overseeing the training of future Foreign Service officers. But, with little or no precedent to follow, the job would be challenging. "I have had to chart a relatively uncharted sea," Mill later admitted.[38]

Mill worked hard and fast to put together the program. The committee decided to establish PFATP in the summer of 1945, and commenced it in December. Mill had only about three months before the arrival of the first group of Filipino trainees. But by December, everything was set. As Mill recalled:

> Plans have, however, now been completed to bring several groups of Filipino trainees here for training in the Department. On Monday the first small group will enter the general sessions of the Foreign Service Officer's Training School then. I have worked closely with the officers of this School mapping out a program of Filipino participation. This lasts for six weeks. After that time the trainees will be assigned to my Division for further lectures and conferences with federal officials. Following that period they will be assigned to American consulates abroad for actual training in the field. We plan to keep this training program going up to the date of Philippine Independence on 04 July 1946.
> As the administrator of this program I have an excellent opportunity to get a detailed, over-all knowledge of the Department and the Foreign Service. Next week I plan about three lectures on the organization of the Department and the Foreign Service. I have drawn up an extensive bibliography of reading materials for the trainees.[39]

Mill acquainted himself with the bureaucracy of the State Department so he could explain the management of the Foreign Service to the Filipino trainees. To teach American diplomatic and consular work, he sought the help of the P. Jester, chief of the Foreign Service Officer's Training School, and many Division officers of the State Department. Everyone cooperated with Mill in the training of the Filipino trainees cognizant of the historic experiment being carried out. As Mill wrote his wife Wilma:

> On Dec. 3 the first group of five Filipino trainees entered the Department for training. These trainees are now participating in most of the sessions of the regular Foreign Service Officer's Training School. They assemble each morning with

me before the formal lectures for general instructions. At the end of each week we held a two-hour review session in my office. Our first week was a most gratifying one.

As you can readily see this is a very historic program. It is the first time in the Department's history that it has ever sought to train the prospective future officers of another country's foreign affairs establishment. As you can see it gives me a unique opportunity to help set up a Department of Foreign Affairs which may play a crucial role in the history of the Pacific. I have the responsibility of training the foreign affairs representatives of the first subject people to attain independence in the Far East.[40]

Halfway through the training of the first batch of Filipino trainees, Mill was immensely pleased over the eagerness and ability of the Filipino trainees, as they had done a very creditable job. He also admitted that he did more teaching for the training program than he expected:

Our Philippine Foreign Affairs Training Program is going along in excellent fashion. I am probably doing more concentrated teaching that I have ever done in my life. I am also going through the regular Foreign Service School with the trainees. This is a very interesting and generally good school. The present session has two more weeks to run.[41]

Mill put his charges through an intensive training program under his immediate supervision. "Although the trainees participate in the regular Foreign Service School and orientation lectures where possible, the greatest burden of the work falls on me," Mill noted. "This means that I must be prepared to lecture to them on almost every conceivable range of activity within the Department. It also means that I must prepare reading lists and outlines for them, prepare and grade examinations, and be on hand constantly to counsel with them. These men are eager and determined and press one day in and out in pursuance of their work."[42]

For the training in consular and diplomatic work, the Filipino trainees were taught how to organize a Foreign Office and administer it after it was set up. They were also taught all details of operating a consulate and were briefed on the governments of different countries. In addition, the Filipino trainees were assigned to various divisions of the State Department for specialized training and a few were selected for still further instruction abroad at American embassies. To round out the training of these future diplomats, their mentor saw to it that they made interesting friends in Washington and organized parties and informal discussion groups for their entertainment. On weekends he took them on trips to places of such historical interest as Hyde Park in New York, Mount Vernon, Monticello, and Arlington National Cemetery in Virginia.[43]

Mill developed excellent relations with the Filipino trainees. He became so close to them that the Filipinos treated him like family. When Manuel Adeva completed a two and a half-week trip to Sydney, Australia for assignment at the American Consulate General there, despite arriving exhausted, he quickly sent a telegram to Mill: "Arrived here this morning and reported immediately to American Consulate. Please advise my wife."[44]

Although he was younger than the majority of the trainees, Mill was like a father to them. After the completion of his training, Benjamin Tirona, a member of Group V, sent a letter to Mill saying: "I lack the proper words to reiterate to you again, my profound thanks and gratitude for all that you have done for me. The telling influence and effects of your wisdom and fatherly treatment to me shall always be a living ember in my memory and may the future give me the fullest chance to render to you the maximum of service within the bounds of my humble limitations. I have looked upon to you as a mentor and as a father, and as such you shall continue to occupy a distinct place in my heart."[45]

Mill shelved his initial plan to stay only in the State Department for six months to one year. His work in the State Department had been very gratifying as he was permitted a great deal of freedom of judgment, had been able to contribute materially to the formation of American policy regarding the Philippines, and was also helping to set up the proposed new Philippine Department of Foreign Affairs which would be operational after Philippine independence. For this, he derived a deep sense of pride in his role as director of the training program. As he wrote to his friend: "I am directing

"Father of the Philippine Foreign Service" 271

a Philippine Foreign Affairs Training Program in the Department. This Program is designed to train a group of outstanding Filipinos to carry on the foreign relations of their country after independence. I thus have a Foreign Service School all of my own."[46]

In the presidential elections held in April 1945, Manuel A. Roxas emerged as the winner, beating incumbent Sergio Osmeña. Roxas thus became the last president of the Philippine Commonwealth and the first president of the new Philippine Republic. As president-elect he visited Washington, D.C. on 10 to 17 May 1945 seeking more financial aid for the war-torn Philippines. As the date of Philippine independence approached, it was evident that the two groups of Filipino foreign affairs trainees, numbering ten, were too small for the needs of the new Philippine Department of Foreign Affairs and Foreign Service. Thus Roxas formally requested the U.S. Secretary of State to continue the Philippine Foreign Affairs Training Program. He received unexpected and considerable help from Mill. It is worth quoting Mill's personal memorandum at length about this episode of his career in the State Department:

> I first met Gen. Roxas (Roxas held the rank of general during the war.) Saturday afternoon, 11 May, when I attended a press conference which he gave at Blair House where he has been quartered during his stay. He handled himself very well at this press conference held jointly with Mr. McNutt. No one asked him the embarrassing question of whether he had actually collaborated with the Japanese or not; Gen. MacArthur has stated flatly that Roxas was no collaborationist. After the conference was over, Mr. Lockhart took me up and introduced me to the President-elect, mentioning that I was the one who had been in charge of the Philippine Foreign Affairs Training Program.
> Thursday noon I attended a luncheon at the National Press Club at which Gen. Roxas spoke. He delivered a very able address proving himself to be an excellent orator though not of the excellence of Gen. Romulo. He was warmly applauded. Thursday afternoon I attended another reception for the General. At this reception I had a very good chance to talk to him. He had been fully informed by Gen. Romulo

of my role in establishing the Philippine Foreign Affairs Training Program, and we talked considerably about this. In due course, he confided in me that he would appreciate my drawing up for his signatures drafts of certain letters to the Secretary of State. He specifically requested that I draw up (a) a letter to the Secretary requesting the US to represent Philippine interests abroad after independence (b) a letter to the Secretary requesting the continuance of the training program (c) a letter to the Secretary requesting an American adviser to assist him in setting up the new Philippine Department of Foreign Affairs, and (d) a letter to the Secretary requesting that a provisional agreement be signed between the two countries pending the coming into force of the regular treaties. I told the President-elect that I would be happy to do my best in the matter.

I then returned to the Department and worked on the requested drafts. By the next morning I had completed the drafts, and Mr. Lockhart and Mr. Vincent presented the draft to Roxas. I was surprised to learn in the afternoon that the drafts had been entirely acceptable to the President-elect and that he was to sign them before his departure. I drew these up very hastily, so I would not have been surprised if they had been rejected.

My writing these letters to the Secretary of State for the new President of the Philippines was a very new and unusual experience and one that does not happen very often, I imagine, in the conduct of relations between nations. This evening at 5:30 Mr. Lockhart and I went to the Mayflower Hotel to the largest reception thus far for the new President. As I shook the President's hand, he said to me, "thanks for everything." I am glad to have this word of appreciation since I had kept my word to him to get the drafts before him.[47]

Mill was more than happy to write the letters of President Roxas, just as he was pleased that his work as director of the training program and his plans for setting up the Philippine Department of Foreign Affairs were recognized by no less than the new Philippine president. Mill's name was also firmly associated with the training of Filipino diplomats thanks mainly to the press releases in Philippine newspapers.

Even Mill's friends in the Philippines were excited to see Mill's growing popularity in the country and to hear rumors about his being hired for a teaching position in Manila. One of them even encouraged him to accept the offer:

> I have heard many favorable comments about the Philippine Foreign Affairs Training Program of the Department of State. You have quite a reputation here in Manila. As a matter of fact, I heard your name mentioned for a teaching position in the Foreign Service School of the University of the Philippines. I am sure that if you do come to the Philippines you will not regret such a decision. Here in Manila you will find a keen interest in the field of Foreign Service. Most of the leading universities have established Foreign Service Departments. In order to give you an idea of the type of program being offered, I am sending you a copy of the University of Manila catalogue.[48]

By October 1946, three groups of Filipino trainees had completed the training program at the State Department. Their performance had greatly impressed their mentor. Mill for his part was all praises for his wards. He was confident that the trainees would help foster good relations between the United States and the Philippines.

After the completion of the fifth training group in October 1947, the Philippine Government decided not to send another batch of trainees to the State Department. Emilio Torres, a member of the fifth group, in his appreciation letter to the Secretary of State lauded Mill's outstanding efforts. "Special mention is made of Mr. Edward W. Mill, Acting Assistant Chief of the Philippine Affairs Division, with whom the Filipino trainees have the honor and pleasure of associating more lengthily. Mr. Mill's inspiring guidance on the whole has been delightfully unique. His scholarly approach to the whole course has made the Filipino trainees realize and feel that they can learn only by giving their utmost and doing their best."[49] Thus the graduates of the Philippine Foreign Affairs Training Program were collectively called "Mill's Boys" or sometimes "Millmen" in honor of Edward W. Mill.

Even the Philippine media shared the State Department Boys' gratitude to their training director. As a Philippine magazine noted: "Today the Philippines can gratefully feel that it has acquired a sort of an elite corps in the science of diplomacy with which to buttress the foundation of its fledgling Foreign Service. No modern nation has had this unusual advantage or good luck of having a young but highly competent mentor put his whole heart and soul into such a vital mission."[50] When Mill received news from his "boys" about their difficulties and struggles in the incipient Philippine Foreign Service, he would sooth their worries and pledge this full support to them. Once he got a letter from Eduardo Rosal who had doubts about his future in the Foreign Service notwithstanding his excellent performance in the State Department training program. Mill chided him but at the same time assured him of his friendship and support. "If there is one thing, Ed, on which you are still in doubt, then let me say that in me you have had probably one of the very best, if not the very best, friends and supporters you have ever had. I have boosted your stock day in and day out, but sometimes when I hear comments from you, I wonder if you really appreciate what I have done for you. I really don't have to do all this boosting of your stock. I can sit back and take things easy. But my heart has been tied up in helping you boys to the maximum, and I want you to always remember that! (Underscoring by Mill himself) You have never had a more outspoken and effective friend and supporter."[51]

Treaty of General Relations

Even before the request of President-elect Roxas to the Secretary of State that a provisional agreement be signed between the Philippines and the United States pending the coming into force of the regular treaties, Mill was already busy working on the Treaty of General Relations between the Philippines and the United States. The treaty provided a broad outline on the following subjects: (1) Recognition of the independence of the Philippines on 04 July 1946; (2) Establishment of diplomatic relations; (3) Assumption of governmental indebtedness by the Philippine Republic; (4) Continued review by the US Supreme Court of cases pending at the time of independence; Settlement of claims; and (6) Notification of independence to other governments and a few other matters.[52]

The Treaty of General Relations became the first bilateral agreement signed by the Philippines and the United States right after the ceremony of Philippine independence. Most of the treaties that the Philippines subsequently negotiated with other countries have been patterned after this original treaty. As the author of the treaty, Mill was very proud of his achievement. He described the Treaty as the decisive treaty of separation of sovereign ties. As he wrote his parents months later:

> I have been very busy and unable to do much writing of late. I do want to take the time now to send you a copy of the Treaty of General Relations as recently released to the press by the State Department. The significance to you of this treaty is that I wrote the treaty one Saturday afternoon about six months ago. It is a very historic treaty, the first of its kind in American history. There were few, if any, precedents for it, so it is a very original job. I am happy to have been able to write it.[53]

Aside from the Treaty of General Relations, another historic document that Mill authored was President Truman's Statement on Philippine Independence on 04 July 1946 for which he was immensely proud of. As he wrote his wife, Wilma:

> What made the Philippine independence personally significant to me was that I wrote the now-famous PROCLAMATION OF INDEPENDENCE for the President and in addition both his other statements and those of the Secretary of State. As incidental historical notations it may be interesting to note that I wrote the Proclamation of Independence, the first such document in our history and a rare type of document in the world's history, in about 35 minutes one Tuesday night about three weeks ago. I glanced at a few other Proclamations to get the legal phraseology and then sat down and quickly wrote it. Now, of course, it is history and in every newspaper in the land. Lowell Thomas especially commended it on his 04 July broadcast.[54]

Notwithstanding his hectic schedule, Mill remained a prolific writer. He was able to squeeze time to write and publish academic articles on the Philippines. Mill also wrote press releases and articles on the Philippine Foreign Affairs Training Program all published in the *Department of State Bulletin*. He wrote two important articles, namely "The Philippines Prepares for Independence" and "The New Republic of the Philippines," published in the *Department of State Bulletin* on 9 June and 15 September 1946 respectively. These articles were some of the first comprehensive treatises on Philippine-American relations and clearly reflected Mill's mastery of Philippine affairs. His writing was a model of scholarly succinctness for which he received a lot of praises. One of those he valued most came from Narciso Ramos, then minister counselor in the Philippine Embassy in Washington and a future Secretary of Foreign Affairs. In his letter to Mill, Ramos said: "I have received the copies of the Department of State Bulletin which you have been good enough to send me. I have read with interest your articles regarding the Republic of the Philippines and I wish to reiterate my admiration for your knowledge and understanding of matters pertaining to my country." Mill considered this "one of the nicest compliments I have ever received in my Philippine work."[55]

When Frank Lockhart retired from the State Department, Mill was appointed Acting Chief of the Division of Philippine Affairs, which he considered "an unusually excellent job." It was also at the time that the State Department abandoned the Old Executive Office Building that it shared with the War and Navy Department and transferred to its new building on E Street, in a place called "Foggy Bottom." It was a transfer that Mill disliked. "We are now in the new building. Almost everyone greatly regretted leaving the old building next to the White House. While this building is more modern and I personally have an office to myself now, the location of the building is most inconvenient for me and requires a trip lasting an hour and 15 minutes from my home."[56]

His promotion to Acting Chief also changed some of Mill's immediate plans. He had to put on hold his plan to pursue a doctorate degree and resume his academic career. He did a lot of soul searching as he declined teaching offers from the University of Wisconsin and Northwestern University. He considered them good offers since he did not yet have a doctorate degree but he was sought primarily out of recognition of his work and achievements in the State Department. Declining the offers placed Mill in a dilemma and he agonized on whether or not he made a wise decision. He considered actual government work, particularly at the policy-making level, as personally preferable to work in academe.

Assignment to Manila

Mill's tenure, however, in the State Department remained uncertain. After several months, Richard Ely, another veteran Foreign Service officer, occupied the chieftainship left by Frank Lockhart, and Mill reverted back as assistant chief. At about that time, Mill received a tentative offer from the Philippine government to reorganize the Department of Political Science of the University of the Philippines and to act as consultant to the Philippine Department of Foreign Affairs.[57] The $11,000 a year position, however, did not materialize.

In February 1948, the U.S. Senate confirmed Mill's nomination as a Foreign Service Reserve Officer Class IV. This qualified Mill for an overseas assignment. In fact, a month before his confirmation, Mill was already sounded off by Thomas H. Lockett, the incoming *chargé d'affaires* at the U.S. embassy in Manila, for an assignment as political officer at the embassy and to serve as his "right-hand man." Mill politely refused Lockett's offer despite regarding Lockett as "one of the finest men this country has ever sent to the Far East."

Lockett, however, was not easily discouraged. As it turned out Lockett approached Richard D. Weigle, the executive officer of the Far East Affairs Bureau, and requested him to prod Mill to accept the Manila assignment. Weigle summoned Mill and they had a serious talk about Mill's career, although it was pretty obvious to Mill that Weigle was pushing him to consider the Manila posting. Weigle stressed "the importance of departmental people getting out of the file and acquiring field experience." They also talked about the possibility of Mill being appointed Division Chief after his foreign assignment since by the time he returned to Washington, D.C., Ely would already be nearing retirement age. "I agreed with Mr. Weigle that there was much logic in what he said and that I would consider the Manila (offer) very carefully and let him know next week. If I did not go I told him that I would probably leave the Department in June with a view to returning to graduate teaching."[58]

Mill also confided to Pablo Peña, a member of Group III of the State Department trainees, that he had been thinking of leaving government for some time. "As long as the Philippine Foreign Affairs Training Program was going on," Mill said in his letter, "I had a particular incentive to remain in government. With that program seemingly over, considerable of the incentive for staying here is gone. Unless therefore I have a sudden change of mind, I shall be out of the (State) Department in June. I shall always keep up my writings of the Philippines and shall continue to be closely interested in Philippine affairs and particularly in the activities of you men."[59]

In the end, Mill decided to accept the assignment to the Philippines. The following day Mill phoned Lockett who was then staying in Allies Inn. He explained that contrary to his previous refusal, he was now agreeable to going to Manila. He added that his high regard for Lockett had a lot to do with his decision to join him. Lockett was pleased with Mill's decision and they agreed to take the same ship, the *President Cleveland*, to Manila.[60] In his letter to Hortencio J. Brillantes, Mill admitted that "one of my prime reasons for accepting the post was to see you boys again. With so many coming back here and going elsewhere, I hope a few of you will remain in the Department. We should have some very good times together again... I hope all the former trainees will be at the dock with Mr. Lockett to greet me when I arrive early in May."

Mill did not have to worry about with the kind of welcome that he would receive upon his arrival in Manila. His former trainees already got wind of his assignment to Manila and were excitedly making the preparations for his arrival. As Brillantes wrote him, "To us, however, the most significant thing in the present maneuverings of fate is the news of your appointment as second secretary at the American embassy in Manila. Your name is now travelling like wildfire among the people of the Department and they all look forward to the day when one way or another they will have a chance to meet you. There is, however, another set of employees in the Department who feel somewhat depressed with your appointment. These men are the prospective Philippine trainees in the Department of State. They will, of course, miss you and they are apprehensive that their training would not be as thorough as the one we had."[62]

On 26 April, fifteen former State Department trainees then working at the Department of Foreign Affairs gave Mill a most cordial welcome upon arrival in the port of Manila, extremely pleased and excited to meet their former mentor again. But behind the festive reception, Mill would later learn that his arrival had in fact caused a protocol snafu that even President Elpidio Quirino himself got involved in. The Manila newspapers as expected had a field day covering the incident.

Prior to Mill's arrival, the State Department graduates had actually planned a surprise welcome reception for Mill not just at the seaport but at Manila Bay. The plan consisted of renting a fast boat to meet the *President Cleveland* and whisk Mill off to the Manila Hotel for a special breakfast. They coordinated with and received clearance for their plans from the US Embassy and the local American President Lines office. But when the State Department graduates motored out in their boat and approached the *President Cleveland*, and in accordance with the prior approval given them, attempted to board, the chief mate rudely ordered them away from the vessel. When the ship finally docked, Luis Moreno Salcedo, then Chief of Protocol of the DFA, and Jose Alejandrino were able to board the ship. Moreno Salcedo was incensed and protested the discourtesy they received from the ship's officer, vowing to report the incident to President Quirino. Mill tried to mollify Moreno Salcedo but in vain. As it turned out, the incident was one of a series involving the American President Liners in the Philippines. Mill was surprised to learn that President Quirino took a vigorous personal interest in the case by protesting to the APL management about the incident. In the end, it was unfortunate for the State Department graduates whose creative reception plan was spoiled, not to mention that they spent their own money for the boat rental.

Mill was thrilled by his arrival in Manila. As he wrote to Juanito Dionisio: "I arrived in Manila on 26 April and was given a splendid reception by the boys from the Department of Foreign Affairs. They have been extremely kind to me at all times. I have had numerous long talks with Undersecretary Africa and have also talked with the President Quirino on two occasions."[63] Some of Mill's Filipino friends were not surprised by the princely treatment that Mill received in Manila. As Consul General Roberto Regala of the Philippine Consulate General in San Francisco noted: "I am not at all surprised that you should be able to make your way in the official circles of the Department of Foreign Affairs, including the President himself. Especially with respect to the men who underwent training in the Department of State, I can imagine how popular you can be."[64]

Mill assumed his position as second secretary to the US Embassy and reported directly to *Chargé d'Affaires* Lockett. His main task was to develop a new Political Section of the embassy. As chief of the Political Section, he kept in close contact with the top officials of the Philippine government and reported regularly on political developments transpiring in the country. "The Political Section of any American Embassy is usually considered the nerve center of the embassy," Mill proudly stated, "and an officer placed in charge of such section inevitably has a heavy responsibility in the running of the Embassy." In the Political Section, Mill supervised three to four junior officers, a biographical research assistant and three general clerks. Although he carried the main load of actual reporting himself, Mill also trained his junior officers on the techniques and method of political reporting so that they could eventually take a larger share of the workload.

During the first year of his tour of duty, Mill's energy and patience were both tested by the notoriety of Philippine politics and Manila traffic. He saw at close range how the Philippine political pot boiled. He reported on the worsening split in the ruling Liberal Party as a new political realignment took shape. Party stalwarts Jose Avelino, former senate president, and Mariano Jesus Cuenco, the new senate president, bitterly fought for the presidency and both announced that they would take over the Senate. The tension was defused at the last minute, however, when Avelino backed out, announcing he would desist from action until the Supreme Court ruled on the legality of the new body. As Mill wrote to a friend back in the States: "These terrific political events have kept me working almost 12 hours a day. The strain is killing at times. I will be glad when I can rest. It is not easy to go at this pace here in the tropics. Sometimes I have felt as if I couldn't take anymore, but next morning, I have to be there pitching."[65]

In the same letter, Mill's observation made more than sixty years ago about Manila's notorious traffic remains true today. "Manila traffic continues to be something for the books. They say if you can drive here you can drive anywhere in the world. The first week I was here I shuddered at the thought of driving here, but I have now become accustomed to it. What complicate matter so much are the presence of thousands of jeepneys converted to passenger use and great, big lumbering buses which have a habit of breaking down right in the middle of the road and snarling up traffic hopelessly for hours."[66]

More importantly, from his position in the US Embassy, Mill was able to exert influence on the Department of Foreign Affairs hierarchy in getting the State Department Boys their permanent appointments in the Philippine Foreign Service. Mill also deemed it important to highlight and disseminate information on the Philippine Foreign Affairs Training Program in Washington, D.C. so that the Filipino public would have a better understanding of the importance of the undertaking and at the same time to honor the trainees. Just two months after his arrival, Mill organized a reception at the U.S. embassy to honor ten State Department graduates who were in Manila at the time—Jose Alejandrino, Marcelino Bernardo, Hortencio J. Brillantes, Irineo D. Cornista, Carlos Faustino, Engracio Guerzon, Generoso Provido, Rodolfo Severino, Roman Ubaldo, Emilio Bejasa and Tiburcio Baja - some of whom brought their wives to the ceremony. Close to a hundred guests including the U.S. embassy and staff members of the Department of Foreign Affairs were present at the affair.[67] Mill likewise held a party for his former wards in his residence in Ambassador Apartments, a write up of which appeared in the social page of the *Manila Bulletin*.[68]

Mill maintained close contact with other top officials of the Philippine Foreign Service. Narciso Ramos, the number two man in the Philippine embassy in Washington, D.C. would consult Mill from time to time on Philippines-United States relations and would seek his comments so that he would know if "he spoke out of turn."[69] Mill also became a much sought-after speaker on Philippine-

American relations and the Foreign Service by universities, churches and alumni associations where his oratorical skills and intelligence made a great impression. Mill became a kind of celebrity in Manila's social circle. The magazine *Philippine Trends* even featured an article on him in its June 1949 edition entitled "Edward W. Mill, Young Man with a Mission." It was, however, around this time, at the height of his popularity, that he received instructions from the State Department reassigning him to Indonesia.

Tour of Duty in Indonesia

After two years in Manila, Mill was assigned to the U.S. embassy in Indonesia in 1950. Following a brief stint as consul at Batavia (Jakarta), he was assigned as Consul and Principal Officer in Surabaya, the second largest city in Indonesia. He was then the first Foreign Service Reserve Office ever to be appointed as Principal Officer. His main task was to reopen and re-establish an American consulate there. The American consulate had officially operated in Surabaya since 1918 but it was forced to close in 1942 during the Japanese occupation. In addition, the new American Consulate also included a new section, the office of the United States Public Information Service or USIS to disseminate factual information about the United States. His consular district presumably includes East Java, part of Borneo, the lesser Sundas, Celebes, Halmahera, Ceram and part of Timor and New Guinea.[70]

Mill received a warm welcome in Surabaya, which led him to believe that the reestablishment of the American Consulate would help to further the cordial relations between the United States and the new nation of Indonesia. It will be recalled that the United States initially hesitated to recognize Indonesia when that country gained its independence on 27 December 1949. Mill developed close ties with prominent Indonesian military and civilian leaders. As in Manila, he moved with ease in social circles. A regrettable experience that Mill had in Indonesia was when his automobile was stolen. He reportedly went to and from official functions in a pedicab until the Indonesia police succeeded in retrieving his car. The incident made Mill even more famous.[71]

During his stint in Surabaya, Mill received a visit from a former State Department trainee, Tagakotta Sotto, who was then assigned as consul to the Philippine Consulate in Karachi, the news of which was released to the Indonesian press by the United States Information Service in Surabaya. Mill also maintained excellent relations with the Filipino community in the city. As a tribute to his birthday on 14 June 1950, the Filipino Association in Surabaya led by Francisco Baltazar requested the State Department graduates and Mill's family to write congratulatory messages for Mill. A good number of them from all parts of the globe responded to the call with flattering but splendid remarks, the most notable of which came from Tiburcio C. Baja, the first secretary and consul at the Philippine Legation in Sydney. He wrote:

> ...Mr. Edward W. Mill is not only a friend of the Philippines –he is also a great champion of the Filipino cause. In his interest in the welfare of the Philippine Republic, few there are that can excel him. His services as trainer of Filipino Foreign Service men will always shine in letters of gold in the annals of the foreign affairs of our country. To Mr. Edward W. Mill, the Filipino is a man, equal and brother to any other man. In his relations with us he has extolled our virtues; guided us in our weaknesses, developed our inherent capacities.[72]

Mill also received a heart-warming letter from Luis Moreno Salcedo, the chief of protocol at the Department of Foreign Affairs, about his promotion.

> It will probably please you to know that two days ago, upon the recommendation of General Romulo, the President signed my appointment as a Foreign Affairs Class Officer, Class II, top grade. On that happy occasion my thoughts turned to you and to days I spent in the State Department. I feel sure that were it not for the technical training I obtained in the Department of State under your sympathetic and unselfish guidance, it would have taken me years and years to obtain the promotion that has now been given me. And so whatever success I might achieve must give you and the State Department a certain amount of satisfaction since you have been instrumental in shaping my career. On the

other hand, whatever failure I may have will likewise be considered as a reflection on the training you gave me, brief though it was.[73]

Back to Academe

After four years in the Foreign Service, Mill decided to return to his other love – academic work. Mill had been contemplating completing a doctorate degree and to pursue a career in academe. His failure to get a promotion to a P-7 Foreign Affairs Officer in the US Foreign Service, however, pushed Mill to resign from the U.S. Foreign Service. He was upset that despite receiving excellent performance ratings during his stint in the State Department and tours of duty in the Philippines and Indonesia and notwithstanding the strong recommendations of his superiors, he had no promotion since 1946 other than automatic, in-grade promotions. His petition to the U.S. Civil Service Commission to take the required examinations for promotion was turned down because of the non-availability of items.

Mill took advantage of an offer from the University of California at Berkeley as a lecturer in political science, specifically to teach a course on Philippine Affairs. Although the teaching job was not great from a financial standpoint, Mill used the opportunity to re-integrate himself into academic life. It was also during this time that Mill decided to remarry after his marriage with Wilma Stevenson fell apart in 1944. In March 1953, he married Virginia Dare.

Mill considered pursuing a PhD at Berkeley but in the end decided to go east. He was admitted to the Department of Politics at Princeton University where he obtained a doctorate degree in 1954. He wrote his dissertation on "The Conduct of Philippine Foreign Relations," a comprehensive study of the administration of Philippine foreign affairs since 1946. It was the first treatise on the subject. In order to complete his research, Mill applied for and obtained a fellowship from the Ford Foundation, which gave him a $7,900 grant to carry out his research in the Philippines. As part of his research, Mill served as a visiting professor of political science at the University of the Philippines from 1953 to1954. With a detached location, surrounded by rolling hills, wide fields of grass and mountainous background, Mill considered the new University of the Philippines campus in Diliman, Quezon City as may be "the most beautiful of any university either in the Philippines or United States."[74]

Mill derived satisfaction from the fact that as a Ford Foundation fellow, he also had the privilege of making a world tour. He visited the Philippine Foreign Service posts in Tokyo, Singapore, Rome, Paris, London, Washington, New York, Chicago and Honolulu where he met with former State Department trainees stationed there. Mill proudly concluded, "Everywhere, one found a keen remembrance of State Department days and a feeling of affection for Washington and the United States."

While at the University of the Philippines, Mill taught a course entitled, "The Conduct of Foreign Relations," twice a week at the Political Science Department. He received no remuneration and was regarded as a "peso a year" man. He was, however, provided with free transportation between his residence and the university. Mill lived in a modest house located at 941 Dakota St. Malate, Manila. Mill complained over the high cost of living in Manila. In a letter to the Ford Foundation, he said: "Prices in Manila are fabulously high, almost double or triple prices in the United States. My previous experience here, sheltered somewhat as it was by embassy walls, had not made this clear to me."[75]

Mill's arrival in Manila coincided with the presidential election, which was won by Ramon Magsaysay, a former Congressman from the province of Zambales. He had also served as Defense Secretary in the Quirino Administration. For the inauguration, Mill was invited to attend the ceremony and sat only a few rows from Magsaysay at the grandstand. Mill was greatly impressed by the new Philippine president. "Magsaysay has great popular appeal, more than I have seen in any other leader in Asia, including Sukarno. He can do great things for his country, Asia, and the world," Mill wrote Jonathan King of The Ford Foundation. Unfortunately Magsaysay died in a plane crash on 17 March 1957.

After only four months, Mill decided to cut short his stay and go back to the United States. His main reason for going to Manila had been to conduct research but he found the state of Philippine archives and libraries weak, if not in a bad state. The National Bureau of Public Libraries was razed during the war and what was left of its collection was still disorganized. Mill assessed that materials on the Philippines at the Library of Congress in Washington, D.C. were ten times more than those found in all the libraries in the Philippines. In February 1954, he turned over the teaching of his class to Professor Pedro Baldoria who Mill had replaced when he came to the Philippines. In his letter dated 10 February 1954 to Dr. Tomas Fonacier, dean of the College of Liberal Arts, Mill bid farewell and thanked the UP officials and staff for their friendly assistance and cooperation.

Mill continued to publish articles on the development of the Philippine Foreign Service and the Philippines's place in the international community. These articles later became the core of his PhD dissertation at Princeton. He would later on submit a book proposal on "The Conduct of Philippine Foreign Relations" to the University of the Philippines Press for publication, but for an unknown reason, Mill did not receive any response from the UP Press. He told Luis Moreno Salcedo about his frustration and the latter tried to encourage him: "…I am sorry to hear that the UP has not answered your letter about your book. It certainly deserves to be published in the Philippines, if only because of its intrinsic value and the fact that it is the only study of its kind of our Foreign Service. Unfortunately, the favorable decision never came.

Notwithstanding the fact the "The Conduct of Philippine Foreign Relations" was not published as a book, Mill published some chapters as separate articles in the *Philippine Social Sciences and Humanities Review* of the University of the Philippines. He also published an article in the *American Foreign Service Journal* in May 1956 entitled "The Philippine Foreign Affairs Training Program: A Decade Later" to commemorate the 10th anniversary of the training program at the State Department. Mill sent copies of the article to the State Department Boys who were more than glad to read their mentor's article about them. "Despite the disappointment and disillusion that many of us trainees have suffered in the service, it was a comfort to read your article. At least, we can take pride in being still the backbone of the service. It is also gratifying to know that you are keeping in touch with developments concerning your 'boys,' including me, who remember you with gratitude and affection," Delfin R. Garcia wrote to Mill.[76]

In September 1957, Mill published an article on "The Personnel of Philippine Diplomacy." It received raving reviews from former State Department trainees. Luis Moreno Salcedo wrote Mill: "I have just received a copy of the reprint your article on *The Personnel of Philippine Diplomacy*. It is even more thorough and documented than I expected, and I felicitate you and your objectivity. You have done our Foreign Service a great service by writing its history, analyzing its problems, and suggesting ways of improving our personnel."[77] Jose Alejandrino, for his part, said, "I think you are the best informed person, inside and outside my country, on the historic development of the organizational structure and personnel of the Department of Foreign Affairs and of the Foreign Service of the Philippines."[78]

After finishing his PhD at Princeton, Mill also completed postdoctoral study at the Institut d'Etudes Politiques in Paris. In 1955 he accepted an associate professorship at the University of Hawaii. His primary assignment was to develop a program on Southeast Asian studies and to teach a course in public administration. He also developed courses on American Foreign Policy. In the fall of that year, he spearheaded the establishment of a Center of Foreign Affairs Training at the UH to train university students for service abroad with the U.S. government, the United Nations, or private business.[79] Mill also continued his interest in Philippine affairs. He was instrumental in paving the way for the conferment of an honorary doctorate degree of the University of Hawaii to Carlos P. Romulo. This, he accomplished with the help of his former State Department student, Emilio D. Bejasa, who at the time was the Philippine consul in Honolulu. Mill regularly invited Bejasa to speak in his class. But Mill's stint in Hawaii was short. Before the end of 1955, he moved back to his home state of Illinois and served as a full-time professor and Chairman of the Political Science Department at Rockford College, an old liberal arts college, founded in 1847, with the sponsorship of the Congregational Church.

In 1959, Mill received an offer from Long Island University (LIU). At about the same time he was offered the presidency of a well-known West Coast university but Mill opted for the LIU position. He went to New York to organize a new LIU Political Science Department at the university's Brooklyn Center. During the next three years, he developed new undergraduate and graduate programs in political science and international relations at Long Island University. When Mill established the Political Science program, there were only three undergraduate majors. Three years later, in 1962, the number of political science majors reached 90.

Mill also introduced and headed a graduate program on international relations, which attracted outstanding students from the United States, and abroad.[80] The program was designed primarily for students preparing for a career in diplomacy. Among the first ten foreign students admitted in the graduate program, two were Filipino students: Rosario Gonzales, a Foreign Service officer, and Esmeralda Constantino, a lawyer. Gonzales would later be known as Rosario Manalo after marrying a fellow Filipino diplomat. She was one of the first two Filipino women who passed the Philippine Foreign Affairs Officer Examination in 1959. She would be appointed as Undersecretary of Foreign Affairs in 1996.

Mill also kept himself abreast of the news about his former trainees. Any updates about their promotion and foreign assignment were always a source of joy and pride. "Most of the "boys" from the State Department days have done very well," he wrote to Juanito C. Dionisio in November 1961. "Of the 40 trainees, I think that about 15 or more are now Ministers or Ambassadors including Adeva, Imperial, Alejandrino, Moreno Salcedo, Abubakar, Tirona, Roxas, Singian, and yourself. Naturally, their records are a source of much satisfaction to me."[81]

Mill's peripatetic academic career did not end in New York. In September 1962, he decided to go west and accepted an appointment in Occidental College in California as Chevalier Professor of Diplomacy and World Affairs. He taught classes in U.S. Foreign Policy, the United Nations, Government and Politics of Southeast Asia and a seminar in United States Foreign Relations. His extracurricular activities included membership in the American Political Science Association, the American Society of International Law, and the American Society of Public Administration.[82]

In the summer of 1963, Mill and his wife Virginia toured Asia and spent three weeks in the Philippines. His visit there was, as expected, mainly to visit his "boys." As he wrote to Hortencio J. Brillantes, "Speaking of the PFATP, this summer brought about quite a reunion with "the boys" all over Asia. We spent three weeks in the Philippines and were on the go constantly. (Secretary of Foreign Affairs) S.P. Lopez gave an especially fine luncheon for us at his new Quezon City home and invited practically the entire Foreign Office. He also recommended me for an award which I may write you more about later. I saw Simeon Roxas, Pablo Peña, Ed Rosal, Aurelio Ramos, etc. Nena (Rosario Gonzales Manalo) was indeed playing a very active role as acting chief of the Personnel Division. She served as Master of Ceremonies at a belated Flag Day Birthday party for me at the Filipinas Hotel... In the field we visited Abu(bakar) in Kuala Lumpur and Ben Tirona in Rangoon. They both showed us a wonderful time. Abu is as full of pep and zing as ever. Ben makes a fine showing in Rangoon... We also saw Romy Busuego in Karachi and Joe Alejandrino in Paris. Joe was a fine host in Paris... I almost forgot Bartolome in Saigon... Thanks mainly to Judge Regala, I had a very fine, unhurried one-hour meeting with President Macapagal. The first thing he said to me was "Congratulations on your ambassadors."[83]

It was during his tenure at Occidental College when Mill received the Order of Sikatuna, the highest diplomatic award given by the Philippine Government to Heads of State, Foreign Ministers and distinguished persons of outstanding services in the field of international relations. On 08 June 1964, in a ceremony held at the President Lounge at Occidental, Philippine Consul General in Los Angeles Alejandro F. Holigores, conferred the Sikatuna award on Mill on behalf of the Philippine Government.[84]

On 22 September 1969, during his visit to the Philippines to attend the investiture of S.P. Lopez as president of the University of the Philippines, Mill paid a courtesy call on President Ferdinand E. Marcos at Malacañang Palace. Narciso Ramos, then Secretary of Foreign Affairs, accompanied Mill to meet President Marcos. The meeting was subsequently featured on TV in "The President's Diary" on Channel 9, where Mill was referred to as the "Father of the Philippine Foreign Service." The *Philippine Herald* also had a photo caption of the meeting the following day. "Somehow, on this trip more than almost any other, I seem to have been given more recognition than ever in this nation as "the Father of the Philippine Foreign Service," Mill noted. "What with the *Philippine Herald* photo and captions of yesterday, coupled with TV identification tonight, this "Father of the Philippine Foreign Service" description seems to have been wider circulation than ever.[85]

Mill would continue to maintain his interest in Philippine affairs but he would expand his expertise to Asian and Pacific affairs, the field he first specialized in at the University of Michigan in the 1940s. He would be eventually known in America as a specialist on Southeast Asia. He also served as an observer in the 1967 national elections in South Vietnam. He co-authored two textbooks on political science with longtime mentor and friend William Ebenstein of Princeton University. He also remained a strong advocate of Foreign Service training and so-called grass roots diplomacy, both on the part of career diplomats and private citizens in international business as well. In a newspaper interview in January 1975, Mill said: "Traditional diplomacy emphasized dealings on the part of the ambassador, the foreign minister and other key persons. Some of that has to be maintained, of course. But along with it, our Foreign Service personnel have to be geared toward getting out and making contacts with the people, knowing their culture, and, if possible, their language."[86]

Mill's sudden death on 13 July 1977 at the age of 61 was indeed a great loss. After his death, his family led by his sister Dorothy and nephew Harold E. Meinheit, who became a U.S. Foreign Service officer himself, turned over Mill's personal collection to the Michigan Historical Collection, now known as the Bentley Historical Library, of the University of Michigan. It houses the largest and most important collection of papers and materials on the Philippines second only to the Library of Congress.

In September 1978, following Mill's personal wish, Dorothy Mill Walls donated part of Mill's memorabilia consisting of letters, articles and photographs to Philippine Consul General to Chicago Rodolfo Sanchez for safekeeping at the Department of Foreign Affairs archives in Manila in a simple ceremony held at the Walls home in Rockford, Illinois. In her brief remarks, Mrs. Walls said that Dr. Mill's "untiring efforts" on behalf of his students "earned for him their respect, admiration and affection and many warm and lasting friendships were formed."[87]

Mill's collection at the Bentley Historical Library is unique because it is the only collection in the United States that preserves a large part of the history and development of the Philippine Foreign Service. Very much aware of the importance of records of the Philippine Foreign Affairs Training Program, Mill collected original and copies of relevant personal and official records on the Philippines and its Foreign Service during and after his stint in the State Department. It also helped that in late December 1955, when Mill was already a full-time academic, he received a letter from Lewis G. Vander Velde, Director of the Michigan Historical Collection, inviting him to place some of his materials in their collection.[88] This inspired Mill to devote part of his time and energy in amassing and preserving his papers. Thus, Edward W. Mill was not only informally called the "Father of the Philippine Foreign Service" but he was also the principal custodian of the records of the beginnings of the Philippine Foreign Service.

9

Leaving a Legacy

Romeo Busuego, the last surviving State Department graduate, died in Manila on 12 March 2009. An unassuming, soft-spoken person, he reportedly "passed away peacefully" at age 93.[1] Busuego had a successful diplomatic career occupying various positions in the Foreign Service, including as Philippine ambassador to Malaysia and India. He also served as acting undersecretary of Foreign Affairs in the early 1960s, at a time when the DFA only had one undersecretary. After his retirement in the Foreign Service, he lived with his daughter in Sydney, Australia. His death marks the end of an era as far as the annals of the Philippine Foreign Service are concerned. The American-trained pioneer Filipino career diplomats are now all gone.

The new generation of Filipinos hardly knows anything about the *pensionados*—the government scholars who were educated or trained in the United States during the American occupation. In the same vein, the present Filipino diplomats only know very little, if at all, about the so-called State Department Boys, the Foreign Service *pensionados* of the Republic and what their group did. These new diplomats relied mainly on scanty recollection of certain active seniors in the Foreign Service whose memory of the State Department Boys is inexorably fading. Thus, there is a need to document the stories of the State Department Boys for the present and for posterity to appreciate more what legacy they left to the country.

In 1948, a year after the end of the Philippine Foreign Affairs Training Program in the US State Department, Edward W. Mill published an article entitled "The First Career Diplomats of the Philippines." Towards the end of said article, he writes:

> The graduates of the Philippine Foreign Affairs Training Program represent the first career Foreign Service officers of the Republic of the Philippines. They are a historic group in that they were the pioneer Foreign Service men of their country. *Succeeding generations will be very much concerned with the manner in which they were recruited and the records they have made.*[2] (Emphasis added)

It seems as though Mill wrote these lines with this book or other works of similar theme in mind. In a way, Mill was a man of foresight. He knew the historical significance of the Philippine Foreign Affairs Training Program at the State Department and the role of the Filipino trainees in the future growth and development of the Philippine Foreign Service.

As early as July 1950, Luis Moreno Salcedo already made an attempt to do a comprehensive study of the lives and careers of the State Department Boys. While teaching part-time at the Far Eastern University in Manila, he tasked his students to do research on "The Philippine Foreign Affairs Training Program in the Department of State – A Study of its Objectives, Program, and Graduates." He was inspired by the project of Professor David Sutherland who gathered materials for a series of articles in the *Saturday Evening Post* on the accomplishments of the Filipino scholars (*pensionados*) to the United States, including the State Department trainees. "While it is too early to evaluate the result of the Philippine Foreign Affairs Training Program in the Department of State, I feel that we should facilitate the work of future researchers by making available to them such materials as may be at hand now," he wrote to Mill. Unfortunately the result of Moreno Salcedo's study was never published and perhaps lost forever when his house in Manila was destroyed by fire in the 1960s.

The State Department Boys lived and made their impact on the Foreign Service during the period which we could call "the golden age" of Philippine diplomacy (1946-1968) since the Philippines was one of the most active among the newly independent states at the time. It was also an era when a number of prominent men dominated the Foreign Service such as Carlos Romulo, Narciso Ramos, Roberto Regala, Bernabe Africa, Felino Neri, Leon Ma. Guerrero, Salvador P. Lopez, Mauro Mendez, and Felixberto Serrano, who out-ranked and over-shadowed the State Department Boys in the Foreign Service hierarchy. The meteoric rise of these brilliant men to the echelon of the Philippine Foreign Service, however, can be attributed to their political and intellectual exploits and connections. In essence, their reputation and credentials were already built elsewhere even before they entered the world of diplomacy.

On the other hand, the State Department Boys had forged their careers exclusively in the bosom of the Foreign Service, learning the nuts and bolts of diplomacy and ultimately making themselves experts on its nuances and subtleties. The nature of their work and responsibilities made them low key, working mainly behind the scenes and often not getting, if ever given, any credit for their contribution. Their collective work, however, had made the Foreign Service, especially during the first decades of Philippine independence, among the most respected in the developing world. As Edward W. Mill wrote on the tenth anniversary of the Philippine Foreign Affairs Training Program in 1955:

> It must be recalled that this past decade has been a period of building for the Republic of the Philippines and its Department of Foreign Affairs and Foreign Service. The principle of a career Foreign Service has had to be enunciated and fortified, an organizational framework abroad and at home created, standards of performance set, and the foreign policy goals and objectives of the Republic clarified. In other words, it has been a pioneering time for career foreign affairs officers. It would be fallacious to credit the graduates of this program with having accomplished all these things. Many non-graduates of the program must share credit with the graduates for building accomplished during this period. But there can be little doubt that the Philippine Foreign Affairs Training Program graduates have been the active

spearhead of the movement to build a career foreign affairs establishment for the Philippines.[3]

Indeed, many of the State Department Boys quickly established themselves as experts in the different fields of diplomacy. A good example is Luis Moreno Salcedo who, after graduating from the State Department training program, was appointed as chief of protocol of the Department of Foreign Affairs by Vice President and Secretary of Foreign Affairs Elpidio Quirino. It was a fitting recognition of Moreno Salcedo's superior intellect, attitude, and physical attributes. With his serious demeanor, good looks and with his 5' 11" frame, he was taller than the average Filipino. During his last years in the Foreign Service, he was often referred to as "every inch the distinguished diplomat." At any rate, Moreno Salcedo would distinguish himself initially as the author of *A Guide to Protocol*, the first book written by a Filipino diplomat on that subject.[4]

The book contains rules on the Foreign Service, diplomatic communications, social gatherings, and others. Two chapters of the book deal with the protocols in the Foreign Service (Chapter 3: The Secretary of Foreign Affairs and Diplomatic and Consular Officers; Chapter 4: Officers of the Foreign Service of the Philippines). It lists down the officials and personnel in the Foreign Service and defines their respective duties and functions. It also presents samples of diplomatic communications and discusses military courtesies and protocol.

A book review written by Emilio D. Bejasa, another State Department graduate, praised the book for being "convenient, reliable and practical book." After citing its merits, however, Bejasa also points out that "the work suffers from hasty editing and unbalanced treatment of the subject matter."[5]

Nevertheless, *A Guide to Protocol* became the main reference book of the Philippine Foreign Service on matters of protocol since its inception. Since its publication in 1950, the book has never been updated or expanded until now. Indonesian diplomats also used Moreno Salcedo's book during the early years of their Foreign Service. Juan A. Ona, Moreno Salcedo's deputy in the Philippine embassy in Moscow in the 1970s, recalled how the Indonesian diplomats posted there were impressed by Moreno Salcedo's reputation.

As Ona recalled:

> In October 1977, when Indonesian Ambassador Choesin heard that Ambassador Luis Moreno Salcedo was coming to Moscow, awe-struck he excitedly asked me: "Is he the ambassador who wrote the book on diplomatic practice?" I said yes. Then he told me that when Indonesia gained independence, he was assigned to the Protocol Office. The only books for their guidance were Ernest Satow's *Guide to Diplomatic Practice* and Luis Moreno Salcedo's *A Guide to Protocol*. Since Satow was too theoretical, Moreno Salcedo's book became their bible.[6]

Another State Department Boy, Jose Alejandrino, published a seminal work, this time, on international law. After obtaining his doctorate degree in Law from the Universidad Central de Madrid, Alejandrino's doctoral dissertation *Suez y el derecho internacional*[7] (Suez and International Law) was published in 1959 by the Instituto Francisco Vitoria of the prestigious Higher Council of Scientific Research of Spain (CSIC). Alejandrino defended his dissertation in 1957 before a panel composed of top Spanish jurists, who included Jose de Yanguas Messia, former foreign minister of Spain, who was also the dissertation director. After his successful dissertation defense, Alejandrino received the grade of *sobresaliente cum laude* (excellent with honors).

In his dissertation, Alejandrino demonstrates with well-reasoned arguments that the Egyptian nationalization of the Suez Canal Company is not contrary to any rule established by international law. Besides, it also shows the wisdom on the part of the Western Powers that respects the awakened Arab nationalism and recognizes the sovereign rights of the countries of the Middle East. Without this respect and this recognition, it seems difficult, perhaps impossible, the channeling of all the Arab sentiments toward relations of mutual cooperation and friendship with the West, notwithstanding the fact that this is the best market for the principal Arab wealth which is oil.[8]

The challenge of writing his dissertation in legal Spanish was not at all difficult for Alejandrino because of his mastery of the language. Earlier, in 1949, his translation of the book of his uncle and name sake, Jose Alejandrino, *The Price of Freedom: Episodes and Anecdotes of Our Struggle for Freedom* was published.[9] The elder Jose Alejandrino was one of the leading Filipino generals during the Philippine Revolution against Spain. He was also the acting head of the Department of War of the Aguinaldo Government during the Philippine-American War. He eventually surrendered to the American Forces in May 1901, two months after the capture of General Aguinaldo.

After Moreno Salcedo and Alejandrino, another State Department graduate, Carlos Faustino, Alejandrino's batch mate at the State Department training program, would make an important contribution to the Foreign Service in the field of publication. Faustino authored the *Revised Foreign Service Regulations of the Philippines* in 1962. Faustino's revision would stand for twenty years before the Philippine Foreign Service Code of 1983 superseded it.

The State Department graduates were adept at drafting laws and legal opinions that would govern and guide the Foreign Service. Since a majority of them had legal background, many were relied on for this task. One of them, Simeon Roxas, dedicated a great deal of his professional life to it. Roxas, a member of Group V of the State Department trainees, distinguished himself first as chief of the Treaties Division and later as one of the longest serving heads of the Legal Office at the Department of Foreign Affairs. Roxas had trained at the Treaties Division of the State Department.

Roxas was a gentleman of the first order. He was half-Spanish and lived the old traditional pre-World War II upper middle class life. He spoke and wrote in Spanish and was probably the last of the generation of Filipino lawyers who read the *Codigo Civil* and *Codigo Penal* in Spanish. He was a man of modest means but his wife, Soledad, was a rich landowner from the southern Tagalog region. At the old DFA building at Padre Faura, Roxas was chauffeured-driven in his personal 1954 Buick limo while he was head of the Legal Office.

During the Ferdinand Marcos murder trial before the Pacific War, Roxas was a member of the defense team from the Francisco Law Office whom Marcos hired to handle his case. Marcos was eventually acquitted and never forgot Attorney Simeon Roxas. During the Macapagal administration (1961–1965), Roxas, already a Foreign Service officer, was appointed to head the freezer section called "the Sabah Claims office" at the DFA. When Marcos became president in 1966, Roxas got a call from Malacañang, the presidential palace, and was told to pick his choice of posts, except the Philippine embassy in Washington. Roxas reportedly asked to be assigned as Philippine consul general to Hong Kong due to its proximity to Manila and for health reasons. It was his last post before retirement. Marcos was amazed by the simple request and immediately granted his wish. Roxas retired in 1972 and attended to his farm in Lipa and Quezon.[10]

In the summer of 1975, President Marcos plucked Roxas out of retirement to help the Department of Foreign Affairs craft a new entity that would allow the Philippine government to legally continue its presence in Taipei without antagonizing Communist China. When the Philippines established diplomatic relations with the People's Republic of China on 8 June 1975, it meant severing ties with Taiwan in accordance with the "One China Policy." The Philippine government was at a loss on how to prepare for an alternative representation in Taipei.

The choice of Roxas was based on his credentials as an international law expert and one of the few "China hands" in the Foreign Service. In October 1975, Roxas submitted a report with recommendations for the establishment of a unique and novel entity – the Asian Exchange Center Taipei Incorporated (ASECTAI), a private non-stock, non-profit corporation organized under the laws of the Philippines and duly registered with the Philippine Securities and Exchange Commission. Since the mission of ASECTAI is similar to a Foreign Service post, Roxas devised a scheme whereby corporate titles are equated to those used in an embassy or consulate.[11] In short, ASECTAI would practically function like an embassy but in name. ASECTAI is now known as the Manila Economic and Cultural Office (MECO).

After masterminding the creation of ASECTAI, Roxas was appointed as its first head and primary incorporator of the Center. To maintain its low profile, "the Center shall be operated in a very discreet manner and there must be no publicity of its work in order to avoid complicating Philippine relations... because Philippine relations with Taiwan are those of an independently functioning although unrecognized government, and because at the same time the conduct of those relations would have implications for Philippine relations with the People's Republic of China, the Department of Foreign Affairs should exercise close supervision and control of the Center just as it does in the case of Philippine embassies abroad."[12]

The successful establishment of the ASECTAI caught the attention of the American embassy in Taipei. In March 1977, Roxas wrote a confidential report to the Department of Foreign Affairs in Manila:

> It might be pertinent to mention that the political counselor of the American embassy, Mr. Frank N. Burnell, recently called on the undersigned on two separate occasions. This was rather surprising, considering that I am not formally accredited to the diplomatic or consular corps of Taipei and I should not have been accorded this courtesy, especially by the number two man of the [U.S.] embassy. During the course of our conversation, Mr. Burnell made discreet inquiries as to how we were operating as a Center.
> In view of this friendly "sounding out" it can be inferred that it is highly possible that the US Government is thinking of setting up in Taipei some sort of a non-political establishment similar in nature to the Asian Exchange Center, Inc. or the Chinese/Japanese Interchange Association which has replaced the former Japanese embassy here. This would mean the pull out of the U.S. embassy in Taipei and its transfer to Peking.[13]

Roxas' hunch about the possible change of U.S. policy *vis-à-vis* China proved correct. Two years later, the United States and the People's Republic of China normalized their bilateral relations and Washington subsequently cut its diplomatic ties with Taipei. Nevertheless, the U.S. Congress passed the Taiwan Relations Act in 1979 to maintain America's unofficial relations with Taiwan.

In 1982, Roxas retired for the second time. He was replaced by Benjamin Tirona, his batch mate at the State Department training program, at the helm of ASECTAI. Tirona would head the Center until 1984. By that time, the control of ASECTAI was transferred to the Office of the Philippine President by virtue of Executive Order No. 931 dated 16 January 1984. The transfer was done ostensibly "to make the ASECTAI separate and distinct from the regular official diplomatic posts, to give it more flexibility and to avoid complete control by the Department of Foreign Affairs."[14]

Benjamin Tirona himself had already retired from the Foreign Service as Philippine ambassador to South Korea. His last days in the Foreign Service, however, were marred by controversy over his deanship of the diplomatic corps in Seoul. As Juan Ona, a retired Philippine ambassador, recounted:

> Ambassador Tirona was the dean of the diplomatic corps in Seoul when he reached the age of retirement in the late 1970s. The Foreign Ministry gave him the customary send off and so did the diplomatic corps and there was even a turnover of the deanship. But after all this, Tirona got an extension of his service and tour of duty. On top of this, he had the effrontery to reclaim the deanship of the diplomatic corps. The diplomatic corps was in an uproar because the new dean refused to recognize him. The ambassadors did not know what to do. The Foreign Ministry was reluctant to intervene and passed on the problem to the President of South Korea. The President, however, did not know what to do either because he did not want to antagonize the Philippines. So for several months, the diplomatic corps was in limbo until Ambassador Tirona finally left.[15]

The late Philippine ambassador, Rodolfo S. Sanchez, confirmed the embarrassing account on Tirona's last days in Seoul. As Sanchez explained: "Ambassador Ona's narration about BTT (Benjamin T. Tirona) last days in Korea was true. It was a bad ending to a good career. He was a great public relations man, the best I have ever known. His tale did not end there. After retirement, he wangled another assignment—to head our pseudo-diplomatic post in Taipei—until again he was eased out by Narciso Ramos, father of President Fidel V. Ramos, certainly a much senior man. And BTT drifted away into oblivion."[16]

Benito B. Valeriano, Philippine consul general to Dubai, corroborated Sanchez' account on Tirona's quest to get the Taipei Center as his retirement post. As Valeriano narrated: "One fine day in 1981, Tirona, his State Department colleague, came to visit Taipei. Pleasantly surprised, Roxas welcomed him and gave him his best hospitality to rekindle their good old days in Washington as trainees. Little did he know that Tirona was on a "field reconnaissance," surreptitiously casing the joints, and true to his thoughts, Taipei was a good retirement post back then. Months later, President Marcos now sick and often dazed, Roxas was recalled and retired for the second time in 1982."[17]

Although Tirona is remembered more in the Philippine Foreign Service for his diplomatic scandal in South Korea and his controversial posting in Taipei, the people of his home province of Cavite, south of Manila, immortalized him by naming a town in Cavite in his honor.

Another retired State Department Boy who was "recycled" to serve in the Foreign Service was Emilio D. Bejasa. Bejasa retired as Philippine ambassador to Brazil in 1979 but was appointed by President Marcos in 1981 as deputy chief of mission at the Philippine Embassy in Saudi Arabia to help Ambassador Benjamin "Kokoy" Romualdez, Marcos' brother-in-law. After helping Ambassador Romualdez settle in Jeddah, Bejasa was re-assigned as Philippine ambassador to India in 1983, in anticipation of a visit by President and Mrs. Marcos there. Mrs. Marcos did make the trip, not to return the earlier visit of Prime Minister Indira Gandhi, but to attend the latter's funeral in November 1984.

Aside from Bejasa's equanimity and English manners, he was also a master wordsmith. Retired Philippine ambassador, Jose A. Zaide, formerly Bejasa's deputy in New Delhi and himself a famed writer, wrote the following account of Bejasa:

> I used to kid Ambassador Bejasa about what he must be worth in a dowry as a widower and a recycled envoy. But even upstarts know their betters. I would discover his caliber (he was formerly editor of the *UP Collegian*) when I wrote a rejoinder to a *Times of India* editorial, which hit the Philippine President below the belt. I was too emotionally

charged in my riposte that I literally ran up a fever. With his deft blue pen—very lightly changing a word here, a word there; and with a reordering of sequence of sentences, he made the difference. I gave to Bejasa a draft in cast iron; he returned it in tempered steel.[18]

Rodolfo A. Arizala, a retired Filipino ambassador, was another witness to Bejasa's equanimity and ingenuity. He remembered how Bejasa extricated the Philippine delegation from a sticky issue during a UN conference in Argentina. As Arizala recalled:

Ambassador Bejasa was one of our best diplomats. Soft-spoken, with a Mona Lisa smile, well-measured movement, cool under fire, and even if we did not receive instructions from the Department of Foreign Affairs during a UN Water Conference in Rosario City, Argentina, he did not panic. He simply told me and the other members of the Philippine delegation to "play it by ear." But a voting on a sensitive issue came up. Bangladesh and India were quarrelling over rights from a river originating from the Himalayas down to India and then to Bangladesh. Bangladesh called for a roll call vote. Bejasa, as chairman of the Philippine delegation, quietly told us, "Let us get out of the room one-by-one discreetly." In our hurry, one of us forgot his jacket hanging at the back of the chair in front of the desk for the Philippine delegation. When the name of the Philippines was called by the conference chairman to cast its vote and found that the Philippine delegation desk was empty, he announced loudly over the microphone: "Philippines, absent, except a jacket hanging at the back of the chair!" We could hear from the outside subdued laughter, and then the chairman called on the next country. When the head of the Indian delegation approached Ambassador Bejasa after the roll call vote asking, "My friend, what happened?" Ambassador Bejasa simply smiled and the Indian delegate understood. We don't like to antagonize any of them – Bangladesh or India. We did not tell him that we have not received any instruction.[19]

Bejasa retired from the Foreign Service for the second time in 1986 after the People Power Revolution toppled the Marcos regime. Bejasa died at the age of 88 in November 2002 in Chicago, Illinois where he settled after retirement. Following his expressed wishes, his cremated remains were brought back to the Philippines for burial in his hometown of Bauan, Batangas. The majority of his twelve children who came from distant and different corners of the world came back to do the last honors for their father.[20]

Bejasa is regarded as one of the topnotch diplomats of all time. Joe Guevara, a famous columnist of *Manila Bulletin*, wrote a tribute to Bejasa in his column on 08 November 2002: "An original in the Foreign Service, Ambassador Bejasa ranks among the country's very best along with such ambassadors as Carlos P. Romulo, Salvador P. Lopez, Luis Moreno Salcedo, Leon Ma. Guerrero, Emmanuel Pelaez, Jose D. Ingles, Romeo Arguelles, Pacifico Castro, Rodolfo Severino and Domingo Siazon."[21]

The previously cited UN Conference incident involving Bejasa needs to be clarified. Although Bejasa's career in the Foreign Service was mostly confined to bilateral posts, Bejasa also served as deputy permanent representative at the Philippine Mission to the United Nations from 1968 to 1971. A number of State Department Boys also made their marked in multilateral diplomacy such as Alejandro Yango, Luis Moreno Salcedo, and Hortencio Brillantes. Yango and Moreno Salcedo succeeded each other as Permanent Representative to the United Nations in New York in the early 1980s. Many Filipino Foreign Service officers remember Yango for his long assignment to the Philippine Mission to the United Nations in New York and as an expert on UN matters, especially the international law of the sea.

Yango started his career in the Foreign Service as a consular officer. He served as Philippine vice consul in Sydney, Jakarta, Hong Kong, and Agana (1948–1956), then as consul in Tokyo and Honolulu (1956–1966). His exposure to multilateral diplomacy started in1966 when he was posted as minister counselor to the Philippine Mission to the United Nations in New York from (1966–1971).[22] After serving in Manila for three years as Assistant Secretary for United Nations Affairs and International Conferences (UNAIC), Yango was assigned again to the Philippine Mission in New York as Deputy Permanent Representative (1974 –1977). He was finally appointed Ambassador Extraordinary and Plenipotentiary and served as Permanent Representative to the United Nations from 1979 to 1982. Upon his retirement, Yango settled in Honolulu where some of his children live. Yango died at Castle Hospital in June 1999 at the age of 82.[23]

On the other hand, Luis Moreno Salcedo capped his Foreign Service career as Permanent Representative to the United Nations in New York. He had a varied and illustrious diplomatic career. He was assigned as ambassador to Argentina, Vietnam, France, Soviet Union, and finally to the Philippine Mission to the United Nations in New York. Towards the end of his tour of duty in Vietnam, Moreno Salcedo and his wife had a brush with death. In February 1968, Salcedo Moreno's official residence was bombarded with heavy artillery by the Viet Cong. As his wife, Hermelinda Ycasiano Moreno, recalled:

> It was 2:30 in the morning in early February 1968 in Saigon, South Vietnam. The night was quiet, a welcome respite from the ongoing weeklong Tet Celebration or the Vietnamese New Year. Suddenly, a powerful explosion rocked the house and shattered the glass windows. This was followed by another explosion! "Oh God, have mercy on our poor USAID neighbor. He is being bombed", I prayed. Little did I know that we were the ones being bombed until the maid came running to the room. She said there were a dozen men shooting at our gate, our cars were burning, and the house was going to burn, too. We rushed to the balcony at the rear of the house. One of the Filipino soldiers guarding the house put a bamboo ladder against the wall. He went up the ladder, stood on the narrow balcony ledge and directed our escape. In spite of his being much smaller than I was, he lifted me over the balcony railing, which I was trying to climb unsuccessfully. Thank God he did not fall over backwards! We rushed down the ladder. Another explosion shattered the remaining glass windows, hitting us as we ran.
> We were brought to the service bathroom as this was supposed to be the safest place. For more than two hours, our

three soldiers and the attackers exchanged gunfire. The bullets were whizzing past us. The soldiers kept radioing their headquarters for more men and more ammunition. They were afraid the enemy would overpower them. They were also running out of bullets.

Unfortunately, all the roads were blocked as the Vietnamese communist forces, as part of what is now known as the 1968 Tet Offensive, were attacking the whole city. One of the soldiers approached Luis (Ambassador Luis Moreno Salcedo), gave him a grenade and said, "Sir, when we are gone, they will come in. Remove the pin from the grenade and throw it at them. My husband kept asking the guard for the time. He probably wanted to know what time he would die, I thought. All of a sudden, my feet felt very cold. It was only then that we realized that I was barefooted. In my hurry to leave the house, I forgot to put on my shoes. Luis gave me his shoes, which I gratefully accepted. It was a lovely gesture in a desperate situation.

At the break of dawn, we were told that the attack was over. The attackers had left. The Vietnamese policeman guarding our gate was dead, so were several passers-by and our neighbor's maid who tried to see what was going on from their balcony. Thank God we were unscathed. An even bigger unexploded bomb was found in our yard. The bomb squad quickly defused this. As soon as we entered the house, my husband typed his report to the DFA, complete with the time the incidents happened. No wonder he kept asking the time. What a perfect example of duty under fire![24]

Even after retirement in 1985, Moreno Salcedo was appointed special adviser to Vice President and Secretary of Foreign Affairs Salvador Laurel during the latter's official visit to some European countries in 1986. Pablo A. Araque, then the newly appointed Assistant Secretary for European Affairs at the DFA, and was a member of the Philippine delegation, recalled: "Ambassador Moreno was with us and his presence was greatly reassuring to me especially. He was a solid, experienced hand in European affairs and he was close to the Laurels. He was a kind and gentle person, a gentleman *"de primera clase"* (firs class). It was much later that I found out that even at the time that we were travelling together, he had already been diagnosed as suffering from cancer of the liver. It was not long afterwards that he died."[25]

But among the State Department Boys, it was Hortencio J. Brillantes who served the longest in a multilateral post. He started his long and brilliant career in the Foreign Service as chief of the Passport and Visa Division at the DFA from 1949 to 1951. After a brief stint as executive officer of the Office of Political and Cultural Affairs, he was assigned as consul to the Philippine Consulate in Seattle from 1952 to 1956. From Seattle, Brillantes was transferred to New York where he served as adviser and executive secretary at the Philippine Mission to the United Nations in New York for nine years (1956–1965). He was subsequently assigned to the Philippine Mission to the United Nations in Geneva as Deputy Chief of Mission in 1966, then as Permanent Representative from 1966 to 1973. He also became concurrent Philippine ambassador to Switzerland and non-resident ambassador to Austria and Czechoslovakia from 1973 to 1979.[26]

Throughout his life, Brillantes maintained a close relationship with Mill, his mentor at the U.S. State Department, and never failed to update Mill of the progress in his diplomatic career. While serving as Philippine permanent representative to the United Nations in Geneva in 1972, Brillantes wrote:

> I send herewith a picture which marks another very touching event in my humble life. You were present when I was elected President of the Trade and Development Board of UNCTAD. As I was being nominated for the Presidency of the Industrial Development Board of UNIDO I recalled how affectionately you congratulated me on my UNCTAD presidency. I know you would have done no less were you with in Vienna at the time. As a personal note I find satisfaction in the fact that it's only in my case where there had been an overlapping presidents in a span of months in 1971-72. My term as President of the Trade and Development Board will not expire until sometime in October and I was elected President of the Industrial Development Board in May.

I know you will be pleased not only because you continue to be my mentor and more meaningfully you have been the "master" who has imparted to the career ambassadors of the Philippine Foreign Service the right perspective and a balance sense of values so indispensable if one means to succeed in the field of diplomacy.[27]

Brillantes, however, would fail in his bid to be elected Secretary General of the United Nations Conference on Trade and Development (UNCTAD) in 1974. Another State Department graduate, Carlos A. Faustino, then Philippine ambassador to Belgium, broke the news to Mill: "I wonder if you knew that Tencing Brillantes almost became Secretary General of the UNCTAD, in the end he lost out to the Ambassador of Sri Lanka to the E.E.C. (European Economic Community), somebody said, because of his age being over that of retirement in the UN."[28]

At any rate, Brillantes is widely remembered in the Foreign Service as "Mr.UNCTAD." In particular, the late Ambassador Pablo A. Araque, who was a former student of Brillantes, recalled that Brillantes "was a very charming person." Araque continued: "He was my professor in immigration law at the University of Manila when I was taking my Foreign Service course and a very good one, too. What impressed me most about the way he taught the subject was his prodigious memory – he recited provisions of the Immigration Law almost verbatim. I was to learn later that he was the passport and visa officer of the Department of Foreign Affairs. His prodigious memory served him well in UNCTAD, where he was considered the authority and mentor of delegates. In the course of my tours of duty, I met a number of foreign diplomats from both East and West who spoke highly of him. He stayed for a very long time in Geneva as permanent representative to UNCTAD."[29]

Indeed, Brillantes became a "permanent fixture" at Philippine Mission in the United Nations in Geneva and was never recalled back to Manila. After his retirement as Permanent Representative to the United Nations in Geneva, Brillantes was appointed by President Marcos as presidential adviser on economic affairs on detail, again, to the Philippine Mission in Geneva.

One major criticism hurled against the State Department Boys was that they were too fixated on foreign assignments. In fact, some of them retired from the Service without even serving in the Home Office. Indeed, many stayed long years abroad. Manuel Adeva, Jose Imperial, Tiburcio Baja, Yusup Abubakar, and Delfin Garcia, for example, hardly served in the Home Office during their entire career. This is perhaps understandable because during that time Filipino diplomats had no fix tenure abroad. It was only with the passage of Foreign Service Law of 1991 when the tour of duty was limited to six years and strict rotation policy was enforced. Besides, the low pay discouraged them to stay in Manila.

There was, of course, an exemption to the rule. Rodolfo H. Severino was among the few State Department graduates who served long and well at the Home Office. Severino joined the Foreign Office in 1948 and was appointed Foreign Affairs officer the following year. He worked at the Division of Asian and Pacific Affairs, becoming its expert on Philippine-Republic of China (Taiwan) relations and later on the Korean War. He served as Chief of the Division of Eastern Political Affairs from 1955 to 1961. His first foreign assignment was in Madrid in 1961 as first secretary and consul general, after which he was assigned to Djakarta in 1963 as minister counselor. In 1965, he was recalled to Manila and designated assistant secretary for Coordination and Planning, and later as head the Department's Consular Office. In 1968, he assumed his post as minister counselor in the Philippine Embassy in the Court of St. James, his last post. Upon reaching the age of 65, Severino retired on 22 March 1970. Although he reached the Chief of Mission rank, he never became an ambassador extraordinary and plenipotentiary.

Rodolfo C. Severino, Jr., son of the Rodolfo H. Severino who became a career Philippine ambassador and served as undersecretary of Foreign Affairs for Policy of the DFA (1992-1997) provided a concise account of his father's career:

> There are three things I remember most about him and wish to bring to the attention of the current crop of Foreign Service officers. One is that he was a man of the utmost integrity. He died poor, and, in life, he rejected the practice of pulling strings to get promotions or choice assignments. I remember him agonizing intensely when he could no longer stand being left behind in the promotions because he had refused to seek favors from politicians, until he was

forced to approach a senator-friend to put in a good word for him. This gave him no end of discomfort. Hard as it is to believe, things were as bad then in terms of patronage as they are now -- perhaps, worse. The second thing is the seriousness that he brought to his job. He was posted in Jakarta at the time of the Gestapu that ended Sukarno's rule, the sequence of events that began on 30 September 1965. In the midst of those critical events, the DFA blithely recalled him to Manila. When he got to Manila, nobody -- nobody -- bothered to debrief him on what was taking place in the country next door. To him, it was incomprehensible as well as appalling. The third thing I remember most about my father is his insistence on the correct and precise use of language. His thinking was that since English was our language of communication we should use it accurately and well. He irritated colleagues by pointing out instances of the cavalier use of language, which reflected fuzzy thinking.[30]

Just days after his arrival in London, Rodolfo H. Severino was appointed *chargé d'affaires* ad interim of the Philippine embassy. At the same time two controversial issues exploded during his watch — fake Philippine passports and fake jobs for Filipinos. In early 1968, 518 special passports were confiscated by the Philippine police after verification showed that they were falsified. Severino coordinated with Thomas de la Rue & Co., Ltd. London, the official printers of Philippine passports, regarding the case of the fake passports. In the end, Severino reported to the Home Office that the passports in question were not printed by Thomas de la Rue. Upon close scrutiny of the serial numbers of the fake passports, it became evident that the passports bear the serial number S-40901 to S-46000. The investigation concluded that the manufacturers of fake currency bills might have branched out into passport-making.[31]

Severino likewise issued a warning to Filipino job seekers against employment agencies in England and other Commonwealth countries that offered services through advertisements in Manila newspapers. After coordinating with the Migration and Visa Department of the Foreign and Commonwealth Office, Severino reported on the investigation being conducted by the London police on the racket. "The object of these agencies is to take advantage of the desire of persons abroad to emigrate to the United Kingdom and to other countries. Their advertisements do not mention the procedures, which must be complied with by persons wishing to enter the United Kingdom for employment. It is considered most unlikely that the agencies in question are able to fulfill the promises made in their advertisements and persons seeking employment in the United Kingdom would be ill-advised to remit any money to them or indeed to have any dealings with them at all," the report said. Severino, in his letter to the Department of Foreign Affairs in Manila, recommended that the DFA undertake a public information campaign on the matter inasmuch as many Filipinos had already been victimized by misleading advertisements for employment to England, Canada and other countries.[32]

While serving at the Home Office, Severino moonlighted as a professor in Manila universities and colleges just like many of his Foreign Service colleagues. His students rated Severino as an excellent professor of political science at the Philippine Law School. One of his students wrote the following:

> Perfectly versed in the subject that he teaches, perplexing problems proounded by the inquisitive students are easily tackled by him [Severino]. His students derive much from his masterly discourse on every topic especially when it comes to diplomatic affairs. Gifted with a keen memory, he still vividly recollects numerous principles in physics which we found to be very relevant to the study of law. Patient and understanding, he takes pairs in entertaining every question, even philosophical ones, to the delight and satisfaction of the students. His timely humorous cracks enliven his class.[33]

Some Filipino Foreign Service officers who worked with the State Department Boys remember them for being stickler for English and good writing style. Many of them have excellent penmanship, at time when good handwriting was valued as a mark of education. Besides, many of the State Department graduates did not know how to use a typewriter and relied on their assistants to type their reports. Also their refined manner of dressing became a hallmark of their group. They were remembered for their sartorial looks, especially Bejasa and Yango who often wore their trademark double-breasted suits. The following depiction of Severino by his student would most likely apply to all the State Department graduates: "Our professor (Rodolfo H. Severino) is always seen in sartorial splendor outmatching our taste for fine clothes. He, certainly, is not of our age, but his picture proves his countenance is still radiant with the sparkle of youth..."[34] But what accentuated their looks was the way they exude confidence. "The State Department Boys walked with a kind of swagger," recalled one retired ambassador.

As to the State Department Boys' working style and attitude towards their work, a retired Philippine ambassador Rodolfo A. Arizala, who worked directly with three of them - Eutiquio Sta. Romana, Roman Ubaldo, and Alejandro Yango – made the following remarks:

> "From all of them I learned or have imbibed from them, aside from the rudiments of consular and diplomatic practice, professionalism, loyalty to service and thorough studies/research before acting on important papers or decisions. All of them, as a general rule, would ask for the PR or previous records of the case or documents of the subject before they have to act on it. Thus, ensuring continuity of action and not divert from the established policy and if they think there is a need for change of approach or policy, they make a memorandum for the ambassador or higher authorities stating why they believe there should be a change of approach or policy. Thus, from them, I learned how to make memoranda and to keep faithful records of all my communications or of what I have acted upon.[35]

The State Department Boys as a group had made a historic contribution to the advancement of their country. Ambassador Delfin Garcia, however, was quite reticent in taking too much credit for being a State Department graduate and a pioneer in the Philippine Foreign Service. He claimed that they were simply fortunate to be among the first. They were only ordinary diplomats who tackled more or less the same problems like what the new generation of Filipino diplomats confronts nowadays.[36] He was just self-effacing. When Garcia was the dean of the diplomatic corps in Singapore in the 1970s, Edward W. Mill described him as "brilliant and highly experienced – a "picture-book type of ambassador."[37] Garcia served as Philippine Ambassador to Netherlands, Singapore, and East Germany before he finally retired from the Foreign Service in 1987, the last State Department graduate to do so.

This reticence for claiming credit as the Republic's first career diplomats might have been tempered by the fact that anti-American sentiment in the Philippines was on the rise during the 1960s. It was clearly demonstrated when President Macapagal decreed that the changing of the date of the celebration of Philippine independence from 4 July to 12 June. As US-trained officers, the State Department Boys perhaps thought it wise to maintain a low profile. As Lewis Gleeck, an American diplomat and scholar, observed:

> It was symbolic that the pride taken by the graduates of the State Department's own in-house educational facility was, after the first decade, replaced by a reluctance to refer to the fact that their individual careers had begun as American trainees.[38]

This reluctance is of course not a new thing. Even during the conduct of the Philippine Foreign Affairs Training Program in 1947, some observers had suspected it of being a means to indoctrinate the trainees with the American perspective and views. An article published by the *New York Herald Tribune* in March 1947 already tackled this issue head on.

> While the Filipino trainees are shown some working samples of reports from American diplomatic and consular reports and gain access to statements of American policy, there is no attempt to indoctrinate them with State Department views, it was explained. Instead, their training consists of lectures and reading or writing political and economic reports, passport and visa controls, protocol and conduct and contacts in foreign countries. Observers point out that the training course here may bring results of incalculable value

if Philippine diplomats draw heavily upon their lessons in Washington to help chart a progressive and peaceful course for the restless millions in the Far East.[39]

The *Manila Post* in its article "State Department Trains P.I. Diplomatic Corps" of 22 March 1947 basically rehashed and echoed the *New York Herald Tribune* article. This claim of no U.S. indoctrination is debatable. The fact is that the State Department trainees were largely exposed to American diplomatic and consular practice. It could be argued, however, that their stay in Washington was brief, on the average three to six months, although some of them received extended field training for about two months in selected U.S. Foreign Service posts. Their training was intensive enough to familiarize themselves with the American style of diplomacy and foreign relations. Thus, the State Department trainees developed a strong bond with America and its people.

One of the objectives of the training program was to strengthen American-Philippine bilateral relations. A press release from the State Department states, "A majority of the members of the Philippine Foreign Service has received training under the program. The United States Government hopes to contribute in this manner to the creation of a foreign affairs establishment for the Philippine Republic which will play a significant role in world affairs and cement further the close ties now existing between the two countries."[40]

The Philippine Foreign Affairs Training Program was by no means the only training program conducted by the U.S. government for the Philippines. The Philippine Rehabilitation Act of 1946 provided for the training of 850 Filipinos in the United States in eight different government agencies: The Federal Works Agency, the Corps of Engineers of the U.S. army, the Public Health Service of the Federal Security Agency, the U.S. Maritime Commission, the Weather Bureau, the Coast and Geodetic Survey of the Department of Commerce, and the Fish and Wildlife Service of the Department of Interior.[41]

It appears that the State Department boys did not form themselves into a cohesive group after their training in Washington as they went on their separate ways. Although the State Department graduates set up the Philippine Foreign Service Association in Washington in March 1947, the Association ran out of steam when they returned back to Manila or were assigned abroad. Clicks, however, existed among the State Department Boys. Five of them, Yusup Abubakar, Pelayo Llamas, Eutiquio Sta. Romana, Renato Urquiola, and Alejandro Yango were members of Class of 1940 of the UP College of Law. Emilio Bejasa and Simeon Roxas both worked as lawyers at the Francisco Law Office. Anastacio Bartolome and Marcelino Bernardo both taught business courses at the University of Manila.

The only lynch pin of the group was their mentor Edward W. Mill who tried to gather them together in 1948 when he was assigned to the American embassy in Manila or his individual visits to the State Department Boys in their foreign posts. As a junior officer stationed in Burma, the late Ambassador Rodolfo Sanchez met Mill in Rangoon in 1962 when the latter was visiting Benjamin T. Tirona, then Philippine ambassador to Rangoon. He noticed that Mill, who was about the same age level as the trainees he taught in the State Department, was very close to his "boys" and was travelling at that time to check on how they were doing. "I listened to the two men talking about their Washington experience like old buddies, not teacher-student. I imagined they had a lot of fun."[42] After Mill's death in 1977, the strong and personal bond was broken. The State Department had no one to fill the void left by Mill. At the same time, many of the State Department Boys had already retired or passed away.

Even then one legacy that some State Department Boys bequeathed to the Foreign Service is their descendants and relatives who followed their footsteps. Looking at the roster of Filipino diplomats, a second, sometimes, and third generation of them are related to the State Department Boys. Former Undersecretary of Foreign Affairs for Policy Rodolfo Severino, Jr. (1992-1998) is the son of Rodolfo H. Severino. Former Permanent Representative to the United Nations in New York, Lauro Baja, is a nephew of Tiburcio C. Baja. Leslie Baja, Philippine ambassador to Switzerland, is also related to Tiburcio C. Baja. Tiburcio is Leslie's grandfather's first cousin. Tiburcio C. Baja also has a grandson in the American Foreign Service, Scott Williams, son of his daughter, Ruth and jazz musician Charles Williams. Scott is currently assigned to the US Embassy in Portugal. Evan Garcia, the current Undersecretary for Policy, is the son of Delfin R. Garcia. The brothers Anthony and Rene Cornista, assigned to the Philippine Embassy in Tokyo and the Philippine Consulate General in San Francisco respectively, are the sons of Irineo Cornista. The late Ambassador Alice Ramos and Consul Leticia Ramos are daughters of Aurelio Ramos.

The Philippine Foreign Service has gone a long way since the last batch of Filipino trainees graduated from the State Department training program in 1947. But we can always look back with pride at the auspicious beginning of the Philippine Foreign Service and the American diplomatic heritage that permeated it as vital factors in the successful conduct of Philippine foreign relations.

While some State Department Boys left the Foreign Service to join the academic and corporate world or due to their frustration over the rampant politics at the Foreign Service during its early years, majority continued to persevere and made diplomacy as their life-long career. Luis Moreno Salcedo, the apotheosis of an outstanding State Department graduate in this study, described diplomacy in the following terms: "Few professions are as demanding, lonely or financially unrewarding as that of a career diplomat. On the other hand, in few other professions can one find as much fulfillment, courage, loyalty, patience and integrity, or serve one's country and countrymen with as much effectiveness and devotion as in diplomacy."[43]

On whether or not he made a contribution as a diplomat, Moreno Salcedo reckoned that: "I do not know if I have accomplished anything important, or if what I have done will be remembered. However, instead of cursing the darkness of greed and indifference that sometimes envelops us, I have sought to light a candle of devotion to duty and service to our countrymen, in the hope that it will help to dissipate the shadows of selfishness and despair."[44]

On the sacrifice that he had made for the sake of serving his country, Moreno Salcedo said: "In the years of loneliness, financial constraints and separation from our children that followed, I adhered to my decision to remain in the Foreign Service. As year followed year, and I was given greater responsibilities and more opportunities to serve meaningfully, the feeling that what I was doing was like a grain of sand used in forming the blocks of granite that would support and strengthen an enduring Republic of the Philippines, grew in me and filled me with satisfaction."[45]

As he grew older, Moreno Salcedo exhibited an air of elegance. Beth Day Romulo, the American wife of then Foreign Secretary Carlos P. Romulo, met Moreno Salcedo in Paris in 1974. She described him as "a tall, elegant, white-haired man, he was every inch the distinguished diplomat, meticulously attired, in one of these trademark white suits), soft spoken, beautifully-mannered..." "As a professor, then diplomat, Luis had a fine command of history, and he played an important role in the development of the foreign policy of the Philippines. Upon his retirement, he was made Dean of Foreign Service Department of Lyceum. So long as he was physically able to serve, he had something to contribute," wrote Beth Day Romulo. "I respected and admired Ambassador Moreno Salcedo. He fulfilled all his assignments with distinction and brought credit to his country. Luis was what is called in show business "a class act." An act that is very hard to follow."[46] When Luis Moreno Salcedo died in March 1988, it was reported that "his friends in the media filled the pages of the metropolitan press with deserved eulogies celebrating his life and work, his principles and patriotism. He died, they said, a poor man."[47]

Poverty is not necessarily the common fate of retired Filipino diplomats, let alone the State Department Boys. Although Moreno Salcedo reportedly "died poor," retirement from the Philippine Foreign Service does not mean automatic financial ruin for Filipino diplomats. Aside from collecting their modest pension, Foreign Service personnel could also get the money value of leave credits earned both at the Home Office and abroad. The value of leave credits earned abroad is also several times higher than those earned in Manila since they are computed on the basis of 2:1 Philippine peso-US dollar exchange rate. Thus, the retired officers and employees of the Foreign Service, at least those who served before 1977, received a sort of financial windfall upon retirement. Again, a State Department graduate was responsible in making this policy.

Upon his retirement in the Foreign Service in February 1975, Jose M. Alejandrino, who previously served as Philippine ambassador to Pakistan, France, and Italy, filed a legal case against the Commission on Audit and the Department of Foreign Affairs regarding the computation of his terminal leave. The case went all the way to the Philippine Supreme Court. Alejandrino argued that the basis for computation of the Department of Foreign Affairs, the General Accounting Office Memorandum Circular No. 618, cannot be "validly applied to personnel of the Philippine Foreign Service." Instead, he insisted that it should be the relevant provisions of

Republic Act No. 708, otherwise known as the Philippine Foreign Service Act of 1952, which should be applied to officers and employees in the Philippine Foreign Service.[48]

After weighing Alejandrino's argument, the Supreme Court sustained it: "Since the petitioner was admittedly a member of the Foreign Service, his leave rights are governed by the Foreign Service Act, and the regulation issued pursuant thereto. "Sec. 4 Supplementary rules and regulations. – The Secretary, with the approval of the Philippines, may issue such supplementary rules and regulations as may be necessary to implement the provisions of this Act." (Title IV 1. Foreign Service Act.)

Since both the Commission on Audit and the Department of Foreign Affairs did not dispute Alejandrino's statement, the Supreme Court ordered the payment of Alejandrino's terminal leave amounting to "360 days less any amounts already paid." The success of Alejandrino's court case benefited not just himself and other State Department Boys but also all the other officers and employees of the Foreign Service. The landmark case is now referred to as the "Alejandrino Doctrine."

Finally, there is one important detail that should be pointed out here. When the Supreme Court ruled in favor of Alejandrino, the associate justices were perhaps not aware that Alejandrino was one of the authors of the Philippine Foreign Service Act of 1952, which was originally patterned after, one can guess, the U.S. Foreign Service Act of 1946.

Appendix

Profile of the State Department Trainees

Name	Date/Place of Birth	Education	Occupation
First Group			
Manuel A. Adeva	12 October 1901 Silay, Negros Occidental	Bachelor of Laws National University, Manila Master of Laws New York University	Chief, Nationals Division, Philippine Commonwealth Government-in-Exile, Washington, D.C.
Tiburcio C. Baja	11 August 1903, Batangas, Batangas	B.S. and M.A. Education University of the Philippines M.A. Foreign Service University of Southern California	Language Editor and Radio Presenter, U.S. Office of War Information, San Francisco
Candido T. Elbo	Santa Cruz, Laguna	No data available	Assistant Secretary to the President of the Philippine Commonwealth
Jose F. Imperial	26 February 1902 San Jose, Camarines Sur	St. Mary's College, USA M.A. and Ph.D. in Foreign Service, Georgetown University	Member, Technical Committee, Office of Philippine Commonwealth President
Vicente I. Singian	23 January 1914 San Fernando, Pampanga	B.A., Ateneo de Manila University Bachelor of Laws University of Santo Tomas M.A. and Ph.D. Foreign Service, Georgetown University	Assistant to the Resident Commissioner to the United States
Second Group			
Tomas G. de Castro	20 August 1907 Bulan, Sorsogon	Bachelor of Laws University of the Philippines	Technical Assistant, Office of the Resident Commissioner to the United States
Delfin Garcia	22 November 1921 Manila	B.S. Foreign Service University of the Philippines	Staff, Division of Foreign Affairs, Office of the President of the Philippine Commonwealth
Pelayo F. Llamas	20 June 1916 Pagsanjan, Laguna	Bachelor of Laws University of the Philippines	Private Secretary to the Second Deputy Commissioner of Immigration
Leopoldo T. Ruiz	15 November 1894 Capiz, Aklan	A.B., University of California M.A., Columbia University Ph.D., University of Southern California	Senior Analyst, Technical Committee, Office of the President of the Philippine Commonwealth
Doroteo V. Vite	6 February 1912 Lapog, Ilocos Sur	B.A., George Washington University	Serviceman, U.S. Army
Third Group			
Anastacio B. Bartolome	27 August 1909 Piddig, Ilocos Norte	B.A. Business Administration and Economics and M.A. Business Administration University of Oregon	Supply Officer, Philippine Relief and Rehabilitation Administration Assistant Professor University of Manila
Emilio D. Bejasa	28 February 1914 Bauan, Batangas	Associate of Arts Ateneo de Manila University Bachelor of Laws University of the Philippines	Lawyer, Francisco Law Office, Manila Chief, Investigation Division, Emergency Control Administration
Francisco P. Claravall	2 April 1910 Ilagan, Isabela	Associate of Arts, Bachelor of Laws and B.S. Foreign Service, University of Santo Tomas	Assistant Attorney, Chicote and Arnaiz Law Office, Manila
Juanito C. Dionisio	2 May 1910 Kalibo, Aklan	A.B. Journalism, University of Washington	Senior Assistant, Office of the Resident Commissioner to the United States, San Francisco
Pablo A. Peña	25 January 1911 Davao City	Associate of Arts University of the Philippines Bachelor of Laws Philippine Law School	Technical Assistant, Philippine National Assembly
Aurelio M. Ramos	28 October 1908 Balanga, Batangas	Bachelor of Laws Far Eastern University, Manila	Technical Assistant, Office of the Philippine Resident Commissioner to the United States, San Francisco
Eutiquio O. Sta. Romana	21 November 1915 Cabanatuan City, Nueva Ecija	Associate of Arts and Bachelor of Laws University of the Philippines	Special Agent, Philippine Constabulary
Alejandro D. Yango	26 February 1917 Cabanatuan City, Nueva Ecija	Bachelor of Laws University of the Philippines	Staff, Information Division, Philippine Constabulary

Appendix

		Fourth Group	
Jose M. Alejandrino	3 January 1910 Arayat, Pampanga	Associate in Arts and Bachelor of Laws University of the Philippines Harvard Law School 1936-1937	Senior Assistant, Department of Foreign Affairs
Marcelino V. Bernardo	1947, Manila	Ph.D. Economics University of Illinois	Assistant Chief, Division of Commercial Transportation Department of Foreign Affairs
Romeo S. Busuego	7 August 1915 Cabanatuan City, Nueva Ecija	Bachelor of Laws, University of the Philippines	Professor, Philippine Law School
Carlos A. Faustino	8 October 1913 Manila	Bachelor of Laws University of the Philippines	Partner, Cavana Law Office, Manila
Generoso P. Provido	17 July 1908 Janiuay, Iloilo	A.B. and M.A. University of California Ph.D., Stanford University	Senior Assistant, European and African Affairs Division, Department of Foreign Affairs
Rodolfo H. Severino	22 March 1906 Silay, Negros Occidental	Associate of Arts National University, Manila Bachelor of Laws Philippine Law School	Legal Officer, Bureau of Lands
Roman V. Ubaldo	9 August 1906 Santa Ignacia, Tarlac	B.A., University of California Ph.D., Indiana University	Senior Assistant, Office of the Resident Commissioner to the United States, San Francisco
		Fifth Group	
Yusup R. Abubakar	6 October 1917 Jolo, Sulu	Bachelor of Laws University of the Philippines	Circuit Justice of the Peace, Sulu
Hortencio J. Brillantes	7 January 1910 Tayum, Abra	Bachelor of Laws University of the Philippines	Special Researcher, Philippine Senate
Irineo R. Cabatit	16 June 1900 San Marcelino, Zambales	Bachelor of Arts University of Washington	Assistant, Western Division, Office of the Resident Commissioner to the United States, San Francisco
Irineo D. Cornista	26 January 1910 San Pablo, Laguna	Associate of Arts and Bachelor of Laws University of the Philippines	Assistant Attorney, Office of the Government Corporate Counsel, Department of Justice
Engracio D. Guerzon	15 April 1899 Santa Maria, Ilocos Sur	B.A. and M.A., University of California	Section Chief, Bureau of Census and Statistics
Guillermo C. Fonacier	10 February 1903 Laoag, Ilocos Norte	No data available	Clerk, Philippine Consulate General in San Francisco
Marciano A. Joven	4 January 1909 Santa Lucia, Ilocos Sur	Associate in Arts, San Mateo Junior College, USA A.B. Political Science and M.A., University of California	Relief and Welfare Officer, Philippine Relief and Rehabilitation Administration
Reynaldo Lardizabal, Jr.	2 July 1914 Lipa, Batangas	Associate in Arts Ateneo de Manila University	Secretary to Senator Claro M. Recto
Luis Moreno Salcedo	6 September 1918 Sara, Iloilo	Bachelor of Laws University of Santo Tomas	Assistant, Department of Foreign Affairs
Simeon R. Roxas	22 February 1905 Lipa, Batangas	Associate of Arts and Bachelor of Laws University of the Philippines	Senior Assistant, Department of Foreign Affairs
Eduardo L. Rosal	25 June 1913 Cavite City	Bachelor of Laws University of the Philippines	Assistant, Philippine Department of Foreign Affairs
Tagakotta Sotto	1910 Hong Kong	Bachelor of Laws University of Santo Tomas	No data available
Benjamin T. Tirona	16 July 1913 Kawit, Cavite	Bachelor of Laws, Manila Law College	Justice of Peace, Tagaytay City
Emilio Torres	18 October 1909 Manila	B.S. Education and Bachelor of Laws University of the Philippines	Legal Officer, Office of the Resident Commissioner to the United States
Renato A. Urquiola	18 November 1916 Manila	Bachelor of Laws and Master of Laws University of Santo Tomas	Special Assistant, Office of the President of the Philippine Commonwealth

PHILIPPINE FOREIGN SERVICE POSTS

POSTS	1946	1951	1955	1969	1981	1990	1996	2002	2013
Embassy	1	3	4	31	54	54	54	60	60
Mission	1	2	2	2	3	2	2	2	4
Legation	-	7	10	-	-	-	-	-	-
Consulate General	2	2	2	16	20	16	14	18	20
Consulate	-	8	12	-	-	2	3	1	-
Extension Office	-	-	-	-	-	-	1	1	-
Total	4	22	30	49	77	74	74	82	84

FOREIGN SERVICE PERSONNEL

	1946	1948	1955	1968	1972	1978	1981	1991	1996	2012
Home Office	41	187	83	575	587	953	722	1,779	1,183	1,507
Foreign Service	no data available	304	123	279	417	665	1,026	898	1,380	1,194
Total	41	491	206	854	1,004	1,618	1,748	2,677	2,563	2,701

Sources: Division of Protocol, DFA, July 1948; Department of Foreign Affairs Review, Vol. 1, No. 3, (February, 1951); DFA Review, Vol. II, No. 1, (March, 1955); The Ministry of Foreign Affairs for the New Millennium, (Foreign Service Institute, 1983); Annual Report of the Ministry of Foreign Affairs, (Foreign Service Institute, 1981); Annual Report of the Department of Foreign Affairs 1991, (Foreign Service Institute, 1991);Primer on the DFA (Draft), (Foreign Service Institute, 1996);DFA Office of Personnel and Administrative Services, 2002. DFA Office of the Undersecretary for Administration, Accomplishment Report 2012.

Prepared by Marciano R. de Borja, Special Assistant, Office of the Undersecretary for Administration, Department of Foreign Affairs, 15 April 2013.

Bibliography

Archival Sources

Bentley Historical Library. University of Michigan, Ann Arbor, Edward W. Mill Collection
Filipinas Heritage Library. Makati City, Philippines
National Archives and Records Administration. College Park, Maryland.
 Records of the Department of State (Record Group 59)
 Records of Posts and Missions (Record Group 84)
National Library. Manila, Philippines
Rizal Library. Ateneo de Manila University, Philippines.
 American Historical Collection
University of the Philippines Main Library. Quezon City, Philippines
 University Archives and Records Depository
 UP College of Law Library

Books

Alejandrino y Medina, Jose. *Suez y el derecho internacional*. Madrid: CSIC, Instituto Francisco de Vitoria, 1959.
Andrade, Jr. Pio. *The Fooling of America: The Untold Story of Carlos P. Romulo* (Revised Edition), Manila: Ouch Publisher, 1990.
Arizala, Rodolfo A. *A Brief Guide to the Diplomatic History of the Filipino People: From President Emilio F. Aguinaldo to President Fidel V. Ramos 1898-1998*. Lucena City: Enverga University Press, 1998.
Castro, Pacifico A. *Philippine Diplomatic and Consular Practice* (Revised Edition). Manila, 1967.
De Borja, Marciano R. *FSO IV: Starting a Career in the Philippine Foreign Service*. Quezon City: New Day Publishers, 1999.
De Manila, Quijano. *Reportage on Lovers: A Medley of Factual Romances, Happy or Tragic,Most of Which Made News*. Manila: Anvil Publishing Inc., 2009.

De Ocampo, Esteban A. and Alfredo B. Saulo. *First Filipino Diplomat: Felipe Agoncillo (1859–1941)*. Manila: National Historical Institute, 1978.

Domingo, Benjamin B. *The Re-Making of Filipino Foreign Policy*. Quezon City: Asian Center, University of the Philippines, 1993.

Ezpeleta, Mariano. *Memoirs of an Ambassador*. Manila, 1973.

Fernandez, Alejandro M. *International Law in Philippine Relations 1898–1946*. Quezon City: University of the Philippines Press, 1971

Gleeck Jr., Lewis E. *Dissolving the Colonial Bond: American Ambassadors to the Philippines, 1946-1984*. Quezon City: New Day Publishers, 1988.

———.*The American Half-Century (1898-1946)*. Manila: Historical Conservation Society, 1984.

Gopinath, Aruna. *Manuel L. Quezon: The Tutelary Democrat*. Quezon City: New Day Publishers, 1987.

Hartendorp, A.V.H. *History of Industry and Trade of the Philippines: The Magsaysay Administration*. Manila: Philippine Educational Company, 1961.

Ingles, Jose D. *Philippine Foreign Policy*. Manila: Lyceum Press Inc., 1982.

Letters of Apolinario Mabini, Manila: National Heroes Commission, 1965.

Lopez del Castillo, Jose. *Orientaciones Diplomáticas*. Manila: n.p., 1939

Mabini, Apolinario. *The Philippine Revolution* (Translated by Leon Ma. Guerrero). Manila: National Historical Commission, 1969.

Majul, Cesar Adib, *The Political and Constitutional Ideas of the Philippine Revolution*. Quezon City: University of the Philippines, 1957.

Malay, Armando J. *Occupied Philippines*. Manila: Filipiniana Book Guild, 1967.

Meyer, Milton Walter. *A Diplomatic History of the Philippine Republic*. Honolulu: University of Hawaii Press, 1965.

Quirino, Carlos. *Quezon: Paladin of Philippine Freedom*. Manila: Filipiniana Book Guild, 1971.

Regala, Roberto. *The Trends in Modern Diplomatic Practice*. Milano: Dott.A. Giuffre Editore, 1959.

Reynolds, Quentin and Geoffrey Bocca. *Macapagal: The Incorruptible*. New York: David McKay Company. Inc., 1965.

Reyes, Narciso G. *Memories of Diplomacy: A Life in the Philippine Foreign Service*. Pasig City: Anvil Publishing Inc., 1995.

Romulo, Carlos P. with Beth Day Romulo. *The Philippine Presidents: Memoirs*. Quezon City: New Day Publishers, 1988.

———. *A Third World Soldier at the UN*. Tokyo: Toppan Co. Ltd., 1991.

Salamanca, Bonifacio S. *The Filipino Reaction to American Rule 1901–1913*. Quezon City: New Day Publishers, 1984.

———. *Toward a Diplomatic History of the Philippines*. Quezon City: University of the Philippines Press, 1995.

Saulo, Alfredo B. *Let George Do It: A Biography of Jorge B. Vargas.* Quezon City: University of the Philippines Press, 1992.
Serrano, Felixberto. *My Personal Story.* Npp: The Author, 1981.
Soriano D. H., and Isidro L. Retizos, eds. *The Philippines Who's Who,* 2nd edition. Manila: Who's Who Publishers, 1981.
Stuart, Graham H. *American Diplomatic and Consular Practice* (Second Edition). New York: Appleton-Century-Crofts, Inc., 1952.
The World Diplomatic Directory and World Diplomatic Biography, London, 1952.
Velasco, Melandres T.*Nachong: Ambassador Narciso R. Ramos: Patriarch, Journalist, Diplomat,* Public Servant, Manila: Ramos Foundation, Inc. & Media Total Ventures, 2000.
Ventura, Sylvia Mendez. *Mauro Mendez: From Journalism to Diplomacy.* Quezon City: University of the Philippines Press, 1978.
Weissblatt, Franz, ed. *Who's Who Philippines: A Biographical Dictionary of NotableLiving Men in the Philippines,* volume II. Manila, N.p. 1940.
Zaide, Jose, *Bababa Ba?: Anecdotes of a Foreign Service Officer,* Mandaluyong City: Academic Publishing Corporation, 2004.

Department of Foreign Affairs /Foreign Service Institute Publications

Annual Report 1981 Ministry of Foreign Affairs. Manila, 1982.
Annual Report 1982 Ministry of Foreign Affairs. Manila, 1983.
Annual Report 1983 Ministry of Foreign Affairs. Manila, 1984.
Annual Report 1984 Ministry of Foreign Affairs. Manila, 1985.
Annual Report 1990 Department of Foreign Affairs. Manila, 1991.
Annual Report 1991 Department of Foreign Affairs. Manila, December 1992.
Biographic Register, Manila: Department of Foreign Affairs, 15 September 1955.
Biographic Register. Manila: Bureau of Printing, 1970.
Biographic Register, Manila: Department of Foreign Affairs, National Media Production Center, 1975
Biographic Register, Manila, 1984.
DFA Quarterly Review. Vol. I, No. 1, May, 1950.
DFA Quarterly Review. Vol. I, No. 2, August, 1950.
Department of Foreign Affairs Review. Vol. I, No.3, February, 1951.
Department of Foreign Affairs Review. Vol. II, No.1, March, 1955.
Department of Foreign Affairs Review. Vol. II, No.2, January, 1956.
Department of Foreign Affairs Review. Vol. II, No.3, August, 1956.
Department of Foreign Affairs Review. Vol. II, No.4, October, 1957.
Department of Foreign Affairs Review. Vol. III, No.1, April, 1958.
Department of Foreign Affairs Review. Vol. III, No.2, October, 1959.
Department of Foreign Affairs Review. Vol. III, No.3, April, 1960.

Department of Foreign Affairs Review. Vol. III, No.4, December, 1960.
Department of Foreign Affairs Review. Vol. IV, No.1, March, 1963.
Department of Foreign Affairs Review. Vol. IV, No.2, June, 1963.
Department of Foreign Affairs Review. Vol. IV, No.3, December, 1964.
Department of Foreign Affairs Review. Vol. IV, No.4, July, 1965.
Department of Foreign Affairs Review. Vol. IV, No.5, December, 1965.
Foreign Service Directory as of January 1985. Manila, 1985.
Foreign Service Personnel Manual, Provisional Edition, Manila, 1981.
History of the Department of Foreign Affairs 1898-1991. Manila, 1991.
Marcos Diplomacy: Guide to Philippine Bilateral Relations. Manila, 1983.
MFA Newsletter, Vol. 3, No. 7, Oct-Nov. 1985.
MFA Newsletter, Vol.4, No. 1, Jan-Feb. 1986.
MFA Reader 1986. Manila, 1986.
Philippine Diplomacy: Chronology and Documents 1972-1981 (Provisional Edition). Manila, 1981.
Philippine Foreign Service Code. Manila, 1983.
Philippine Foreign Service Reader 1980 (Provisional Edition). Manila, 1980.
Regulations of the Department of Foreign Affairs. Pasay City, 1995.
Romulo Reader on World Affairs. Manila, 1982.
San Pablo-Baviera, Aileen and Lydia N. Yu-Jose, *Philippine External Relations: A Centennial Vista.* Pasay City, 1998.

Articles, Pamphlets, Reports

Arizala, Rodolfo A. "Assistance to Nationals: Concept and Modern Practice."
Foreign Relations Journal, Vol X. No. 1(March 1995): 5-30.
———. "A Commentary on House Bill No. 7092 (Amendments to Philippine Foreign Service Law." Manila: *The Lawyers Review,* Vol. XIII, No. 7, (July 31, 1999): 5-8.
Asia Who's Who 1960. Hong Kong: Pan-Asia Newspaper Alliance, 1960.
Carson, Arthur L. *Silliman University: 1901-1959.* Taiwan: United Board for Christian Higher Education in Asia, 1965.
De Viana, Augusto, V., "The Diplomatic Service of the Philippine Revolutionary Government and the Philippine Republic: For Independence or Tutelage," *UNITAS,* Vol. 72, No. 1, March 1999, 9-32.
Diplomatic List. U.S. Department of State, October 1947.
Fifield, Russell H., "Philippine Foreign Policy," *Far Eastern Survey.* Vol. XX, 21 February 1951, 33–38.
A Friendship of Two Suns: Philippines-Japan Relations. A Centennial Publication of the Philippine Embassy in Tokyo, 1998.
Imperial, Jose F., "The Philippines and Indonesia," *Fookien Times The Philippine Yearbook1952,* Manila, 49-52.

Lazo, Felix L. "A Glimpse of the Department of Foreign Affairs" in *Public Opinion Magazine*, Manila, 24 August 1948, 41-50.
Peña, Pablo A. "Filipino Foreign Service Students in Washington" in *Philippine Free Press*, 14 September 1946, 8
Peña, Pablo A., and Anastacio B. Bartolome. "Philippine Trainees Gain Field Experience," *The American Foreign Service Journal*, Vol. 24, No. 6, June 1947, 12-13 and 46-54.
Philippine Trends, Manila, June 1, 1949, 42-43
The Philippines in Shanghai, Philippine Consulate General, Shanghai, 2005
Protocol. Manila: Far Eastern University, Vol. I, No. 4, December 1949, 4–22.
Querol, M. N. "Freedom and Peace: Foundation of Philippine foreign policy," *Fookien Times, The Philippine Yearbook*, 1950–1951, 16–18.
"Seven Years of Foreign Affairs." *Sunday Times Magazine*, Manila, 6 September 1953, 10-11.
Seventh and Final Report of the High Commissioner to the Philippines, Washington: United States Government Printing Office, 1947.
Severino, Rodolfo H., "Beautiful Isle: Formosa's strategic location is vital to PI defense," *Sunday Times Magazine*, Manila, 17 June 1951 4-6.
Smith, Roger M. "The Philippines and the Southeast Asia Treaty Organization," *Two Papers on Philippine Foreign Policy*, Data Papers Number 38, New York: Cornell University, December 1959, 1-56.
Villanueva, Honesto A. "A Chapter of Filipino Diplomacy." *Philippine Social Science and Humanities Review*, Vol. 17 No. 2, June 1952: 103-186.
Viray, Manuel A., "White House on Arlegui Street" in *The Sunday Times Magazine* (Manila), 24 October 1948, 6-7.

Publications of Edward W. Mill on the Philippine Foreign Service

"The Origins of the Agencies of Philippine Foreign Affairs." *Philippine Social Science and Humanities Review*, Vol. XX. No. 2, June 1955: 107–119.
"Philippine Foreign Affairs Training Program", *Department of State Bulletin*, Vol. XIV, No. 334, 3 February 1946: 148–49.
"The Philippines Prepares for Independence", *Department of State Bulletin*, Vol. XIV, No. 362, 9 June 1946: 980-1014.
"First Philippine Foreign Affairs Training Group", *The American Foreign Service Journal*, Vol. 23, No.4, April 1946: 15-16, 49-50.
"The New Republic of the Philippines", Department of State, Publication 2662, Far Eastern Series, Reprinted from the *Department of State Bulletin* of 15 September 1946: 1-16
"A Career Foreign Service: Bulwark of Democracy" Pedro Baldoria, *Readings: Documents and Literature on Philippine Government and Foreign Relations*. Mimeograph. University of the Philippines, 1954. 540–50.

"The Philippines in the World Setting". *Philippine Social Science and Humanities Review*, Vol. XX. No. 1 March 1955: 3–37.

"The Philippine Foreign Affairs Training Program: A Decade Later." *The American Foreign Service Journal*, May 1956.

"The Personnel of Philippine Diplomacy", *Philippine Social Science and Humanities Review*, Vol. XXII, No. 3. September 1957, 299–340.

"Philippine Foreign Affairs Training Program", *Department of State Bulletin*, Vol. XIV, No. 347, February 24, 1946, pp. 298-299.

"Philippine Foreign Affairs Training Program", *Department of State Bulletin*, Vol. XVI, No. 407, April 20, 1947, pp. 718.

The Conduct of Philippine Foreign Relations, PhD Dissertation, Princeton University, 1954

Unpublished Materials

Barcelo, Angel H. B. The Foreign Relations of the Philippines: A Historical Study 1949–1950, University of Manila, 1950.

Marte, Gonzalo S. The Puppet Republic of the Philippines: Its Foreign Relations, University of Manila, 1949.

Calderon, Eddie Amponin. The Philippines and the United Nations during the Tenure of Carlos P. Romulo, Ph.D. dissertation, University of Minnesota, 1973.

Moreno, Hermelinda Ycasiano. Vietnam War Memoirs, Manila, 2005.

Valeriano, Benito B. The Manila Economic and Cultural Center (MECO): An Interpretation of Philippine Representation in Taiwan, Master's Thesis in Political Science, Lyceum of the Philippines, October 1998.

Internet Sources

www.state.gov
www.dfa.gov.ph
www.bentley.umich.edu/
www.archives.gov/dc-metro/college-park/
www.adst.org/Oral_History.htm

Notes

CHAPTER 1   The Pioneers

1. Jose Lopez del Castillo, *Orientaciones Diplomáticas* (Manila: n.p., 1939), 10.
2. Edward W. Mill, *Philippine Foreign Affairs Training Program*, 2 (unpublished article written in April 1946) Edward W. Collection Box 1, Bentley Historical Library, University of Michigan.
3. Oscar M. Alfonso (editor), *University of the Philippines: The First 75 Years (1908–1983)* (Quezon City: University of the Philippines Press, 1985), 230.
4. *University of the Philippines General Catalogue 1935–1936*, Bulletin No. 16, October 1935 (Manila: University of the Philippine Press, 1935), 310.
5. One of the first graduates of the B.S. Foreign Service from the University of the Philippines who was fortunate to land a job there was Delfin R. Garcia. Upon his graduation in March 1941, Garcia worked in the Division of Foreign Relations in June until the office was disbanded because of the outbreak of the war in the Pacific in December 1941. Garcia would eventually join Group II of the State Department trainees.
6. *The Guerilla*, Manila, 22 August 1945. Quoted in Letter of the American Consul General in Manila Paul P. Steintorf to the Secretary of State dated 23 August 1945 (811B.428-2345).
7. Ibid. At $1 to 2 pesos exchange rate, the budget amounts to $250,000.
8. Letter of Secretary of Finance Jaime Fernandez to Chief of Philippine Affairs Division Frank Lockhart dated 06 January 1945 (811B.021/1-645).
9. Memorandum of Chief of Philippine Affairs Division Frank P. Lockhart dated 10 January 1945.
10. Edward W. Mill, "Philippine Foreign Affairs Program," *Department of State Bulletin*, Vol. XIV. No. 344, 3 February 1946, 148.
11. Memorandum of Resident Commissioner Carlos P. Romulo to Chief of Philippine Affairs Division Frank Lockhart dated 25 July 1945 (120.31/7-2545).

12. Memorandum of Chief of Philippine Affairs Division Frank P. Lockhart to State Department officials—Mr. Harrington and Mr. Willoughby, 10 September 1945.
13. Ibid.
14. The Acting Secretary of State to the American Consular Officer in charge in Manila, 20 September 1945 (811B.42/8-2345).
15. Edward W. Mill, "The Origins of the Agencies of Philippine Foreign Affairs," *Philippine Social Science and Humanities Review*, Vol. XX, No. 2, June 1955, 114.
16. Report of the American Consul General in Manila Paul P. Steintorf to the Secretary of State, 13 October 1945 (811B.42/10-1345).
17. Memorandum of Conversation on "Participation of Filipino Foreign Service Trainees in the Session of Foreign Service Officers Training School beginning December 3,"14 November 1945 (811B.42/11-1445).
18. Letter of the Secretary of State to the Philippine Resident Commissioner to the United States (Romulo), 20 November 1945 (811B.4211-2045).
19. Secretary of State in a telegram to the American Consul General in Manila, 20 November 1945 (811B.42/10-1345 CS/LE).
20. The Secretary of State to the American Consular Officer in Charge in Manila, 23 November 1945 (811B.42/10-1345).
21. The Secretary of State to the American Consular Officer in Charge in Manila, 28 November 1945 (811B.42/10-1345 CS/LE).
22. The American Consul General in Manila to the Secretary of State, 04 January 1946 (811B.42/1-446).
23. The American Consul in Manila to the Secretary of State, 12 December 1945 (811B.42/12-1245).
24. The Secretary of State to the American Consul in Manila, 21 November 1945 (811B.42/11-2145 CS/LE).
25. The Secretary of State to the American Consular Officer in Charge in Manila, 28 November 1945 (811B.42/10-1345 CS/LE).
26. The American Consul General in Manila to the Secretary of State, 04 January 1946 (811B.42/1-446).
27. The American Consul in Manila to the Secretary of State, 27 November 1945 (811B.42/11-2745).
28. The Secretary of State to the American Consular Officer in Charge in Manila, 28 November 1945 (811B.42/11-2745 CS/LE).
29. The Secretary of State to the American Consular Officer in Charge in Manila, 11 December 1945 (811B.42/12-1145 CS/LE); Also see Edward W. Mill, "Philippine Foreign Affairs Program", *Department of State Bulletin*, Vol. XIV. No. 344, 3 February 1946, 148.
30. Edward W. Mill, "The Origins of the Agencies of Philippine Foreign Affairs," Philippine Social Science and Humanities Review, Vol. XX, No. 2, June 1955, 114.

31 Biographic Register of the Department of Foreign Affairs. Manila, 15 September 1955, 19. Unless otherwise stated, the background information on the all the Filipino trainees comes from this source and the Biographic Register of the Department of Foreign Affairs, Manila: Bureau of Printing, 1970.
32 Edward W. Mill, "The First Philippine Foreign Affairs Training Group," *The American Foreign Service Journal*, Vol. 23, No.4, April 1946, 16. See also List of officials and employees Commonwealth Government in Washington, D.C. as of 27 February 1945.
33 Edward W. Mill, "The Personnel of Philippine Diplomacy," 327–328.List of officials and employees Commonwealth Government in Washington, D.C. as of 27 February 1945.
34 Edward W. Mill, *The Conduct of Philippine Foreign Relations* (Princeton University, 1954), 72.
35 Press Release on Tiburcio C. Baja from the Office of the Resident Commissioner of the Philippines to the United States, 22 April 1946.
36 Interview with Ruth Baja Williams, 02 July 2009. Also see Williams's book Detour Berlin, 2001, 13.
37 Edward W. Mill, "The Personnel of Philippine Diplomacy," *Philippine Social Science and Humanities Review*, Vol. XX, No. 3, September 1957, 309.
38 Ibid, 310.
39 Ibid.
40 The Secretary of State to the American Consul in Manila, 13 February 1946 (811B.42/12-1245 CS/LF).
41 The American Consul General in Manila to the Secretary of State, 04 January 1946 (811B.42/1-446 CS/D).
42 Summary of Work of Philippine Foreign Affairs Trainees (undated report) Edward W. Mill Collection.
43 Biographical Sketch of Doroteo V. Vite as attachment to Note Verbale from the Philippine Embassy to the U.S. Department of State dated 31 January 1947 (701.9611/1-3147).
44 Interview with Ambassador Delfin Garcia, DFA Executive Lounge, 10 March 1997.
45 Acting Secretary of State Dean Acheson to the American Consul in Manila, 21 June 1946 (811B.42/6-2146 CS/RH).
46 Bertrand D. Hulen, "Washington Trains Filipinos: State Department Helps Build Foreign Staff for Service Here and in Asia", *The New York Times*, 22 September 1946, E 9.
47 Letter of President Manuel Roxas to the Secretary of State dated 01 June 1946 (811B.42/6-146 CS/RH).
48 Ibid.

49 American Consul General in Manila (Steintorf) to the Secretary of State, 16 April 1946 (811B.42/4-1646).
50 American Consul General in Manila (Steintorf) to the Secretary of State, 2 May 1946 (811B.42/5-246).
51 Pablo A. Peña, "Filipino Foreign Students in Washington "*Philippines Free Press*, 14 September 1946, 8. Also see Pablo Peña, *The Glamour and Grind of Foreign Service Training* (unpublished memoir, 14 pages dated 1946 included in the Edward W. Mill Collection)
52 Email of Amb. Eduardo Montilla to Amb. Juan Ona, Wednesday, 06 February 2000.
53 Memorandum of Edward W. Mill's Talk with Minister-Counselor of the Philippine Embassy Concerning Records of the Fifth Philippine Foreign Affairs Training Group, 21 July 1947, 2.
54 Memorandum from Edward W. Mill to Mr. Ely on the Fourth Philippine Foreign Affairs Training Group, 18 December 1946.
55 Biographical Sketch of Emilio Torres, Note Verbale dated 12 August 1948 from the Philippine Embassy in Washington, D.C. to the U.S. Department of State.
56 Letter of Edward W. Mill to Anastacio Bartolome, 24 March 1947. Estela R. Sulit would become the first woman consul of the Philippines and would later get appointed as Philippine ambassador to Portugal during the latter part of her diplomatic career. There were other Filipino applicants who were already U.S.-based such as Diomedes I. Galindo from Woodbury College, Los Angeles, and Mamerto S. Ventura, graduate student in Law and International Relations at Columbia University. Both Galindo and Ventura applied to the State Department to be able to attend the training program, but the State Department turned the two down because it was the Philippine Government who had the sole prerogative to nominate suitable candidates.
57 Letter of Edward W. Mill to Richard Butrick, 14 January 1947.
58 Letter of Hortencio J. Brillantes to Edward W. Mill from Honolulu (on his way back to Manila) about Emilio Torres, 22 September 1947.
59 Letter of Edward W. Mill to Hortencio J. Brillantes, 30 October 1947. In his publications and talks about the Philippine Foreign Affairs Training Program, Mill excluded Torres from the list of the graduates of the State Department, perhaps not to offend the other State Department Boys.
60 Press Release, "Philippine Foreign Affairs Program", *Department of State Bulletin*, Vol. XIV. No. 407, 20 April 1947, 718.

CHAPTER 2   Diplomatic and Consular Training

1 "Filipino Young Men Training for Foreign Service: Under Edward Mill."*Manila Daily Bulletin*, vol. 137, no. 74.28 March 1949, section 4, 28.

2 The building is now known as Lothrop Mansion and serves as the Office of the Trade Representative of the Russian Federation.
3 Transcript of the 24th of series of 1949 Radio Broadcast, International Information and Cultural Activities Division, Department of Foreign Affairs, 7.
4 Edward W. Mill, "Philippine Foreign Affairs Program", *Department of State Bulletin*, Vol. XIV. No. 344, 3 February 1946, 148-149.
5 Edward W. Mill, "The Origins of the Agencies of Philippine Foreign Affaire", *Philippine Social Science and Humanities Review*, Vol. XX, No. 2, June 1955, 115.
6 Pablo Peña, *The Glamour and Grind of Foreign Service Training*, page 12 (unpublished memoir, 14 pages, 1946) Edward W. Mill Papers Reel No. 1, Bentley Historical Library, University of Michigan.
7 "Filipino Young Men Training for Foreign Service: Under Edward Mill."*Manila Daily Bulletin*, vol. 137, no. 74.28 March 1949, section 4, 28.
8 Discussion on the Philippine Foreign Affairs Training Program adapted for radio by Manuel A. Adeva and Jose I. Imperial, undated from the Edward W. Mill Collection.
9 The Secretary of State to the American Consular Officer in Charge in Manila, 14 January 1946 (811B.42/1-1446 CS/LE).
10 Memorandum of Conversation on the Filipino Foreign Service Trainees between Frank P. Lockhart and Carlos P. Romulo, 06 February 1946 (120.313/2-2046). Lockhart proposed Dr. Rodrigo Tugade, dean of the Law School at Silliman University (in Dumaguete City, Philippines) for the consideration of the Commonwealth Government. Nothing, however, happened to his proposal.
11 Press Release, "Philippine Foreign Affairs Program", *Department of State Bulletin*, Vol. XIV. No. 347, 24 February 1946, 298.
12 Division of Philippine Affairs to Division of Foreign Service, 11 February 1946.
13 Division of Foreign Service to Division of Philippine Affairs, 20 February 1946 (120.313/2-2046).
14 The Secretary of State to the American Consul in Sydney, 8 March 1946 (811B.42/3-846 CS/VJ). Similar instructions were sent to the American consulate general in Montreal and the American embassies in Havana, Mexico City, and Santiago.
15 The Secretary of State to the American Consular Officer in charge in Manila, 25 January 1946 (811B.42/1-2546 CS/D).
16 Letter of Assistant Secretary of State Donald Russell to Resident Commissioner Carlos P. Romulo, 12 March 1946 (811B.42/3-1246 CSD).
17 Press Release on Tiburcio C. Baja from the Office of the Resident Commissioner of the Philippines to the United States, 22 April 1946.

18 The Acting Secretary of State to the American Consular Officer in charge in Montreal, 17 May 1946 (811B.42/5-1746).
19 The American Consular Officer in Montreal to the Secretary of State, 20 May 1946 (811B.42/5-2046).
20 Manuel A. Adeva to the Secretary of State through the American Consulate General in Sydney, 29 May 1946 (811B.42/5-2946 CS/SMS).
21 Memorandum of Arthur Richards of BC to Division of Philippine Affairs, 24 June 1946.
22 Manuel A. Adeva to the Secretary of State through the American Consulate General in Sydney, 29 May 1946 (811B.42/5-2946).
23 Memorandum of Frank P. Lockhart to DF and Special Deposits, 01 July 1946 (811B.42/7-146).
24 Minutes of the First General Meeting of the Philippine Foreign Affairs Training Program, 26 June 1946.
25 The Acting Secretary of State to the American Ambassador in Mexico City, 12 June 1946 (811B.42/6-1246).
26 The American Embassy in Mexico City (First Secretary and Consul General M.L. Stafford) to the Secretary of State, 24 June 1946 (811B.42/6-2446).
27 The American Embassy in Havana (Chargé d'Affaires, a.i. Robert F. Woodward) to the Secretary of State, 01 July 1946 (811B.42/7-1146 CS/V).
28 Letter of Vicente I. Singian to Edward W. Mill, 29 May 1946.
29 Letter of Vicente I. Singian to Edward W. Mill, 19 June 1946.
30 The American Ambassador in Ottawa (Atherton) to the Secretary of State, 25 June 1946 (811B.42/6-2546).
31 Edward W. Mill, "The Origins of the Agencies of Philippine Foreign Affairs," *Philippine Social Science and Humanities Review*, Vol. XX, No. 2, June 1955, 115-116.
32 Memo from Edward W. Mill to Mr. Ely on the Fourth Philippine Foreign Affairs Training Group, 18 December 1946.
33 Pablo A. Peña, "Filipino Foreign Service Students in Washington," in *Philippine Free Press*, 14 September 1946, 8.
34 Letter of Edward W. Mill to Richard P. Butrick, 17 September 1946.
35 Letter of Mill to Professor Kenneth Colegrove, Department of Political Science, Northwestern University, 17 September 1946.
36 Letter of Edward W. Mill to Professor Harold W. Vinacke, Department of Political Science, University of Cincinnati, 10 October 1946.
37 Letter of Edward W. Mill to Charlotte, 28 August 1946.
38 Letter of Edward W. Mill to Richard P. Butrick, 17 September 1946.
39 Letter of Richard P. Butrick to Edward W. Mill, 8 November 1946.
40 Letter of Edward W. Mill to Richard P. Butrick, 17 September 1946.
41 Letter of Pablo Peña to Edward W. Mill dated September 22, 1946.

42 Ibid.
43 Letter of Pablo Peña to Edward W. Mill, 29 September 1946.
44 Pablo Peña, "Philippine Trainees Gain Field Experience," in *The American Foreign Service Journal*, Vol. 24, No. 6, June 1947, 13.
45 Ibid, 46.
46 Mill's Letter to Pablo Peña, 21 August 1946.
47 Letter of Anastacio B. Bartolome to Edward W. Mill, 19 December 1946.
48 Ibid.
49 Letter of Edward W. Mill to Anastacio B. Bartolome, 30 December 1946.
50 Letter of Edward W. Mill to Tiburcio C. Baja, 31 December 1946.

51 Memo of Edward W. Mill to Mr. Ely on Conference with Vice President Quirino on Philippine Foreign Affairs Training Program.13 May 1947, 2.
52 Letter of Edward W. Mill to Delfin R. Garcia, 11 March 1947.
53 Letter of Jose Alejandrino to Edward W. Mill, 25 June 1947.
54 Letter of Mill to Ben (Benjamin T. Tirona), 1 October 1947.
55 Letter of Carlos A. Faustino to Edward W. Mill, 11 May 1947.
56 Transcript of the 24th of series of 1949 Radio Broadcast, International Information and Cultural Activities Division, Department of Foreign Affairs, 13-13 A. Edward W. Mill Collection, Box 4. Folder 1.
57 Ibid.
58 Ibid., 10–12.
59 Letter of Hortencio J. Brillantes to Edward W. Mill, 31 July 1947.
60 Letter of Eduardo Rosal to Edward W. Mill, 10 September 1947. Rosal was referring to Graham Stuart's book on *American Diplomatic and Consular Practice* which was one of the main subjects that the Filipino trainees had to master during their training.
61 Memorandum of Mill's Talk with Minister Counselor of the Philippine Embassy Concerning Records of the Fifth Philippine Foreign Affairs Training Group, 21 July 1947.
62 Note Verbale of the Department of State to the chargé d'affaires *ad interim* of the Philippines on the records compiled by each of the members of the Fifth Philippine Foreign Affairs Training Group during their period of training in the Department of State, 18 September 1947.
63 Letter of Undersecretary Bernabe Africa to Raymond D. Muir, 13 March 1947.
64 Memorandum of Mr. Ely to Ms. Shipley (PD–Passport Division), 3 July 1947, on the Special Training Assignment in PD for Mr. Hortencio J. Brillantes.
65 Memorandum of Mill to Mr. Hibbard, 21 July 1947 on Hortencio J. Brillantes.

66 Letter of Hortencio J. Brillantes to Edward W. Mill, 25 August 1947.
67 Letter of Edward W. Mill to Jose Alejandrino, 8 September 1947.
68 Letter of Edward W. Mill to Jack, 20 October 1947.
69 Transcript of the 24th of series of 1949 Radio Broadcast, International Information and Cultural Activities Division, Department of Foreign Affairs, 16.
70 Memorandum of Edward W. Mill to Richard Ely, 6 March 1947.
71 Personal History-Summary of E. Edward Schefer, Edward W. Mill Collection, Box 5, Bentley Historical Library, University of Michigan.
72 Letter of Edward W. Mill to Ms. Mordaunt, 15 September 1946.
73 Memorandum of Edward W. Mill to Richard Ely, 16 April 1947 regarding the Remarks of Ambassador Elizalde concerning Philippine Foreign Affairs Training Program.
74 Letter of Emilio Torres to the Secretary of State (unsigned), 15 October 1947 and Letter of Hortencio J. Brillantes to the Secretary of State, 3 September 1947.
75 Letter of Elpidio Quirino to Edward W. Mill, May 1947.

CHAPTER 3   A Foreign Office for a New Nation

1 Teodoro A. Agoncillo and Oscar M. Alfonso, *A Short History of the Filipino People* (Quezon City: University of the Philippines, 1961), 220-222.
2 *Act of Proclamation of Philippine Independence, Cavite Viejo*, June 12, 1898 (Manila: The Independence Day National Committee, 1971).
3 The Aguinaldo Government allocated a budget for the operation of the Department of Foreign Affairs. Its budget was mainly divided into the Office of the Secretary whose budget for personnel amounted to 3,240 pesos and for supplies, 1,200 pesos. The diplomatic and consular corps had 12,600 pesos for personnel and 60,000 pesos for unforeseen expenses. Archive of foreign affairs was not itemized but a budget for unforeseen expenses was set at 12,000 pesos. See Ambeth Ocampo, "Budgets, then and now" in *Philippine Daily Inquirer*, 22 November 2002. Online version–www.inq7.net/opl/2002/nov/22/text/opl_arocampo-1-p.htm.
4 The decision to recognizing Mabini as the first Secretary of Foreign Affairs is contained in a Memorandum of the National Historical Institute to the Honorable Emmanuel Pelaez, Secretary of Foreign Affairs, dated February 28, 1962. This Memorandum was prepared by Prof. Nicolas Zafra, a noted Filipino historian, as the official position of the Philippine Historical Association on the matter in question.
5 Cesar Adib Majul, *Apolinario Mabini: Revolutionary* (Manila: National Heroes Commission, 1964), 88–89.
6 *Letters of Apolinario Mabini*, 74.
7 Apolinario Mabini, *The Philippine Revolution*, Translated by Leon Ma. Guerrero (Manila: National Historical Commission, 1969), 56.

8 *Letters of Apolinario Mabini*, 172.
9 Edward W. Mill, "The Origins of the Agencies of Philippine Affairs," *Philippine Social Science and Humanities Review*, Vol. XX, No. June 1955, 109.
10 Ibid.
11 Interview with Ambassador Delfin Garcia, DFA Executive Lounge, 10 March 1997. In June 1941, Garcia joined the Division of the Foreign Relations right after graduating with a Bachelor of Science in Foreign Service degree from the University of the Philippines.
12 Graham H. Stuart, *Department of State: A History of its Organization, Procedure and Personnel* (New York: The MacMillan Company, 1949), 319.
13 The assignment of an American consular officer in the Philippines during the Commonwealth period was considered by some scholars as absurd as the Philippines was still under U.S. sovereignty. See Luke T. Lee, *Consular Law and Practice*, 2nd Edition, New York: Oxford University Press, 1991, 30. Also see Philip C. Jessup, "Philippine Independence", 29 *American Journal of International Law*, 1935, 83-87.
14 *The Second Annual Report of the U.S. High Commissioner to the Philippine Islands to the President and Congress of the United States covering the calendar year 1937 with a Review of Government Finances for the Years 1935, 1936 and 1937*, Manila, September 1, 1938, 18.
15 *Fifth Annual Report of the U.S. High Commissioner to the Philippine Islands covering Fiscal Year 1941* (Washington, United States Government Printing Office, 1943), 17.
16 Ibid. *Fifth Annual Report of the U.S. High Commissioner to the Philippine Islands covering Fiscal Year 1941*.
17 Ibid.
18 Speech of President Sergio Osmeña during the re-opening of the Philippine Congress, *Free Philippines*, Monday, 11 June 1945.
19 Ibid.
20 Edward W. Mill, "The Origins of the Agencies of Philippine Affairs", 110.
21 Alejandro M. Fernandez, *International Law in Philippine Relations 1898-1946* (Quezon City: University of the Philippines Press, 1971), 197.
22 Edward W. Mill, "The Origins of the Agencies of Philippine Affairs", 111.
23 Ricardo T. Jose, "Test of Wills: Diplomacy between Japan and the Laurel Government," *Philippines-Japan Relations*, edited by Ikehata Setsuho and Lydia N. Yu Jose (Quezon City: Ateneo de Manila University Press, 2003), 200-201.
24 Armando J. Malay, Occupied Philippines: *The Role of Jorge B. Vargas during the Japanese Occupation*, Manila: Filipiniana Book Guild, 1967, 128-129.
25 Jose, 217-218.

26 Lorna E. Barile, *The Role of Jorge B. Vargas during the Japanese Occupation, 1942-1945* (Master's thesis, University of the Philippines-Diliman, 1976), 118-122. Strictly speaking, Jorge B. Vargas was the first Filipino ambassador extraordinary and plenipotentiary in the real sense of the world. The distinction of being the first Filipino diplomat belongs to Felipe Agoncillo but he was not accredited by any receiving state because the Philippines was not yet independent.

27 Malay, *Occupied Philippines*, 129.

28 Barile, 120.

29 Malay, *Occupied Philippines*, 129-130. Also see Leon Ma. Guerrero, Twilight in Tokyo (Manila: *Manila Times* Publishing Co., 1946), pp. 101-02.

30 Jose, 201.

31 Claro M. Recto, *Three Years of Enemy Occupation: The Issue of Political Collaboration in the Philippines* (Manila: People's Publishers, 1946), 10.

32 Rose Laurel Aveceña and Ileana Maramag, Days of Courage: *The Legacy of Dr. Jose P. Laurel* (Philippines, 1980), 161-165. Also see, Jose P. Laurel, *War Memoirs* (Manila: JPL Foundation, 1962), 39-45.

33 Commonwealth Act No. 683 "An Act to Organize the Office of Foreign Relations and for other Purpose", 25 September 1945.

34 Vicente G. Sinco, "The Foreign Affairs of the Philippine Commonwealth" as Enclosure No. 1013 dated 3 April 1946 from the American Consulate General at Manila, entitled "Organization and Activities of the Office of Foreign Relations of the Philippine Commonwealth Government."

35 *Seventh and Final Report of the High Commissioner to the Philippines*, Washington: United States Government Printing Office, 1947. 88-89.

36 Letter of Secretary of State James F. Byrnes to Resident Commissioner Carlos P. Romulo dated 31 May 1945 (811B.42/4-2446 CS/VJ).

37 The American Consulate General in Manila to the Department of State dated 02 July 1946 (811B.42/7-246).

38 Letter of Nathaniel P. Davis, Counselor at the American Embassy in Manila, to his mother dated 7 July 1946 as quoted in Lewis E. Gleek, Jr. *Dissolving the Colonial Bond: American Ambassadors to the Philippines, 1946-1984* (Quezon City: New Day Publishers, 1988), 17.

39 Ibid.

40 J. Eduardo Malaya and Jonathan E. Malaya, *...So Help Me God: The Presidents of the Philippines and their Inaugural Addresses* (Manila: Anvil Publishing Inc., 2004), 126.

41 *Seventh and Final Report of the High Commissioner to the Philippines* (Washington: United States Government Printing Office, 1947), 101.

42 Letter of President Manuel A. Roxas to the Secretary of State, 01 June 1946.

43 Telegram of the American Embassy in Manila to the U.S. Department of State dated 07 June 1947 (811B.01A/6-746) Steintorf joined MacArthur during the Leyte landing and opened the U.S. Consulate General as soon as Manila was liberated.
44 *The Second Annual Report of the U.S. High Commissioner to the Philippine Islands to the President and Congress of the United States covering the calendar year 1937 with a Review of Government Finances for the Years 1935, 1936 and 1937*, Manila, September 1, 1938, 34-35.
45 Memorandum of Telephone Conversation by Frank Lockhart, U.S. Department of State dated 11 June 1946 (F.W. 811B.01A/6-746).
46 Ibid.
47 Telegram of Acting Secretary of State Dean Acheson to the American Consul in Manila dated 17 June 1946 (811B. 01A/6-746).
48 Telegram from the American Consulate General in Manila to the Department of State dated 17 June 1946 (811B.01A/6-1746 LRC).
49 Telegram from the American Consulate General to the U.S. Department of Stated dated 19 June 1946 (811B.01A/6-1946).
50 *Initial Interview with Richard P. Butrick by Charles Stuart Kennedy*, 25 March 1993, The Association for Diplomatic Studies and Training Foreign Affairs Oral History Project. www.adst.org.
51 The U.S. Foreign Service was still divided then between the diplomatic and the consular corps. The two branches were merged with the passage of the Rogers Act in 1924.
52 Letter of the Secretary of State to Ambassador Paul V. McNutt, 20 July 1946.
53 Minutes of the First General Meeting of the Philippine Foreign Affairs Training Program, 26 June 1946.
54 Letter of Richard P. Butrick to Edward W. Mill, 28 August 1946.
55 Interview with Ambassador Delfin Garcia, DFA Executive Lounge, 10 March 1997.
56 Letter of Richard P. Butrick to Edward W. Mill, 28 August 1946.
57 Letter of Richard P. Butrick to Edward W. Mill, 8 November 1946.
58 Telegram from the American Embassy in Manila to the U.S. Department of State dated 05 September 1946 (701.9600/9-546 LRC).
59 Secret Telegram from the U.S. Department of State to the American Embassy in Manila for Butrick, dated 06 September 1946 ((701.9600/9-646).
60 Memorandum of Ely of Philippine Affairs Division to Ferris of Office of Foreign Service on the Continuation of Services of FSO Richard P. Butrick as Adviser on Foreign Relations to the Republic of the Philippines, 5 February 1947.
61 Attachment to the Memorandum of Ely of PI to Ferris of OFS, 15 May 1947.

62 *Initial Interview with Richard P. Butrick by Charles Stuart Kennedy*, 25 March 1993, The Association for Diplomatic Studies and Training Foreign Affairs Oral History Project, www.adst.org.
63 Email of Rachel Davies Butrick, the widow of Richard Butrick, dated 29 January 2008. After his retirement from the Foreign Service, Butrick briefly joined academe and he later became a professor emeritus at the Department of Philosophy in Ohio University. He edited the book "American University Men in China", a fascinating account of early Chinese students in America. He also set up a lecture fund at Hamilton College in New York State. He died in 1997 at the ripe age of 103. His death was not caused by any illness; he just expired like a candle.
64 Letter of Edward W. Mill to Richard P. Butrick, 14 October 1946.
65 Letter of Richard P. Butrick to Edward W. Mill, 1 November 1946.
66 Letter of Richard P. Butrick to Edward W. Mill, 18 October 1946.
67 Letter of Edward W. Mill to Richard P. Butrick, 28 October 1946.
68 Dispatch from the American Embassy in Manila to the U.S. Department of State, dated 19 September 1946 ((701.9600/9-646).
69 Telegram from the American Embassy in Manila to the U.S. Department of State, dated 20 September 1946 (701.9600/9-2046).
70 Telegram from the American Embassy in Manila to the U.S. Department of State, dated 20 September 1946 (701.9600/9-2046).
71 Edward W. Mill, "The Philippine Foreign Affairs Training Program: A Decade Later," *The American Foreign Service Journal*, May 1956, 12.
72 Edward W. Mill, *The Conduct of Philippine Foreign Relations*, Princeton University, 1954, 72-73.
73 Statement of President Manuel Roxas Establishing the Organization and Operation of the Department of Foreign Affairs and of the Foreign Service.
74 Edward W. Mill, *Conduct of Philippine Foreign Relations*, Princeton University, PhD Dissertation, 1954, 258.
75 "Roxas Sets Basic Policy on PI Foreign Service," *Manila Times*, 18 September 1946, 1, 15.
76 Letter of Richard P. Butrick to Edward W. Mill, 1 November 1946.
77 Carlos P. Romulo with Beth Day Romulo, *The Philippine Presidents* (Quezon City: New Day Publishers, 1968), 81–90.
78 Ibid., 82.
79 Biographical Sketch of Bernabe Africa as contained in Note Verbale of the Philippine Embassy in Washington, DC to the Department of State dated 27 September 1948 (701.9694/9-2748 CS/V).
80 Edward W. Mill, "The Personnel of Philippine Diplomacy", *Philippine Social Science and Humanities Review*, Vol. XXII, No. 3. September 1957, 334.

81 Quentin Reynolds and Geoffrey Bocca, Macapagal: *The Incorruptible* (New York: David Mckay Company, Inc., 1965), 71, 74_79.
82 Letter of Edward W. Mill to Eduardo Rosal, 14 October 1948.
83 Letter of Richard P. Butrick to Edward W. Mill, 16 September 1946. In his letter to Butrick dated 14 October 1946. Mill also expressed satisfaction that Section 17 of E.O. 18 blanketed automatically the State Department trainees.
84 Edward W. Mill, "The Personnel of Philippine Diplomacy", 299-340.
85 Letter of Richard P. Butrick to Edward W. Mill, 16 September 1946.
86 Carrie Lorenzana. "Cory's 'White House' on Arlegui." *Sunday Malaya*, 11 May 1986, 14-15.
87 Notes on the photo of the Arlegui Property from the American Historical Collection, Jose Rizal Library, Ateneo de Manila University.
88 Felix L. Lazo, "A Glimpse of the Department of Foreign Affairs" in *Public Opinion Magazine* (Manila), 24 August 1948, 41.
89 Manuel A. Viray, "White House on Arlegui Street" in *The Sunday Times Magazine* (Manila), 24 October 1948, 6-7.
90 Edward W. Mill, *Conduct of Philippine Foreign Relations*, Princeton University, PhD Dissertation, 1954, 251.
91 Letter of Luis Moreno Salcedo to Edward W. Mill, 19 March 1952.
92 *Department of Foreign Affairs Review*, Vol. I, No. 3 (February, 1951), 206.
93 Introduction of Senate Bill No. 424 by Senator Zulueta at the Senate (Third Session of the Second Congress of the Republic of the Philippines).
94 Memorandum of Minister Narciso Ramos of the Philippine Legation in Buenos Aires to the Secretary of Foreign Affairs entitled "Comments of the Macapagal-Tizon Bill (HB No. 47)", 15 October 1951.
95 Introduction of Senate Bill No. 424 by Senator Zulueta at the Senate (Third Session of the Second Congress of the Republic of the Philippines).
96 Letter of Consul Librado Cayco of the Philippine Consulate General in New York to Edward W. Mill, 14 February 1955.
97 Foreign Service Act of the Philippines, 5 June 1952. Part B, Section 1 (C).
98 Hermenegildo C. Cruz, In Search of Merit: *The Spoils System in the Department of Foreign Affairs*, Quezon City: Central Book Supply, Inc. 2007, 256-257.

CHAPTER 4   Dealing with America

1 A detailed discussion of the dispute between the Philippine Assembly and the Philippine Commission on the appointment of Resident Commissioner can be found in Aruna Gopinath, Manuel L. Quezon: Tutelary Democrat (Quezon City: New Day Publishers, 1987), 3-4.

2 Edward W. Mill, "The Origins of the Agencies of Philippine Affairs", *Philippine Social Science and Humanities Review*, Vol. XX, No. June 1955, 110.
3 Memorandum of Lockhart, PI, to Vincent, FE, dated 23 May 1946 (701.9611/5-2346)
4 Ibid.
5 Carlos P. Romulo with Beth Day Romulo, *The Philippine Presidents*, 73.
6 Milton Walter Meyer, *A Diplomatic History of the Republic of the Philippines* (University of Hawaii Press, 1965), 33.
7 For a detailed discussion on the Elizalde family in the Philippines, see Marciano R. de Borja, *Basques in the Philippines*, Reno & Las Vegas: University of Nevada Press, 2005 and Franz Weissblatt, editor. *Who's Who in the Philippines: A Biographical Dictionary of Notable Living Men in the Philippines* 1940–41, volume II. Manila: Franz Weissblatt, 1940, 57.
8 Editorial of Evening Herald, Sunday, 11 July 1946.
9 Editorial of *Manila Morning Sun*, Sunday 11 July 1946.
10 http://en.wikipedia.org/wiki/Embassy_Row.
11 Letter of Mill to his wife Wilma, 25th (no month and year) could be July 1946.
12 The American Embassy in Manila to the U.S. Secretary of State, 01 October, 1946 (701.9611/10-146 CS/A).
13 Letter of Secretary of Justice Roman Ozaeta to the Auditor General dated 27 October 1946 as attachment to the Report of the American Embassy in Manila to the U.S. Secretary of State, 09 October 1946.
14 Letter of Narciso Ramos to Edward W. Mill, 17 October 1946.
15 Letter of Narciso Ramos to Edward W. Mill, 30 April 1954.
16 The American Embassy in Manila to the Secretary of State on the Philippine Diplomatic Mission to Argentina; Background of Narciso Ramos, newly appointed Envoy Extraordinary and Minister Plenipotentiary, 8 December 1948 (701.9635/12-848).
17 Franz Weissblatt (editor). *Who's Who Philippines: A Biographical Dictionary of Notable Living Men in the Philippines*, volume II. Manila: Franz Weissblatt, 1940, pp. 69-70. Biographical Sketch of Melquiades J. Gamboa as attachment to Note Verbale from the Philippine Embassy to the U.S. Department of State dated 16 August 1946 (701.9611/8-1646 CSHH).
18 Biographical Sketch of Tomas G. de Castro as attachment to Note Verbale from the Philippine Embassy to the U.S. Department of State dated 16 August 1946 (701.9611/8-1646 CSHH).
19 Biographical Sketch of Leopoldo T. Ruiz as attachment to Note Verbale from the Philippine Embassy to the U.S. Department of State dated 16 August 1946 (701.9611/8-1646 CSHH).
20 Biographical Sketch of Godofredo Rivera as attachment to Note Verbale

from the Philippine Embassy to the U.S. Department of State dated 16 August 1946 (701.9611/8-1646 CSHH).
21 In 1947, Torres joined the fifth and last batch of Filipino trainees in the State Department as a last minute participant after he secured a clearance from the U.S. Army Counter Intelligence Corps in Manila. He was one of those initially disqualified by the State Department due to his record during the Japanese occupation (as a lawyer in the Department of Justice, 1941-1944).
22 Biographical Sketch of Lt. Col. Manuel Q. Salientes as attachment to Note Verbale from the Philippine Embassy to the U.S. Department of State dated 16 August 1946 (701.9611/8-1646 CSHH).
23 Biographical Sketch of Octavio L. Maloles as attachment to Note Verbale from the Philippine Embassy to the U.S. Department of State dated November 29, 1946 (701.9611/11-2946).
24 Benitez was selected by the Philippine Commonwealth to attend the PFTAP in the State Department but his nomination was disapproved after U.S. Army intelligence report ascertained that Benitez served in the Ministry of Foreign Affairs during the Japanese regime.
25 Report of the American Consul General to the Secretary of State dated 15 November 1946 (701.9611/11-1546). Elpidio Quirino, who as a senator in 1945, accused Benitez of being "opportunist and morally unfit for the Foreign Service." Quirino, however, changed his mind when he became Vice President and Secretary of Foreign Affairs and appointed Benitez as second secretary in Washington.
26 Augusto V. de Viana, *Kulaborator: The Issue of Political Collaboration during World War II* (Manila: University of Santo Tomas Publishing House, 2003), 171–213.
27 Biographical Sketch of Abelardo L. Valencia as attachment to Note Verbale from the Philippine Embassy to the U.S. Department of State dated 26 February 1947 (701.9611/2-2647 CS/A).
28 Biographical Sketch of First Lt. Senador Valeriano as attachment to Note Verbale from the Philippine Embassy to the U.S. Department of State dated January 31, 1947 (701.9611/1-3147).
29 Interview with Mr. Benito Valeriano by the author, May 19, 2007.
30 Melandres T. Velasco, *Nachong: An Enduring Legacy: Ambassador Narciso R. Ramos – Patriarch, Journalist, Diplomat, And Public Servant*. Manila, Ramos Foundation, Inc., 2000, 55.
31 Letter of Secretary of Justice Roman Ozaeta to the Auditor General dated 27 October 1946.
32 Milton Walter Meyer, *A Diplomatic History of the Republic of the Philippines*, University of Hawaii Press, 1965. 9.
33 *Seventh and Final Report of the High Commissioner to the Philippines*, Washington: United States Government Printing Office, 1947, 101.

34 Edward W. Mill, "One Year of the Philippine Republic" in *Department of State Bulletin*, 29 June 1947 (reprint) ,1280-1281.
35 Oral History Interview with Walter Trohan by Jerry N. Hess, Washington, D.C, 7 October 1970. www.trumanlibrary.org/oralhist/trohan.htm. Walter Trohan was Chief of the Washington Bureau of the Chicago Tribune.
36 *The World Diplomatic Directory and World Diplomatic Biography 1950*, London, England.268, 784.
37 Letter of Pablo A. Peña to Edward W. Mill, 9 March 1949.
38 Tiburcio C. Baja and Eliseo Alampay. *Mr. Justice Roberto Regala: His Life and Times* (Quezon City: Phoenix Press, Inc., 1970), 1–5.
39 *The World Diplomatic Directory*, 268.
40 *The World Diplomatic Directory*, 268.
41 Mill, *Conduct of Philippine Foreign Relations*, 8.
42 *The World Diplomatic Directory*, 785.
43 Ibid., 784.
44 Letter of Vicente Villamin to Mill, 12 March 1948 (with an article reprinted from *Manila Bulletin*).
45 Graham H. Stuart, *Department of State: A History of its Organization, Procedure and Personnel* (New York: The MacMillan Company, 1949), 319.
46 Memorandum of Lockhart of PI to Mrs. Mathieu of DP, 20 September 1945.
47 Email of Christopher Morrison, Office of the Historian, U.S. Department of State to the author dated 14 November 2007.
48 Note Verbale from the Philippine Embassy to the U.S. Department of State dated 27 April 1947 (701.9611/Taxation/4-2747 CS/H).
49 Letter of Stanley Woodward to John Russell Young dated 2 May 1947 (701.9611/Taxation/4-2747 CS/H).
50 Letter of Doroteo V. Vite to Edward W. Mill, 29 May 1948.
51 *Evening News Service*, Washington, 13 May 1947 as quoted in *The Memoirs of Elpidio Quirino* (Manila: National Historical Institute, 1990), 98.
52 Times, 15 May 1947 as quoted in *The Memoirs of Elpidio Quirino*, 99.
53 Ibid. Quirino's second visit to America was as Philippine president. President Truman again received him in the White House on 4 February 1950. This time Truman was accompanied by Secretary of State Acheson as protocol dictated. Elizalde was at Quirino's side.
54 The American Embassy in Manila to the U.S. Secretary of State, 23 November 1948 (701.9611/11-2348).
55 Ibid.
56 "Elizalde Quitting?"*Philippine Trends*, 15 June 1949, 4.
57 Romulo assumed both as ambassador at the Philippine Embassy in Washington and as chief delegate at the Philippine Mission to the Unit-

ed Nations. The two concurrent diplomatic positions would be separated in 1954 during the start of the term of President Ramon Magsaysay.

CHAPTER 5   On the International Stage

1 Pacifico A. Castro, *Philippine Diplomatic and Consular Practice*, rev. ed. (Manila: Jacobo and Sons, 1967), 5.
2 Vicente G. Sinco, "The Foreign Affairs of the Philippine Commonwealth" as Enclosure No. 1013 dated 3 April 1946 from the American Consulate General at Manila, entitled "Organization and Activities of the Office of Foreign Relations of the Philippine Commonwealth Government."
3 Quoted from the "Philippine Foreign Affairs Development, 1936–1956: A Resume," *Department of Foreign Affairs Review*, Vol. II, No.3, August 1956, 58.
4 Ibid.
5 Carlos P. Romulo with Beth Day Romulo, *A Third World Soldier in the UN* (Tokyo: Toppan Co., Ltd., 1991), 1.
6 Ibid., 20.
7 Poland was not represented in the San Francisco Conference but signed the Charter later. This is the reason there were fifty participating countries in the Conference but fifty-one countries signed the Charter as founding members of the United Nations.
8 Eddie Amponin Calderón, *The Philippines and the United Nations during the Tenure of Carlos P. Romulo*, unpublished Ph.D. dissertation, University of Minnesota, 1973, 169–170.
9 Ibid., 170–171.
10 Ibid., 172.
11 Ibid. Also see Rodolfo A. Arizala, "The First Philippine Delegation to the United Nations" *Philippine Panorama*, 23 April 1995, 5.
12 Romulo, *A Third World Soldier in the UN*, 23.
13 Letter of Carlos P. Romulo to Edward W. Mill, 11 December 1947.
14 Bonifacio S. Salamanca, *Toward a Diplomatic History of the Philippines* (Quezon City: University of the Philippines Press, 1995), 15.
15 Carlos P. Romulo with Beth Day Romulo, *The Philippine Presidents*, 76.
16 Russell H. Fifield, "Philippine Foreign Policy," in *Far Eastern Survey* Vol. XX, 21 February 1951, 33.
17 *New York World Telegram*, Tuesday, 17 September 1946, 78.
18 *The World Diplomatic Directory and World Diplomatic Biography* 1950, London, 1950, 268.
19 *New York Times*, Real Estate Section, Sunday, 30 April 2000, 9.
20 Romulo, *A Third World Soldier in the UN*, 47.
21 Interview with Carlos P. Romulo / Interviewer, William Powell (New

22 Ibid., 20–22.
23 Ibid., 76–78.
24 Jose A. Zaide, *Bababa Ba?:Anecdotes of a Foreign Service Officer* (Mandaluyong City: Academic Publishing Corporation, 2004), 79.
25 *Department of Foreign Affairs Review*, Vol. III. No. 4, December 1960, 133-122.
26 Oral History Interview with Francis O. Wilcox by Donald A. Ritchie of the Senate Historical Office. Washington, D.C. April 13, 1984 Source: http://www.trumanlibrary.org/oralhist/wilcox4.htm. Wilcox was formerly Chief of Staff, Senate Foreign Relations Committee, 1947–1955.
27 Gladys Zehnpfennig, *General Carlos P. Romulo: Defender of Freedom* (Minneapolis: T.S. Denison & Company, Inc.), 1965.
28 Narciso G. Reyes, *Memories of Diplomacy: A Life in the Philippine Foreign Service* (Pasig City: Anvil Publishing Inc., 1995), 74.
29 Editorial, *Manila Morning Sun*, Sunday, 11 July 1946.
30 *Remembering Carlos P. Romulo* (Makati: Carlos P. Romulo Foundation, 1998), 23.
31 Privado G. Jimenez, "The Fourth General Assembly," in *Quarterly Review*, Manila: Vol. I, No. 1, May 1950, 24.
32 Ibid., 25.
33 Pio Andrade, Jr. *The Fooling of America: The Untold Story of Carlos P. Romulo*, Revised Edition (Manila: Ouch Publisher, 1990), 92.
34 Reyes, *Memories of Diplomacy: A Life in the Philippine Foreign Service*, 74.
35 The book of Pio Andrade, Jr., *The Fooling of America: The Untold Story of Carlos P. Romulo*, is a good example of Romulo-bashing.
36 Zaide, *Bababa Ba?*, 77.
37 Reyes, *Memories of Diplomacy*, 74.
38 Romulo, *A Third World Soldier in the UN*, 67.
39 Ibid., 68.
40 Jose D. Ingles, *Philippine Foreign Policy* (Manila: Lyceum Press, Inc., Manila, 1882), 10.
41 Interview with Carlos P. Romulo / Interviewer, William Powell, New York: UN, 30 October 1982, UN Oral History Project series, UN Dag Hammarskjold Library.
42 Calderon, *The Philippines and the United Nations during the Tenure of Carlos P. Romulo*, 91–92.
43 Ibid., 92.
44 Mill, *The Conduct of Philippine Foreign Relations*, 33. See also Carlos P. Romulo, "Fundamental of our Foreign Policy," 25 May 1951, 20–21.
45 United Nations Yearbook, 1946, 67.

46 Ibid., 34.
47 Ibid., 35

CHAPTER 6   Reaching Out to a Larger World

1 Letter of Tiburcio C. Baja from Mexico City to President Manuel A. Roxas, 28 May 1946.
2 The Acting Secretary of State to the United States High Commissioner to the Philippines (McNutt) dated 21 June 1946 in United States Foreign Relations, 1946, Vol. III, 887-888.
3 Milton Walter Meyer, *A Diplomatic History of the Philippine Republic*, University of Hawaii Press, 1965. p. 33.
4 Note Verbale of the Philippine Embassy in Washington to the U.S. Department of State dated 02 November 1946 (701.9600/11-246 CS/V).
5 The American Embassy in Manila to the U.S. Secretary of State on the subject "Philippine Diplomatic Service," dated 18 August 1948 (701.9600/8-1847 CS/V).
6 The American Embassy in Manila to the U.S. Secretary of State on the subject "Philippine diplomatic representation abroad," dated 17 July 1947 (701.9600/7-1746 CS/A).
7 The American Embassy in Manila to the U.S. Secretary of State on the subject "Philippine diplomatic and consular service," dated 30 September 1947 (701.9600/9-3047 CS/V).
8 Russel H. Fifield, *"Philippine Foreign Policy"* in *Far Eastern Survey*. Vol. XX, 21 February 1951, 34.
9 "Seven Years of Foreign Affairs," *Sunday Times Magazine*, 6 September 1953, 10-11.
10 In January 1951, for instance, the Philippine Legations in Madrid and Jakarta were raised to Embassy respectively. The Philippine Legation in London followed in October 1954. In 1956, the Philippine Mission to Tokyo was elevated to Embassy upon the successful conclusion of the Philippines-Japan War Reparation Talks. By the 1960's, the term legation and mission (except the UN Mission) were no longer existent in the Philippine Foreign Service as all of the them were already raised to embassies.
11 "Nations' Envoys Flock to Manila, New International Listening Post" *Philippine Trends*, August 1949, 13.
12 Felix L. Lazo, "A Glimpse of the Department of Foreign Affairs" in *Public Opinion Magazine*, Manila, 24 August 1948, 50.
13 "Seven Years of Foreign Affairs," *Sunday Times Magazine*, 6 September 1953, 10-11.
14 Telegram from Ambassador Paul V. McNutt to the Secretary of State, 20 September 1946 (701.9693/9-2046).

15 The American Embassy in Manila to the U.S. Secretary of State on the subject "Philippine diplomatic and consular service," dated 30 September 1947 (701.9600/9-3047 CS/V).
16 The American Embassy in Manila to the U.S. Secretary of Stated dated 18 August 1947 (701.9600/8-1847 CS/V).
17 The American Embassy in Manila to the U.S. Secretary of State dated 27 October 1948 (701.9693/10-2748 HH).
18 Interview with Amb. Delfin Garcia, DFA Executive Lounge, March 10, 1997.
19 Interview with Mr. Benito Valeriano by the author, 19 May 2007. Valeriano was the Philippine Consul General to Xiamen (formerly Amoy) when the Consulate General was reopened in February 1995.
20 *The Philippines in Shanghai*, Philippine Consulate General, Shanghai, 2005, 18.
21 Ibid.
22 Letter of Eutiquio O. Sta. Romana to Edward W. Mill, 14 June 1948.
23 Letter of Eutiquio O. Sta. Romana to Edward W. Mill, 2 September 1948.
24 The American Embassy in Manila to the U.S. Secretary of State dated 29 December 1949 (701.9693/12-2948 HH).
25 Rodolfo H. Severino, "Beautiful Isle: Formosa's Strategic Location is Vital to PI Defense," *Sunday Times Magazine*, 17 June 1951, 16.
26 The Commission was automatically disbanded when Japan accepted and signed the terms of surrender on 8 September 1951 as specified in the San Francisco Peace Treaty.
27 Bernabe Africa, "Our Foreign Policy Towards Japan" in *Protocol*, Manila, Vol. I. No. 4, December 1949, 6.
28 Telegram from the Department of State to the Supreme Commander for the Allied Powers in Tokyo dated 09 October 1948 (701.9694/10-948 CSA).
29 Note Verbal from the Philippine Embassy in Washington to the Secretary of State, 15 December 1948. 701.9694/12-1548.
30 Note Verbale from the U.S. State Department to the Ambassador of the Philippines, 22 October 1948 (701.9694/9-2748 CS/SMS).
31 The United States Political Adviser to Japan to the U.S. State Department on the Establishment of the Philippine Mission in Japan, 22 December 1948 (701.9694/12-2248 CS/A).
32 A Friendship of Two Suns: *Philippines-Japan Relations*, A Centennial Publication of the Philippine Embassy in Tokyo, 1998. p. 48-49.
33 Milton Walter Meyer, *A Diplomatic History of the Philippine Republic*, University of Hawaii Press, 1965, 140.
34 Dr. Marcelino V. Bernardo, "Reparations: A Philippine View" in *Quarterly Review* of the Department of Foreign Affairs, Manila: Vol. I, No. 1, May 1950, 11-12.

35 Memo between Richard Ely and Edward W. Mill on Current Philippine Attitude Towards Japan, 20 February 1948. Carlos P. Romulo at that time was the chief delegate of the Philippines to the United Nations.
36 Carlos P. Romulo, "Our Fight for Reparations in the Far Eastern Commission," Official Text Address before the Manila Junior Chamber of Commerce, 21 August 1951, and released by the Division of International Information, Department of Foreign Affairs, Arlegui, Manila, 1.
37 Mill, *Conduct of Philippine Foreign Relations*, 12-13.
38 Ibid, 16-17.
39 Ibid.
40 The American Embassy in Manila to the Secretary of State on the Report on political maneuvering for London diplomatic post, 8 January 1947 (701.9641/1-847).
41 Ibid.
42 Memorandum of Richard Ely to Mr. Vincent and Mr. Penfield of FE, 24 January 1947.
43 Letter of Everett F. Drumright to Edward W. Mill, 16 January 1947.
44 Letter of Everett F. Drumright to Edward W. Mill, 8 January 1947.
45 Letter of Mill to Everett Drumright, First Secretary, U.S. Embassy, London, 21 January 1948.
46 Letter of Everett F. Drumright to Edward W. Mill, 4 June 1947.
47 John Hooper, *The New Spaniards* (second edition), London: Penguin Group, 1995, 12-13. Also see *United Nations Yearbook* 1946, 67.
48 The American Consulate General to the Secretary of State on the Activities of Tabacalera during the Occupation of the Philippines, 28 June 1945 (811B.5034/6-2845).
49 Confidential Memorandum of Richard Ely to Mr. Penfield of FE, 11 September 1947.
50 The chancery of the Philippine legation was located at Calle Velasquez 87.
51 The American Embassy in Madrid to the Secretary of State on Press Article about the Philippine Charge d'Affaires Nieto: Political Differences with the Philippine Legation, 7 October 1948.
52 Ibid.
53 Secretary of Foreign Affairs Carlos P. Romulo expressed this viewpoint in a speech in Rio de Janeiro on 24 October 1950. The Philippine voted in favor of the resolution supporting this policy that was approved by the UN General Assembly on 4 November 1950 Russel H. Fifield, *"Philippine Foreign Policy"* in *Far Eastern Survey*. Vol. XX, 21 February 1951, 34. Also see The New York Times, 25 October 1950.
54 Sebastian had a successful career in politics and government service, although he was well known as a judge. He was first elected representative

of the second district of Cagayan (1922-25), and later provincial governor of Cagayan. He was appointed judge-at-large before the war.
55 Telegram from Lockett of the American Embassy in Manila to the Secretary of State, 12 August 1948 (701.9665/8-1248).
56 Telegram from Lockett of the American Embassy in Manila to the Secretary of State, 17 May 1948 (701.9665/5-1748).
57 Edward W. Mill, "Personnel of Philippine Diplomacy" in *Philippine Social Sciences and Humanities Review*, September 1947, 329.
58 In 1951, the Philippines had a healthy trade surplus vis-a-vis Italy. Philippines exports to Italy were valued at 15,493,773 pesos and imports from Italy were valued at 5,383,358 pesos. See Mill, *The Conduct of Philippine Foreign Relations*, 12.
59 Letter of Alejandro D. Yango to Edward W. Mill, 27 March 1948.
60 Philippine Foreign Affairs Development, 1936-1956: A Resume in *The Department of Foreign Affairs Review*, Vol. 11, No. 3, August, 1956, 58-84.
61 *Department of Foreign Affairs Review*, Vol. I, No. 1, May 1950, 33.
62 Jose F. Imperial, "The Philippines and Indonesia" in *Fookien's The Philippine Yearbook 1952*, 49-52.released as a special feature bulletin by the Division of International Information, DFA, Manila series of 1952, 2 December 1952. Imperial, a State Department graduate, served as minister in Djakarta.
63 Ibid.
64 Telegram from the American Embassy in Manila to the Department of State dated 14 February 1949 (701.9692/2-749).
65 Ibid.
66 Air gram from the American Embassy in Manila to the Department of State dated 25 April 1949 (701.9692/4-2549 HH).
67 Confidential Air gram from the American Embassy in Manila to the Secretary of State, 06 May 1949 (701.9692/4-2549).
68 Ibid.
69 Ibid.
70 Email of Ambassador Rodolfo Arizala to Consul Lourdes Tabamo, 07 May 2008. The funds used in purchasing the lot for the embassy complex was partly taken from the excise tax which accumulated during World War II which the British Government paid to the Philippine Government for coconut exports to the UK.
71 Mill, *Conduct of Philippine Foreign Relations*, 166.
72 Ibid., 165-166.
73 "Ramos Asks Indian Press to Identify PI as Banana Republic," *The Sunday Times*, 4 April 1954, 3.
74 Ibid.
75 "Bueno to Open Korean Legation", *Manila Bulletin*, 8 April 1953, 2.

76 Mill, *Conduct of Philippine Foreign Relations*, 164.
77 Memorandum of Conversation on Philippine Interests-Cuba between Dr (Melquiades) Gamboa, Philippine Embassy, and Ms. Wolberg, DS, 23 December 1949.
78 The American Embassy in Manila to the Secretary of State on the Philippine Diplomatic Mission to Argentina; Background of Narciso Ramos, newly appointed Envoy Extraordinary and Minister Plenipotentiary, 8 December 1948 (701.9635/12-848).
79 Ibid.
80 Estela Sulit was the former Estela Romualdez, sister of Daniel Romualdez, the former speaker of Congress and the daughter of Don Miguel Romualdez, the former mayor of Manila. She was married to Captain Sulit, a Filipino war veteran residing in San Francisco. Estela Sulit would later be appointed Philippine Ambassador to Lisbon. See Mariano Ezpeleta, *Memoires of an Ambassador*, Manila, 1973, 79.
81 Ibid., 90.
82 List of Officials and Employees of the Department of Foreign Affairs as of July 1, 1955. *Department of Foreign Affairs Review*, Vol. II, No. 1 (March 1955), 110-113. The Philippine Consulate in Cairo opened in September 1955 with Yusuf Abubakar as Consul. The Consulate in Vancouver was also established before the end of the year. See "Philippine Foreign Affairs Development, 1946-1956" in *Department of Foreign Affairs Review*, Vol. II, No. 3 (August 1956).
83 Directory of the Department of Foreign Affairs as of June 30, 1957, *Department of Foreign Affairs Review*, Vol. II, No. 4 (October 1957), 40-45.
84 Letters of Credence, *Department of Foreign Affairs Review*, Vol. IV, No. 2 (June, 1963), 266.
85 Press Releases, *Department of Foreign Affairs Review*, Vol. IV, No. 3 (December, 1964), 137.
86 Department Circular No. 10-65 dated April 30, 1965, *Department of Foreign Affairs Review*, Vol. IV, No. 4 (July, 1965), 105-106

CHAPTER 7 Surviving the Foreign Service

1 U.S. Department of State to the American Embassy in Manila (For Butrick) 06 September 1946 (701.9600/9-546 CS/A). Foreign Affairs Officers (FAO), later changed to Foreign Service Officers, begin with the rank of Class IV in the Home Office. This rank is equivalent to third secretary or vice consul when the FAO is assigned to an embassy and consulate respectively.
2 The American Embassy in Manila to the U.S. Department of State, 10 September 1946 (701.9600/9-1046).
3 The U.S. Department of State to the American Embassy in Manila (For Butrick), 13 September 1946 (701.9600/9-1046 CS/V).

4 Letter of Richard P. Butrick to Edward W. Mill, 16 September 1946.
5 Letter of Richard P. Butrick to Edward W. Mill, 16 September 1946.
6 Letter of Emilio Torres to the Secretary of State (unsigned), 15 October 1947.
7 Letter of Delfin R. Garcia to Edward W. Mill, 7 April 1949.
8 *Department of State Press Release*, No. 280, 4 April 1947.
9 Letter Edward W. Mill to Tiburcio Baja, 31 December 1946.
10 Letter Edward W. Mill to Richard P. Butrick, 14 November 1946.
11 Letter of Vicente I. Singian to Edward Mill, 25 October 1946 (Manila).
12 Letter Edward W. Mill to Richard P. Butrick, 2 December 1946.
13 Butrick's Comment on Imperial, 18 October 1946.
14 Letter of Edward W. Mill to Everett F. Drumright, 8 January 1947.
15 *Department of State Press Release*, No. 280, 4 April 1947.
16 *Biographic Register of the Department of Foreign Affairs*, Manila: Bureau of Printing, 1970, 71.
17 Letter of Generoso Provido to Edward Mill, 11 July 1947 (from Manila DFA).
18 *Department of Foreign Affairs Review*, Vol. II, No. 3, August, 1956, 60.
19 Letter of Eutiquio O. Santa Romana to Edward W. Mill, 25 April 1947.
20 Letter of Edward W. Mill to Eutiquio O. Sta. Romana, 7 May 1947.
21 Letter of Mill to Eutiquio Sta. Romana, 27 October 1946.
22 Letter from Maria Soledad Sta. Romana Reverente to the Author, 28 February 2010.
23 Letter of Eutiquio O. Sta. Romana to Edward W. Mill, 10 February 1953.
24 Letter of Rodolfo H. Severino to Edward Mill, undated (204 Ayala Building, Manila).
25 Letter of Carlos A. Faustino to Edward W. Mill, 18 June 1947. The sad experience of Carlos A. Faustino and Rodolfo H. Severino was not an isolated case. Many *pensionados* (government scholars) coming back from the U.S. were suspected of becoming too Americanized and suffered cold treatment, even to the extent of ridicule. They were often branded as "Americanized" or "American Boys." For an elaborate discussion on the pensionados, please see Lewis E. Gleek, Jr., *American Institutions in the Philippines* (1898–1941) (Manila: Historical Conservation Society, 1976), 49–52.
26 Letter of Edward W. Mill to Carlos A. Faustino, 26 June 1947.
27 Letter of Roman V. Ubaldo to Edward W. Mill, 01 February 1948.
28 "Filipino Young Men Training for Foreign Service: Under Edward Mill" *Manila Daily Bulletin*, Vol. 137, no. 74.28 March 1949, section 4, 28.
29 Letter of Mill to Benjamin Tirona, 7 September 1947.
30 Letter of Edward W. Mill to Tagakotta Soto, 20 October 1947.
31 Letter Edward W. Mill to Generoso Provido, 28 August 1947.

32 Letter of Tiburcio C. Baja to Edward W. Mill, 10 January 1947.
33 Letter of Tiburcio C. Baja to Edward W. Mill, 10 July 1947.
34 Letter of Edward W. Mill to Delfin R. Garcia, 18 November 1946.
35 Letter of Anastacio B. Bartolome to Edward W. Mill (in Surabaya), 11 July 1950.
36 Letter of Yusup Abubakar to Edward W. Mill, 31 July 1950.
37 Letter of Doroteo V. Vite to Edward W. Mill, 21 September 1948.
38 Letter of Tiburcio C. Baja to Edward W. Mill, 19 May 1948. The preponderance of lawyers during the early years of the Philippine Foreign Service was obvious. In 1952, out of the 112 officers and staff of the Home Office and the Foreign Service, 77 were lawyers.
39 Letter of Delfin R. Garcia to Edward W. Mill, 16 May 1951.
40 Letter of Tiburcio C. Baja to Edward W. Mill, 14 March 1951.
41 Letter of Edward W. Mill to Delfin R. Garcia, 23 May 1951.
42 Email of Ambassador Eduardo Montilla to Ambassador Juan Ona, 15 February 2000.
43 Carson, Arthur L. *Silliman University*: 1901–1959 (Taiwan: United Board for Christian Higher Education in Asia, 1965), 344, 433-35.
44 "Arlegui Revamp Due, "*Manila Times*, 24 January 1954, 1 and 15.
45 Ibid., 15.
46 "An Unwise Proposal," The *Manila Times*, 23 January 1954, 13.
47 "It's the Spoil System," *The Evening News*, 23 January 1954, 10.
48 Benigno S. Aquino, "Focus on Asia," The *Manila Times*, 23 January 1954, 3.
49 "Diplomatic Axe poised," *Manila Times*, 10 February 1954, 15.
50 *Manila Bulletin*, 22 January 1954, 22 Quoted in Edward W. Mill, *The Conduct of Philippine Foreign Relations*, Ph.D. dissertation, Princeton University, 1954, 302-30.
51 Mill, *The Conduct of Philippine Foreign Relations*, 305.
52 Opinion No. 82, 1954 as contained in the Letter of Secretary of Justice Pedro Tuason to the Secretary of Foreign Affairs, 3 April 1954.
53 "Solon Disputes Tuason Opinion" *Philippines Herald*, 21 June 1954.
54 Letter of Roberto Regala to Edward W. Mill, 14 May 1954.
55 Letter of Edward W. Mill to Roberto Regala, 24 May 1954.
56 Letter of Roberto Regala to Edward W. Mill, 24 June 1954.
57 Mill, *The Conduct of Philippine Foreign Relations*, 51.
58 Letter of Roberto Regala to Edward W. Mill, 24 June 1954.
59 "Tuason Restores Ousted Foreign Service Officers," *Manila Bulletin*, 24 June 1954, 1 and 19. Quoted in *The Conduct of Philippine Foreign Relations*, 308.
60 *Manila Bulletin*, 15 June 1954, 12.Quoted in *The Conduct of Philippine Foreign Relations*, 309.

61 Letter of Angela V. Ramos to Edward W. Mill, 4 January 1954.
62 Letter of Narciso Ramos to Edward W. Mill, 30 April 1954.
63 Letter of Roberto Regala, Minister to Australia, to Edward W. Mill, 12 August 1954.
64 Letter of Delfin R. Garcia to Edward W. Mill, 2 August 1954.
65 Letter of Anastacio Bartolome to Dr. & Mrs. Mill, 19 July 1957 attaching a clipping of *The Manila Chronicle*, 18 July 1957. Source: Edward W. Mill Papers, Personal/Biographical, Materials Box 1.
66 *Philippine Free Press*, February 12, 1955, 64.
67 Letter of Luis Moreno Salcedo to Edward W. Mill, 17 February 1955.
68 Letter of Hortencio J. Brillantes to Edward W. Mill, 24 December 1957.
69 *Department of Foreign Affairs Review*, Vo. 11. No. 3, August 1956, p. 61 and 63.
70 *Department of Foreign Affairs Review*, Vo. 11. No. 3, August 1956. p. 74.
71 Interview with Ambassador Delfin Garcia, DFA Executive Lounge, 10 March 1997.
72 Edward W. Mill, "The Philippine Foreign Affairs Training Program: A Decade Later," *Foreign Service Journal*, May 1956, 44.
73 Ibid.
74 Ibid., 12.
75 Letter of Anastacio Bartolome to Edward W. Mill, Manila, 4 November 1959.
76 Letter of Edward W. Mill to Anastacio Bartolome, 14 November 1959.
77 Letter to Tiburcio C. Baja to Edward W. Mill, 25 August 1965.
78 Celso G. Cabrera, "Why Our Diplomats Prefer Posts Abroad" in Inside Malacañang, *Manila Bulletin*, 1968, 5.
79 Email of Amb. Juan A. Ona to the DFA Tattlers, 2 June 2005.
80 Edward W. Mill Papers, Correspondences 1965–1968, Box 3.

CHAPTER 8   "Father of the Philippine Foreign Service"

1 Letter of Virginia Mill to Bill, 20 July 1978, Edward W. Mill Collection, Box 1.
2 Telegram of Carlos P. Romulo, Secretary of Foreign Affairs to Mrs. Virginia Mill, 19 July 1977, Mill Collection, Box 1.
3 Undated letter of Philippine Consul General to Los Angeles Armando C. Fernandez to Virginia Mill, Mill Collection Box 1.
4 Letter of Juan M. Arreglado, Secretary General of the Philippine Ambassadors Association, to Virginia Mill, 17 April 1978. Mill Collection, Box 1.
5 Letter of Edward W. Mill to Marie E. Mill, 30 August 1937.
6 Mill's Diary, Tuesday, 14 June 1938. Unless otherwise indicated Diary refers to E.W. Mill's Diary.

7 Diary, Monday, 17 June 1940.
8 Diary, 27 October 1941.
9 Letter of Edward W. Mill to his Folks, 2 April 1942.
10 Diary, Tuesday, 19 March 1942.
11 Diary, Saturday afternoon, 26 April 1941.
12 Letter of Mill to Bill, 21 September 1942.
13 Letter of Mill to Stan, 27 September 1942.
14 Letter of Mill to his aunt Ida, 3 December 1942.
15 Letter of J.R. Hayden, 25 June 1942; Mill later on gave two other reasons that prevented him from accepting the Quezon job offer – the status of his draft application to the Navy and the pursuit of a PhD degree.
16 Letter of R.A. Kleindienst, Administrative Officer, 20 July 1942, U.S. Department of the Interior, Office of the Secretary, Division of Territories and Island Possessions.
17 Letter of Mill to Goodwin Watson, 27 February 1943.
18 Mill's letter to his folks, 5 March 1943.
19 Mill's letter to his Aunt Ida, 1 May 1943.
20 Mill's letter to his folks, 10 May 1943.
21 Mill's letter to his folks, 10 May 1943.
22 Letter of Mill to his folks, 27 November 1943.
23 Letter of Mill to his folks, 12 June 1944.
24 Letter of Mill to Prof. Everett. S. Brown, Department of Political Science, University of Michigan.
25 Letter of Mill to his folks, 30 August 1944.
26 Letter of J.R. Hayden to Gen. W. J. Donovan, OSS, 4 September 1944.
27 Letter of J.R. Hayden to E.W. Mill dated 20 November 1944.
28 Letter of Mill to his folks, 19 September 1944.
29 Letter of Mill to his sister Dorothy, 24 September 1944.
30 Letter of Mill to his folks, 25 October 1944.
31 Letter of Mill to John, 28 December 1944.
32 Letter of Mill to his folks, 18 March 1945.
33 Letter of Mill to Prof. William Ebenstein, Department of Political Science, University of Wisconsin, 27 March 1945.
34 Letter of Mill to his folks, 21 April 1945.
35 Letter of Mill to Lloyd S. Millegan, 2 May 1945.
36 Letter of Mill to his folks, 3 November 1945.
37 Letter of Mill to his folks, 3 November 1945.
38 Letter of Mill to Prof. Kenneth Colegrove, Department of Political Science, Northwestern University, 1 December 1945.
39 Letter of Mill to Prof. Kenneth Colegrove, Department of Political Science, Northwestern University, 1 December 1945.
40 Letter of Mill to his wife Wilma, 9 December 1945.

41 Letter to Professor Kenneth Colegrove, Department of Political Science, Northwestern University, 2 January 1946.
42 Memorandum of Edward W. Mill to Mr. Ely on the Fourth Philippine Foreign Affairs Training Group, 18 December 1946.
43 "Filipino Young Men Training for Foreign Service under Edward Mill." *Manila Daily Bulletin*, vol. 137, no. 74.28 March 1949, section 4, 28.
44 The American Consulate General in Sydney to the Secretary of State dated 20 May 1945 (811B.42/5-2046).
45 Letter of Benjamin T. Tirona to Edward W. Mill, 26 July 1947.
46 Letter of Edward W. Mill to Professor Warren Smith, Chairman, Department of Geology, University of Oregon, 15 January 1946.
47 Mill's Personal Memorandum on the Visit of Manuel A. Roxas, President-elect of the Philippine to the United States, May 10-17, 1946.
48 Letter of Edgar F. Love, Acting Chief of Administration, Branch G-4 Section, U.S. Army in Manila, 1 July 1947.
49 Letter of Emilio Torres to the Secretary of State (unsigned) dated 15 October 1947.
50 *Philippine Trends*, 1 June 1949, 42.
51 Letter of Mill to Eduardo Rosal, 1 October 1947.
52 Letter of Mill to Frank Lockhart, Saturday, 2 March 1946, 4:15 P.M.
53 Letter of Mill to his folks, 4 November 1946.
54 Letter of Mill to his wife Wilma, 6 July 1946.
55 Letter of Mill to his folks, 28 October 1946.
56 Letter of Mill to Andrew F. Rolle, American Consulate General, Genoa, Italy, 26 June 1947.
57 Letter of Mill to Prof. William Ebenstein, Department of Government, Princeton University.
58 Talk with Mr. Weigle about Assignment and Effect of Future Status in FE (9 January 1948).
59 Letter of Mill to Pablo Peña, 6 January 1948.
60 Mill's note, dated 10 January 1948.
61 Letter of Mill of Hortencio J. Brillantes, 1 March 1948.
62 Letter from Hortencio Brillantes to Edward W. Mill, 24 February 1948.
63 Letter of Mill to Juanito Dionisio, 03 June 1948.
64 Letter of Roberto Regala to Mill, 31 May 1948.
65 Letter of Mill to Kay, 25 February 1949.
66 Letter of Mill to Kay, 25 February 1949.
67 *Manila Bulletin*, 18 June 1948, 5. Also see *The Manila Chronicle*, 18 June 1948, 32.
68 Bessie Hacket, "Around Manila," *Manila Bulletin*, 6 November 1948, missing page number. Mill regularly appeared in social pages of The *Manila Bulletin*, especially in the column of Bessie Hacket, "Around Manila."

69 Letter of Narciso Ramos to Edward W. Mill, 03 December 1948.
70 Supplementary Statement to Accompany Form 57, Examination for Foreign Affairs Officers, P-6 to P-8 EC-23.
71 Letter of Luis Moreno Salcedo to Mill, 9 July 1950.
72 Letter of Tiburcio C. Baja dated 22 May 1950.
73 Letter of Luis Moreno Salcedo to Edward W. Mill, 11 January 1951.
74 Letter of Edward W. Mill to Dean Valenzuela, 17 May 1951.
75 Letter to Jonathan King, The Ford Foundation, New York, 01 December 1953.
76 Letter of Delfin R. Garcia to Edward W. Mill, 2 August 1954.
77 Letter of Luis Moreno Salcedo to Edward W. Mill, 19 November 1957.
78 Letter of Jose Alejandrino to Edward W. Mill, 3 December 1957.
79 *Honolulu Star-Bulletin*, Thursday, 14 April 1955.
80 Long Island University Newsletter, 16 April 1962.
81 Letter of Edward W. Mill to Juanito C. Dionisio, 29 November 1961.
82 *The Occidental*, 28 September 1962, 8.
83 Letter of Edward W. Mill to Hortencio J. Brillantes, 12 September 1963.
84 *Wisconsin Alumnus*, October 1964, 28. Also see The *Manila Times*, 16 June 1964, 2-A.
85 As presented over TV on "The President's Diary," Channel 9, Manila, 9:30 PM Monday night, 22 September 1969.
86 "World Diplomacy Is Big Business Today," *Los Angeles Herald-Examiner*, 7 January 1975, B1.
87 "Father of RP Foreign Service" collection received by Sanchez," *Philippines Herald*, 3 September 1978, Chicago, Illinois, 20. When the DFA building at Padre Faura caught fire in December 1986, the Mill collection was among the records lost. Fortunately before the Mill family turned over the collection to the Philippine Consulate General in Chicago, the collection was microfilmed by the Bentley Historical Library of the University of Michigan in Ann Arbor and it is still preserved there.
88 Letter of Mill to Lewis G. Vander Velde, Director of the Michigan Historical Collection, University of Michigan, 26 December 1955.

CHAPTER 9   Leaving a Legacy

1 The author would have wanted to interview Ambassador Romeo Busuego but was told that Busuego was living in Sydney, Australia and had become reclusive.
2 Edward W. Mill, *The First Career Diplomats of the Philippine Republic*, 14 December 1948, 6. Edward W. Mill Papers, Box I. Bentley Historical Library, University of Michigan. The article was published by Protocol, Manila, January 1949. Protocol was a publication by the Far Eastern University whose editor was Luis Moreno Salcedo, a member of Group V of the State Department trainees.

3 Edward W. Mill, "The Philippine Foreign Affairs Training Program: A Decade Later," *Foreign Service Journal*, May 1956, 44.
4 Luis Moreno Salcedo, *A Guide to Protocol*, Manila: Protocol Club of the Far Eastern University, 1950.
5 Emilio D. Bejasa, Book Review of *A Guide to Protocol* by Luis Moreno Salcedo inDepartment of Foreign Affairs *Quarterly Review*, Manila, Vol. I, No. 1, May 1950, 43.
6 Email of Ambassador Juan A Ona to the DFA Tattlers dated 15 May 2005.
7 Jose Alejandrino y Medina, *Suez y el derecho internacional*, Madrid: Instituto Francisco de Vitoria, 1959. Jose Alejandrino, Jr. told the author that Egyptian President Gamal Nasser gave a presidential citation to his father in recognition of his book on the legal dimension of the nationalization of the Suez Canal. The author sent an official letter to the Egyptian Embassy in Madrid in July 2008 to verify said award to Alejandrino but did not receive a reply.
8 Ibid. See book's jacket.
9 Alejandrino, Jose. *The Price of Freedom: Episodes and Anecdotes of Our Struggle for Freedom*, Translated from Spanish by Jose M. Alejandrino and Prologue by Teodoro M. Kalaw (Manila: M. Colcol & Company, 1949). The original title in Spanish is La Senda del Sacrificio.
10 Letter of Philippine Consul General to Dubai Benito B. Valeriano to the Author dated 16 July 2008. Valeriano is now the Philippine ambassador to India.
11 Benito B. Valeriano, *The Manila Economic and Cultural Center (MECO): An Interpretation of Philippine Representation in Taiwan*, Master's thesis in Political Science, Lyceum of the Philippines, October 1998, 90–91.
12 DFA Memorandum to the President No. 846-75, 20 October 1975. Quoted from Valeriano's thesis.
13 Letter (Restricted) of Simeon R. Roxas to the Department of Foreign Affairs, 25 March 1977. Quoted from Valeriano's thesis, 100-101.
14 Executive Order No. 931, 16 January 1984. Quoted in Valeriano's thesis, 101.
15 Email of Ambassador Juan A. Ona to the DFA Tattlers, 25 May 2002.
16 Email of Ambassador Rodolfo S. Sanchez to the Author, 28 May 2002.
17 Letter of Benito B. Valeriano to the Author, 16 July 2008.
18 Jose A. Zaide, *Bababa Ba? Anecdotes of a Foreign Service Officer* (Mandaluyong: Academic Publishing Corporation, 2004), 92.
19 Email of Ambassador Rodolfo A. Arizala to Ambassador Juan Ona and the DFA Tattlers, 22 November 2002.
20 Email of Ambassador Pablo A. Araque to the Author, 19 November 2002.
21 The tribute given to Bejasa was even more impressive taking into account the fact that he almost left the Foreign Service in disgrace. His

career was almost ruined when he was involved in a romantic relationship, although he was already a widower at that time, with his German secretary/interpreter when he was the Philippine ambassador to West Germany in the late 1960s. The Bejasa affair became a big scandal in Manila. Not only did the Manila press had a field day covering the account but the Philippine Congress also summoned Bejasa back to Manila to personally explain his love affair. See Quijano de Manila, *Reportage on Lovers: A Medley of Factual Romances, Happy or Tragical, Most of Which Made News*, Manila: Anvil, 2009.

22 *Philippine Foreign Service Reader 1981*, Manila: Foreign Service Institute, 1981, 171.
23 Star Bulletin, Obituaries, Honolulu, 24 June 1999.
24 Hermelinda Ycasiano Moreno, Vietnam War Memoirs, Manila, 2005. *Mrs. Hermelinda Ycasiano Moreno is the wife of the late Hon. Luis Salcedo Moreno, former Philippine Ambassador to Vietnam, Saigon.*
25 Email of Ambassador Pablo A. Araque to the Author, 12 November 2002.
26 *The Philippine Foreign Service Reader* 1981, 163.
27 Letter of Hortencio J. Brillantes, the Philippine Ambassador to the UN, Geneva, to Edward W. Mill, 14 June 1972.
28 Letter of Carlos A. Faustino, then Philippine Ambassador to Belgium, to Mill, 13 February 1974.
29 Email of Ambassador Pablo A. Araque to the Author, 12 November 2002.
30 Email of Ambassador Rodolfo C. Severino, Jr. to the Author, 27 March 2008. Severino also served Secretary General of the Association of Southeast Asian Nations (ASEAN) from 1998 to 2002.
31 *Manila Bulletin*, 4 March 1968.
32 *Manila Chronicle*, 24 February 1969.
33 Arturo Bernales, "Faculty Line–Up" in *Philippine Law School Newsletter*, 1960.
34 Ibid.
35 Email of Ambassador Rodolfo A. Arizala to the Author, 19 July 2010.
36 Interview by the author with Ambassador Delfin R. Garcia, 10 March 1997, DFA Executive Lounge.
37 Quoted from Mill's advice to his friend on contacts for Asian Trip, July 1976.
38 Lewis E. Gleek, Jr., Dissolving the Colonial Bonds: American Ambassadors to the Philippines, 1946-1984, Quezon City: New Day Publishers, 1988. 22.
39 Jay Reid, "U.S. Training Filipinos for Diplomat Corps: Unique State Department Program, 2 Years Old, Tightens Nations' Links," *New York Herald Tribune*, 16 March 1947.
40 Press Release, "Philippine Foreign Affairs Program", *Department of State Bulletin*, Vol. XIV. No. 407, 20 April 1947, 718.

41 *Department of State Press Release* No. 814, 14 November 1946.
42 Email of Amb. Juan Ona to Amb. Rodolfo Sanchez to, Thursday, 23 May 2002.
43 Luis Moreno Salcedo, "At the end of the day (Post Scriptum)," *Manila Bulletin*, Tuesday, 8 March 1988, 7.
44 Ibid.
45 Ibid.
46 Beth Day Romulo, "A gallant diplomat," *Manila Bulletin* (author's source was undated).
47 Aurora Cruz, Having it all (City Diary), *Malaya*, 11 March 1988.
48 *Jose M. Alejandrino, petitioner, vs. The Honorable Francisco S. Tantuico, Acting Chairman, Commission on Audit, The Honorable Carlos P. Romulo, as Secretary of Foreign Affairs, respondents*, G.R. No. L-44928, 30 October 1981. There is also an online version of the case. An online version of the case is available: athttp://www.lawphil.net/judjuris/juri1981/oct1981/gr_44928_1981.html.

Index

Abad Santos, Vicente, 8
Abello, Emilio, 63, 119, 131
Abrera, Bernardo P., 177
Abrera, Sofronio, 125
Abubakar, Yusuf R., 18, 46, 47, 49, 50, 125, 189, 214, 219–221, 238, 241, 288–289, 309
Acheson, Dean, 67, 72, 82, 111, 167
Adeva, Manuel A., 7–10, 14, 28, 30–31, 80, 109, 138, 173, 175, 201–202, 204, 217–218, 231, 238, 242, 288, 309
Africa, Bernabe, 37, 48, 67, 79, 83–84, 171, 176–177, 280, 295
Agoncillo, Felipe, 56–57
Aguinaldo, Emilio, 55–56, 108, 298
Alejandrino, Jose M., 12, 17 18, 42–43, 50, 92, 189, 191–193, 203, 210, 233, 241, 281, 287–289, 297–298, 317
Alzate, Manuel A., 188, 231
Angeles, Estanislao P., 177
Aquino, Benigno, Jr., 225
Aquino, Benigno, Sr., 63, 87
Araneta, Salvador, 181
Araque, Pablo A., 306
Arellano, Cayetano, 56–57
Arlegui House, 86–89
Arizala, Rodolfo A., 303, 312
Austin, Warren, 145

Baja, Tiburcio C., 7–10, 14, 28, 30–31, 124, 165, 178, 189, 201–202, 204, 214, 216–218, 220, 229, 239–241, 281, 283, 309, 315

Baluyut, Sotero, 191, 203
Barreto, Juan Antonio, 117
Bartolome, Anastacio B., 11, 14, 16, 35–37, 40–41, 124, 201, 207, 218, 233, 239, 241, 315
Bautista, Amado N., 142
Bejasa, Emilio D., 11, 14–16, 35, 37, 90, 174, 188, 201, 207–208, 233, 241–242, 281, 287, 296, 302–303, 315
Benitez, Tomas C., 8, 59, 67, 118, 120
Bernardo, Marcelino V., 17–18, 41, 44, 50, 178, 210, 220–221, 242, 281, 315
Bevin, Ernest, 83
Borja, Jacinto, 59
Brillantes, Hortencio J., 11, 18–20, 44, 46, 48–50, 52, 214, 234, 241–242, 278, 281, 288, 304, 307
Boncan, Marcelo T., 125
Buencamino III, Felipe, 187–188
Bueno, Maximo, 195
Burman, Robert A., 19, 127
Busuego, Romeo S., 12, 17–18, 42–43, 183, 184, 210, 241, 289, 293
Butrick, Richard P., 17, 19, 34, 70–78, 79, 80, 85, 121, 172, 183, 201–202, 204–205, 217
Byrnes, James F., 2, 68, 70
Cabatit, Irineo R., 18, 49, 124, 214, 242
Cabili, Tomas, 226
Calingo, Mauro, 59, 64, 79
Camacho, Augusto, 145

Cayco, Librado, 93
Chiang Kai-shek, 172, 174
Claravall, Francisco P., 11, 14, 16, 35, 185, 201–202, 207
Collantes, Manuel, 241
Columbia University, 13 150
Constantino, Esmeralda, 288
Cornista, Irineo D., 18, 48, 125, 214, 239, 241, 281, 316
Cuenco, Mariano Jesus, 142, 280
Cristobal, Romeo T., 144

Day, Henry B., 40, 60
de Aguilar y Salas, Teodomiro, 184
de Castro, Tomas G., 13, 14, 117, 120, 180, 189, 195, 201–202, 233, 238, 241
Delgado, Francisco A., 138
Department of Foreign Affairs, Philippines, 4, 28, 33, 46, 48, 49, 51, 53, 55, 56, 59, 66–70, 78–80, 132, 201–202, 208, 211–212, 214, 219, 222–223, 225, 229, 237, 241; counselors, 83–84; Foreign Affairs Cooperative Association (FACA), 87; home office/headquarters, 86–89; politics in 218-220; reorganization, 222–229 (*see also* Foreign Service Act of 1952); secretary, 81-82; undersecretary, 83
Department of State building, 24
Dewey, George, 56
Dionisio, Juanito C., 14, 15, 35, 109, 124, 201, 207, 233, 241, 279, 288
Division of Foreign Relations, 2, 58–61
Drumright, Everett F., 39, 43, 182–184, 206

Elbo, Candido T., 10, 28, 29, 31–32, 124, 201, 204, 220–221, 242
Elizalde, Joaquin M., 3, 20, 38, 50, 52, 85, 109–110, 112–114, 116–117, 119–121, 131–132, 195
Ely, Richard, 48,49, 179, 185, 277

Escudero, Manuel, 186, 196
Evangelista, Jose, 59
Evangelista, Teodoro, 59–60, 64, 83–84, 209
Executive Order No. 18, 78–81
Ezpeleta, Mariano, 173, 197

Far Eastern Commission (FEC), 175–176
Far Eastern University, 294
Farol, Meynardo, 189, 193
Farolan, Modesto, 124–125
Faustino, Carlos A., 12, 17, 44, 191–192, 211–213, 233, 241, 281, 298,308
Fernandez, Jaime, 3
Fernandez, Ramon J., 184,
Filipino Central Committee, 58
Fonacier, Guillermo C., 18, 47–49, 124, 204, 214, 242
Foreign Affairs officers (FAO) Examinations, 94
Foreign Service Act of 1952, 91–95, 120, 223, 225–228, 318
Foreign Service Law of 1991, 309
Foreign Service Officers Training School, 4–9, 24, 25, 27, 48
Foreign Service Regulations of the Philippines, 80, 121, 298
Formosa, 69, 169,174,
Franco, Francisco, 184

Gallego, Manuel V., 115, 142, 190
Gamboa, Melquiades J., 70, 85, 117, 120
Garcia, Carlos P., 138, 195, 222–225, 238
Garcia, Delfin R., 13–14, 34, 59, 67, 75, 80, 90, 172–173, 201, 204–205, 217, 220–221, 233, 241–242, 286, 309, 312, 315
Garcia, Enrique M., 176–177
Garcia, Leon T., 189
Georgetown University, 10, 11, 207
German Consulate, 61, 87
Gonzales, Rosario, 288, 289

Guerrero, Leon Ma., 64, 85, 222, 230, 295, 304
Guerzon, Engracio D., 12, 18, 20, 47–48, 204, 214, 242, 281

Hare-Hawes-Cutting Law, 82
Harrington, Julian, 6
Hayashi, Yoshihide, 63
Hayden, Joseph R., 110, 256, 259–263
Hull, Cordell, 136–137

Ibn–Saud, 156
Imperial, Domingo, 187, 192
Imperial, Jose F., 7–10, 27, 28, 30, 68, 79–80, 117, 121, 124, 138, 178, 180, 184, 201, 202, 204, 204, 208, 217, 238, 240–241, 288, 309
Ingles, Jose D., 142, 144, 157, 304,
International Labor Organization (ILO), 37, 38, 162, 210
International Monetary Fund (IMF), 4, 136, 162,
Israel, State of, 155–159

Jacobs, Joseph E., 60, 126
Japanese collaboration issue, 8, 110, 118–119, 131, 267
Japanese invasion and occupation, 62–65
Jones Law of 1916, 108
Joven, Marciano A., 12, 20, 190, 214, 239, 241

Kalaw, Maximo, 138
Khrushchev, Nikita, 148–149,

Lardizabal Jr., Reynaldo, 18, 120, 214, 242
Laurel, Jose P., 63–65
Legarda, Benito, Sr., 108
Leuterio, Raul t., 142, 228
Liberal Party, 93, 171, 181, 222, 223, 232, 280
Lie, Trygvie, 38
Llamas, Pelayo F., 13, 125, 173, 180, 198, 201–202, 205, 233, 241, 314
Lockett, Thomas H., 277–278
Lockhart, Frank, 3–7, 27, 70–72, 110, 127, 264, 266, 272, 276–277
Lopez, Pedro, 138, 142
Lopez, Salvador P., 64, 67, 141–142, 144, 198, 289, 295, 304
Lothrop House, 17, 24

Mabini, Apolinario, 57–58
Macapagal, Diosdado, 78, 83, 84, 92, 120, 198, 227, 240, 298
MacArthur, Douglas, 61, 68, 263–265
Magsaysay, Ramon, 222, 229, 231–233, 235–238, 285
Makalintal, Querube, 64
Maloles, Octavio, 11, 67, 118, 120, 183, 184, 188
Malvar, Miguel, 58
Manalo, Rosario, 288–289
Manglapus, Raul, 85
Manila Bulletin, 94, 210, 230, 281, 304
Manila Economic and Cultural Office (MECO), 299
Manila Times, 150, 224 225
Mao Zedong, 174
Marcos, Ferdinand E., 117, 232, 240–241, 289, 298–299
McKinley, William, 57
McMicking, Joseph, 181–182
McNutt, Paul, 69, 73–74, 79, 111–112, 122
Melchor, Alejandro, 138
Melencio, Jose, 85, 124, 126
Mendez, Mauro, 144, 295
Merril, Gregor C., 60
Mill, Edward W., 4, 7, 17, 19, 24, 35–36, 50, 53, 234, 253, 291; family and married life, 254–255, 258, 288; education and academic career, 255–258, 284–288; other employment, 259–267, 282–284; in Manila, 277–282; service in PFATP, 114,

127, 179, 202, 204–205, 267–274; writings, 286–287, 294–295
Ministry of Foreign Affairs, 62–66
Molotov, Vyacheslav, 137, 146
Mondonedo, Osmundo, 120
Montilla, Eduardo,16
Moreno, Jose, 125
Moreno Salcedo, Luis, 12, 18–20, 46, 47, 48, 49, 197, 214, 234, 241–242, 279, 283, 286–288, 294, 296–297, 304–306, 316–317
Muir, Raymond D., 48
Murata, Syozo, 65

Nacionalista Party, 93,108, 114, 222, 225, 232
Nakayama, Kazuma, 64
Neri, Felino, 191, 295
Nieto, Manuel, 185–186, 196
Non–Aligned Movement (NAM), 163

Ocampo, Pablo, 108
Office of Foreign Relations, 6, 11, 12, 27, 66–68
Office of Strategic Services, 114, 260, 261–266
Oira, Francisco, 187
Orlanes, Remedios S., 178
Osmeña, Sergio, 14, 59–61, 66, 109, 136, 138, 151, 263, 267, 271
Ozaeta, Roman, 115–116, 181

Pardo de Tavera, Trinidad, 56
Pastrana, Vicente L., 120, 190
Pelaez, Emmanuel, 198, 304
Peña, Pablo A., 12, 14, 26, 34, 35, 37, 50, 124, 182–183, 201, 207, 241, 278, 289
Pensionado Examinations, 11–12
Philippine Assembly, 108
Philippine Bill of 1902, 107
Philippine Club of Washington, 127–128
Philippine Commission, 108
Philippine Commonwealth, 59, 66, 82, 109, 136, 262, 267;exiled in Washington, 61–62
Philippine Congress, 119, 122
Philippine foreign posts (Mission/ Legation/ Embassy/ Consulate, Consulate General), in Australia, 188–189; Bangkok, Thailand, 190–193; Brussels, Belgium, 198; Buenos Aires, Argentina, 195–196; Burma, 242; Cairo, Egypt, 197, 238; Copenhagen, 198; Denmark, 60, 184, 198; Hamburg, 198; Hong Kong, 169, 198, 241, 299; Calcutta and New Delhi, India, 193–194; Cambodia, 189; Havana, Cuba, 195; Jakarta, Indonesia, 189–190; Karachi, Pakistan, 170, 189; Kuala Lumpur, 199; London, Legation in, 180–184; Madrid, Spain, 184–187; Mexico, 197; Nanking and Amoy, China, 171–175; New York, 123–124; Paris, France, 187; San Francisco, 124; Seoul, South Korea, 19–195; Tokyo, Japan, 175–180; Rome, Italy, 187–188; Singapore, 189, 198; United Nations, 144–145; Washington, United States, 107–121
Philippine Foreign Affairs Training Program (PFATP), 3–7; candidates, 7–9; first group, 9–11, 24–33, 201, 204; second group, 13–14, 33–34, 201; third group, 14–17, 34–37, 201, 208; fourth group, 17– 18, 42–44; fifth group, 18–21, 44–47, 214. *See also* Edward Mill; Richard Butrick
Philippine Herald, 109, 119, 289
Philippine Independence Act (1946), see Tydings–McDuffie Act
Philippine Rehabilitation Act, 121,

314
Philippine Resident Commissioner to the U.S., Office of, 107–110. *See also* Carlos P. Romulo; Joaquin M. Elizalde
Philippine Veterans Board, 122
Philippines–Japan War Reparations Talks, 170
Princeton University, 284
Progresista Party, 108
Provido, Generoso P., 17, 18, 207, 210, 239, 241, 281
Puyat, Gil J., 226,

Quezon, Manuel L., 59–62, 81, 108–109, 135–136, 151, 187, 238, 263
Quintero, Eduardo, 8, 59, 75
Quirino, Carlos, 183
Quirino, Elpidio, 37, 41, 43, 53, 68, 75–77, 79, 81–82, 111, 126, 117, 119, 125, 129–132, 142, 168, 171–172, 181, 183–187, 190, 208–209, 279–280, 296

Ramirez, Pedro G., 125
Ramos, Aurelio M., 12, 15, 35, 124, 201, 207, 233, 242, 289
Ramos Narciso, 17, 19, 20, 47, 52, 85, 91,113–116, 119–120, 131, 181, 193–194, 196–197, 216, 231–232, 240, 276, 281, 289, 295, 301
Recto, Claro M., 63
Regala, Roberto, 59, 75, 79, 83, 84, 85, 124, 126, 189, 228, 229, 231–232, 280, 295
Reyes, Narciso G., 144, 154–155
Rhee, Syngman, 195
Rivera, Godofredo, 117
Romualdez, Benjamin, 242, 302
Romulo, Carlos P., 4, 27, 40, 109, 114, 262, 283, 295, 304, 316; biography, 149–155; Ambassador to the U.S., 132–133; Ambassador to the U.N., 40, 138–140, 145–149, 155–160, 175; Resident Commissioner to the U.S., 4, 27, 68, 70–72, 109, 132; Secretary of Foreign Affairs, 132, 179, 190, 253
Roosevelt, Franklin, 135,
Rosal, Eduardo L., 12, 18, 19,20, 47–48, 125, 175, 214, 240, 242, 274, 289
Roxas, Manuel, 14, 67–68, 70–71, 73, 82, 85,111–112, 122, 130, 142, 165–166, 238, 271–272
Roxas, Simeon R., 18, 48–50, 163, 214, 233, 239, 288, 298, 315
Russell, Donald, 29
Ruiz, Leopoldo T., 13, 62, 117–118, 124, 172, 201–202, 205, 221–222, 242

Salientes, Manuel Q., 118
Sanchez, Rodolfo S., 301, 315
Schefer, Edward, 51, 127
Schneider, Agnes, 42
Sebastian, Proceso, 171, 173,187
Secretaria de Relaciones Exteriores, 55–56
Serrano, Felixberto, 238, 295
Severino, Rodolfo H., 12, 17, 211, 213, 233, 239, 242, 281, 309–312, 315
Silliman University, 222
Sinco, Vicente G., 27, 66,79,138, 198
Singian, Vicente I., 8, 10, 11, 27, 28, 29, 30, 32,174, 198, 201–202, 204, 239, 242, 288
Sison, Antonio, 8
Soriente, Isidro A., 177
Sotto, Tagakotta, 18, 19, 49, 124, 189, 214–215, 229, 236, 242, 282
Southeast East Asia Treaty Organization (SEATO), 163
Spanish–American War, 56
Sta. Romana, Eutiquio O., 12, 15, 16, 35, 173–174, 201, 208, 242, 312, 315
Steintorf, Paul, 9, 14, 71, 73,119, 266
Stettinius, Edward M., 138, 265
Sukarno, 190, 285

Sulit, Estela R., 19
Sumulong, Lorenzo, 142, 148, 203, 226
Sychangco, Faustino, 64

Teodoro, Jose, Jr., 120,
Tirona, Benjamin T., 18, 48, 50, 124–125, 215, 242, 270, 288–289, 300–301, 315
Tojo, Hideki, 63–64
Torres, Emilio, 8, 18–20, 52, 62, 117–118, 204, 214, 221, 242, 273
Treaty of General Relations (1946), 96, 112, 167, 199, 274–275
Treaty of Paris (1898), 57, 58
Truman, Harry S., 43, 67–68, 112–113, 122, 129, 153, 155–156, 275
Tuason, Pedro, 226, 230
Tydings–McDuffie Act, 58–59, 68, 127

Ubaldo, Roman V., 17, 18, 42–43, 109, 211, 213, 242, 281, 312
Umayam, Bartolome A., 120
United Nations: Balkan Commission, 147; Charter, 137–139, 141, 143, 154; Commission on Human Rights, 141, 162; Commission on the Unification and Rehabilitation of Korea (UNCURK), 195; Economic Commission for Asia and the Far East, 48; Food and Agriculture Organization (FAO), 137, 188; General Assembly, 117, 140, 153, 156; headquarters, 142–144; Palestine Question, 155–159 163; Relief and Rehabilitation Administration (UNRRA), 118, 136, 173;
Security Council, 139–140, 148, 153, 160, 162; Educational, Scientific and Cultural Organization (UNESCO), 139, 141, 162; Philippine membership in, 135, 137–142
Universal Postal Union, 135, 162
Universidad Central de Madrid, 297
University of California, 284
University of Hawaii, 287
University of Manila, 294, 308, 315
University of Michigan, 255–258, 260, 290
University of the Philippines (UP), 2, 81, 138, 150–151, 171, 191, 221, 277, 284–286, 289, 314
University of Santo Tomas (UST), 2
Urquiola, Renato A., 12, 18, 20, 125, 214, 242, 314,
U.S. Army Forces in the Far East (USAFFE), 61, 65
U.S. Congress, 108, 122
U.S. Consulate General in Manila, 7, 9
U.S. Embassy in Manila, 116, 178, 187, 191–192, 220, 277
U.S. State Department, 107, 138, 166–169, 173, 177; Office (later Division) of Philippine Affairs, 126–127, 179. *See also* Richard Ely

Valencia, Abelardo L., 119–120
Valeriano, Benito B., 301–302
Valeriano, Senador D., 119
Vargas, Jorge, 63–64, 177,
Velasco, Constancio R., 178
Velasquez, Jaime C., 120
Verlinden, Michael, 40
Vincent, John Carter, 110
Virata, Leonides, S., 70, 142
Vite, Doroteo V., 13, 33, 117, 119–120, 128, 201, 205, 219, 221, 242

Washington Post, 129, 130
Willoughby, Woodbury, 6
Woodward, Robert, 32
Woodward, Stanley, 128
World Bank, 41, 44, 136, 162
Yango, Alejandro D., 12, 15–16, 35,

37, 188, 201, 207, 208, 242, 304, 312, 315
Yasuda, Iwajiro, 65
Young, John Russell, 128
Yulo, Jose, 110–111

Zaide, Jose A., 154, 190, 302
Zafra, Urbano A., 113, 117, 120, 138
Zulueta, Jose C., 92, 94, 131

Marciano R. de Borja is a career diplomat in the Philippine Foreign Service, currently Special Assistant in the Office of the Undersecretary for Administration at the Department of Foreign Affairs in Manila. He most recently served as Minister at the Philippine Mission to the United Nations in New York. Previously he served in the Philippine embassies in Japan, Chile, and Spain and was director for the United States Division in the Department of Foreign Affairs. He holds degrees from the University of the Philippines and the University of Navarra (Spain). He also studied International Politics at the University of Tokyo. He is the author of *FSO IV: Starting a Career in the Philippine Foreign Service* (Quezon City: New Day Publishers, 1999) and *Basques in the Philippines* (Reno & Las Vegas: University of Nevada Press, 2005).

www.ingramcontent.com/pod-product-compliance
Lightning Source LLC
Chambersburg PA
CBHW020730160426
43192CB00006B/174